HISTORICAL LINGUISTICS 1999

SELECTED PAPERS FROM THE 14TH INTERNATIONAL
CONFERENCE ON HISTORICAL LINGUISTICS,
VANCOUVER, 9–13 AUGUST 1999

Edited by

LAUREL J. BRINTON
University of British Columbia

with the editorial assistance of
Desireé Lundström

JOHN BENJAMINS PUBLISHING COMPANY
AMSTERDAM/PHILADELPHIA

™ The paper used in this publication meets the minimum requirements of American National Standard for Information Sciences – Permanence of Paper for Printed Library Materials, ANSI Z39.48-1984.

Library of Congress Cataloging-in-Publication Data

International Conference on Historical Linguistics (14th : 1999 : Vancouver, B.C.)
    Historical linguistics 1999 : selected papers from the 14th International Conference on Historical Linguistics, Vancouver, 9–13 August 1999 / edited by Laurel J. Brinton.
    p. cm. (Current Issues in Linguistic Theory, ISSN 0304–0763 ; v. 215)
    Includes bibliographical references and index.
       1. Historical linguistics--Congresses. I. Brinton, Laurel J. II. Title. III. Series.

P140.I5   2001
417'.7--dc21   2001035020
ISBN 90 272 3722 0 (Eur.) / 1 58811 064 8 (US) (Hb; alk. paper)

John Benjamins Publishing Co. · P.O.Box 36224· 1020 ME Amsterdam · The Netherlands
John Benjamins North America · P.O.Box 27519 · Philadelphia PA 19118-0519 · USA

HISTORICAL LINGUISTICS 1999

AMSTERDAM STUDIES IN THE THEORY AND HISTORY OF LINGUISTIC SCIENCE

General Editor

E. F. KONRAD KOERNER

(University of Ottawa)

Series IV – CURRENT ISSUES IN LINGUISTIC THEORY

Advisory Editorial Board

Volume 215

Laurel J. Brinton (ed.)

Historical Linguistics 1999. Selected papers from the 14th International Conference on Historical Linguistics, Vancouver, 9-13 August 1999

This volume is dedicated to the memory of
Suzanne Fleischman
(1948–2000)

Table of contents

Contributors' addresses

Minoji Akimoto
Aoyama Gakuin University
Department of English
4–4–25 Shibuya, Shibuya-ku
Tokyo 150, Japan
miha-ru@cc.aoyama.ac.jp

Gregory D.S. Anderson
University of Manchester
Department of Linguistics
Oxford Road
Manchester M13 9PL, U.K.
greg.anderson@man.ac.uk

Janice Aski
The Ohio State University
Department of French and Italian
248 Cunz Hall
1841 Millikin Rd.
Columbus, OH 43210, U.S.A.
aski.1@osu.edu

Kristin Bech
University of Bergen
Department of English
Sydnesplass 7
N-5007 Bergen, Norway
Kristin.Bech@eng.uib.no

Delia Bentley and Thórhallur Eythórsson
University of Manchester
Department of Linguistics
Manchester M13 9PL, U.K.
delia.bentley@man.ac.uk, tolli@man.ac.uk

Vit Bubenik
Memorial University of Newfoundland
Department of Linguistics
St. John's, NF A1B 3X9, Canada
vbubenik@morgan.ucs.mun.ca

Young-mee Cho
Rutgers University
Department of Asian Languages
330 Scott Hall, College Avenue
New Brunswick, NJ 08901, U.S.A.
yucho@rci.rutgers.edu

Karen Dakin
Universidad Nacional Autonoma de
Mexico
Instituto de Investigaciones Filologicas
CTO. Mario de la Cueva S/n
04510 Mexico, D.F.
dakin@servidor.unam.mx

David Denison
University of Manchester
Department of English and American
Studies
Manchester M13 9PL, U.K.
d.denison@man.ac.uk

Randall Gess
University of Utah
Department of Linguistics
255 S. Central Campus Dr., Rm. 2328
Salt Lake City, UT 84112, U.S.A.
randall.gess@m.cc.utah.edu

Gunnar Ólafur Hansson
University of Chicago
Department of Linguistics
1010 East 59th Street
Chicago, IL 60637, U.S.A.
gunnar@socrates.berkeley.edu

Jacob Hoeksema
University of Groningen
Faculty of Letters, P.O. Box 716
9700 AS Groningen, The Netherlands
hoeksema@let.rug.nl

Maria Manoliu
University of California, Davis
Department of French and Italian
509 Sproul Hall
Davis, CA 95616, U.S.A.
mimanoliu@ucdavis.edu

Ana Maria Martins
Faculdade de Letras da Universidade de
Lisboa
Departamento de Linguística Geral e
Românica
Alameda da Universidade
1600–214 Lisboa, Portugal
anamartins@ip.pt

D. Gary Miller
University of Florida
Department of Classics
P.O. Box 117435
Gainesville, FL 32611–7435, U.S.A.
dgm@classics.ufl.edu

Marianne Mithun
University of California, Santa Barbara
Department of Linguistics
Santa Barbara, CA 93106–3100, U.S.A.
mithun@humanitas.ucsb.edu

Johanna Nichols
University of California, Berkeley
Department of Slavic Languages, #2979
Berkeley, CA 94720–2979, U.S.A.
jbn@socrates.berkeley.edu

Anette Rosenbach
Heinrich Heine University
Department of English Linguistics
(Anglistik III)
Universitätsstr. 1
D-40225 Düsseldorf, Germany
ar@phil-fak.uni-duesseldorf.de

Gregory Stump
University of Kentucky
Department of English
1215 Patterson Office Tower
Lexington, KY 40506–0027, U.S.A.
gstump@pop.uky.edu

Marie-Lucie Tarpent
Mount Saint Vincent University
Department of Modern Languages
166 Bedford Highway
Halifax, NS B3M 2S6, Canada
marie-lucie.tarpent@msvu.ca

Donald N. Tuten
Emory University
Department of Spanish
Atlanta, Georgia 30322, U.S.A.
dtuten@emory.edu

Annette Veerman-Leichsenring
University of Leiden
Department of Comparative Linguistics
P.O. Box 9515
2300 RA Leiden, The Netherlands
veerman.al@wolmail.nl

Theo Vennemann
University of Munich
Schellingstr. 3 RG
D-80799 Munich, Germany
Vennemann@germanistik.uni-
muenchen.de

Norman H. Zide
University of Chicago
1030 E. 59th Street
Chicago, IL 60637, U.S.A.
n-zide@uchicago.edu

Preface

The volume contains a selection of papers from the 14th International Conference on Historical Linguistics (ICHL 14) held August 9–13, 1999, at the University of British Columbia in Vancouver, B.C., Canada. Attendance at the conference included over 220 participants from 27 countries ranging from Iceland to Vanuatu. In addition to the pleasures of Vancouver and its surroundings, participants enjoyed a rich and diverse program of papers on historical linguistics. Over the five days of the conference, there were 4 plenary addresses, 117 papers in three parallel sessions, and 42 papers in 4 workshops (on Historical Pragmatics, Japanese and Korean Linguistics, Patterns of Actualization in Language Change, and Grammatical Relations and Grammatical Change). The choice of just twenty-three papers — intended to display the state of current research in the field of historical linguistics — from such a broad display of scholarship posed quite a daunting task. This volume would have been impossible without the expert opinions of a large group of anonymous referees, who gave generously of their time and advice in this very difficult selection process.

I would like to take this opportunity to thank as well those organizations and individuals who contributed to the success of the conference itself. External funding for the conference was supplied by the Social Sciences and Humanities Research Council of Canada under the "Aid to Occasional Research Conferences and International Congresses in Canada" (Grant #646–98–1047). Local funding was extended by the Dean of Arts, the Dean of Graduate Studies, the Vice President Research, the Department of English, the Department of Linguistics, and the Department of Language Education of the University of British Columbia. The Dean of Arts of York University (Ontario, Canada) also provided support for the conference, as did the City of Vancouver. Cambridge University Press, Oxford University Press, Mouton de Gruyter, Rodopi, and John Benjamins provided funding, books, and/or displays at the conference. I would like to thank all of these organizations for their financial support.

While financial support is, of course, essential, the contribution of individuals is invaluable to the smooth running of a conference. For their special assistance, I extend a large debt of gratitude to my colleagues in the English Department, especially Leslie Arnovick and Lilita Rodman, to Dieter Stein of Heinrich Heine Universität, Düsseldorf, to Sheila Embleton of York University, to David Denison of Manchester University, and to Henning Andersen of University of California, Los Angeles. The support staff in the Department of English at UBC was extremely helpful to conferees during the course of the conference; I am also very grateful to Mrs. Patricia Lackie, whose knowledge of the intricacies of university financial accounting was invaluable both before and for many months after the conference. Beth at the UBC Conference Centre provided assistance in the planning stages of the conference. For vetting the abstracts of papers that were presented at the conference, I would like to thank the Executive Committee of the International Society of Historical Linguistics, Barry Blake, Kate Burridge, Dorothy Disterheft, Sheila Embleton, Alice Harris, and Dieter Stein, as well as my colleague Leslie Arnovick and a number of other specialists. I am indebted to Ralph Brands for computer assistance, especially in the early stages of organizing the conference. To my graduate student assistants, Michael Lapointe, Desireé Lundstöm, and Gudrun Dreher, who both before and during the conference put in effort beyond the call of duty (and learned a little about historical linguistics in exchange), I extend my sincerest gratitude. I would especially like to thank Monika Schmid and Alex Bergs, from Düsseldorf, who generously volunteered both their time and their conference-organizing expertise (gained at ICHL 13).

Finally, I extend my thanks to Anke de Looper of John Benjamins for her invaluable editorial expertise and to Desireé Lundstöm for countless hours of assistance in the editing of this volume. I greatly appreciated Desireé's patience, hard work, attention to detail, sound sense, and good cheer, even when doing battle with 'special characters' and apparently recalcitrant computer files.

Laurel J. Brinton
Vancouver, B. C.
1 November 2000

How far has *far from* become grammaticalized?*

Minoji Akimoto
Aoyama Gakuin University

1. Introduction

Far from has an interesting history, tracing back to the Old English period. At that time, the phrase had only a literal meaning, i.e., physical distance. It is only around the seventeenth century that it began to have metaphorical/idiomatic meanings as well. This paper discusses the change of *far from* in relation to grammaticalization and idiomatization from the 15th to the 20th centuries, briefly touching on the Middle English period. During these periods, *far from* gradually expanded its uses grammatically, and semantically from literal to metaphorical.

Data for this study were collected from three texts from each century consisting of approximately 60,000 words. The corpus covers a variety of genres, such as novels, letters, and drama, representing a gradient from formality to colloquialism in each text type (see the list of texts at the end of the paper). But because of the scarcity of examples (40), I made use of the OED CD-ROM and COBUILD (in Modern English) as primary sources.

2. A note on previous studies

There are very few studies relating to the *far from* phrase. Traditional grammars such as Jespersen (1942:IV23.6(2)), Quirk et al. (1985:1390 fn.) and Poutsma (1926:502) touch very briefly on this phrase. Kajita (1977), from the viewpoint of generative-transformational grammar, takes up *far from* for discussion as an example of syntactic reinterpretation which reverses the head-nonhead relation in adjective phrases. He describes the case as follows:

(1) a. The airport is far from the city.
         [$_{AP}$ [$_{Adj}$ far] [$_{PP}$ from the city]]

b.   Those people are far from innocent.
[$_{AP}$ [$_{Adv}$ far from] [$_{Adj}$ innocent]]
cf.   Those people are hardly innocent.
[$_{AP}$ [$_{Adv}$ hardly] [$_{Adj}$ innocent]]

Thus, *far from* has turned into an adverbial phrase as a result of syntactic reinterpretation. However, as I discuss later, *far from* has seen a further development from adverbial phrase to conjunctive/discoursal phrase.

3.   Survey of the data

Far from is used in the sense of "great distance" in early Middle English. The following examples are cited from *The Oxford English Dictionary* (OED) and *The Middle English Dictionary* (MED) respectively.

(2)   c1205 Lay. 543
Achalon heihte an flum þe nes noht *feor from* heom.
"Achalon is called a river which is not far from them"
(OED; s.v. *far*)

(3)   c1275 (c 1250) *Prov. Head.* st. 18:
Fer from eye, *fer from* herte.
"far from the eye, far from the heart"
(MED; s.v. *fer*)

Note that the element which follows *far from* is an NP in its literal sense.

Beginning in late Middle English, the variety of complements[1] following *far from* increases. To obtain a sufficient number of examples, I made an electronic search of the OED CD-ROM. Table 1 shows the frequency of *far from*, with its different complement types from the 16th to the early 20th centuries. Although the OED represents a fairly random collection of data collected for no specific grammatical purpose, and therefore there is danger in making quantitative judgements based on OED data, it can still be used to show general trends. Furthermore, the data collected from my corpus (given below) may remedy the arbitrariness of the OED data to a certain extent.

The following are examples corresponding to the types in Table 1:

(4)   a.   Not *far from* Chester, I knew an odd, foul-mouthed knave, called Charles the Friar ... (Nashe: 87)
b.   Verily they be *far from* good reason, in mine opinion, which ... (Elyot: 43)
c.   i.   ... men that are so *far from* being episcopall that they are thought to be anabaptiste ... (Pepys: 124)
ii.   So *far from its being* proscribed by Utilitarian notions, they demand its existence. (OED 1830 *Westm. Rev.* Jan. 3)

    iii. *Far from there being* any noticeable improvement in the quality of rela-
         tionship as practised among freaks … (OED 1971 *Ink* 7/3)
d.   "I was so *far from* imagining they stood still …" (Boswell: 100)
e.   … Mrs Dauberry, who, I am afraid, is *far from* well. (Wilde: 146)
f.   From the time of St. Louis, the feudal power in France was scotched, though
    far from killed. (OED 1894 Baring-Gould *Deserts S. France* II.115)
g.   The truly religious tone … not unmixed, indeed, *far from it*, but unmistak-
    able. (OED 1882 Wicksteed tr. *Kuenen's Hibbert Lect.* iii.127)
h.   What Mr. Bouton characterizes as peculiarly German Socialist, defeatist and
    pacifist attitude of "a class apart" is *far from that.* (OED 1930 *Sun* (Balti-
    more) 31 Dec. 6/2)

Table 1. Complements of *far from* by century (data from the OED)

	16th	17th	18th	19th	20th
(a) count NP	13	57	64	90	56
(b) abstract NP	8	23	5	15	29
(c) *being (its being, there being)*		15	34	41	52
(d) other *-ing*	1	38	33	44	29
(e) Adj		3	9	42	29
(f) past participle		1		1	3
(g) *it*				2	3
(h) *that*					1
Total	22	137	145	235	202

In my corpus, I found 40 examples of *far from* + complement. Table 2 shows the
frequency of the examples and complement types by century. My result generally
confirms the OED data in Table 1. That is, *far from* comes to be frequent in the 19th
century and the use of the *-ing* complement begins to be frequent particularly after
the 18th century.

Table 2. Complements of *far from* by century (data from the corpus used in this paper)

	15th	16th	17th	18th	19th	early 20th
(a) NP	1	6	3	1	1	2
(b) *-ing*			2	8	10	2
(c) *it*			1	1		
(d) *well*					2	
Total	1	6	6	10	13	4

As can be seen in Table 1 and as is confirmed also in Table 2, the following tendencies for the development of *far from* are noteworthy.

a.   In the 17th century, *far from* begins to increase. Particularly in the 19th century, *far from* comes to be frequent, with some decline in the 20th century.
b.   The use of *-ing* forms begins to be frequent from the 17th century onwards.[2]
c.   Adjectives after *far from* come to be frequent particularly from the 19th century onwards.
d.   *Being* also begins to be frequent particularly after the 18th century.

There is a variety of adjectives modified by *far from*, but what is interesting in the 19th century is that there are many negative adjectives, such as *uncheerful, dissocial, incompatible, disagreeable, inconsonant, unsatisfactory, inconsiderable, inexpugnable,* and *unlearned*.[3] In the construction *far from being*, elements which follow *being* are mostly nouns, adjectives, and past participles. In the 18th, 19th, and early 20th centuries, *far from being* + adjective and *far from* + adjective are both used.

To see general trends in the range of complement types in Modern English, I selected 100 examples at random from COBUILD. Table 3 shows the breakdown of elements after *far from*.

Table 3. Complements of *far from* in Modern English *(data from COBUILD)*

(a) concrete NP	5
(b) abstract NP	34
(c) *being*	13
(d) other *-ing*	10
(e) Adj	26
(f) past participle	3
(g) Adv	2
(h) *wh*	2
(i) Pro (*each other*)	1
(j) *it*	4

4.   Grammaticalization and idiomatization

The development of *far from* can be seen as involving not only grammaticalization, but also idiomatization.

4.1 Grammaticalization

Grammaticalization has been discussed extensively in recent years (see, for example, Hopper 1991; Hopper & Traugott 1993; Bybee et al. 1994). While the category of

adjective is by no means one of the major grammatical categories where grammaticalization is thought to take place — grammaticalization studies have usually
concentrated on verbs (auxiliaries) and nouns — I shall take up some aspects of
grammaticalization in relation to the *far from* construction.

The following are recognized processes of change in grammaticalization.

a. A shift from concreteness to abstractness (Hopper & Traugott 1993);
b. Decategorialization (Hopper 1991);
c. Retention of original meaning (Bybee et al. 1994); and
d. Change from propositional to textual to emotive meaning (from objective to
    subjective meaning) (Traugott 1982).

Far from exemplifies these processes of grammaticalization in most respects. *Far
from* originally expressed only a concrete meaning, i.e., physical distance, but began
to express mental/abstract distance later on, as in:

(5) *Far from* the purpose of his coming hither, He makes excuses for his being there.
     (OED 1593 Shakes. *Lucrece* 113)

Far from has maintained both literal (6) and metaphorical meanings (7) since the
17th century:

(6) In the midland parts *far from* the sea. (OED 1601 Holland *Pliny* I.40)

(7) I am *far from* their opinion who damne it for superstition to portract that Glori-
     ous Virgin or her Babe. (OED 1610 J. Guillim *Heraldry* iii.xxiv.243)

Far from mostly occurred as a predicate adjective in early English, but gradually it
became decategorialized from adjective to adverb (8) and then to interjectional
intensifier (9):

(8) She is very *far from* strong, and requires a deal of watching over.
     (OED 1903 Mrs. De La Pasture *Cornelius* xvi.183)

(9) His heir was a nephew... not a bad boy, but not a chip off the old block, no, sir,
     far from it. (OED 1947 W.S. Maugham *Creatures of Circumstance* 7)

Far from predominantly takes a concrete noun complement expressing literal
meaning, but abstract nouns become increasingly common (see Table 3), as the
construction assumes metaphorical meaning. Metaphorical meaning is strength-
ened by the occurrence of *-ing* forms from the 17th century onwards. *Far from* as a
whole still maintains its adjectival nature, but as it comes to take adjectives and past
participles as complements in the 19th century, its function changes from adjective
to intensifier adverb. To the extent that *far from* takes an *it* complement, the phrase
also develops a discourse function, since the pronoun usually refers back to the
previous discourse; *far from* connects two portions of text, and therefore its

function is textual. Furthermore, as *far from* acquired a metaphorical meaning, the strong negation "not at all" which *far from* begins to express in due course also denotes an emotional attitude of a speaker, as in:

> (10)   NZ is about to become a banana # republic. *Far from it*, because NZ is in better
>   shape. (COBUILD)

Far from can thus be said to follow the general trend of semantic change which Traugott (1982) proposes as follows:

> propositional → textual → interpersonal/emotive/subjective

4.2   The relation between semantic and syntactic change: Idiomatization

Grammaticalization is an area where both syntactic and semantic changes converge.

Far from takes different complements in its history, from concrete nouns to abstract nouns, to -*ing* forms to adjectives/past participles, and finally to *it. Far from* also changes in meaning from concrete to abstract. This raises the question of the relationship between the changes in complement-types and the meanings of *far from*, that is, the relation between syntactic and semantic changes. Do the syntactic changes precede and bring about the semantic change, or do the semantic changes permit the expansion of the *far from* construction into other syntactic environments and thus lead to grammaticalization?

A generative approach to linguistic change, for example, that of Lightfoot (1978: 61), claims that syntactic change takes place independently of meaning. In contrast, when discussing the *be going to* construction, Hopper and Traugott (1993: 61–62, 87–88) emphasize the semantic parts of grammaticalization, including metonymic processes and bleaching, as well as generalization of meaning (96–100). Although they refer very briefly to idiomatization (64–65), they do not go into any detail concerning this process. This suggests that idiomatization is not a major factor in their framework of grammaticalization. Yet generalization of meaning, in particular the shift from concreteness to abstractness, is a central aspect of idiomatization, which focuses on the gradual indecipherability of an expression. According to Nunberg et al. (1994: 529–530), idiomatization has the tendency to map from concrete to abstract situations. For an idiom to have flexible uses, it must have an abstract meaning (for example, *pulling (the) strings* = "exerting influence"). A further example provided by Nunberg et al. (1994: 530) involves some idioms associated with the word *horse*, idiomatic meanings of which apply to an abstract entity (the example is slightly modified):

a. *look a gift horse in the mouth*
    horse = "something that has been freely offered"
b. *flog a dead horse*
    horse = "something that can no longer give satisfaction"
c. *change horses in midstream*
    horses = "course of action"

It seems safe to say that it is the semantic shift from concrete to abstract meaning in *far from* which brings about syntactic flexibility in the construction, making possible its expansion in complement-type from NP to *-ing*, and finally to adjectives and past participles.[4] In the process of the syntactic and semantic changes, re-analysis[5] takes place as follows:

		status of *far from*:	
		syntactic	semantic
a.	X + [*be* + *far*] [*from* + Y]	adjective	literal
	Y = Head (concrete N)		
b.	X + *be* + [*far from*] + Y	adjective	metaphorical[6]
	Y = Head (abstract N, *-ing*)		
c.	X + *be* + [*far from*] + Y	adverb	
	Y = Modifier (Adj, participle)		idiomatic
d.	Far from it	interjection	

The following examples correspond to the process of reanalysis leading to idiomaticity.

(11) a. And not *far from* hence be great forests and woods ... (Malory: 166) — (a)
      b. But what need we to search so *far from* us, since we have sufficient examples near unto us? (Elyot: 11) — (a)
      c. I was so *far from* imagining they stood still ... (Boswell: 100) — (b)
      d. *Far from* going to the inn, Mr. Holmes, I should be pleased if ... (Doyle: 670) — (b)
      e. Mayor Brian Burke, said the sealing issue was *far from* dead. (COBUILD) — (c)
      f. Cup soccer campaign in Sweden, beaten but *far from* disgraced in matches against ... (COBUID) — (c)
      g. NZ is about to become a banana # republic. *Far from it*, because NZ is in better shape. (COBUILD) — (d)

In the process of *far from* becoming an idiom, it has come to take different kinds of complements, as discussed before. Interestingly, the change of complement-types reflects a loss of 'nouniness' (cf. Ross 1973) as follows:

Noun ^{concrete}
↓
Noun ^{abstract}
↓
-*ing* gerund
↓
being (+ NP/Adj/past participle)
↓
adjective/past participle

Morphosyntactically, therefore, idiomatization involves decategorialization of the nouns. Semantically, it is precipitated by the change from concreteness to abstractness. Reanalysis resulting mainly from a combination of these factors takes place to make an integrated form. The phrase *far from,* has undergone various stages in the process of idiomatization. Stage (a) presents a typical predicate structure with no idiomatic meaning. Stage (b) still expresses a predicate structure, but with a change of meaning. Stage (c) shows both changes — syntactic and semantic. Finally, stage (d) sees a further development in the syntactic structure and change of meaning, making the phrase idiomatic in its entirety. Taking into account the functional reanalysis of *far from* from (a) to (d), mentioned before, I consider the stage of change from concrete noun to -*ing* gerund as metaphorical. To become an idiom, *far from* must change its meaning and must be syntactically fixed. It is at the next stage (i.e., *being* NP/Adj —; Adj/past participle —) that these conditions are met, and *far from* behaves idiomatically.

Finally, a recurrent question is why some particular items undergo reanalysis and others do not. How is reanalysis licensed in the particular case of *far from*? Similar cases of patterning, such as *apart from, near to* and *next to* are not as productive as *far from*. A cursory examination of examples of *apart from* from the OED CD-ROM, for instance, demonstrates that, while there is a shift from a complement adverb phrase placed after *be* to a discourse phrase placed in head position particularly in 20th century usage, as in

(12)   *Apart from* the intellectual ravage, they should be restrained from blackening the sub-fuscous. (OED 1904 *Sat. Rev.*30 Jan.140)

the phrase *apart from* has never developed the function of modification like that of *far from*. The phrases *near to* and *next to* have developed the function of modifying the following adjectives, as in

(13)   I was *near to* distracted. (Defoe M 101, from Jespersen 1942:387)

(14)   I'm *next to* certain I should have heard the whole truth.
(Collins W. 478, from Jespersen 1942:387)

but they have not developed discoursal functions. While *apart from, near to*, and *next to* have undergone reanalysis to a restricted extent, *far from* exhibits all stages of reanalysis (see above). This difference of flexibility — both semantic and syntactic — is reflected in the development of the phrase *far from*.[7]

5. Conclusion

I have confined myself to the analysis of *far from*. This is because the phrase is frequent and shows an interesting change from Middle English to present-day English. I have discussed its change in relation to grammaticalization and idiomatization on the basis of the OED CD-ROM and COBUILD data complemented by my collected data. In my view, idiomatization is not independent of grammaticalization, but a subpart of it, possibly located at the final stage of grammaticalization. If this is the case, the incorporation of idiomatization into grammaticalization will enrich the theory of grammaticalization.

Notes

* I would like to thank Laurel Brinton and an anonymous reader for their helpful comments.

1. For convenience's sake, the term 'complement' in this paper refers to any constituent following *far from*.

2. There seems to be no restriction on verbs taking *-ing* except that *having* appears rather constantly throughout the periods.

3. Although the *Longman Dictionary of Contemporary English* (1995) refers to the collocation of *far from pleased/happy*, the *happy* collocation is not frequent, and the *pleased* collocation was not found even once in the OED and COBUILD data.

4. An opposite view is expressed by Gronemeyer (1999), where it is suggested that the syntactic construction functions as a strong constraint on meaning changes in grammaticalization and that the establishment of a new semantic domain is contingent upon structural analysis (37).

5. Without going into detailed discussion on reanalysis, I shall use Crystal's (1997:322) definition of reanalysis as "a development which alters the structure or function of a linguistic form".

6. By 'metaphorical' I mean that this (b) process serves the function of being in between literal and idiomatic parts.

7. I owe this observation to Laurel Brinton.

References

Corpus

Austen, Jane. 1990. *Pride and Prejudice* ed. by J. Kinsley. Oxford: Oxford University Press. [1813]
The Book of Margery Kempe. 1961. Ed. by M. S. Brown. London, New York, & Toronto: Oxford University Press. [1436?]
Boswell, James. 1980. *Life of Johnson* ed. by R. W. Chapman. Oxford: Oxford University Press. [1771]
Bunyan, John. 1965. *The Pilgrim's Progress* ed. by R. Sharrock. Harmondsworth: Penguin. [1678]
Burney, Fanny. 1992. *Evelina* ed. by E. A. Bloom. Oxford: Oxford University Press. [1778]
Chesterton, G. K. 1986. *The Man who was Thursday* introduced by Kingsley Amis. Harmondsworth: Penguin. [1911]
Deloney, Thomas. 1969. *The Works of Thomas Deloney* ed. by F. O. Mann. Oxford: Clarendon Press. [1583–1600]
Doyle, A. C. 1966. *The Complete Sherlock Holmes Short Stories*. London: John Murry. [1904]
Dryden, John. 1971. *The Works of John Dryden* ed. by S. H. Monk & A. E. W. Maurer. Berkeley & Los Angeles: University of California Press. [1668–1691]
Elyot, Sir Thomas. 1970. *The Governor* (= Everyman's Library 227) ed. by S. E. Lehmberg. London: Dent. [1531]
Le Morte D' Arthur. 1994. (Modern Library edition.) New York: Random House. [1485]
Lord Chesterfield. 1992. *Lord Chesterfield's Letters* ed. by D. Robert. Oxford: Oxford University Press. [1774]
Nashe, Thomas. 1972. *The Unfortunate Traveller and Other Works* ed. by J. V. Steane. Harmondsworth: Penguin. [1594]
The Oxford Book of Letters. 1995. Ed. by F. Kermode & A. Kermode. Oxford: Oxford University Press. [1553–1985]
Paston Letters and Papers of the Fifteenth Century. 1971. Ed. by N. Davies. Vol. 1. Oxford: Oxford University Press. [1429–1489]
Pepys, Samuel. 1993. *The Shorter Pepys* ed. by R. Latham. Harmondsworth: Penguin. [1660–1669]
Wilde, Oscar. 1995. *The Importance of Being Earnest and Other Plays* ed. by P. Raby. Oxford: Oxford University Press. [1893–95]
Woolf, Virginia. 1992. *To the Lighthouse* ed. by S. McNichol. Harmondsworth: Penguin. [1927]

Secondary Sources

Bybee, Joan, Revere Perkins, & William Pagliuca. 1994. *The Evolution of Grammar: Tense, aspect, and modality in the languages of the world*. Chicago: Chicago University Press.
COBUILD Written and Spoken Corpus. Birmingham.
Crystal, David. 1997. *A Dictionary of Linguistics and Phonetics*. 4th ed. Oxford: Blackwell.
Gronemeyer, Claire. 1999. "On Deriving Complex Polysemy: The grammaticalization of *get*". *English Language and Linguistics* 3.1–39.
Hopper, Paul. 1991. "On Some Principles of Grammaticization". *Approaches to Grammaticalization* (= *Typological Studies in Language*, 19) ed. by Elizabeth C. Traugott & Bernd Heine, vol. 1, 17–35. Amsterdam & Philadelphia: John Benjamins.
Hopper, Paul & Elizabeth C. Traugott. 1993. *Grammaticalization*. Cambridge: Cambridge University Press.
Jespersen, Otto. 1942. *A Modern English Grammar on Historical Principles*, vols. IV and V. London: George Allen & Unwin. Copenhagen: Ejnar Munksgaard.

Kajita, Masaru. 1977. "Towards a Dynamic Model of Syntax". *Studies in English Linguistics* 5: *To Akira Ota in his sixtieth birthday* ed. by Masaru Kajita, Toshio Nakao, & Masatomo Ukaji, 44–76. Tokyo: Asahi Press.

Longman Dictionary of Contemporary English. 1995. London: Longman.

Lightfoot, David. 1979. *Principles of Diachronic Syntax.* Cambridge: Cambridge University Press.

Middle English Dictionary. 1952–present. Ed. by Hans Kurath, Sherman M. Kuhn, John Reidy, & Robert E. Lewis. Ann Arbor: University of Michigan Press. [= MED]

Nunberg, Geoffrey, Ivan A. Sag, & Thomas Wasow. 1994. "Idioms". *Language* 70.491–538.

Oxford English Dictionary on CD-ROM (Version 2.0) [= OED CD-ROM]

Poutsma, Hendrik. 1926. *A Grammar of Late Modern English*, Part I, First Half. Groningen: P. Noordhoff.

Quirk, Randolph, Sidney Greenbaum, Geoffrey Leech, & Jan Svartivik. 1985. *A Comprehensive Grammar of the English Language.* London: Longman.

Ross, John R. 1973. "Nouniness". *Three Dimensions of Linguistic Theory* ed. by Osamu Fujimura, 137–258. Tokyo: TEC.

Simpson, J.A. & E.S.C. Weiner, eds. 1989. *The Oxford English Dictionary.* 2nd ed. Oxford: Oxford University Press. [= OED]

Traugott, Elizabeth C. 1982. "From Propositional to Textual and Expressive Meanings: Some semantic-pragmatic aspects of grammaticalization". *Perspectives on Historical Linguistics* ed. by Winfred P. Lehmann & Yakov Malkiel, 245–271. Amsterdam & Philadelphia: John Benjamins.

Recent advances in the reconstruction of the Proto-Munda verb

Gregory D.S. Anderson and Norman H. Zide
University of Manchester / University of Chicago

1. Introduction

The languages of the Munda family are spoken by 7 to 8 million so-called 'tribals' predominantly in the eastern and central Indian states of Orissa and Bihar and adjacent areas. The Munda languages represent the westernmost branch of the Austroasiatic (AA) language family.[1] When exactly the Munda-speaking peoples entered India is unknown, but they appear to be the oldest surviving linguistic stratum in many of the areas of their current distribution.

Ever since Pater Schmidt established the relation of the Munda and Mon-Khmer languages at the beginning of this century (1906), researchers of comparative AA have been troubled by the apparent typological distance between many modern Mon-Khmer languages on the one hand, and the Munda languages on the other. Some consider the Munda languages to have acquired their often quite complicated structure along with SOV constituent order as the result of diffusion from neighboring non-Munda languages of South Asia, i.e., local Dravidian and Indo-Aryan languages (cf. Donegan 1993; Donegan & Stampe 1983), in many cases, presumably, independently in the individual Munda languages or sub-groups.[2] Others, e.g., Pinnow (1963), suggest that Proto-Austroasiatic was more like Munda, with rather extensive morphological complexity; the present authors maintain this latter position. Nominal morphology in various vestigial forms is found throughout the AA family; various components of the Proto-AA nominal system have been inferred, e.g., an infixed nominalizer in *-n-, prefixed syllabic nasals, a prefixal formative in *k(V)-, a prefixed pronominal case formant/augment in *a-, etc. (see Anderson & Zide forthc.). Characteristics of the Proto-Munda verb not of South Asian origin are of particular interest in the reconstruction of the heretofore elusive Proto-Austroasiatic verbal system due to the overall paucity of (especially inflectional) verbal morphology in many Austroasiatic languages.[3]

The Munda languages have without question been profoundly influenced by the other languages of India: for example, the developed system of auxiliary verbs seen throughout the Munda family, as well as the shift to subject-object-verb word order, both reflect influences of the South Asian *Sprachbund.* Nevertheless, a careful comparison of the Munda languages, starting with recent studies by Zide and Anderson (forthc.) and Anderson (1999a), has revealed a considerable amount of old, morphologically realized categories that must be reconstructed all the way back to the Proto-Munda ancestor language. These include, but are not limited to, such categories as causative, reciprocal, negative, a transitive and intransitive past, a non-past, a reduplicated habitual, an intransitive imperative, at least one participial construction, as well as a set of subject proclitics and object suffixes. Among other features which are not soundly reconstructible, but nevertheless may still be old in the Munda family, is a limited system of verb-noun stem compounding — that is, a type of noun-incorporation — in Proto-South Munda which is lacking in North Munda but which has parallels in other Austroasiatic languages (e.g., Nicobarese or Khasi).[4]

In the following sections we examine a number of categories of the Proto-Munda verb that were realized morphologically, offering parallels to other Austroasiatic languages where warranted. The categories examined include the causative (2), the complex system of referent indexing in the Proto-Munda verb (3), and various parts of the Proto-Munda tense-mood-aspect system (4).

2.   Causative in Proto-Munda

While a range of causative constructions may be found in the individual members of the Munda language family, there is one that appears to be cognate throughout the family which we reconstruct for the Proto-Munda ancestor language. The causative morpheme in Proto-Munda was marked by a prefix consisting of a labial consonant (with an accompanying initial vowel) which was used with monosyllabic stems, and a corresponding preglottalized labial infix allomorph used with stems longer than one syllable. In Proto-North Munda, only a small number of stems preserved the old prefix in a lexicalized form. The vast majority of Kherwarian languages innovated a new productive causative suffix. Korku, on the other hand, lost the morphological causative altogether. The infixed causative seems to have been lost already by the Proto-North Munda stage. In Proto-South Munda, on the other hand, as well as in all the modern attested South Munda langauges, both causative allomorphs remained and remain highly productive.

(1)   *Mundari*   a-jal- "make s.o. lick"
                   a-kiriŋ- "sell" (Osada 1992:94)
      Bhumij   a-jom- "feed"
                   a-nuʔ(u)- "give to drink" (Ramaswami 1992:86)

Kharia	ob-puḍ-na
	CAUS-jump-INF
	"to make jump" (Malhotra 1982:165)
	o-leŋ-na
	CAUS-fly-INF
	"to cause to fly" (Malhotra 1982:165)
	ḍo-b-ko-na (< ḍoko)
	sit-CAUS-sit-INF
	"make sit, seat" (Malhotra 1982:165)
	ob-ḍo-b-ko-yoʔ
	CAUS-sit-CAUS-sit-PAST.II
	"he made him make her sit" (Malhotra 1982:166)
Juray	ər-ə'b-ti-tiy-əm
	NEG.CAUS-REDUP-give-2
	"I can't give you (any)" (A. Zide 1983:120)
Remo	ɔ-gi-ge'b
	CAUS-REDUP-heat
	"cause to heat up, burn" (Bhattacharya 1968:12)
Gorum[5]	bu-p-toŋ-u
	fear-CAUS-fear-TRANS.INF
	"to frighten" (A. Zide, field notes)
	ab-geb-u
	CAUS-burn-TRANS.INF
	"to burn" (A. Zide, field notes)
Gtaʔ	ṇ-aʔ-coŋ-ke
	1-CAUS-eat- PAST.B
	"I fed" (Mahapatra et al. 1989:29)

Therefore, we propose a reconstruction of a causative affix in Proto-Munda and its daughter proto-languages as in (2), with both prefixed and infixed allomorphs.

(2) Proto-Munda   *a'b/*o'b- (1-σ), *-'b- (1+-σ)
     Proto-South Munda *a('b)/*o('b) (1-α), *-(o)'b- (1+-α)
     Proto-North Munda *a-

Many Mon-Khmer languages show forms cognate with the Proto-Munda causative formation. In a range of languages, for example, Katu, Kentakbong (Aslian), Bahnar, Khasi, or Middle Khmer, only the prefix has been preserved, and in many of these languages, only in a restricted set of lexical items (cf. Proto-North Munda). However, both the prefix and infix have been preserved in such geographically and genetically distant languages as Kammu (Khmuʔic) and Nancowry Nicobarese, with exactly the same distribution as in Proto-Munda. See examples in (3).

(3) a.   *Khasi*   *ph-rung* "penetrate"
                             < *rung* "enter" (Henderson 1976: 487)
                             ph-láit "clear away"
                             < *láit* "be free" (Henderson 1976: 487)
                             b-ta "wash/besmear face" (Henderson 1976: 487)

     Middle Khmer   *ph-tiŋ* "inform"
                             < *tyiŋ* "know" (Jacob 1976: 611)

     Bahnar   *po-lôch* "kill"
                             < *lôch* "die" (Banker 1964: 105)
                             po-ji "hurt s.o."
                             < *ji* "be hurt" (Banker 1964: 105)

     Kentakbong   *pi-lay* "bathe s.o."
                             < *ʔilay* "bathe" (Haji Omar 1976: 955)
                             pi-ci "feed"
                             < *ci* "eat" (Haji Omar 1976: 955)
                             pi-tɛg "cause to sleep"
                             < *tɛg* "sleep" (Haji Omar 1976: 955)

     Katu   *pamut* "make run"
                             < *mut* "run" (Costello 1965: 35)
                             pantôq "make fall"
                             < *ntôq* "fall" (Costello 1965: 35)
                             pagoot "cause to cut hair"
                             < *goot* "cut hair" (Costello 1965: 34)

  b.   *Nancowry*   *ha-kah-naŋ*
                             "make understand" (Radhakrishnan 1981: 87)
                             p-um-lóʔ
                             "make lose" (Radhakrishnan 1981: 54)
                             h-um-kah
                             "make know" (Radhakrishnan 1981: 55)

     Kammu (Khmuʔic)   *p-háan* "kill"
                             < *háan* "die" (Svantesson 1983: 104)
                             p-rəh "raise"
                             < *rəh* "rise" (Svantesson 1983: 104)
                             k-m-sés "drop"
                             < *k-sés* "fall" (Svantesson 1983: 104)
                             t-m-lùuy "hang (TRANS)"
                             < *t-luy* "hang" (Svantesson 1983: 104)

This correspondence between Proto-Munda on the one hand and Khmuʔic and Nicobarese on the other cannot be due to chance, and therefore we propose the tentative, schematic reconstruction given in (4) for Proto-Austroasiatic. Note that the Proto-Munda preglottalized infixed allomorph may have been phonetically nasalized in Proto-Austroasiatic, as it is in many modern Munda languages; subsequently this developed into an actual labial nasal in the eastern Austroasiatic languages, preserved in both Kammu and Nancowry Nicobarese.

(4)   Proto-Austroasiatic CAUS
       *B- (1-α), *-(')b-[6] ~ *-m-] (1+-σ)

*B was realized as b-, p-, ph-, pV-, bV-, ha-, V(')b-, etc. in various daughter languages.

3.   Referent indexing in Proto-Munda

A set of both subject proclitics and object suffixes needs to be reconstructed for
Proto-Munda for first and second person subjects; third person (dual/plural) forms
were invariably marked by suffixes, if at all.[7] For Proto-South Munda, both subject
prefixes and object suffixes may be relatively straightforwardly reconstructed, based
on correspondences between Juang and Gorum.

(5)   a. Subject prefixes
       Juang   mɛ-jɔ-ki-ñ
                2-see-PRES.II-1
                "you see me" (Matson 1964:35)
                ni-kib-tan
                1PL-do-COND
                "if we do (it)" (Matson 1964:35)
                ba-ama-gitɔ-ke
                1DL-NEG-sing-PRES.I
                "we-2 don't sing" (Matson 1964:53)
       Gorum   mo-taʔy-iŋ
                2-give-1
                "you gave me" (Aze 1973:249)
       b.   Object prefixes
       Juang   jɔ-ɔ-k-ɔm
                see-1-PRES.II-2
                "I see you" (Matson 1964:35)
                e-jo-e-neniñ
                2PL-see-FUT.II-1PL
                "y'all will see us" (Matson 1964:35)
                ḍi-mi-ñ-ɛ-pa-kia
                give-3FUT-give-FUT.II-2DL-DL
                "they-2 will push you-2" (Pinnow 1960-ms.:131)
       Gorum   ne-aʔy-t-om
                1-splash.AFF-NONPAST-2
                "I will splash you" (Aze 1973:250)

Other South Munda languages show a range of individual developments, such as
the loss of the object suffixes in Proto-Gutob-Remo-Gtaʔ, or the loss of subject prefixes
(other than in the first and second plural) in Sora. Tentative reconstructions for

Proto-South Munda and its various daughter proto-languages Proto-Kharia-Juang, Proto-Sora-Gorum, and Proto-Gutob-Remo-Gtaʔ are given in (6)–(9).

(6)

	Proto-Kharia-Juang SUBJ			Proto-Kharia-Juang OBJ		
	SG	DL	PL	SG	DL	PL
1	*-V-	*ba-	*nV-	*-ñ	*-ba	*-nen
2	*mV-	*ha-	*V-	*-(n)om	*-pa	*-pe
3		(*-ki-ar)	(*-ki)			*-ki

(7)

	Proto-Sora-Gorum SUBJ		Proto-Sora-Gorum OBJ	
	SG	PL	SG	PL
1	*ne-	*le-	*-iñ/ŋ	*-ileŋ
2	*mo-	*bV-	*-Vm	*-iben
3		*-gi		*(-gi)

(8)

	Proto-Gutob-Remo-Gtaʔ SUBJ			
	SG	DL	PL.incl	PL.excl
1	*ŋ-	*naŋ-	*ne/ɛ-	*naj-
2	*na-	*pa-		*pe-

(9)

	Proto-South Munda SUBJ				Proto-South Munda OBJ		
	SG	DL	PL.incl	PL.excl	SG	DL	PL
1	*ŋ/ŋ-	*na(ŋ)-	*n/le-	*naj-	*-iŋ/ñ	?	*-len/ŋ
2	*m(o)-	*pa-		*pe-	*-Vm	*-pa	*-pe(N)
3	*–	(*-ki-ar)	*-ki			(*ki-(b)ar)	(*-ki)

The North Munda languages present a slightly different and more complicated picture. Object marking is found in all the attested North Munda languages, and presumably was characteristic of Proto-North Munda as well.

(10) *Korku*   kul-kiñ-bà
                 send-3DL-FIN
                 "sends them-2" (N. Zide, field notes)
      Santali   Kumbṛabad-te-ko əgu-ke-'t-le-a
                 K-LOC/ALL-PL   bring-ASP-TRANS-1PL-FIN
                 "they brought us to Kumbrabad" (Bodding 1929:208)

The correspondences between Proto-South Munda and Proto-North Munda object suffixes suggest that these should be reconstructed all the way back to the Proto-

Munda ancestor language.

One of the noteworthy aspects of subject marking in the Kherwarian languages (and Proto-Kherwarian and perhaps Proto-North Munda as well) is that the subject markers are preferentially attached to the word immediately preceding the verb; see examples in (11).

(11)   *Mundari*   *hola   Ranchi-te-ñ sen-ke-n-a*
                 yesterday R-ALL-1   GO-ASP-INTRANS-FIN
                 "yesterday I went to Ranchi" (Cook 1965:228)
      Santali   *hḕ iñ-iñ cala'k-a*
                 yes I-1.go-FIN
                 "yes I will go" (Bodding 1929:58)
      Mundari   *ka-ko   jom-ke-d-a*
                 NEG-PL eat-ASP-TRANS-FIN
                 "they didn't eat (it)" (Osada 1992:39)
      Santali   *alo-m   læi-a-e-a*
                 PROHIB-2 tell-BEN-3-FIN
                 "don't tell him" (Bodding 1929:81)

Note that this is not a mere Wackernagel second position clitic, as it is always on the word immediately preceding the verb that the subject is indexed on, regardless of that word's position in the clause. Most striking in this regard is the fact that the immediately pre-verbal subject agreement markers will even appear on an overt subject pronoun, if that happens to be the word in the appropriate position; cf. the first Santali form given in (11) above.

In Kherwarian clauses consisting of only a single verb, and optionally in other clauses, subject marking was found enclitic to the verb complex, following the finitizer or predicator suffix (*-(w)a) which was innovated at the Proto-North Munda level.

(12)   *Santali*   *dal-iñ-kan-a-e*
                 beat-1-PROG-FIN-3
                 "he is beating me" (Ghosh 1994:95)
      Bhumij   *ape nuʔu-e-a-pe*
                 y'all drink-FUT-FIN-2PL
                 "y'all will drink (it)" (Ramaswami 1992:92)

In order to account for the correspondences between the Proto-South Munda prefixes and the Proto-Kherwarian/-North Munda system where subject was indexed on the word immediately preceding the verb, we propose that there was a boundary reanalysis in Proto-North Munda, whereby the original Proto-Munda subject *proclitics* were reinterpreted as *enclitics* belonging to the preceding word. In other words, there was a mismatch between the phonological and morphological word in Proto-North Munda (and Proto-Kherwarian and modern Kherwarian as well). This highly marked phenomenon was subsequently lost in Korku, where subject marking is restricted to third person subjects of various locative copulas and nominal predicates in the locative case.

(13) *Korku*   *de-èn taàkha-ku*
                 there be.there-PL
                 "they are there" (N. Zide, field notes)
                 di-kiñ   Sikag-òn-kiñ
                 s/he-DL Chicago-LOC-DL
                 "they-2 are in Chicago" (N. Zide, field notes)

Note that in Proto-Kherwarian language (and possibly in Proto-North Munda as well, though Korku subject data is mostly lacking), the subject clitics and object suffixes were apparently formally identical, their function being determined by their position in the verb: if the element appears either bound within the verbal complex preceding the finitizer or even the transitivity marker in some cases, it refers to an object of some kind ('direct', 'indirect', 'beneficiary') or a possessor; if the element appears enclitic to the preceding word, or in absolute final position following the finitizer, it marks subject (14).

(14)   **Proto-North Munda**

	SG	incl	DL	incl	PL
1	*-(i)ñ/ŋ*	*-laŋ*	*-liŋ/ñ*	*-bu(N)*	*-le*
2	*-me*		*-ben*		*-pe*
3	*-e/ij*		*-kiŋ/ñ*		*-ku/o*

A preliminary reconstruction of the Proto-Munda agreement affixes may be found in (15).

(15)   **Proto-Munda OBJ**

	SG	DL	PL
1	*-iñ/ŋ*	(*-laŋ*) (12) (*-liŋ*) (13)	*-le*
2	*-(V)m/mV*	*-pa(n)*	*-pe(n)*
3	*-e/ij*		(*-kV*)

	Proto-Munda SUBJ		
	SG	DL	PL
1	*ŋ-/ŋ-*	*laŋ-* (12) *liŋ-* (13)	*l/ne-*
2	*mV-*	*pa-*	*pe-*
3			(*-kV*)

Our proposals for the developments in the system of subject marking in Proto-Munda and its various daughter proto-languages are schematized in (16).

(16) PM X α=y–β >   PSM X α–Y–β   > PSJG, PKhJ X α–Y–β PGRG X α–Y
                          PNM X=α Y–β–FIN > Korku X Y–β–FIN
                                             PKher. X=αy–β–FIN ~ x y–β–FIN=α
      X = word preceding the verb, Y = verb stem, α = SUBJ, β= OBJ
      = is a clitic boundary; – is an affix boundary

      PM=   Proto-Munda
      PSM=   Proto-South Munda
      PNM=   Proto-North Munda
      PSJM=   Proto-Sora-Juray-Gorum
      PKhJ=   Proto-Kharia-Juang
      PGRG=   Proto-Gutob-Remo-Gitaʔ
      PKher.=   Proto-Kherwarian

Note that object marking in Proto-Munda was probably not limited to patients or direct objects alone, but rather probably also included the salient animate non-patient arguments of certain common ditransitive verbs, e.g. 'give', 'tell', etc. This can be found in both South Munda languages (17) and North Munda languages (18).[8]

(17) *Juang*   ḍi-mi-ñ-ɔm
                         give-3FUT-give-2
                         "he will give (it to) you" (Pinnow 1960-ms.: 110)
                         gata-y-ɔ-ñba
                         talk-CNCTV-PAST.II-1DL
                         "(he) talked to us-2" (Matson 1964:61)
      Juray   e'd-tiːy-l-iñ
                         NEG-give-PAST-1
                         "(you) didn't give me" (A. Zide 1983:116)
      Gorum   mo-taʔy-iŋ
                         2-give-1
                         "you gave me" (Aze 1973:249)

(18) *Hazaribagh Korwa* mene-m em-gad-iñ-a
                         NEG-2   given-ASP-1-FIN
                         "you haven't given to me" (Grierson 1906:161)
      Birhor   kahiː-kiːch-aː-e
                         tell-ASP.TRANS.3-FIN-3
                         "he told him" (Grierson 1906:103)
      Koda[9]   kaː-m äːm-taː-t-iñ-aːm
                         NEG-2 give-ASP-TRANS-1-FIN-2
                         "you didn't give me (it)" (Grierson 1906:112)

The transitive imperative in Proto-Munda was characterized by both object agreement and subject agreement. However, unlike the indicative where subject was marked prefixally and object suffixally, the order was probably Verb-OBJ-SUBJ in Proto-Munda. This reconstruction is based on identical patterning in imperatives in North Munda Khwerwarian (e.g., Ho) and South Munda Sora. This variation between prefixal subject marking and suffixal marking in the imperative may have aided the development of the alternate post-verbal subject marking system that became characteristic of Kherwarian.[10]

(19)   *Sora*   *ti'-iñ-ba*
                  give-1–2PL
                  "give (it) to me (you-PL)" (Ramamurti 1931: 141)

       Ho   *eto-ñ-me*
                  teach-1–2
                  "teach me!" (Deeney 1979: 18)
                  jom-e-ben
                  eat-INAN-2DL
                  "eat it you-2!" (Deeney 1979: 14)

Unlike the causative, our proposed referent indexing system of Proto-Munda is not likely to go all the way back to Proto-Austroasiatic. Nevertheless, forms that resemble probable earlier stages in the grammaticalization and fusing of the Proto-Munda subject proclitics can be found in various Mon-Khmer languages, either in the form of resumptive pronouns in such languages as Pacŏh and Katu (20), or the development, as in Proto-South Munda, of actual subject prefixes in the Aslian language Temiar (21). It is quite likely that the Proto-Munda system of proclitic SUBJ agreement arose from a system of resumptive pronouns present, perhaps dialectally, even at the Proto-AA level.[11]

(20)   *Pacŏh*   *a-ám anhi acân ŋai pôc*
                  fathers uncles FUT 3PL go
                  "fathers and uncles will go" (Watson 1964: 93)

       Katu   *dó dâh   dó gamak*
                  he quickly he become.big
                  "he quickly became big" (Wallace 1965: 27)
                  yi 'boor pe jaal   yi chô
                  we 2   3   times we return
                  "we returned 2 or 3 times" (Wallace 1965: 27)

(21)   *Temiar*   *kə²an kə²a-sɛhluh*
                  you.2 2DL-blow.pipe
                  "you-2 are blow-piping" (Benjamin 1976: 159)
                  ²i-sɛluh ñam   ²im-rec
                  1-shoot animal 1.FUT-eat
                  "I shot an animal to eat" (Benjamin 1976: 166)

> tɔʔ ha-reñrec   sec   mɛjmɛj   na
> NEG 2-REDUP-eat meat excellent that
> "you didn't eat that good meat" (Benjamin 1976: 167)

The object suffixes in Proto-Munda apparently have no parallels in other Austroasiatic languages. In Proto-Munda, on the other hand, the object suffixes were apparently more bound (in)to the verbal word than the subject prefixes, (and therefore possibly grammaticalized, phonologically reduced, and fused earlier) despite the general tendency (observable cross-linguistically) to mark subject over object in the verb. Note that in some modern Munda languages, object suffixes were either alone, or at least more consistently, preserved than the subject prefixes, for example in Sora, or, more strikingly, in Korku, which, other than in the very restricted locative expressions with third person subjects mentioned above, has lost subject marking altogether on the verb, but object marking remains active.

4. Further topics in comparative Munda: Tense, transitivity, etc.

In addition to the categories discussed in 2 and 3 above, a number of other categories were realized morphologically in the Proto-Munda verb, including a transitive past, an intransitive past, a non-past, a reduplicated habitual, a participial construction, and an intransitive imperative. The transitive past (22) is preserved in almost all Munda languages except Gtaʔ. The intransitive past (23) is justified on the basis of Proto-North Munda correspondences with Juang. The remainder of the South Munda languages innovated a new intransitive past in *-kt.

(22) PAST.TRANS (except Sora-Gorum) *-(H)o'd[12]
    Juang   gita-y-ɔ
               sing-PAST.TRANS
               "he sang" (Matson 1964: 28)
    Birhor   nam-ed-e-a:-e
               find-PAST.TRANS-3-FIN-3
               "he found him" (Grierson 1906: 103)

(23) PAST.INTRANS *-an
    Juang   gelo-an
               play-PAST.INTRANS
               "he played" (Matson 1964: 28)
    Asuri   sen-en-a:
               go-PAST.INTRANS-FIN
               "he went" (Grierson 1906: 139)

In contrast with the past where the two forms were differentiated for transitivity, there seems to have been a single marker of non-past in Proto-Munda (*-tV). This is preserved in the majority of Munda languages. In a few modern languages, there appears to have been a *k-initial allomorph, rather than the *t-initial form of the non-past. This *k-initial non-past was preserved in Santali, Juang, and Plains Gtaʔ.

(24) NONPAST *tV- (~ *kV-)
      Gorum   ne-aʔy-t-om
               1-splash.AFF-NONPAST-2
               "I will splash you" (Aze 1973:250)
      Remo   goy-ta
               die-NONPAST.INTRANS
               "s/he will die" (Bhattacharya 1968:49)
      Bhumij   lel-ta-n-a-i
               see-NONPAST-INTRANS-FIN-1
               "I am seeing/looking at" (Ramaswami 1992:93)

In addition to the two pasts and the non-past, a number of other verbal affixes were found in Proto-Munda. These include an intransitive imperative and a participial formation. Correspondences between Korku and Gutob-Remo-Gtaʔ, which represent opposite ends of the Munda world, are suggestive of these reconstructions for Proto-Munda.

(25) INTRANS.IMP *-e/*-a
      Korku   oḍ-e
               come.out-INTRANS.IMP
               "come out" (N. Zide field notes)
      Gutob   tunon-a
               stand-INTRANS.IMP
               "stand" (N. Zide field notes)
(26) PART *-kVne
      Korku   goj-ken sim
               die-PART chicken
               "dead chicken" (N. Zide field notes)
      Gtaʔ   gwɛʔ-kne gsæŋ
               die-PART chicken
               "dead chicken" (N. Zide field notes)

5. Conclusions

In the preceding pages we have demonstrated that the Proto-Munda language was indeed morphologically complex, and it is far from the case that all such morphological features are attributable to South Asian areal diffusion.[13] In fact, parallels to the Proto-Munda constructions can be found in various branches of the Austroasiatic language family, e.g., Bahnaric, Katuic, Khmuʔic, Aslian, Nicobarese, or Khasic. With this in mind, perhaps it is appropriate to look for concrete internal phonological or Southeast Asian areal/diffusional histories for the reduction of morphological complexity found in various modern Mon-Khmer languages (where influence from Tai-Kadai and Chinese-type languages is at least as prevalent as are South Asian areal features in the Munda languages) and to work towards a reconstruction of Proto-Austroasiatic verb morphology that takes into consideration the probable archaic nature of Proto-Munda verb morphology, and, one that parallels the derivational (and seeming inflectional) complexity of the Proto-AA noun, which may have included such categories as noun-class, or in the case of pronouns, case as well, both of which have correspondences in the Proto-Munda noun.[14]

Abbreviations

AFF – Affective; AGT – Agentive; ALL – Allative; ASP – Aspect; AUX – Auxiliary; B – -ke tense, Gtaʔ; BEN – Benefactive; CAUS – Causative; CMPL – Completive; CNCTV Connective; COND – Conditional; DESID – Desiderative; DIST – Distributive; DL – Dual; excl – exclusive; FIN – Finit(iz)e(r); FUT – Future; IMP – imperative; IMPERF – Imperfect; INAN – Inanimate; incl – inclusive; INCLIN – Inclinative; INF – infinitive; INTRANS – Intransitive; LOC – Locative; NEG – Negative; NONPAST – Non-past; OBJ – Object; PASS – Passive; PERF – Perfect(ive); PL – Plural; POSS – Possessive; PRES – Present; PROHIB – Prohibitive; PROG – Progressive; PART – Participle; RECIP – Reciprocal; REDUP – Reduplication; SG – Singular; SUBJ – Subject; TRANS – Transitive; 1 – 1st person; 2 – 2nd person; 3 – 3rd person

Notes

1. Apart from Munda, Austroasiatic (AA) includes a large number of languages spoken predominantly by so-called 'hill tribes' or 'hill peoples' in geographically and politically inaccessible regions of Southeast Asia, primarily in Vietnam, southern China, Myanmar (Burma), northern Thailand, Cambodia, Laos, and Malaysia. These fall into a large number of subgroups, the internal relationships of which are still disputed: Nicobarese, Khasic, Aslian, Khmer, Monic, Katuic, Bahnaric, Khmuʔic, Pearic, Viet-Muong, and Palaung-Wa. The total number of known or attested AA languages is appoximately 150–160, although this number has grown in recent years in large part because of the tireless efforts of Gérard Diffloth, who, due to an increasingly favorable political climate, periodically unearths speakers of previously unknown or poorly known AA languages or language groups, for example, the recently isolated Angkuic languages (a subgroup of Palaung-Wa). The non-Munda, eastern languages of the Austroasiatic family are often collectively known as Mon-Khmer [MK] (less commonly Khmer-Nicobar). Many modern MK languages are characterized by relatively simple morphological structure and are notable for their unusual syllable structure (with so-called 'minor'-syllables) and their frequently elaborate vowel systems, which combine a number of vocalic contrasts with a complicated system of register or phonation types (e.g., breathy voice, creaky voice, etc.).

2. Indeed, as Donegan and Stampe (1983) and Donegan (1993) put it, the morphemic complexity of Munda has resulted from a shift in the 'rhythmic holism' of the languages from the Austro-

asiatic/Southeast Asian type to the South Asian type. However, they admit (1983:341) that "in fact, the Munda languages are far more agglutinative and polysynthetic than is typical of India".

3. Verbs in Munda languages can be quite complex (i):

(i) *Kharia*   sob bunui ob-soŋ-ḍom-goḍ-sikh-o-may
                   all pig   CAUS-sell-PASS-CMPL.AUX-PERF-PAST.II-PL
                   "all the pigs have been sold" (Malhotra 1982:200)
     Juang   ḍi-mi-ŋ-ɛ-pɛ-kia
                   give-3.FUT-give-FUT.II-2PL-DL
                   "they-2 will give it to you all" (Pinnow 1960-ms:131)
     Remo   o-sum-oʔ-ki-niŋ
                   CAUS-eat-PAST.II-PERF-1
                   "I had caused (s.o.) to eat" (Fernandez 1968:57)
     Mundari   senoʔ-ja-n-a-ko
                   go.INTRANS-ASP-INTRANS-FIN-PL
                   "they just got down by themselves" (Osada 1992:96)
     Santali   dal-e-'t-me-tahɛkan-a-e
                   beat-ASP-TRANS-2-IMPERF-FIN-3
                   "he was beating you" (Ghosh 1994:106)

While the extreme complexity typical of modern Kherwarian and Kharia is not to be attributed to Proto-Munda, and is generally not characteristic of Mon-Khmer languages, it is far from the case that morphemic complexity is entirely alien to the eastern AA languages. In a variety of languages, there are forms which consist of stems in combination with two or even three additional morphemes.

(ii) *Katu*   ta-pa-têêŋ
                              RECIP-CAUS-work
                              "make e.o. work" (Costello 1965:41)
                              ta-pa-gluh
                              RECIP-CAUS-go.outside
                              "make e.o. go outside" (Costello 1965:41)
      Bahnar   jo-po-lôch
                              PERF-CAUS-die
                              "to have killed" (Banker 1964:113)
                              jo-to-yaih
                              PERF-PASS-untie
                              "to have been untied" (Banker 1964:113)
      Nancowry Nicobarese   pa-m-um-huaʔ
                              be.afraid-AGT-CAUS-be.afraid
                              "one who frightens" (Radakrishnan 1981:58)
      Khasi   ya-pɨn-sam-thyaʔ
                              RECIP/DIST-CAUS-INCLIN-feel.sleepy
                              "together make (others) feel sleepy" (Nagaraja 1985:27)
      Kentakbong   maʔ-pi-yin-ʔam
                              DESID-CAUS-NEG-suckle
                              "(she) wants to wean (the baby)" (Haji Omar 1976:955)

4. Nancowry full and combining forms (Radhakrishnan 1981) ʔu(ál)mát "eye" vs. kap-mat "imagine", halepimatri "examine something"; Khasi kti but tiipdeŋ "middle finger" (Rabel 1961:44), khmat but matliʔ "white of eye" also ʔiimat "eye" < "see-eye/face" (Rabel 1961:149).

5. Note also Gorum, *ta-kin* CAUS-die "kill", with possible cognates in Khmer (Gorgoniev 1974:108) and Bahnar (Banker 1964:106).

6. As an anonymous reviewer has pointed out, there is no definitive, internal Mon-Khmer evidence for the existence of preglottalized stops at the Proto-AA level. In Munda, stops in final syllable coda-position are generally phonetically preglottalized. Despite the fact that there are unmotivated stop nasal alternations or correspondences in MK languages (and more generally in languages throughout Eurasia, particularly b ~ m), based on the Munda evidence (where the change *m > 'b is not known) and the well-known, cross-linguistic tendency for (pre)glottalized elements to develop nasal releases (i.e., the process of 'rhinoglottophilia'), we have tentatively set up a preglottalized obstruent allomorph which may have been phonetically nasalized already by the dialectal or late Proto-AA stage.

7. While interesting from a typological point of view, it seems unlikely that the possessor of objects that may be indexed in the Santali verb (as well as in other 'minor' Kherwarian languages like Karmali) seen in (iii) goes all the way back to Proto-Munda:

(iii) *Santali*   *sukri-ko gɔ'c-ke-d-e-tiñ-a*
            pig-PL   die-ASP-TRANS-3-POSS.1-FIN
            "they killed my pig" (Bodding 1929:209)
            hɔpɔn-e hɛč'-en-tiñ-a
            son-3   come-PAST.INTRANS-POSS.1-FIN
            "my son came" (Ghosh 1994:65)
            seta-e dal-e-tiñ-a
            dog-3 beat-ASP-POSS.1-FIN
            "he will beat my dog" (Bhat 1997:247)

Note that the object suffixes themselves in pre-Proto-Munda may have originally been possessive markers.

8. Thus the development of a benefactive or indirect object marker seen in various other North Munda languages (iv) was probably a secondary development.

(iv) *Erŋa Korwa*   *ñaw-ā-iŋ*
               seek-BEN-1
               "seek for me" (Grierson 1906:166)
               kijā-wā-iŋ-a
               buy-BEN-1-FIN
               "buy for me" (Grierson 1906:166)

9. Note that there is a double marking of subject in this Koḍa form. This probably represents an expressive doubling of subject and in any event is optional; double marking of subject is obligatory, however, in (most) Gorum auxiliary verb constructions (Anderson 1999b).

10. This may have been further supported by the fact that third person plural and dual subjects seem to have used the general nominal number markers, which were suffixes — albeit probably only secondarily/optionally. The same may have been true of Kharia as well.

11. Phenomena akin to noun-class concord in Khasi, beyond the scope of the present study, are similarly suggestive of a preverbal clitic position for tracking referents present in Proto-Austroasiatic.

12. The capital-H in the reconstructed form for the transitive past represents a laryngeal feature of unknown phonetics in the proto-language. This reconstruction is justified on the basis of the fact that the transitive past triggers aspiration of certain stem final obstruents in Kharia, and is found with low tone in Korku.

13. In certain instances, it is possible to suggest possible paths of grammaticalization or development from an earlier state, e.g., the development of the Proto-Munda subject prefixes from a system of resumptive pronouns, earlier stages in the grammaticalizaton path of which may be adduced from data in various Katuic languages, where resumptive pronouns are used even in clauses with an overt subject pronoun. In other instances, based on possible lexical sources within individual AA languages or groups cross-linguistic patterns, one can venture to make conjectures about the origin of certain Proto-AA elements, e.g., the labial causative prefix may have derived from a syntactic construction in which the first, semantically bleached element was a verb meaning 'make' (cf. *pi* "make") later grammaticalized and phonologically reduced as the Proto-AA causative prefix (which subsequently developed an infixed allomorph with sesquisyllabic (and disyllabic) stems. Whether there was a restriction as to the semantic class of verbs that the Proto-AA causative prefix could attach to must await further research.

14. For example, there appears to have been a classifier *k(V)- used with animal names or non-human animate beings found in both Munda and other Austroasiatic languages, e.g. Gutob *gusɔʔ* "dog" Gtaʔ [South Munda] *gsæŋ* "chicken" (N. Zide, field notes), Kontoi [Palaung-Wa)] *kətam¹* "crab" (Paulsen 1992:210–213), Somree [Pearic] *kəpih* "shrimp" (Headley 1978:86), Khasi *ksew* "dog" Mynnar [Khasic] *ksem* "bird" (Fournier 1974:86–92), etc. In some languages (e.g., Chong [Pearic] or Shinman [Palaung-Wa]), a certain number of nouns with this element may not be marking original noun class, but rather reflect the fact that this element has been generalized as the unmarked derivational formant to fulfill the "Bimoraic Constraint" on free forms of nouns that characterized Proto-Austroasiatic and many of its daughter languages, including Proto-Munda (see Anderson & Zide forthc.). Also, Proto-Munda had a case *prefix* in *a*-, originally probably used only with pronouns, later generalized to all nouns in languages like Remo. This element has parallels in various Katuic languages used also only with pronouns; see Solntseva (1996) for more details on its use in Ta-ôih (Katuic).

References

Abbi, Anvita, ed. 1997. *Languages of Tribal and Indigenous Peoples of India: The ethnic space*. Delhi: Motilal Banarsidass.

Anderson, Gregory D.S. 1999a. "A New Classification of the Munda Language Family: Evidence from comparative verb morphology". Paper presented at the 209th American Oriental Society Meeting. Baltimore.

Anderson, Gregory D.S. 1999b. "A Typology of Inflection in Auxiliary Verb Constructions: Contributions of 'minor' language data. *CLS 35: Panel on Linguistic Diversity and Linguistic Theory* ed. by Sabrina J. Billings et al., 249–263. Chicago: Chicago Linguistic Society.

Anderson, Gregory D.S. & Norman H. Zide. Forthcoming. "Issues in Proto-Munda and Proto-Austroasiatic Nominal Derivation: The Bimoraic Constraint". To appear in *South-East Asian Linguistics Society X* ed. by M. Macken.

Aze, (F.) Richard. 1973. "Clause Patterns in Parengi-Gorum". *Patterns in Clause, Sentence, Discourse in Selected Languages of India and Nepal* ed. by Robert. L. Trail, 1: 235–312. Norman, OK: SIL.

Banker, Elizabeth M. 1964. "Bahnar Affixation". *Mon-Khmer Studies* I.99–118.

Benjamin, Geoffrey. 1976. "An Outline of Temiar Grammar". Jenner et al. 1976.129–188.

Bhat, D.N. Shankara. 1997. "Noun-Verb Distinction in Munda Languages". Abbi 1997.227–251.

Bhattacharya, S. 1968. *A Bonda Dictionary*. Poona: Deccan College.

Bodding, Paul O. 1929. *Santal Grammar for Beginners*. Dumka: Santal Mission of N. Churches.

Cook, Walter Anthony. 1965. *A Descriptive Analysis of Mundari*. Ph.D. dissertation, Georgetown University.

Costello, Nancy A. 1965. "Affixes in Katu". *Mon-Khmer Studies* II.29–56.

Deeney, Joseph. 1979. *Ho Grammar and Vocabulary*. Chaibasa: Xavier Ho Publications.

Diffloth, Gérard. 1976. "Jah Hut, an Austroasiatic language of Malaysia". *Southeast Asian Linguistic Studies 2. Pacific Linguistics C-42* ed. by Ð.L. Nguyên, 73–118. Canberra: ANU.

Donegan, Patricia J. 1993. "Rhythm and Vocalic Drift in Munda and Mon-Khmer". *Linguistics in the Tibeto-Burman Area* 16/1.

Donegan, Patricia J. & David Stampe. 1983. "Rhythm and the Holistic Organization of Language Structure". *Papers from the Parasession on the Interplay of Phonology, Morphology, and Syntax* ed. by J. Richardson et al., 337–353. Chicago: Chicago Linguistic Society.

Fernandez, Frank 1968. *A Grammatical Sketch of Remo*. Ph.D. dissertation, University of North Carolina.

Fournier, Alain. 1974. "Les Khasi, une population mon-khmer de l'Inde". *Asie du Sud-Est et Monde Insulindien (=Bulletin du Centre de Documentation et de Recherche Scientifique, École des Hautes Études en Sciences Sociales, Paris)* 5: 1.79–96.

Ghosh, Arun. 1994. *Santali: A look into Santali morphology*. New Delhi: Gyan Publishing House.

Gorgoniev, Ju. A. 1974. *Glagol kxmerskogo jazyka*. [The verb of Khmer]. Moscow: Nauka.

Grierson, Sir George. A. 1906. *Linguistic Survey of India. Vol. IV: Munda and Dravidian*. Calcutta: Office of the Superintendent of Government Printing.

Haji Omar, Asmah. 1976. "The Verb in Kentakbong". Jenner et al. 1976.951–970.

Headley, Robert K., Jr. 1978. *An English-Pearic Vocabulary*. *Mon-Khmer Studies* VII: 61–94.

Henderson, Eugenie J.A. 1976. "Vestiges of Morphology in Modern Standard Khasi". Jenner et al. 1976.477–522.

Jacob, Judith M. 1976. "Affixation in Middle Khmer with Old and Modern Comparisons". Jenner et al. 1976.591–624.

Jenner, Philip N., Laurence C. Thompson, & Stanley Starosta, eds. 1976. *Austroasiatic Studies I and II. (Oceanic Linguistics Special Publication*, 13.) Honolulu: University of Hawaii Press.

Mahapatra, Khageshwar (with Dobek Pujari & P.K. Panda). 1989. *Ḍiḍayi* (In Oriya). Academy of Tribal Dialects and Culture, Government of Orissa, Bhubaneshwar.

Malhotra, Veena. 1982. *The Structure of Kharia: A study in linguistic typology and change*. Ph.D. dissertation, J Nehru University.

Matson, Dan M. 1964. *A Grammatical Sketch of Juang*. Ph.D. dissertation, University of Wisconsin.

Nagaraja, K.S. 1985. *Khasi: A descriptive analysis*. Pune: Deccan College.

Osada, Toshiki. 1992. *A Reference Grammar of Mundari*. Tokyo: Institute for the Study of Languages and Cultures of Asia and Africa.

Paulsen, Deborah A 1992. "Phonological Reconstruction of Proto-Plang". *Mon-Khmer Studies* XVIII–XIX.160–222.

Pinnow, Heinz-Jürgen. 1960–ms. *Beiträge zur Kenntnis der Juang-Sprache*. Unpublished-ms. Berlin.

Pinnow, Heinz-Jürgen. 1963. "The Position of the Munda Languages within the Austroasiatic Language Family". *Linguistic Comparison in Southeast Asia and the Pacific* ed. by Henry L. Shorto, 140–152. London: SOAS.

Rabel, Lili. 1961. *Khasi: A Language of Assam*. Baton Rouge: Louisiana State University Press.

Radhakrishnan, R. 1981. *The Nancowry Word*. Edmonton: Linguistic Research, Inc.

Ramamurti, G.V. 1931. *A Manual of the So:ra Language*. Madras: Government Press.

Ramaswami, N. 1992. *Bhumij Grammar*. Mysore: Central Institute of Indian Languages.

Schmidt, P. Wilhelm. 1906. "Die Mon-Khmer Völker: Ein Bindeglied zwischen Völkern Zentralsiens und Austronesiens". *Archiv für Anthropologie* 33 (n.s. 5).59–109.

Solntseva, V. Nina. 1996. "Case-marked Pronouns in the Taoih language". *Mon-Khmer Studies* XXVI.33–36.

Svantesson, Jan-Olaf. 1983. *Kammu Phonology and Morphology.* Malmö (Lund): CWK Gleerup.

Wallace, Judith M. 1965. "Katu Personal Pronouns". *Mon-Khmer Studies* II.19–28.

Watson, Sandra A. 1964. "Personal Pronouns in Pacoh". *Mon-Khmer Studies* I.81–98.

Zide, Arlene R.K. 1983. "The Story of Two Girls (Excerpt from a Juray Text)". *International Journal of Dravidian Linguistics* XII/1.12–25.

Zide, Arlene R.K. n.d. Field Notes on Gorum. Munda Language Project, Chicago.

Zide, Norman H. 1997. "Gutob Pronominal Clitics and Related Phenomena Elsewhere in Gutob-Remo-Gtaʔ". Abbi 1997.307–334.

Zide, Norman H. n.d. Field notes on Gutob, Gtaʔ. Munda Language Project, Chicago.

Zide, Norman H. & Gregory D.S. Anderson. Forthcoming. "Towards an Analysis of the South Munda Verb". To appear in *South-East Asian Linguistics Society VII* ed. by F.K. Lehman.

Multivariable Reanalysis and phonological split[*]

Janice M. Aski
The Ohio State University

1. Introduction

Sound changes resulting in multiple outcomes in a particular phonetic context compromised the cornerstone of the neogrammarian framework, the regularity principle, by forcing Neogrammarians to posit borrowing and analogy for unexpected developments. Lexical Diffusionists responded to multiplicity by interpreting sound change as phonetically abrupt and lexically gradual, and by identifying unaffected lexemes as the residue of an incomplete spread of a sound change through the lexicon. Labov's (1981, 1994) attempt to reconcile these approaches identifies neogrammarian change as operating at an allophonic, non-contrastive level during the early stages of change, and Lexical Diffusion (LD) as involving lexical and grammatical conditioning of the "abrupt substitution of one phoneme for another ..." (1994:542) during the late stages of change.

This paper traces the multiple developments of the voiceless dental and velar plosives followed by yod from Latin into modern Italian. The analysis begins by presenting the multiple outcomes of Latin /tj/ and /kj/ in Italian and examining previous interpretations, which are either invalidated by counter evidence or are forced to resort to borrowing to explain one of the two outcomes. Evidence is then presented against borrowing and in favor of indigenous multiplicity. The second half of this paper demonstrates that a cogent interpretation of the historical development of these indigenous, multiple outcomes can only be achieved by (1) recognizing a phonetically and lexically gradual intermediate phase between Labov's dichotomy of the early and late stages of sound change, and (2) identifying which lexical items were affected during each phase.

The three-phase analysis of a sound change with multiple outcomes will show that prior to palatalization of /tj/, estimated to have been in the second or third century, assimilation of the dental and the velar to the following yod produced a range of surface variants which, in some cases, overlapped, as the articulation of the dental retracted toward the palatal and that of the velar moved forward. This phonetic variation, which was generated during the first stage of change, continued undisturbed until palatalization of /tj/ to a dental affricate forced speakers to assign the range of surface variants to either /tj/ or /kj/, a categorization process based on speakers' perceptions. The intermediate phase of this three-stage model expands upon the variationist perspective of Wanner and Cravens (1980) to show the manner in which phonetic (surface) variation, which Weinreich, Herzog and Labov (1968) identify as the characteristic feature of sound change, and speakers' perceptions of this variation, which is describable as *Multivariable Reanalysis* (MR), may contribute to phonological split.

Once phonological assignments were complete and a split developed in the phoneme inventory, it will be argued that a limited set of verbs, in which the dental + yod produced a palatal affricate, were formed as a result of morphologically constrained Lexical Diffusion during the third and last stage of change.

2. The problem

The following forms are examples of what are traditionally considered to be the expected developments of Latin /tj/ and /kj/ in Italian, since the majority of lexical items evolve in this manner:

/tj/ > /(t)ts/	/kj/ > /(t)tʃ/
LICENTIA > *licenza* "license"	QUERCEA > *quercia* "oak tree"
ACUTIARE > *aguzzare* "to sharpen"	GLACIU > *ghiaccio* "ice"

Latin /tj/ in postconsonantal and intervocalic position emerges as a dental affricate, and /kj/ as a palatal affricate. However, there are a limited number of lexemes in which /tj/ emerges as a palatal affricate and /kj/ as a dental affricate, which are regarded as exceptional developments. These are shown in Tables 1 and 2.

2.1 Neogrammarian interpretations

Traditional neogrammarian interpretations that seek to sort out the phonetic environment conditioning the change are either invalidated by counter-evidence or are forced to look for external motivations for unexpected developments. Meyer-Lübke (1923: 457–458) posits stress as the conditioning environment for the outcomes of /tj/, a position that is refuted by counter-evidence provided by Rohlfs (1966). Puşcariu (1904) declares the postvocalic and postconsonantal positions as the conditioning environments, but is forced to relegate a number of exceptions to borrowings, learned developments, change in declension, or chrono-

Table 1. /tj/ > /(t)tʃ/ in Standard Italian.

*BOCCIA/*BOTTIA >	*boccia* "decanter"/*bozza* "stone polished roughly, jutting out of wall"
*GUTTIA, *GUTTIARE >	*goccia* "drop", *gocciare* "to drip"
*CENTIU >	*cencio* "rag"
*TENTIONE >	*tencione/tenzone* "poetic contest"
*COMIN[I]TIARE >	*cominciare* "to begin"
(*EX)CURTIARE	*(s)corciare* "to shorten"
*EXQUARTIARE (QUARTU) >	*squarciare* "to tear apart"
*TORTIARE (TORTU) >	*torciare* "to twist"
*CORRUPTIARE (CORRUPTU) >	*corrucciar(si)* "to get angry"
*COMPTIARE (COMPTU) >	*conciare* "to tan"
*CAPTIARE >	*cacciare* "to hunt"
*(DIS)*TRACTIARE (TRACTU) >	*(s)tracciare* "to trace/track"
*SUCTIARE (SUCTU) >	*succiare* beside *suzzare* "to absorb"
DUCTIONE, *DUCTIARE >	*doccione* "trough", *docciare* "to shower"
*SOSPECTIARE >	*sospecciare* (O) "to suspect"
*DISROTEOLARE >	*sdrucciolare* "to slip/slide"
*BIROTIU >	*bir/baroccio* "cart with two or four wheels"

Table 2. /kj/ > /(t)ts/ in Standard Italian

*BOCCIA/*BOTTIA >	*boccia/bozza*
*MUCCEU >	*mozzo* "cut off"
LANCEA >	*lanza* (O) "spear"
*LUNCEA >	*lonza* "leopard"
CALCEA >	*calza* "stocking"
HELCIARIU >	*alzaia* "toe path"
*FACIOLU- >	*fazzoletto* (der.) "tissue"
SOLACIU >	*sollazzo* "amusement"
-Ī/U/A/OCIU >	*-izzo/izio, -uzzo, -azzo, -ozzo*

logically later developments.

Later twentieth-century models do not abandon the neogrammarian framework, and consequently also find themselves resorting to borrowing to explain unexpected developments. Tekavčić (1972:257) and Rohlfs (1966:388) posit that the developments of /kj/ to a palatal affricate and /tj/ to a dental affricate are the indigenous Tuscan outcomes, while a dental affricate from /kj/ is a borrowing from the North, since in most areas of Northern Italy /kj/ and /tj/ merge to a dental affricate /ts/. However, since it is not possible to posit a palatal affricate outcome from /tj/ as a direct northern import, Tekavčić still maintains that these terms are borrowed, but in the importation process, the northern dental affricate /ts/ is 'tuscanized' to a palatal affricate /(t)tʃ/. Among the inconsistencies in the borrowing hypothesis, the most troublesome is that it is not clear what would motivate speakers to transform the dental affricate borrowed from the north to a palatal affricate when the dental exists in Tuscan.

2.2 Evidence for indigenous multiplicity

Attempts to identify the phonetic environment conditioning the outcomes of /tj/ and /kj/ have been unsuccessful, and borrowing from external sources has been shown to be unlikely. At the same time, there is sufficient evidence supporting indigenous developments, such as the multiple reflexes of /tj/ and /kj/ in Tuscan toponyms, dialect terms, and suffixal morphemes.

The phonological outcomes of toponyms can be used to identify indigenous developments, since it is unlikely that speakers would borrow the name they assign to their town or city from an external source. The following toponyms from Tuscany in Grosseto, Livorno, Pisa, and Siena, in which Latin /tj/ develops to a palatal affricate and /kj/ to a dental affricate, are cited in Pieri (1969): MAURITIUS > *Samoreci* (a small piazza in Siena near the church of San Maurizio), CASATIANU > *Casaciano* (near Volterra), TERENTIANU > *Terrinciano* (Buonconvento, Siena), QUINCIANU/QUINTIANU > *Guinzano* (regione, Monciano, Grosseto), *Guinciano* (Monteroni d'Arbia), AEDIFICIUM > *Defizio* (farm, Riparbella, Pisa). Although limited in number, these phonological developments in toponyms support the possibility that the unexpected developments of /tj/ and /kj/ are indigenous to Tuscany.

The variable developments of lexical items in the Tuscan dialects provide additional evidence that all outcomes of /tj/ and /kj/ are indigenous. The lexemes in Tables 3–9 deriving from Latin etyma with /tj/ and /kj/[1] were gathered from dialect dictionaries from Pisa, Amiata, Siena, Viareggio, Versilia, the Maremma, and Pitigliano. In some forms (those preceded by •) the Standard has the expected development while the dialects have the unexpected outcomes of /tj/ and /kj/.

For the items preceded by a bullet it is difficult to argue that the unexpected developments are borrowings, since forms borrowed from a distant prestige source would be expected to appear in the Standard and not be limited to dialectal use. Moreover, as previously noted, the terms in which /tj/ develops as a palatal affricate cannot be northern imports since the palatal affricate is geographically limited in northern dialects. An additional indication that the dialect terms with unexpected outcomes of /tj/ and /kj/ are not borrowed from the North is, in many cases, the common semantic content of the words. That is, speakers would not need to borrow the term for "porridge", "vat, tub", "pigs' grass", the verb "to ache", or the adjective "queasy".

The lists of dialect outcomes reveal that /kj/ had multiple realizations in suffixal morphemes as well as in lexemes. Latin suffixes with /tj/ either have the expected outcome or have a voiced palatal affricate variant unrelated to this study, which are

Table 3. The outcomes of Latin /tj/ and /kj/ in the dialect of Pisa

The dialect of Pisa (Malagoli 1939)	Latin	Standard Italian
•*lanza* (15th–16th c.)	LANCEA	*lancia* "lance, spear"
•*pacenzia* (liv. volg., lucch., cors., rom.), •*paciensia* (Pisan texts of 13th c.), *pazienza*	PATIENTIA	*pazienza* "patience"
•*sforcio* (15th–16th c.)	-FORTIA	*sforzo* "effort"
•*tencione* (14th–15th c.)	TENTIONE	*tenzone* "poetic contest"
malacciato/-zzato (Orent)	-ACEU-	*malazzato* "sickly"
tallocci (rural), *-ozzi* (Cecina) "harvest"	-*OCIU	
officio/-zio (15th–17th c.)	OFFICIU	*ufficio/offizio* "office"
calcerotto, Liv: *calzerotto, carcerotto/carzinotto* (B.Ca., Camp., liv. volg.)	CALCEA-	*calzerotto* "wool sock"
incalciare (14th c.)	-CALCEA-	*incalzare* "to pursue"
comenzare (15th–16th c.)	COMINITIARE	*cominciare* "to begin"
solaccio (13th–14th c.)/*solasso* (13th c.)	SOLACIU	*sollazzo* "fun"

The abbreviations indicate the following towns/cities or dialects: B.Ca. – Bagni di Casciana (Pisa), Camp – Campiglia di Marittima (Livorno), Orent – Orentano (Pisa), liv. – dialect of Livorno, volg. – vulgar/popular, rom. – dialect of Rome, lucch. – dialect of Lucca, cors. – Corsican.

discussed in Aski (forthc.). The multiple outcomes of Latin suffixes with /kj/ in Tuscan dialects as well as in the Standard are discussed by Rohlfs (1966:365–372), who provides several examples, a representative sample of which are the following:

-ACEU   > -*accio, -azzo*: *bonaccione* "peaceful, kind man", *amoraccio* "vulgar/ popular love" (Boccaccio: *amorazzo*), *Melazzo* "citizen of Melo in Province of Lucca"

-ĪCIU   > -*iccio, -izzo*: Toscana: *testicciuola* "small head", *stradicciuola* "small street", Lucca: *omizzoro* "small man", *pedizzoro* "small foot"

-*ŏCEU   > -*occio, -ozzo*: *carezzoccia* "undesired caress", *bamboccio* "fat baby/ child", *basciozzo* "crude kiss"

-ŪCEU   > -*uccio, -uzzo*: *gattuccio* "small cat", *pietruzzo* "small stone/pebble"

Given that Tuscan had its own productive suffixes, the onus is on models which posit an external source for one variant to explain why an alternate form would be borrowed from another speech community.

The data presented suggest that the 'unexpected' or 'exceptional' outcomes of Latin /tj/ and /kj/ may indeed be indigenous. The next section offers a variationist interpretation of indigenous multiplicity based on Wanner and Cravens' (1980) account of the role of phonetic variation in sound change, and demonstrates that a three-phase model, rather than Labov's dichotomy between neogrammarian change and Lexical Diffusion, is necessary for understanding multiple outcomes.

Table 4. The outcomes of Latin /tj/ and /kj/ in the dialect of Amiata

The dialect of Amiata (Fatini 1953)	Latin	Standard Italian
•*pacenza* (A, Cp, Ml, P, Sg)	PATIENTIA	*pazienza* "patience"
•*stramaccioni* (Cz, P, R, Sf)	-TIONE	*stramazzoni* "fall"
•*panizza* (A, P, R, Sf)	-ICIA	*paniccia* "porridge"
•*porrazzu* (A, Ar, Cp)	-ACIU	*porraccio* "pigs' grass"
biconcio/•biconzo (Mc)	*BIGONCIU	*bigoncio* "vat, tub"
doliccicà (P)/•*dolizzicà* (Ml)	-ICIU-	*doliccicare* "to ache"
pioviccicà (Ar, Ml)/*piovizzicà* (Cz, P)	-ICIU-	*piovigginare* "drizzle"
piluccicà (Ca, Sg)	-UCIU	*spelluzzicare* "taste"
mantelluccio (Ml)/-*uzzu* (A, Ar, Cz, P) "wool cover for baby"	-UCIU	
paniuzze (Mc)/*paniuzzi* (Cs) "small pieces of wood planted to attract birds"		

The abbreviations indicate the following towns/cities: A – Abbadia S. Salvatore (Siena), Ar – Arcidosso (Grosseto), Ca – Campiglia d'Orcia (fraction of Castiglion d'Orcia), Cp – Casteldelpiano (Siena), Cs – Castiglion d'Orcia (Siena), Cz – Castellazzara (Grosseto), Mc – Monticello Amiata (fraction of Cinigiano, Grosseto), Mg – Montegiovi (Casteldelpiano), Ml – Montelaterone (Arcidosso), P – Piancastagnaio (Siena), R – Radicofani (Siena), Se – Selvena (fraction of Castellazzara), Sf – Santafiora (Grosseto), Sg – Seggiano (Grosseto).

Table 5. The outcomes of Latin /tj/ and /kj/ in the dialect of Siena

The dialect of Siena (Cagliaritano 1975)	Latin	Standard Italian
•*bigonzo* (Si, Rp, Sn, To, Sv, Ci, Pe, Ra)	*BIGONCIU	*bigoncio*
•*pacienzia* (scherz.)/*pazienza*	PATIENTIA	*pazienza*
•*schicchignosu* (Ab)		CZ: Northern *schissa* *schizzinoso* "queasy, pug-nose"
•*dolizzica(re)/doliccica(re)* (Pi)	-ICIU-	*doliccicare*
ficciolo (Si, As, Bn, Mc, Ra, Cd, Cp)/ •-*zzolo* (Si, Sg, As, Rc, Bn, Ci, Ra, Cd, Cp)	*ISICIU	*sicciolo/cicciolo* "fried bits of pork fat"
defizio (Cp)	EDIFICIU	*edificio/-zio* "building"
paltriccio (Mo, Mc, Ml, Sc)/-*izzo* (Ci)	-ICIU	

The abbreviations indicate the following towns/cities: Pi – Piancastagnaio (Piano), Si – Siena, Rp – Rapolano, Sn – Sinalunga, To – Torrita di Siena, Sv – San Giovanni d'Asso, Ci – Chiusdino, Pe – Pienza, Ra – Radicofani, Cp – Casteldelpiano, Mo – Montepulciano, Mc – Monticiano, Mi – Montalcino, Sc – San Casciano Bagni, As – Asciano (Sciano), Cd – Castiglion d'Orcia, Ab – Abbadia San Salvatore, Rc – Radicondoli, Ml – Montalcino, Bn – Buonconvento, Sg – San Gimignano.

Table 6. The outcomes of Latin /tj/ and /kj/ in the dialect of Viareggio

The dialect of Viareggio (Gianni 1993)	Latin	Standard Italian
pitizzà "argue" *torzo/torcio* "wandering aimlessly"	-ICIU	*bisticciare/bischizzare*

Table 7. The outcomes of Latin /tj/ and /kj/ in the dialect of Versilia

The dialect of Versilia (Cocci 1956)	Latin	Standard Italian
•*pacenza/pacenzia*	PATIENTIA	*pazienza*
•*spennazzà* "remove feathers"	-ACEU	*spennacchiare*
calcerotto	CALCEA-	*calzerotto*
spiegaccià/-azzà "sgualcire"	-ACEU	

Table 8. The outcomes of Latin /tj/ and /kj/ in Maremmano

The dialect of Maremma (Barberini 1995)	Latin	Standard Italian
•*bigonzo*	*BIGONCIU	*bigoncio*
•*sdirocciare/-zzare*	*DISROTEOLARE	*dirozzare* "refine"
•*vitizzo*	-ICIU	*viticcio*
pazienza/•pacenza/•pacenzia	PATIENTIA	*pazienza*
•*schicchignoso/schizzignoso*		CZ: Northern *schissa* *schizzignoso*
cavalluccio/-uzzo "astride one's shoulders"	-UCIU	
Cencio		*Vicenzo* "proper name"
scaveccio "type of fish like an eel that derives its name from *scavezzi* 'iron cord'"		

Table 9. The outcomes of Latin /tj/ and /kj/ in the dialect of Pitigliano

The dialect of Pitigliano (Longo 1936)	Latin	Standard Italian
•*bbigonzu*	*BIGONCIU	*bigoncio*
•*pačenza*	PATIENTIA	*pazienza*
panza	PANTEX-ICIS	*pancia* "tummy"
kakkjaččhu		*cazzaccio* "haphazard"

3.   A three-phase model of change

3.1   Phase I: Assimilation to yod produces a range of surface variants

Due to the flurry of discussion on the palatalization of /tj/ to [ts] by fourth- and fifth-century Latin grammarians, such as Servius (Keil 1961:4,445), Papirius (Keil 1961:7,216), Pompeius (Keil 1961:5,286) and Consentius (Keil 1961:5,395), in contrast to their silence on the pronunciation of /kj/, it appears that palatalization of /tj/ preceded that of /kj/, although the periods in which each palatalization process occurred are debated. Based on inscriptional evidence, Aski (1997) places inception of palatalization of /tj/ in lower registers in the second to third centuries A.D. However, incorporation of [ts] into refined registers is postponed to the fourth and fifth centuries, since grammarians' comments on [ts] for /tj/ do not appear until then. Despite the lack of inscriptional data and grammarians' comments on the articulation of /kj/, Aski (1997) provides evidence that by the fourth and fifth centuries this cluster had not yet palatalized in upper-class educated speech. However, the period of palatalization of the velar + yod cluster in any class remains unclear.

An indication that /tj/ and /kj/ may have had similar articulations before palatalization is suggested by orthographic confusion between ⟨ci⟩ and ⟨ti⟩ in Latin documents and inscriptions as early as the 2nd century A.D., such as Greek *Αρουκιανος* for *Aruntianus* in 131 A.D. (Eckinger 1892:99), *mundiciei* for *munditiei* in 136 A.D. (Seelmann 1885:323), *Praestetium* beside *Praesetecium* (for **Praesteticius*) in the 2nd or 3rd century A.D. (Jeanneret 1918:48), *Terciae* in Baetica, 179 A.D., *terminaciones* and *defenicionis* in Mauretania Sitifensis, 222–235 A.D. (Castellani 1980:111), and the forms cited by Schuchardt (1866:154): *tribunitiae* (Or. 957 Steinbach im Els., 222 n.Chr.), *Anitius* (Renier I. A. 90, B, 50 Lambaesa, 218 n.Chr.), *impacientis* (Furlanetto Le ant. lap. Pat. CCXXVII Steinbach im Els., 222 n.Chr.), *ocio* (Grut. 462, 1 389 n. Chr.), *Constancius, milicie* (Le Blant I. Chr. 223 Trier, 5 jahrh. n.Chr.).

Grandgent (1907) posits that in the 2nd and 3rd centuries both clusters merged at an intermediate articulation and were confused. Lindsay (1894:88) makes a similar observation but distinguishes the orthographic variation between ⟨ci⟩ and ⟨ti⟩ before the palatalization of /tj/, which he places in the 5th century, from the variation between these two graphemes which continued well after this period[2] when he states that

> ... *ci* (*ce*) before a vowel underwent the same process of palatalization, as *ti* before a vowel did in the fifth cent. A.D., although interchange of spelling between prevocalic *ci* and *ti* before that time means merely that *cy, ty* were confused, as *cl, tl* were confused ... not that both *cy* and *ty* expressed a sibilant sound.

Prior to palatalization of /tj/ to a dental affricate /(t)ts/, spelling confusion between ⟨ci⟩ and ⟨ti⟩ indicates that the dental and velar plosives were separate phonemes whose allophones were similar due to assimilation to the following yod. The divergent developments of /tj/ and /kj/ as well as the multiple outcomes of each in Italian demonstrate that this merger was incomplete. The realizations of these clusters in the modern Italian dialects may contribute to our understanding of their diachronic development during the assimilation process.

Giannelli (1976: 24) reports that in Florentine /(k)kj/ can be pronounced as a palatalized dental, a postpalatal, or a velar, since he finds all three articulations in *chiave* "key" ([t'ave], [čave], [kjave]) and *occhio* "eye" ([ot't'o], [oččo], [okkjo]). In Arezzo and in the transition zone between Arezzo and Siena, Giannelli (1976: 78) notes that a palatalized dental [t't'] is the realization of /kj/ much more frequently than the postpalatal ([čč]), so that in Arezzo he finds *occhio* realized as [ot't'o] and *bicchiere/i* "(drinking) glass(es)" as [bit't'ere, -i]. In this same area Giannelli (1976: 78) highlights the lack of the dental + yod cluster before a vowel, so that Standard Italian *tiene* "he has/holds" emerges as /kiene/, while *tiepido* "luke-warm" is /kiebbeto/.

In the dialects of the Pisa area Malagoli (1939: xviii) finds that in the country-side around Pisa /tj/ and /kj/ emerge as a velar + yod, so that *chiepito* corresponds to standard *tiepido*. In the Pisa-Livornese hills the result appears to be various degrees of a 'velo-palatal' articulation, or an intermediate articulation probably closer to [kj], while in Calci, in the hills east of Pisa, the dental feature prevails with "qualche sfumatura velo-palatale", so that /kj/ and /tj/ emerge as [tj] and standard *chiave* is *tiave*.

Further evidence of an intermediate articulation between the dental and the velar that is described by Malagoli as a velo-palatal and by Giannelli as a post-palatal are the realizations of /tj/ and /kj/ after /s/ in modern Tuscan dialects. According to Migliorini (1957: 209), the shift from a velar to a dental in forms such as *schiena* "back" and *fischiare* "to whistle", which emerge as [stjena] and [fistiare], was common by the 16th century in Tuscany. Lapucci (1988) reports that in the Tuscan dialect of Montepulciano [skj] easily passes to [stj] in words with this cluster, but that the dental is not a pure sound, since it partially preserves the velar articulation. This intermediate articulation, which to the listener appears to preserve the velar and dental articulations, is attested in several reports of the [skj] cluster in the *Atlante Linguistico Italiano* (ALI) shown in Table 10, where the reflexes in italics demonstrate the transcribers' indecision between the velar and dental articulation.

Moreover, evidence of the opposite development in which [stj] → [skj] in forms such as *bestia* "beast, animal", which emerges as *beschia*, are found in Tuscan dialect dictionaries for Amiata (Fatini 1953), Siena (Cagliaritano 1975), Pisa (Malagoli 1939), the Maremma (Cocci 1956; Barberini 1994).[3]

Table 10. Reports of the [skj] cluster from the Atlante Linguistico Italiano (ALI)

ALI	fischio "whistle"	maschio "male"	raschiamo "we scrape"	schiaffo "slap"	schiena "back"	schiuma "foam"	vischio "mistletoe"
*444 Camu-gnano BO		t′/k′					
*457 San Pietro in Bagno FO				k′ t′/k′			
515 Pistoia		k′/t′		k′/t′			
516 Legri FI	k′/t′	k′	t′/k′	k′/t′			k′/t′
517 Vicchio FI		k′ t′/k′	t t′/k′	t			
521 Tizzana PT	t′/k′ k′/t′	k′/t′	t	k′/t′			k′/t′
523 Firenze		k′ k′		k k′/t			
526 Badìa Tedalda AR	t′/k′	k′/t′		k′/t′		t′/k′	
*556 Perugia Umbria	k′/t′	k′/t′		k′/t′	k′/t′	k′/t′	
568 Capoliveri LI	k′ k′/t′	t′	t′/k′	t′	t′ k′/t′	t′	
587 Isola del Giglio GR				t′/k′		t′/k′	

Abbreviations indicate the following Provinces: BO – Bologna, FO – Forlì, FI – Firenze, PT – Pistoia, AR – Arezzo, LI – Livorno, GR – Grosseto.

The realizations of /tj/ and /kj/ in Tuscan dialects reveals that these clusters are unstable, and succumb easily to assimilation. The Tuscan articulations of /tj/ and /kj/[4] are summarized in Table 11.[5]

Table 11. Summary of the Tuscan articulations of /tj/ and /kj/

	/tj/			/kj/		
	(t)tj	——	(k)kj	(t)tj	——	(k)kj
Florence	(t)tj	**	**	(t′)t′	(č)č	(k)kj
Arezzo	**	**	(k)kj	(t′)t′	(č)č	**
Pisa countryside	**	**	(k)kj	**	**	(k)kj
Pisa-Livorno hills	**	(č)č	**	**	(č)č	**
hill east Pisa	(t)tj	**	**	(t)tj	**	**

These various outcomes as well as the data from the ALI indicate that a range of articulations is produced during assimilation to the following yod as the dental retracts and the velar is pulled forward. This type of allophonic variation during sound change is a key feature of Wanner and Cravens' (1980) account of the voiced/voiceless split development of intervocalic plosives in Tuscan. They posit that a variable voicing rule generated surface variation of degrees of voicing that was constrained by sociolinguistic 'performance' parameters.[6] When this variable rule ceased to operate, the intervocalic obstruents that were not consistently voiced were perceived as voiceless, but those with consistent voicing were interpreted as underlyingly voiced. In this model, the assignment of phonological class identity is a type of Lexical Diffusion, the results of which are lexicalized and resemble an irregular sound change.

Incorporating the principles of Wanner and Cravens' model into a three-stage interpretation of the development of Latin /tj/ and /kj/, we find that in the first phase, an allophonic assimilation rule applies variably and produces surface variation along a continuum of full velar and dental occlusion that is constrained by socio- and extra-linguistic factors. A model of the first phase is presented in Figure 1.

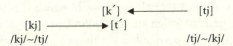

Figure 1. Variable articulations of the allophones of /tj/ and /kj/

3.2 Phase II: Multivariable reanalysis of surface variants

During the second phase, this variation is disturbed by another change in the system. In Wanner and Cravens' (1980) case the variable voicing rule ceased to operate, but here the change is palatalization of /tj/. Once the dental + yod cluster began to palatalize, speakers were forced to identify which surface variants were associated with an underlying /tj/, and thus were candidates for palatalization, and which variants were associated with /kj/. This assignment process would have been similar to that described by Wanner and Cravens for the voiced/voiceless feature of intervocalic plosives, and is identified here as *Multivariable Reanalysis*. For the most part, during reanalysis in the second stage of change, speakers could keep the two phonemes distinct, as demonstrated by the restricted number of unexpected outcomes. However, in some cases, surface variants of /tj/ were perceived to be closer to the velar articulation, while some surface variants of /kj/ were perceived to be closer to the dental articulation, and each restructured accordingly.

Within Wanner and Cravens' (1980) model, the ultimate split in the lexicon represents a case of Lexical Diffusion of the phonological reassignments. However, in this three-stage model of sound change, Multivariable Reanalysis, which occurs in the second phase, relies on variation within the speech community and speaker's perceptions, and thus produces unexpected and unconstrained results. Lexical Diffusion, which according to Labov occurs during the late stages of change and is constrained by lexical or grammatical contexts, only begins after the reassignments of surface variants to underlying phonemes has taken place.[7]

3.3   Phase III: Morphologically-constrained Lexical Diffusion of phonemic substitutions

Some of the items in which /tj/ results in a palatal affricate may have been the result of Lexical Diffusion during the last, third phase of change. Castellani (1980: 112–113) considers the following forms from Table 1 above, *GUTTIARE > gocciare, *COMIN[I]TIARE > cominciare, *EXCURTIARE > scorciare, *CORRUPTIARE (CORRUPTU) > corrucciar(si), *COMPTIARE (COMPTU) > conciare, *CAPTIARE > cacciare, *DISTRACTIARE > stracciare, *TRACTIARE (TRACTU) > tracciare, *SUCTIARE (SUCTU) > succiare beside suzzare, *DUCTIARE > docciare *DISROTEOLARE > sdrucciolare, and points out that all the cases in which /tj/ has a palatal affricate outcome are verbs, none of which are attested in Latin and all of which are formed from nouns, adjectives, or participles. He proposes that these palatal outcomes developed after /tj/ had already assibilated to the dental affricate. This secondary /tj/ could not assibilate, since the assibilation rule had already terminated, but it could have been confused with /kj/ or been involved, at a later stage, in the palatalization of /kj/ to the palatal affricate /tʃ/.[8]

By positing that unattested, derived verbs in which /tj/ became /tʃ/ must be late developments that formed after palatalization of /tj/ had terminated, Castellani's model predicts that unattested, derived verbs, in which /tj/ had the expected outcome /ts/, would not exist. However, the following exceptions demonstrate that lack of attestation in Latin may not necessarily indicate a development that occurred after palatalization of /tj/ had terminated: *ADVITIARE > avvezzare, *ATTITIARE > attizzare, *SINGLUTTIARE > singhiozzare, *ABANTIARE > avanzare. On the other hand, since few unattested, non-verbal items with /tj/ emerge with /tʃ/ (*CENTIU > cencio, *BUTTIA > boccia, *BIROTIU > biroccio, baroccio), Castellani's observation that a relatively large number of verbs were affected suggests that morphological conditioning may have influenced the change.

The fact that some unattested, derived verbs have regular developments suggests that the derived verbs could have formed at a later time, but while palatalization of /tj/ was underway, and both /tj/ and /kj/ still had unpalatalized variants in the speech community. That is, the intermediate articulations of secondary /tj/ could have been interpreted either as dentals, and joined the development of /tj/, or as velars, and joined that of /kj/. This would have been before the fourth or fifth centuries, when evidence suggests that all classes had eliminated the [tj] variant of /tj/ (and the unpalatalized [kj] realization of /kj/ was still maintained, at least by the upper class). The relatively large number of verbs in which the intermediate articulations of secondary /tj/ must have been assigned to /kj/ indicates that this process was implemented by means of morphologically-constrained Lexical Diffusion of phonemic substitutions, in which /tj/ was supplanted by /kj/.[9]

4. Concluding remarks

This model refines our understanding of a variety of sound changes. It can account for regular, neogrammarian-type changes, lexically diffused changes, and all the exceptions which cannot be characterized as a product of either of these models. The three-stage model is summarized in Table 12.

Labov's early stage of change and the first phase of the three-stage model begins as an allophonic rule at a non-contrastive level, which in this case produces variation in terms of degrees of assimilation of the dental and velar to a following yod. This allophonic variation is constrained by socio- and extra-linguistic constraints and, if it continues uninterrupted, the result may be stable variation or the development of a regular, neogrammarian change.

If, however, this socially constrained allophonic variation is disturbed by another change in the system, in this case palatalization of /tj/, which forced speakers to assign surface variants to an underlying dental or velar, there is a strong possibility of multiple outcomes. This assignment process, or Multivariable Reanalysis, relies on speakers' perceptions and is lexically sporadic since it is unconstrained by any type of social or grammatical context.

Once a phonological split develops, phonological substitutions occur in the third phase of a three-stage model, or Labov's late stages of change. At this point, phonemic substitutions are implemented by means of lexically and grammatically conditioned Lexical Diffusion.[10]

This paper has demonstrated that indigenous multiplicity cannot be classified within the Labovian dichotomy of neogrammarian change vs. Lexical Diffusion. Instead, a three-stage model in which Multivariable Reanalysis takes place in the second phase, is an interpretation of sound change that incorporates surface variation, an intrinsic feature of language, and speakers' perception of that variation, to account for a three types of change: regular, or neogrammarian change, phonological split, and constrained Lexical Diffusion.

Table 12. A summary of the three stages of change

First stage: Application of a variable allophonic rule produces surface variation (see Table 11) constrained by socio- and extra-linguistic factors

Second stage: Multivariable Reanalysis of surface variants

/tj/ > /(t)ʃ/	/kj/ > /(t)ts/
*BOCCIA/*BOTTIA > boccia/bozza	*BOCCIA/*BOTTIA > boccia/bozza
*CENTIU > cencio	*MUCCEU > mozzo
*TENTIONE > tencione/tenzone	LANCEA > lanza (O)
*BIROTIU > bir/baroccio	*LUNCEA > lonza
	CALCEA > calza
	HELCIARIU > alzaia
	*FACIOLU- > fazzoletto (der.)
	SOLACIU > sollazzo
	-ō/U/A/OCIU > -izzo/izio, -uzzo, -azzo, -ozzo

Third Stage: Morphologically constrained Lexical Diffusion of /tj/ > /(t)tʃ/

*GUTTIARE > gocciare
*COMIN[I]TIARE > cominciare
*EXCURTIARE > scorciare
*CORRUPTIARE (CORRUPTU) > corrucciar(si)
*COMPTIARE (COMPTU) > conciare
*CAPTIARE > cacciare
*(DIS) TRACTIARE (TRACTU) > (s)tracciare
*SUCTIARE (SUCTU) > succiare/suzzare
*DUCTIARE > docciare
*DISROTEOLARE > sdrucciolare

Notes

* I would like to thank Professors Thomas D. Cravens, Betty S. Phillips, Richard Janda, and Roger Wright for their helpful comments and suggestions. All opinions expressed and any errors are my own.

1. Latin etymologies from Battisti and Alessio (1950) are given when available.

2. Examples of orthographic confusion between ⟨ci⟩ and ⟨ti⟩ after the fourth century are reported in Northern Italian documents by Carlton (1973: 150), Politzer (1949: 47), Corbett (1957: 190), Löfstedt (1961), and Adams (1976). The same confusion in Latin inscriptions and documents in Spain is discussed by Carnoy (1916: 141–144), Muñoz y Rivero (1919: 113), and Puentes Romay (1986). In Gaul, ⟨ci⟩/⟨ti⟩ confusion is examined by Bonnet (1968), Pirson (1901: 71–72), Vielliard (1927), Taylor (1924: 40), and Pei (1932: 97–98).

3. These dialects appear to have a flip-flop rule, by which [stj] > [skj] and [skj] > [stj]. However, it is possible that a lexicographer familiar with Standard Italian /skj/ and confronted with a surface variant [st'] may interpret this nonstandard intermediate realization as 'not /skj/', leaving /stj/ as the

only option. The opposite would occur for /stj/. The intermediate outcomes in Table 10 support this interpretation based on misperception, but this problem requires further investigation.

4. The symbol used by Giannelli to represent the postpalatal in Arezzo and Florentine ([(č)č]) is used to represent the 'velo-palatal' described by Malagoli in the Pisa-Livorno hills.

5. In his discussion of the loss of /tj/ in Arezzo, Giannelli (1976: 78, n.280) points out that the loss of this cluster may have been due to a diachronic tendency to create palatalized dentals, which appears to have withdrawn in Florentine. Since he finds traces of this phenomenon in the southeast and, in a different form, in Elba, with traces in the western dialects, he concludes that it may have been a feature of central Italy. The development of /kj/ in the Tuscan dialects appears to have been similar, with assimilation to yod bringing the articulation of this cluster close to an intermediate postpalatal or a dental articulation.

6. For a discussion of surface variation and its role in the development of /sj/ from Latin to Italian, see Aski (forthc.).

7. Phillips (1999) focuses on the interconnections and interdependencies within the lexicon during the implementation of sound change and submits that "neighborhood density must be incorporated into a psychologically real model of the lexicon and the effect of sound change upon that lexicon" (19). Her research reveals that sound changes that require syntactic, morphological, or phonological analysis during their implementation affect the least frequent words first, while others affect the most frequent words first. Extending these observations to developments of /tj/ and /kj/, the exceptional developments discussed here would be the least frequent words. Although there is no way to confirm this observation, applying the results of modern research to historical data provides a plausible interpretation of the process.

8. Regarding the dental affricate development of /kj/, Castellani does not mention the doublets of Central Italy and only refers to the merger of /tj/ and /kj/ in the South when he remarks that in some territories (Southern Italy and Sardegna) /kj/ followed the outcomes of /tj/ when the latter assibilated.

9. On the other hand, if any secondary /tj/ formed when all classes had adopted the palatalized variant ([ts]) and had rejected [tj] in all phonetic contexts (or, in Castellani's terms, the palatalization of /tj/ had ended), yet /kj/ was still unpalatalized (at least in educated speech), hypercorrection may have influenced the lexical reassignments. That is, speakers could have associated the intermediate variants of secondary /tj/ with the unpalatalized variant of /kj/, which would have been a prestige variant used (at least) by the educated class. The large number of affected verbs suggests, as in the first case, that reassignment to /kj/, in this case motivated by prestige, was implemented by morphologically-constrained Lexical Diffusion.

10. This lexical and grammatical conditioning refines the notion of Lexical Diffusion, making it identifiable as a type of analogical spread. Kiparsky (1995: 647) also identifies LD as a type of analogy within the model of Lexical Phonology. See Phillips (1998) for a contrasting position.

References

Adams, J.N. 1976. *The Text and Language of a Vulgar Latin Chronicle (Anonymous Valesianus II)*. London: Institute of Classical Studies.
Aski, Janice M. Forthcoming. "La sonorizzazione variabile e esiti multipli: Lo sviluppo di /sj/ dal Latino all'Italiano". *Zeitschrift für romanische Philologie*.

Aski, Janice M. 1997. *Panchronic Variation and Multiple Outcomes: The developments of Latin /tj/ and /kj/ in Italian and Romance*. Ph. D. dissertation, University of Wisconsin-Madison.

Barberini, Mario. 1994. *Vocabolario maremmano*. Pisa: Nistri-Lischi.

Battisti, Carlo & Giovanni Alessio. 1950–1957. *Dizionario etimologico italiano*. 5 vols. Florence: Barbèra.

Bonnet, Max. 1968. *Le latin de Grégoire de Tours*. Reprint of 1890 original. Hildesheim: Georg Olms.

Cagliaritano, Ubaldo. 1975. *Vocabolario senese*. Florence: Barbèra.

Carlton, Charles Merritt. 1973. *A Linguistic Analysis of a Collection of Latin Documents Composed in Ravenna between A.D. 445–700*. The Hague: Mouton.

Carnoy, Albert Joseph. 1916. "The Assibilation of ti and di Before a Vowel". *Proceedings of the American Philological Association* 47.145–152.

Castellani, Arrigo. 1980. *Saggi di linguistica e filologia italiana e romanza (1946–1976)*. 2 vols. Rome: Salerno.

Cocci, Gilberto. 1956. *Vocabolario versiliese*. Florence: Barbèra.

Corbett, P. B. 1957. "Local Variations of Spelling in Latin Manuscripts". *Studia Patristica: Papers presented at the Second International Conference on Patristic Studies held at Christ Church, Oxford, 1995* ed. by Kurt Aland & F. L. Cross, vol. 1, 188–193. Berlin: Akademie.

Eckinger, Theodor. 1892. *Die Orthographie lateinischer Wörter in griechischen Inschriften*. Munich: C. Wolf & Sohn.

Fatini, Giuseppe. 1953. *Vocabolario amiatino*. Florence: Barbèra.

Giannelli, Luciano. 1976. *Toscana*. Pisa: Pacini.

Gianni, Iberico. 1993. *Vocabolario viareggino*. Viareggio: Mauro Baroni.

Grandgent, Charles H. 1907. *An Introduction to Vulgar Latin*. Boston: D. C. Heath.

Jeanneret, Maurice. 1918. *La langue des tablettes d'exécration latines*. Paris: Attinger Frères.

Keil, Heinrich. 1961. *Grammatici Latini*. 8 vols. Reprint of 1855–1880 original. Hildesheim: Georg Olms.

Kiparsky, Paul. 1995. "The Phonological Basis of Sound Change". *The Handbook of Phonological Theory* ed. by John A. Goldsmith, 640–670. Cambridge, MA: Blackwell.

Labov, William. 1981. "Resolving the Neogrammarian Controversy". *Language* 57.267–301.

Labov, William. 1994. *Principles of Linguistic Change: Internal factors*. Oxford: Blackwell.

Lapucci, Carlo. 1988. *La parlata di Montepulciano e dintorni*. Montepulciano: Editori del Grifo.

Lindsay, William M. 1894. *The Latin Language*. Oxford: Clarendon Press.

Löfstedt, Bengt. 1961. *Lautliches und Orthographisches zu den ältesten Handschriften von Rotharis Edikt*. Stockholm: Almqvist & Wiksell.

Longo, Vicenzo. 1936. "Il dialetto di Pitigliano (in Provincia di Grosseto)". *Italia Dialettale* 12.19–33, 103–147.

Malagoli, Giuseppe. 1939. *Vocabolario pisano*. Florence: Reale Accademia della Crusca.

Massobrio L. & G. Ronco, eds. 1995–1996. *Atlante Linguistico Italiano. Vols. 1–2: Il corpo umano*. Turin: Istituto Poligrafico e Zecca dello Stato. (Unpublished data also examined).

Meyer-Lübke, Wilhelm. 1923. *Grammaire des langues romanes. Vol. 1*. Trans. Eugène Rabiet. New York: G. E. Strechert.

Migliorini, Bruno. 1957. *Saggi linguistici*. Florence: Felice Le Monnier.

Muñoz y Rivero, Jesús. 1919. *Los códices y documentos españoles de los siglos V–XII*. Madrid: Daniel Jorro.

Pei, Mario. 1932. *The Language of the Eighth-Century Texts in Northern France*. New York: Carranza & Company.

Phillips, Betty S. 1999. "Lexical Diffusion, Lexical Frequency, and Lexical Analysis". Paper presented at the Symposium on Frequency Effects and Emergent Grammar, Carnegie-Mellon University, May 28–30.

Phillips, Betty S. 1998. "Lexical Diffusion is not Lexical Analogy". *Word* 49: 3.369–381.

Pieri, Silvio. 1969. *Toponomastica della Toscana meridionale e dell'Arcipelago toscano.* Siena: Accademia Senese degli Intronati.

Pirson, Jules. 1901. *Le langue des inscriptions latines de la Gaule.* Bruxelles: J. Adam.

Politzer, Robert L. 1949. *A Study of the Language of Eighth-Century Lombardic Documents.* Ph. D. dissertation, Columbia University.

Puentes Romay, José Antonio. 1986. "Acerca de la grafía del latín alto medieval". *Euphrosyne* 14.97–112.

Puşcariu, Sextil. 1904. *Lateinisches TJ und KJ im Rumänischen, Italienischen und Sardischen.* Leipzig: Kommissionverlag von J. A. Barth.

Rohlfs, Gerhard. 1966. *Grammatica storica della lingua italiana e dei suoi dialetti: Fonetica.* Turin: Einaudi.

Schuchardt, Hugo. 1866. *Der Vokalismus des Vulgärlateins.* Leipzig: B. G. Teubner.

Seelmann, Emil. 1885. *Die Aussprache des Latein.* Heilbronn: Gebr. Henninger.

Taylor, Pauline. 1924. *The Latinity of the Liber Historiae Francorum.* New York: [s.n.].

Tekavčić, Pavao. 1972. *Grammatica storica dell'italiano. Vol. 1: Fonematica.* Bologna: Il Mulino.

Vielliard, Jeanne. 1927. *Le latin des diplômes Royaux et Chartes Privées de l'époque Mérovingienne.* Paris: Librairie Ancienne Honoré Champion.

Wanner, Dieter & Thomas D. Cravens. 1980. "Early Intervocalic Voicing in Tuscan". *Papers from the 4th International Conference on Historical Linguistics* ed. by Elizabeth Closs Traugott, Rebecca Labrum, & Susan Shepherd, 339–348. Amsterdam: John Benjamins.

Weinreich, Uriel, William Labov, & Marvin Herzog. 1968. "Empirical Foundations for a Theory of Language Change". *Directions for Historical Linguistics* ed. by Winfred P. Lehmann & Yakov Malkiel, 95–195. Austin: University of Texas Press.

Are Old English conjunct clauses really verb-final?*

Kristin Bech
University of Bergen

1. Introduction

This paper discusses the claim that Old English (OE) conjunct clauses typically have verb-final (SXV)[1] word order, a claim which has almost become axiomatic. The term 'conjunct clause' has been used in various ways, but usually it refers to any declarative main clause introduced by *and, ac,* and, in a few cases, *oððe,* and which has an overt subject. This is the way the term will be understood in this paper.[2]

The observation that conjunct clauses tend to have verb-final order has been made by, among others, Campbell (1964: 191), Mitchell (1964: 119, 1985(I): 694, 1985(II): 967), Kohonen (1978: 36), Denison (1986: 283),[3] van Kemenade (1987: 177), Stockwell and Minkova (1990), Traugott (1992: 277), and Pintzuk (1995: 249 ff.). These authors represent different theoretical frameworks; some, such as van Kemenade, Pintzuk, and Stockwell and Minkova, are concerned with underlying as well as surface structure, while others busy themselves with surface structure only. This makes it hard to compare the studies, especially since generative syntacticians often fail to clarify whether it is underlying or surface structure they are discussing at any given point. Furthermore, the term 'verb-final' may have different meanings; within a generative framework, an SXVX clause may very well be regarded as verb-final, with the postverbal element(s) being derived from an underlying verb-final structure by postposition. Likewise, an SV_1XV_2 clause may be derived from an underlying verb-final structure by verb projection raising. In spite of these differences, it seems to be generally agreed upon that the tendency for conjunct clauses to be verb-final (in surface structure) is far greater than for other main clauses, and it is this claim I wish to devote some time to in this paper. In order to avoid any misunderstanding, let me at this point make it clear that I am concerned with surface structure only.

As far as explanations of the presumed verb-final word order of conjunct clauses are concerned, only a few have been offered, and then usually rather sketchily. Kohonen proposes that in OE, the conjunctions *and/ac* "had the effect of blocking topicalization and causing a dependent clause word order (SXV); i.e., they shared properties of subordinating conjunctions" (1978:154). Traugott (1992:277) suggests that the discourse function of the conjunct clause has a bearing on its word order, while Pintzuk (1995:249ff.) claims that that INFL-final, as opposed to INFL-medial, structure in conjunct clauses is due to syntactic parallelism; i.e., conjoined constituents often have similar structures.

However, a question that does not seem to be asked very often in this context is whether the empirical facts are correct; i.e., whether conjunct clauses really *are* verb-final to the extent they are claimed to be. My first, and main, aim with this paper is thus to disprove the claim that there is a strong tendency for conjunct clauses to be verb-final, which I think is due to a misunderstanding, or perhaps I should rather say a failure to look at the question from the right angle. If we look at word order in general, it soon becomes clear that only a minority of conjunct clauses are verb-final. However, if we turn the whole thing around and look at what word order patterns have the most conjunct clauses, it becomes equally clear that conjunct clauses are more frequent in the verb-final pattern than in other word order patterns. The failure to distinguish between those two points of view is, I think, the source of the misunderstanding.

While the main aim of this paper, to show that it is not the case that most conjunct clauses are verb-final, is easily achieved, the second aim, which is to find out why a majority of verb-final clauses are conjunct clauses, is rather more difficult. I suspect that part of the reason for this distribution is discourse-related, and I shall return to this question in Section 3.

Table 1. The word order of conjunct clauses

Word order patterns	# of conjunct clauses	% of conjunct clauses
SVX	222	27.9
(X)SXV	122	15.3
XSV(X)	101	12.7
XVS(X)	96	12.1
(X)SXVX	89	11.2
$SV_1XV_2(X)$	35	4.4
XXVS(X)	19	2.4
verb-initial	19	2.4
XXSV(X)	11	1.4
(miscellaneous)	(81)	(10.2)
	795	100.0

2. Some facts about conjunct clause word order

Let us first look at some facts about *and/ac* clauses and word order.[4] Table 1 shows that out of 795 conjunct clauses, only 122 (15.3%) have SXV, or verb-final, word order.[5] Furthermore, we see that the word order of conjunct clauses varies greatly, and that in fact, conjunct clauses are much more frequently SVX, or verb-medial, than verb-final.[6]

Below, the various word order patterns are exemplified by one conjunct clause from each pattern:

SVX: *7   se wisdom 7   eac oðre cræftas nabbað   nan lof   ne nænne*
        and the wisdom and also other virtues not-have no   praise nor no
        weorðscipe on ðisse worulde
        honour   in this world
        "and wisdom and other virtues besides have no praise nor honour in this world" (*Boethius*, 104:6)

(X)SXV: *& seo godcunde meht a   staþolfæstlice stondeþ*
        and the divine   might ever firm   stands
        "and the divine might stands ever firm" (*Blickling Homilies*, 19:20)

XSV(X):   *7   on middeweardum hire   rice hio getimbrede Babylonia þa burg*
        and in middle   of-her reign she built   Babylon   the city
        "and in the middle of her reign she built the city of Babylon" (*Orosius*, 37:27)

XVS(X):   *& mid ðære geornfulnesse &   mid þære wilnunge ðisse   worlde & hiere*
        and by the cares   and by the desires of-this world and its
        welena bið asmorod   ðæt sæd Godes   worda
        wealth is smothered the seed of-God's words
        "and by the cares and desires of this world and its wealth the seed of God's words is smothered" (*Cura Pastoralis*, 67:21)

(X)SXVX: *and alexandria seo burh sona wearð afylled mid mycclum cristen-dome . and*
        and Alexandria the city soon was   filled with much   Christianity and
        manegum cyrcum
        many   churches
        "and the city of Alexandria was soon filled with many Christian people and many churches" (*Ælfric's Lives of Saints*, 40:276)

$SV_1XV_2(X)$:   *7   his lichoma wæs ute   bebyrged neah cirican þara   eadiga apostola*
        and his body   was outside buried   near church of-the blessed apostles
        Petrus 7   Paulus
        Peter and Paul
        "and his body was buried outside, near the church of the blessed apostles Peter and Paul" (*Bede*, 104:30)

XXVS(X):   *And ðy us deriað 7   ðearle dyrfað fela ungelimpa*
        and then us harms and severely injures many misfortunes
        "and then many misfortunes will severely harm and injure us" (*Wulfstan's Homilies*, 124:20)

verb-initial: *and wearð micel reownes aweht*
             and was   great storm   raised
             "and a great storm was raised" (*Apollonius of Tyre*, 16:18)

XXSV(X):   *7   þæræfter innan September he for   ofer   sæ into Normandig*
             and thereafter in   September he went across sea into Normandy
             "and thereafter, in September, he went across the sea, into Normandy"
             (*Peterborough Chronicle*, 36:5)

The miscellaneous category includes clauses which for various reasons did not fit into any of the patterns.

Let us return to the statistics again, and to the question of how the claim that conjunct clauses are frequently verb-final could have arisen. Table 2 shows that out of 2500 main clauses altogether, 795 are conjunct clauses.

Table 2. The distribution of conjunct clauses in each word order pattern

Word order patterns	# of clauses altogether	# of conjunct clauses	% of conjunct clauses
(X)SXV	214	122	57.0
(X)SXVX	204	89	43.6
$SV_1XV_2(X)$	83	35	42.2
XXSV(X)	28	11	39.3
SVX	627	222	35.4
XSV(X)	288	101	35.1
XXVS(X)	78	19	24.4
XVS(X)	680	96	14.1
verb-initial	145	19	13.1
(miscellaneous)	(153)	(81)	(52.9)
	2500	795	

If for each word order pattern we calculate how many clauses are conjunct clauses out of the overall number of clauses in that pattern, we get the following result: out of 214 SXV clauses, 122 (57%) are conjunct clauses. In other words, SXV clauses are much more likely to be conjunct clauses than are for example XVS clauses, of which only 14.1% are conjunct clauses. This fact might be what has led to the misconception of conjunct clauses as being verb-final. People have looked at verb-final clauses and noted that they often have an initial coordinating conjunction, and from that deduced that conjunct clauses are usually verb-final. But it is important to keep those two aspects apart: the fact that a majority of verb-final clauses are conjunct clauses does not mean that a majority of conjunct clauses are verb-final.[7]

3.   Word order and information structure

It has by now, I hope, been clearly demonstrated that conjunct clauses are not usually verb-final. It remains an interesting question, however, why verb-final clauses, to the extent that they are used, are often conjunct clauses, whereas XVS clauses, for example, rarely have an initial coordinating conjunction. This distribution cannot be coincidental, and in the following I will attempt to give some answers to this question.

Sections 3.2 and 3.3 deal with SXV and XVS clauses, respectively, and they are structured as follows: first I say something about the nature of the word order pattern, what it is that characterizes it pragmatically. Then I analyze and compare the information structure of conjunct and non-conjunct clauses in the two patterns. In doing this, I hope to be able to say something about why conjunct clauses are "allowed" in the SXV pattern to a greater extent than in the XVS pattern. In other words, the question is *not*: What is it about conjunct clauses that makes them verb-final (we have already seen that only a minority of conjunct clauses are verb-final), but rather: What is it about the verb-final pattern that makes it contain so many conjunct clauses?

3.1   Method of pragmatic analysis

Before I start the analysis of the information structure of the clauses in question, the method used for the pragmatic analysis needs to be explained. Space does not permit an extensive discussion of the problems one inevitably encounters when trying to arrive at a method that may be applied for such an analysis; thus, the following paragraphs must necessarily be more descriptive than argumentative.

I analyze the sentence elements in terms of their degree of 'information value', or 'IV', and I make a binary distinction between 'low IV' elements and 'high IV' elements. My analysis is inspired by Firbas (1992), and the notion of 'communicative dynamism' (CD), by which is understood "the relative extent to which a linguistic element contributes towards the further development of the communication" (1992: 8). However, my method differs considerably from that of Firbas, not only because quite a few objections can be raised against his theory (cf. for example Dyvik 1980; Chafe 1994; Bech 2000/2001), but also because it is very difficult to apply his method to a corpus of any size, as it requires a very detailed study of each clause and its context.

While Firbas takes three factors into consideration in order to assess the degree of communicative dynamism of an element, namely, the contextual factor, the semantic factor, and linear modification, I shall be concerned with the first two factors only. The contextual factor has to do with whether an element is retrievable or irretrievable from the context, or, to put it more simply, whether it has been mentioned before or not. Elements that have been mentioned before, that are 'given', I have labeled as low IV elements, whereas 'new' elements are regarded as high IV elements.[8] The contextual factor is particularly relevant with respect to the analysis of subjects and objects: if the noun phrase has been mentioned in the (relatively immediate) context, it is a low IV element; if not, it is regarded as a high IV element. The same is the case with noun phrases and adjectives functioning as subject complements. Pronominal elements are always regarded as low IV elements, even though they sometimes may have contrastive stress. One reason why I operate with the terms 'low IV' and 'high IV', rather than 'given' and 'new', is that this allows me to include subjects like existential *there* (or *þær*) and anticipatory *it* (or *hit*). These elements are non-referential and can therefore not be analyzed in terms of givenness, but they are both analyzable in terms of degrees of IV, both being low IV elements which act as place fillers in the subject position in order to allow the heavy/high IV notional subject to be placed in clause late or clause final position (cf. Breivik 1981: 10).

The contextual factor is also relevant in the analysis of adverbials, in that adverbials realized by adverbs are classified as low IV elements if they have been mentioned in the previous context; otherwise they are high IV elements. Furthermore, adverbials which link the clause to the previous context, such as *þa/þonne* "then", *siþþan* "afterwards", as well as conjuncts such as *þeah* "however", *forþæm* "therefore", *þus* "thus", are regarded as low IV elements. In these cases, then, the analysis is also based on semantic properties.

The analysis of adverbial prepositional phrases is more problematic, and another reason why the given/new distinction is not completely suitable. Prepositional phrases are potentially heterogeneous as regards information value, in that both the preposition and the prepositional complement contribute to the information content of the phrase. So, for example, the preposition can be given while the prepositional complement is new, or the other way round, or both can be given, or both new. Therefore, it is difficult to classify prepositional phrases as *either* given *or* new. However, I consider the prepositional complement the most important element in the phrase, and I have therefore chosen to analyze prepositional phrases as low or high IV elements according to the contextual givenness of the prepositional complement: if it has been mentioned before, the phrase is analyzed as low IV, if not, it is analyzed as high IV.

Firbas describes the semantic factor as "the impact that the semantic character of a linguistic element, as well as the character of its semantic relations, has on the distributions of degrees of CD" (1992: 41). The semantic factor is particularly relevant for the analysis of verbs. As Chafe (1994: 69) points out, verbs are transient elements; i.e., they are usually not repeated, and will therefore in most cases convey new information. In other words, contextual factors can usually not help us distinguish between low IV and high IV verbs. However, both Chafe and Firbas operate with a category of semantically 'weak' verbs, which Chafe calls 'low-content verbs' (1994:110ff.), and Firbas calls 'verbs of appearance or existence on the scene' (1992:59ff.). Chafe's and Firbas' categories only overlap to a certain extent, and I shall be using Firbas' category of verbs of appearance or existence on the scene (which I, for the sake of simplicity, call 'existential verbs'), mainly because there seems to be good reason, from a historical point of view, to treat these verbs separately from other verbs (cf. for example Firbas 1957, 1992, and Breivik 1990). In addition to the existential verbs, I have also singled out another type of verb with a low semantic content, namely the copula.

Finally, note that clausal elements, such as adverbial clauses, subject clauses, and object clauses have not been analyzed in terms of IV, as these structures are too complex to allow an analysis into binary categories.

3.2 The information structure of non-conjunct and conjunct SXV clauses

Since our point of departure is the word order pattern, rather than the conjunct clause, our first step is to consider what the pragmatic nature of SXV clauses might be. We know that it seems to be a general principle that clauses are structured in such a way that the known precedes the unknown, and that lighter elements precede heavier elements. If that is the case, we would expect a majority of the subjects in SVX clauses to be known, i.e., to be low IV elements. Furthermore, if there is more than one X element between the subject and the verb, we would expect to see a gradual increase in IV; i.e., X elements near the beginning of the clause would be more likely to be low IV elements than elements near the end of the clause. Finally, we would not expect to find copulas and existential verbs to any great extent, as these are too light, or too low in information value, to occur in clause final position. Of course, the SXV pattern may have other characteristic features, but I shall content myself with these for the time being.

Tables 3 and 4 show the distribution of low and high IV elements in non-conjunct clauses and conjunct clauses with verb-final word order. I have distinguished between clauses with one, two, and three X elements between the subject and the verb. In other words, '1 X' means that there is one element between the subject and the verb, '2 X' means that there are two, and '3 X' means that there are three.

Table 3 shows that the distribution of low and high IV elements is largely as expected, if we accept the thesis that in general, the further back in a clause an element occurs, the more important it is from a communicative point of view, and the higher its IV will be. We see that if the clause has only one preverbal element apart from the subject, that element is most likely to be a low IV element. If it has two, both the first and the second are more frequently low IV than high IV, but the first X element is nevertheless more frequently low IV than the second. And if there are three X elements, there is a gradual increase of information value, with the third

Table 3. The distribution of low and high IV elements in non-conjunct SXV clauses

	First X				Second X				Third X			
	low IV		high IV		low IV		high IV		low IV		high IV	
	#	%	#	%	#	%	#	%	#	%	#	%
1 X	27	65.9	14	34.2								
2 X	18	64.3	10	35.7	17	60.7	11	39.3				
3 X	14	73.7	5	26.3	9	52.9	8	47.1	4	22.2	14	77.8

element being most often high IV.

Table 4 shows the distribution of low vs high IV elements in verb-final conjunct clauses. Here we see a different pattern, with a generally higher proportion of high IV elements throughout. Though it is not shown in the table, this is also the case with the subjects, with 87.5% low IV subjects in non-conjunct clauses, and 70.8% in conjunct clauses. As regards the distribution of copulas and existential verbs, there is no significant difference between conjunct clauses and non-conjunct clauses, but in the SXV pattern in general, these 'light' verbs are rare: only 11.7%, as opposed to 33.5% in the XVS pattern.

Table 4. The distribution of low and high IV elements in conjunct SXV clauses

	First X				Second X				Third X			
	low IV		high IV		low IV		high IV		low IV		high IV	
	#	%	#	%	#	%	#	%	#	%	#	%
1 X	27	50.0	27	50.0								
2 X	23	45.1	28	54.9	15	29.4	36	70.6				
3 X	6	66.7	3	33.3	2	22.2	7	77.8	2	22.2	7	77.8

All in all, then, verb-final conjunct clauses seem to be heavier informationally than non-conjunct clauses.

Let us sum up what we have found out so far about the relationship between the SXV pattern and conjunct clauses. First, since only a minority of conjunct clauses are verb-final, whatever needs to be expressed by conjunct clauses does not require that it is expressed with verb-final word order. Second, since a majority of verb-final clauses are conjunct clauses, we can deduce that whatever needs to be expressed with this word order is often expressed in conjunct clauses. In other words, there is a basic asymmetry here: conjunct clauses do not favor verb-final word order, but the verb-final pattern favors conjunct clauses.

As observed in Tables 3 and 4, verb-final conjunct clauses contain a higher proportion of high IV elements than verb-final non-conjunct clauses. It may very well be that this is the case for conjunct clauses in general: if one of its functions is to elaborate on and modify the main clause (Traugott 1992:277), we might expect the conjunct clause to be heavier informationally than the first clause. However, although the IV of the clause elements would be expected to influence the order in which they occur, it would not necessarily induce verb-*final* word order, and we would therefore not expect the frequency of verb-final conjunct clauses to be particularly high, which it is indeed not, as we have seen.

As was mentioned above, copulas and existential verbs are rare in the SXV pattern. From the absence of these types of verb, we can perhaps deduce that verbs need to be either heavy in weight or heavy informationally (those two aspects often coincide, of course) in this pattern. As regards the question of the high frequency of conjunct clauses in the SXV pattern, then, one possible line of reasoning would be as follows: in a conjunct clause the verb *may* occur in final position more easily than in a non-conjunct clause (which does not mean that it necessarily *does*). This is because in the first of two conjoined clauses, or in an independent main clause, the verb needs to appear early, since it is important to establish what is going on; what the action is. In the conjunct clause, on the other hand, the importance does not lie in establishing what the action is, but rather how it relates to the preceding clause, by expressing elaboration and contrast, for example. The verbs in these clauses are therefore potentially more eligible for the informationally heavy final position. Thus, if the information value of the conjunct clause elements is such that the verb is a high IV element, the verb-final pattern can, and will, be used. In other types of clauses this possibility may not occur to the same extent. Seen from this angle, then, the high frequency of conjunct clauses in the SXV pattern is not surprising.

3.3 The information structure of non-conjunct and conjunct XVS clauses

Let us now consider the nature and information structure of XVS clauses. In an XVS clause we would expect the initial X element to be a low IV element, often a link to the previous context. Furthermore, copulas and existential verbs would probably occur more often than in most other word order patterns, given the verbal position. As regards the subject, we would expect it to be a high IV element more often than subjects in other word order patterns. In other words, from a pragmatic point of view, XVS word order is suitable for the introduction of new referents, and it is therefore not difficult to imagine why this word order is not favored for conjunct clauses, which usually relate to the previous discourse, and in which the subject therefore is likely to be known already.

Table 5 shows that, like SXV conjunct clauses, XVS conjunct clauses seem to have a generally higher distribution of high IV elements, both with respect to the

Table 5. The information structure of non-conjunct and conjunct XVS clauses

	Non-conjunct clauses		Conjunct clauses	
	#	%	#	%
nit X low IV	525	89.6	66	67.7
nit X high IV	39	6.7	18	18.8
Init X ad. cl.[a]	22	3.8	13	13.5
Total	586	100.1	97	100.0
Subj. low IV	313	54.1	26	27.1
Subj. high IV	229	39.6	60	62.5
Subj. clause	37	6.4	10	10.4
Total	579[b]	100.1	96	100.0

[a] "Initial X element is an adverbial clause".

[b] The reason why the number is lower (579, rather than 586) is that not all subjects could be analyzed in terms of either low or high IV. For example, in *þa sæde he Pompeius þæt he þær drycræftas geleornode* (*Or*, 23:27), the subject is an apposition with both a pronominal and a nominal element, *he Pompeius*.

initial X element and the subject. As regards verbs, there is a clear difference between conjunct and non-conjunct clauses in the distribution of existential verbs, in that the frequency of these verbs is higher in conjunct clauses than in non-conjunct clauses (37.5% vs 19.7%). This fact may be seen in connection with the high proportion of high IV subjects in XVS conjunct clauses, since the presence of an existential verb often signals the introduction of a new referent.

We have seen that there is asymmetry in the frequency of verb-final conjunct clauses vs the frequency of conjunct clauses in the SXV pattern. As regards the relation between the XVS pattern and conjunct clauses, however, there is symmetry: conjunct clauses do not favor the XVS pattern and the XVS pattern does not favor conjunct clauses. As for the former, there is no reason, from a pragmatic point of view, why conjunct clauses should favor XVS word order more than other word orders, just as there is no reason why verb-final order would be preferred. As we have seen, conjunct clauses seem to be more marked than non-conjunct clauses; i.e., they contain more high IV elements. What these elements are varies, however, and word order is chosen on the basis of where the communicative focus lies in a given context. It is not surprising either that the XVS pattern does not favor conjunct clauses if this word order is particularly suitable for the introduction of a new turn of events, or a new referent. However, once in a while we find conjunct clauses with XVS word order, and in these clauses the subject is very often a high IV element. This could indicate that the XVS order is used in cases where the subject contrasts with the subject in the preceding clause, and therefore needs to occur late in the clause.

4. Conclusion

I had two aims with this paper. Most importantly, I wanted to show that the common belief that conjunct clauses to a great extent are verb-final is not confirmed by the empirical data. A simple count involving 795 conjunct clauses shows that only 15.3% of them are verb-final. However, it is not so strange that this misconception has arisen, because if we look at each word order pattern, it becomes equally clear that within the verb-final pattern, a majority (57%) of the clauses are conjunct clauses. The failure to distinguish between those two points of view is, I think, what has led to the misunderstanding.

The second aim of this paper was to try to explain this asymmetry; i.e., why verb-final conjunct clauses are relatively rare, whereas there is a high frequency of conjunct clauses in the verb-final pattern. In doing this, I found it useful to compare the SXV pattern to the XVS pattern, where there is symmetry; i.e., conjunct clauses with XVS word order are rare, and the frequency of conjunct clauses in the XVS pattern is low. I suspected that the explanation for this distribution is at least partly functional; that it has to do both with the discourse function of the various word orders, and the discourse function of the conjunct clause.[9] Consequently, I sketched some possible features of the pragmatic nature of SXV and XVS word order, before I attempted an analysis of the information structure of conjunct and non-conjunct clauses in these two patterns.

What I found was basically this: the high frequency of conjunct clauses in the SXV pattern, and the low frequency in the XVS pattern, may be explained on the basis of the pragmatic nature of the word order patterns. In other words, the pragmatic nature of the SXV pattern, i.e., the way information must be structured in this pattern according to general pragmatic principles, corresponds to a great extent to the way information *may be* structured in conjunct clauses. In other words, the pragmatic requirements of SXV word order can be met more easily by conjunct clauses than by other main clauses, which leads to the situation we have seen, with a majority of SXV clauses being conjunct clauses. The inverse does not apply, however: a majority of conjunct clauses are not verb-final. This is because whatever needs to be expressed by conjunct clauses does not require that it be expressed with SXV word order. For the XVS pattern, the situation is different, in that the way information must be structured in XVS clauses does not in general correspond to the way information may be structured in conjunct clauses. Nor do the characteristics of the conjunct clause make it favor the XVS pattern. Therefore we see neither a great proportion of conjunct clauses in the XVS pattern nor a high frequency of conjunct clauses with XVS word order.

Notes

* I would like to thank two anonymous referees, whose comments and suggestions I have attempted to incorporate in the revision.

1. In clauses with verb-final (SXV) word order, the finite verb occurs in clause final position, and there must be one or more elements intervening between the subject and the verb. Thus, a clause with the word order XSV, for example, is not verb-final, but rather verb-medial, since the subject precedes the verb immediately.

2. Bean (1983), Denison (1986), and Stockwell and Minkova (1990) use the term 'conjunct clause' for *and/ac*-clauses with no expressed subject. As regards clauses with an expressed subject, Bean, unlike Denison and Stockwell and Minkova, does not distinguish between *and/ac* clauses and other main clauses.

3. Denison (1986:281), as well as Stockwell and Minkova (1990:507), finds that the tendency for verb-final order is greater in *and/ac* clauses without an expressed subject than in *and/ac* clauses with an expressed subject. It should be mentioned that their corpus consists of only one text, the 892–900 segment of the *Parker Chronicle*.

4. The corpus consists of excerpts from nine Old English texts (see reference list), with samples varying between 150 and 500 declarative main clauses from each text.

5. Of course, if SXVX clauses are regarded as verb-final as well, the percentage becomes higher.

6. Note that in the SXV, SXVX, SV_1XV_2, and SVX patterns, "X" may represent *one or more* constituents. This is because, from a typological point of view, the number of X constituents is not relevant; a verb-final clause, for example, is verb-final no matter how many elements intervene between the subject and the verb. In the XVS, XSV, XXVS, and XXSV patterns, on the other hand, "X" represents *only one* constituent, since here it does matter how many initial X elements there are. XVS clauses are verb-second; XXVS clauses are not, or at least, they have not been counted as such here. (X) means that there may be one or more optional elements in that position. Note also that XVS includes XVXS, XV_1XSV_2, etc. The main point is that the finite verb is in second position.

7. Interestingly enough, Dahlstedt (1901:14) observes that verb-final position in Old English "is especially to be found after *and*", Davis (1953:61) writes that verb-final order is "very commonly [found] in co-ordinate clauses joined to the main clause by *and* (also *ac*)", and according to McLaughlin (1983:68), "SOV order tends to occur most frequently in embedded clauses (dependent), and in the second member of conjoined clauses". In other words, it seems that what these authors claim is not that conjunct clauses are verb-final, but rather that verb-final clauses are often conjunct clauses, which is also my point. However, they do not distinguish between the two points of view, which makes it hard to tell whether their formulations are chosen for reasons of precision, or whether it is a coincidence that they express themselves in this particular manner. The matter is complicated further by the fact that these authors are sometimes cited in support of the view that conjunct clauses are verb-final.

8. In this connection the question of how long givenness lasts arises, for it is obvious that an element does not remain given forever; the reader will have to be reminded of it from time to time. I shall not attempt to solve this problem here, but rather admit that a certain degree of subjectivity is unavoidable in the analysis. In ambiguous cases, one must determine whether an element is more likely to be given or new in that particular context.

9. In other words, I agree with Allen (1995:33) in her belief that "at least some of the OE constituent order facts are to be accounted for better by assuming that different orders performed different functions, rather than postulating structural constraints".

References

Primary sources

Bately, Janet, ed. 1980. *The Old English Orosius.* (= *EETS* s.s., 6.) London: Oxford University Press.

Bethurum, Dorothy, ed. 1957. *The Homilies of Wulfstan.* Oxford: Clarendon Press.

Clark, Cecily, ed. 1958. *The Peterborough Chronicle 1070–1154.* London: Oxford University Press.

Goolden, Peter, ed. 1958. *The Old English "Apollonius of Tyre".* London: Oxford University Press.

Miller, Thomas, ed. 1890. *The Old English Version of Bede's Ecclesiastical History of the English People.* (= *EETS* o.s., 95, 96.) London: Trübner & Co.

Morris, Richard, ed. 1967 [1874–1880]. *The Blickling Homilies.* (= *EETS* o.s., 58, 63, 73.) London: Oxford University Press.

Sedgefield, Walter J., ed. 1968 [1899]. *King Alfred's Old English Version of Boethius "De Consolatione Philosophiae".* Darmstadt: Wissenschaftliche Buchgesellschaft.

Skeat, Walter W., ed. 1881–1885. *Ælfric's Lives of Saints,* vols. I, i & ii. (= *EETS* o.s., 76, 82.) London: Trübner & Co.

Sweet, Henry, ed. 1909 [1871]. *King Alfred's West Saxon Version of Gregory's Pastoral Care.* (= *EETS* o.s., 45.) London: Trübner & Co. and Oxford University Press.

Thorpe, Benjamin, ed. 1834. *The Anglo-Saxon Version of the Story of Apollonius of Tyre.* London: John & Arthur Arch.

Secondary sources

Allen, Cynthia L. 1995. *Case Marking and Reanalysis. Grammatical relations from Old to Early Modern English.* Oxford: Clarendon Press.

Bean, Marian C. 1983. *The Development of Word Order Patterns in Old English.* London & Canberra: Croom Helm.

Bech, Kristin. 2000/2001. *Word Order Patterns in Old and Middle English: A syntactic and pragmatic study.* Doctoral dissertation, University of Bergen.

Breivik, Leiv Egil. 1981. "On the Interpretation of Existential *there*". *Language* 57: 1.1–25.

Breivik, Leiv Egil. 1990. *Existential* there: *A synchronic and diachronic study.* 2nd ed. Oslo: Novus Press.

Campbell, A. 1964. Review of *La structure de la phrase verbale à l'époque Alfrédienne* (= *Publications de la Faculté des Lettres de l'Université de Strasbourg. Paris, 1962*) by Paul Bacquet. *The Review of English Studies* 15.190–193.

Chafe, Wallace. 1994. *Discourse, Consciousness and Time. The flow and displacement of conscious experience in speaking and writing.* Chicago: The University of Chicago Press.

Dahlstedt, August. 1901. *Rhythm and Word-Order in Anglo-Saxon and Semi-Saxon.* Lund: E. Malmström.

Davis, Norman, ed. 1953. *Sweet's Anglo-Saxon Primer.* 9th ed. Oxford: Clarendon Press.

Denison, David. 1986. "On Word Order in Old English". *Dutch Quarterly Review of Anglo-American Letters* 16.277–295.

Dyvik, Helge. 1980. "Om definisjonen av 'tema' i tema/rema-analysen". *Egenproduksjon* nr. 8, skriftserie ved Nordisk institutt, Universitetet i Bergen, 50–77.

Firbas, Jan. 1957. "Some Thoughts on the Function of Word-Order in Old English and Modern English". *Sborník Prací Filosofické Fakulty Brněnské University* A5, 72–100.

Firbas, Jan. 1992. *Functional Sentence Perspective in Written and Spoken Communication.* Cambridge: Cambridge University Press.

Kemenade, Ans van. 1987. *Syntactic Case and Morphological Case in the History of English.* Dordrecht: Foris Publications.

Kohonen, Viljo. 1978. *On the Development of English Word Order in Religious Prose around 1000 and 1200 A.D.: A quantitative study of word order in context.* Åbo: Åbo Akademi Foundation.

McLaughlin, John. 1983. *Old English Syntax. A handbook.* Tübingen: Niemeyer.

Mitchell, Bruce. 1964. "Syntax and Word Order in *The Peterborough Chronicle*". *Neuphilologische Mitteilungen* 65.113–144.

Mitchell, Bruce. 1985. *Old English Syntax,* vols. I & II. Oxford: Clarendon Press.

Pintzuk, Susan. 1995. "Variation and Change in Old English Clause Structure". *Language Variation and Change* 7 ed. by David Sankoff, William Labov, & Anthony Kroch, 229–260. Cambridge: Cambridge University Press (1996).

Stockwell, Robert & Donka Minkova. 1990. "Verb-Phrase Conjunction in Old English". *Historical Linguistics 1987* ed. by Henning Andersen & Konrad Koerner, 499–515. Amsterdam & Philadelphia: John Benjamins.

Traugott, Elizabeth Closs. 1992. "Syntax". *The Cambridge History of the English Language, vol. I: The beginnings to 1066* ed. by Richard M. Hogg, 168–289. Cambridge: Cambridge University Press.

Alternation according to person in Italo-Romance[*]

Delia Bentley and Thórhallur Eythórsson
University of Manchester

1. Introduction

In a number of dialects of Italy (and Catalonia) the perfective auxiliaries "have" and "be" alternate according to person (the *mixed paradigm*). In this paper we propose that historically the spread of "be" into the domain of "have" is triggered by a phonological factor, i.e., the fact that the 2nd and 3rd singular atonic forms of "have" coincide. The emergence of "be" in the paradigm of transitives and unergatives gives rise to alternation according to person and may result in the loss of alternation according to verb class. In these dialects perfective auxiliaries have been reanalyzed as grammatical person markers.

2. Patterns of alternation according to verb class

In order to make our account of the mixed paradigm comprehensible, it is necessary to sketch the situation in languages with perfective auxiliary alternation according to verb class. In Romance languages such as standard Italian and French "be" is used with unaccusatives and reflexives and "have" with transitives and unergatives. The class of unaccusatives which select "be" is smaller in some languages (e.g., French) than in others (e.g., Italian). An analogous situation is found in the Germanic languages (e.g., Danish and German), except that there reflexives select "have". A number of Romance and Germanic languages (e.g., Spanish and English) do not exhibit auxiliary alternation according to verb class (or person) and take "have" as the only perfective auxiliary.

3.   Patterns of alternation according to person: The mixed paradigm

The mixed paradigm occurs in a number of Italian dialects (spoken in Abruzzo, Piemonte, Veneto, Toscana, Marche, Lazio, Campania, and Puglia; cf. Rohlfs 1969: §730; Giammarco 1973; Tuttle 1986; Lorenzetti 1995). It also occurs in certain dialects of Catalonia (Tuttle 1986). There are various patterns of mixed paradigm: alternation according to (i) person only, (ii) person and verb class, and (iii) person, verb class, and tense. Number can also play a role in the mixed paradigm, with auxiliary alternation in the singular persons, but not in the plural, or with one auxiliary in the singular persons and the other one in the plural persons.

Alternation according to person only is found, for example, in Eastern Abruzzese, where 1st and 2nd person singular and plural take "be" while the 3rd person singular and plural take "have" (Hastings 1996). The paradigm in (1) exemplifies the pattern found in the dialect of L'Aquila:

(1)   *sò   šcrittu, sci   šcrittu, a   šcrittu*
       be.1SG written, be.2SG written, have.3SG written
       sémo šcrittu, séte   šcrittu, au   šcrittu
       be.1PL written, be.2PL written, have.3PL written
       "I have written, you (SG) have written, s/he has written, we have written, you
       (PL) have written, they have written"
       (Giammarco 1973: 71)

In Western Abruzzese, on the other hand, "be" is found in the 2nd person singular only, as in the dialect of Introdacqua (2):

(2)   *ɛjjə   scréttə, sci   scréttə, a   scréttə*
       have.1SG written, be.2SG written, have.3SG written
       "I have written, you have written, s/he has written"
       (Giammarco 1973: 71–72)

This appears to be a common pattern. A less frequent one involves the 1st singular only (e.g., the dialect of Notaresco).

Alternation according to person and verb class occurs in a number of dialects. In Altamurano (Puglia) there is free variation of "be" and "have" in some or most persons and alternation according to verb class in the 3rd person (Loporcaro 1988a: 279–280). In a variety of Salentino (Puglia) "be" occurs in the 3rd person singular of all verbs and in the 3rd person plural of unaccusatives and reflexives only (La Fauci and Loporcaro 1989: 167). In some varieties of Sorrentino (Campania) "be" occurs in the 3rd person singular of verbs denoting change of state (Cennamo 1999b).

Finally, alternation according to person, verb class, and tense is found in the dialects of the Castelli Romani (Lazio). Typically, the mixed paradigm is restricted to the present perfect of transitives and unergatives, while "be" occurs in the other tenses and with unaccusatives (Lorenzetti 1995: 246 ff.; Tufi 2000).

In addition to these alternating patterns, "be" occurs as the only perfective auxiliary in Terracinese.[1] However, "have" figures in the 3rd person in an older variety of this dialect, indicating a mixed pattern at an earlier stage (Tuttle 1986: 267–269).

4. Previous accounts of the diachronic development

Giammarco (1973) claimed that "be" with transitives and unergatives originates directly from the perfect of Latin deponent verbs, which have passive morphosyntax, requiring "be" as a perfective auxiliary and subject past participle agreement (*proficiscor* "I set out" / *profectus sum* "I have set out", *hortor* "I incite" / *hortatus sum* "I have incited"), and from a resultative construction of the type *cenatus est* "he has eaten and is therefore full". The main argument for this claim is the subject agreement of transitive past participles in dialects such as the one of Introdacqua (cf. (4)).

This view is at odds with the standard account of perfective auxiliaries in Romance (Vincent 1982). According to this account, *esse* "be", which was the perfective auxiliary of all deponents in Classical Latin, became restricted to deponents with patient/theme subjects (i.e., unaccusative deponents) in Late Latin, and, later, to all unaccusatives.

As a result of a parallel development in the formation of perfective tenses, Latin possessive constructions with *habere* "have" and an NP modified by a past participle (3a) were reanalyzed as perfective constructions where the subject of auxiliary "have" and that of the participle coincide (3b).

(3) a. *Pecunias   magnas   collocatas   habent.*
         capital.ACC.PL great.ACC.PL invested.ACC.PL have.3PL
         "They have great capital invested."
     b. "They have invested great capital." (Vincent 1982)

Giammarco's proposal does not combine easily with this account of the development of perfective auxiliaries. Since transitive deponents are not attested in the earliest Romance documents, they must have been lost at a very early stage. The alleged development would have to have taken place before they were lost. To our knowledge, however, there is no evidence attested for the mixed paradigm within early Romance. Moreover, no principled account is given by Giammarco of the emergence of the mixed paradigm. It should be noted that "have" is not distributed at random in the dialects with the mixed paradigm. In fact, a number of these dialects also show alternation according to verb class. In addition, vestiges of an earlier stage with "have" in the 3rd person occur in the speech of elderly Terracinese speakers, while current Terracinese has generalized "be". This shows that the mixed paradigm requires the assumption of the spread of "be" to the domain of "have". Hence, any diachronic account of alternation of "have" and "be" according to person presupposes a system like that of standard Italian, where the alternation is according to verb class.

This point was, in fact, emphasized by Tuttle (1986) in a seminal article on auxiliary alternation according to person in Italo-Romance. Tuttle's main argument for this assumption is the lack of subject past participle agreement with transitives and unergatives in most of the dialects in question. While, for the reasons given above, we accept the view that the mixed paradigm derives from a system like the standard Italian one, we have doubts about Tuttle's argument. In fact, agreement could have been lost by generalization of the transitive pattern with "have". Also, in some cases, subject agreement is found in transitives and unergatives in the mixed paradigm, as in the dialect of Introdacqua (4). Here the past participle agrees in number with the subject with both "be" (2SG) and "have" (all other persons):

(4)   ɛjjə   maɲɲatə
      have.1SG eaten.SG
      ši   maɲɲatə
      be.2SG eaten.SG
      á   maɲɲatə
      have.3SG eaten.SG
      avɛmmə mɛɲɲétə[2]
      have.1PL eaten.PL
      (Tuttle 1986:272)

Tuttle further argues that the spread of "be" originated from reflexives and from the correspondence between the dative of interest construction (involving reflexive pronouns and "be") and, on the other hand, its transitive counterpart (cf. Rohlfs 1969: §730). The structure in (5a) exemplifies the dative of interest with "be", which expresses empathy with the grammatical subject, while (5b) is a corresponding transitive construction with "have":

(5)   a.   *Mi   sono   comprata   una camicia.*
           REFL be.1SG bought.FEM a   shirt
           "I have bought myself a shirt."
      b.   *Ho   comprato un camicia.*
           have.1SG bought   a   shirt
           "I have bought a shirt."

Moreover, Tuttle claims that the occurrence of "be" in the 1st and the 2nd persons only might depend on a tendency for the animate persons to express empathy (1986:277–278). No evidence is provided, however, for such a tendency. In fact, the dative of interest also occurs in the 3rd person in Italian (6):

(6) *Si   è   mangiata un panino.*
     REFL be.3SG eaten.FEM a   sandwich
     "She has eaten a sandwich."

In addition, in the dialect of Notaresco (Abruzzo) the 3rd person of transitives normally takes the reflexive pronoun unlike the 1st and 2nd persons, which do not (Giammarco 1973:73). This situation contrasts with Tuttle's (1986) account, contradicting some of his basic assumptions.

In some dialects the perfective auxiliary "be" is associated with the 3rd person, while "have" occurs in other persons. In a variety of Salentino (Puglia) "be" is the only auxiliary found in the 3rd person singular of transitives and unergatives. As for unaccusatives and reflexives, it occurs in the 3rd person singular and plural in free variation with "have" (cf. Fanciullo in La Fauci & Loporcaro 1989:167 fn. 9). In some varieties of Sorrentino (a Campanian dialect), "be" figures either in the 3rd or in the 2nd and 3rd person singular of a subclass of unaccusatives, while all other persons take "have" (Cennamo 2001).

Lastly, "have" is common with reflexives in Italo-Romance, especially in the southern dialects (cf. Rohlfs 1969:§731). This is a further indication that Tuttle's idea of the spread of perfective "be" from reflexives is not plausible.[3]

5. The origins of the mixed paradigm

In this section we present a novel account of the origins and development of the mixed paradigm. We argue that the spread of "be" is triggered by a phonological factor, i.e., the fact that the atonic forms of the 2SG and 3SG persons of the present of "have" may coincide (*a(i)*, *a'* (2SG) – *a* (3SG) (Rohlfs 1969:§541)).[4] This is illustrated by the following example from the dialect of Santeramo (Puglia):

(7) a. /tu   a: ši:/
         you have.2SG go
         "You will go."
     b. /kud: a: ši:/
         he   have.3SG go
         "He will go."
         (Loporcaro 1988a:286)

The starting point of our analysis is the observation that when "be" occurs only in one person, this is normally the 2SG (Hastings 1996:34). The emergence of "be" in the 2SG of transitives and unergatives gives rise to alternation according to person and may eventually result in the loss of alternation according to verb class.

5.1 Outline of the development

As argued above, any diachronic account of the mixed paradigm presupposes a system like that of standard Italian, with perfective auxiliary alternation according to verb class (transitives and unergatives with "have" and unaccusatives with "be"). In a number of languages "have" has spread to the domain of "be" to various extents. In French "be" occurs with a limited class of unaccusatives (*aller* "go", *venir* "come", *sortir* "go out", *naître* "be born", *mourir* "die", *devenir* "become", *décéder* "decease", etc.), while in (Daco-)Romanian, a number of Italo-Romance dialects (e.g., Sicilian), Catalan, and Spanish, "have" has been generalized, occurring with predicates of all verb classes. It is important to note that the spread of "have" does not occur at random, but rather according to semantic gradients of unaccusativity. As noted by Sorace (1993, 2000) "have" occurs first with "peripheral unaccusatives" (verbs of existence and continuation of condition) and later with "core unaccusatives" (verbs expressing telic change of condition and telic change of location) (cf. Cennamo 1997, 1999). In diachronic terms, it would appear that generalization of "have" is due to paradigmatic leveling in accordance with Sorace's Unaccusative Hierarchy, leading to the loss of alternation according to verb class.

Another possible development involves the spread of "be" to the domain of "have". This gives rise to the mixed paradigm and may lead to the loss of alternation according to verb class, ultimately resulting in the generalization of "be". As stated above, we assume that the mixed paradigm in Italo-Romance has its origins in a phonological merger, typically of the 2nd and 3rd person singular of the atonic forms of "have". Starting with a paradigm with "have" in all three persons of transitives and unergatives, the similarity of the 2nd and 3rd person would give rise to a paradigm with "be" in the 2nd person singular (cf. the dialect of Introdacqua). Subsequently, "be" would spread from the 2nd person to the 1st person singular and, by analogy, to the 1st and 2nd plural (cf. the dialect of L'Aquila). When "be" is introduced in the 2nd person singular, "have" and "be" acquire the function of markers of grammatical person in addition to the function of marking tense and aspect and verb valency.

Table 1 confronts perfective auxiliaries in two varieties of Abruzzese, where alternation according to verb class has been eliminated, and in standard Italian, which preserves this distinction.

As shown in Table 1, in Western Abruzzese (cf. the dialects of Introdacqua and Scanno; Giammarco 1973:73) "be" occurs in the 2nd person singular only (*sci*), while in Eastern Abruzzese (cf. the dialect of L'Aquila) it occurs both in the 1st and in the 2nd persons (*sò* and *sì*, *sci*). Diachronically speaking, the situation found in the western varieties would seem to represent an earlier stage than that of the eastern ones. The same situation is found in Puglia, for example in Biscegliese. By contrast, a split between the 2nd person singular and plural and all other persons

Table 1. Variation in perfective auxiliary alternation

Standard Italian		Western Abruzzese	Eastern Abruzzese
ho have.1sg	*sono* be.1sg	*èjjə* have.1sg	*sò* be.1sg
hai have.2sg	*sei* be.2sg	*sci* be.2sg	*sì, sci* be.2sg
ha have.3sg	*è* be.3sg	*a* have.3sg	*a* have.3sg

occurs in Lazio (cf. the dialects of Cassino, Amaseno, Veroli) where "have" alternates freely with "be" in the 1st person singular and plural, but "be" is the only auxiliary found in the 2nd person singular and plural (Giammarco 1973:74).[5]

The fact that the 1st and 2nd persons tend to take the same auxiliary is in accordance with a person hierarchy observed in linguistic change. The 3rd person is less likely to be affected by analogical change than the other persons. This may be due to its formally and semantically unmarked status in the paradigm (Benveniste 1946; Kuryłowicz 1947; Watkins 1962; Saxon 1999). However, as already mentioned, there are a few dialects (for example Salentino and Sorrentino) in which the 3rd person tends to be marked with "be", as opposed to all other persons, which take "have". We suggest that in these cases the phonological clash was resolved by the introduction of "be" into the 3rd person, and not into the 2nd, as is more often the case.[6] While this process is somewhat unusual from a typological perspective, it does not constitute a counterexample to our account. The fact that the 3rd person is normally the last one to be affected by analogical change is after all only a tendency and by no means the result of a universal law. On the other hand, the patterns with "be" in the 3rd person and "have" in the others are highly problematic for any account associating either auxiliary with a particular person (e.g., Tuttle 1986; Kayne 1993).

It is to be expected that in the type of change with which we are concerned here there should be intermediate stages of free variation of "have" and "be" in the same grammatical persons. In fact, this situation is found in a number of dialects, for example in Altamurano (Loporcaro 1988a: 279–280).

The final stage in this development is represented by Terracinese, which has only "be". As pointed out above, however, there are vestiges of alternation according to person in the idolect of elderly Terracinese speakers. In principle, "be" may be generalized from a stage involving alternation according to person and verb class, or from a stage with alternation according to person only, which amounts to loss of alternation according to verb class. While the latter stage necessarily presupposes the former, the converse does not hold. Either possibility will result in the loss of alternation according to person. In the dialects of the Castelli Romani "be" occurs in all persons and all verb classes in tenses other than the present perfect of unergatives and transitives. Presumably, the present perfect retains the alternation due to its higher relative frequency.[7]

5.2 Alternation according to person in the future periphrasis

In a number of Italo-Romance dialects, including some of those with the mixed paradigm, the future/deontic periphrasis with "have" plus particle and infinitive exhibits the particle *da* (from the Latin prepositions *de* "of" and *ab* "from") in certain persons, while the outcome of the Latin preposition *ad* "to" figures in other persons (Rohlfs 1968: § 591). This pattern is found in Altamurano (8), a dialect which exhibits alternation according to person in the perfect.

(8) a. *a*   *(d)a ši*
         have.2SG PART go
         "You will go."
     b. *a(v)'   a   ggi*
         have.3SG PART go
         "S/he will go."
         (Loporcaro 1999: 87)

According to Rohlfs (1968: § 591) the use of *da* in the 2nd person singular (8a) vis-à-vis *a* in the 3rd singular (8b) and elsewhere in the paradigm is to be attributed to the fact that *a*, the 2nd person singular form of "have", and the particle *a* would merge. We suggest that this case is parallel to the mixed paradigm: the alternation of *a* and *da* is part of the person marking system of the relevant dialects.[8] Note that although in Altamurano (as in many other dialects) the dental of /da/ is optionally elided, the contrast between *a* from *ad* and *a* from *de ab* is overtly marked by syntactic doubling (SD), which only applies after the former particle.[9]

6.   What is the mixed paradigm?

In the languages with alternation according to verb class, perfective auxiliaries are markers of tense and aspect.[10] In dialects with the mixed paradigm, auxiliaries mark grammatical person in addition to tense and aspect. Where there is alternation according to both verb class and person, auxiliary selection is semantically determined, insofar as the marking of grammatical person only applies to some verb classes (typically transitives and unergatives). In languages with alternation according to person only, auxiliary choice is not semantically determined, as there is no distinction in the marking of different verb classes.

It has been proposed that auxiliary alternation according to person is a manifestation of the strength or weakness of a feature person on subject NPs (Kayne 1993). On this analysis the fact that the 1st and 2nd persons exhibit "be" in some dialects depends on a strong feature of the subject NP, while "have" in the 3rd person depends on a weak feature. Such an approach, however, is problematic in view of theoretical considerations and empirical evidence, including cases in which "be" figures in the 3rd person as against "have" elsewhere, as in the dialect of Sorrento (cf. Bentley & Eythórsson 1999).

Contrasting with this and other accounts (e.g., Tuttle 1986), the mixed paradigm does not appear to be attributable to syntactic or semantic principles associating each auxiliary with a particular grammatical person. This possibility is ruled out by the variety of existing patterns. While in the majority of cases "be" is found in the 2nd and/or 1st person, there are, as mentioned, dialects in which "be" occurs in the 3rd person and "have" in the others.[11] Thus we would not subscribe to the view that there is a rule of auxiliary selection according to person.[12]

7. Conclusion

Puzzling though it may seem at a first glance, alternation according to person turns out to have a relatively simple explanation, deriving from a homonymity clash with subsequent spread of "be". Thus, the ultimate origins of the mixed paradigm are to be ascribed to a phonological factor, while the spread of "be" tends to occur in accordance with cross-linguistic patterns of person hierarchy which have been observed to hold in analogical change. On the other hand, we hope to have shown that the process is not motivated by a syntactic or a semantic rule, applying to the 1st and 2nd persons only (cf. Kayne 1993; Tuttle 1986). We also consider it unlikely that the mixed paradigm, which is found in a limited number of modern dialects, has its roots in Late Latin, as is implicit in Giammarco's (1973) account.

Our analysis leads us to conclude that there is only one criterion of perfective auxiliary selection: the morphosyntactic marking of unaccusative as against transitive and unergative clauses. The marking of unaccusativity may vary across languages according to an implicational hierarchy determining gradients of unaccusativity (Sorace 2000). On the other hand, alternation according to person is part of a grammatical person marking system on verbs. In view of this, the various patterns of auxiliary alternation are unlikely to be captured by a single (albeit "modular") synchronic rule such as that of Kayne (1993).

Notes

* The research reported here is part of a project on the historical morphosyntax of European languages, which is funded through a British Academy Institutional Fellowship. The authors take joint responsibility for the entire article. We wish to thank Michela Cennamo, Robert Hastings,

Michele Loporcaro, Luca Lorenzetti, Nigel Vincent, and two anonymous reviewers for their comments on a previous version of this article.

1. Within Germanic the same situation is found in one dialect, viz. Shetlandic (Robertson & Graham 1991).

2. In the dialect of Introdacqua both singular and plural participles end in /ə/. However, number agreement is marked by the metaphonic raising of the stressed vowel of the plural participles (cf. plural *meɲɲétə* vs. singular *maɲɲatə*). This indicates a previous stage with distinct endings on the singular and plural participles.

3. Moreover, the use of "have" with reflexives is found in Tuscan and Italian until the seventeenth century (Rohlfs 1969: § 731).

4. Observe that the 2nd and 3rd person singular of the perfect would not coincide if syntactic doubling (SD) were at work in the 3rd person, as indeed is the case in standard Italian (/a f:atto/ "has done"). However, in the dialects of the Centre-South under discussion here (Puglia, Lucania, Campania, Abruzzo) the conditions which determine SD differ substantially from those which apply to standard Italian. In the latter variety SD is triggered by the final stressed vowel of (i) monosyllables and bisyllables originally ending in a consonant and (ii) monosyllables and bisyllables which are etymologically different, but have been affected by the extension of the rule. By contrast, in the dialects of the Centre-South SD is only found if the consonant is still present and assimilates to the first consonant of the following word (Fanciullo 1986; Loporcaro 1988b). Northern dialects have lost doubling altogether.

5. In the dialects of Notaresco and Atri (Abruzzo) "be" only occurs in the 1st person singular (Giammarco 1973:74). This might be counterevidence to our account of the rise of the mixed paradigm, which presupposes a phonological clash between the 2nd and 3rd persons. This situation, however, might originate from a paradigm involving "be" in both 2nd and 1st persons, as in Eastern Abruzzese and various other dialects. Notaresco would then represent a reversal of the tendency for "be" to spread, with leveling in the opposite direction, in favour of "have".

6. In fact, Cennamo's (2001) recent findings suggest that the spread of "be" in a number of Campanian varieties has started from the 3rd person singular.

7. As mentioned earlier, the mixed paradigm is also found in a number of Catalan dialects (Tuttle 1986). Ideally, it ought to be possible to account for this phenomenon in a similar way as for the Italo-Romance dialects discussed in this paper. In Catalan, though, the forms of the perfective auxiliary "have" are partly different from those of Italo-Romance. Crucially, in the standard variety the form of the 2nd person singular is *has*. Hence, there does not seem to be any basis for assuming a phonological clash with the 3rd person *ha*. However, the situation in the dialects with alternation according to person is not well documented. Accordingly, it is difficult to work out a diachronic analysis on the basis of synchronic variation. Therefore, Catalan cannot be used to either confirm or falsify the account proposed here.

8. A similar pattern is found in a number of Abruzzese dialects, where *da* occurs with the 2nd and 3rd person singular and with the 3rd plural (Rohlfs 1968: § 591). In Tollese the particle *a/da* has become an affix of the auxiliary "have". In the 1st person singular and in the 3rd singular and plural persons it is a suffix. In the 2nd person singular and plural and in the 1st person plural it is an infix occurring between the stem and the ending (*ajja fa* "I will do", *adi fa* "you will do", *ada fa* "s/he will do", *adama fa* "we will do", *adata fa* "you will do", *ada fa* "they will do") (R. Hastings, p.c.). This suggests that the particle is now part of the person marking system in the future periphrasis.

9. M. Loporcaro (p.c.) comments that there is no contrast between 2nd and 3rd person when SD does not apply or applies vacuously. Accordingly, the alternation of *a* and *da* in the future

periphrasis would not be a parallel to the mixed paradigm. In our view, however, the facts pointed out by Loporcaro do not invalidate our account. To be sure, on the surface SD (and hence person alternation) occurs in a limited number of contexts (with infinitives beginning in a consonant which does not geminate vacuously). However, the 2nd and 3rd person may contrast at the underlying level. Accordingly, the underlying form of *a* < *da* (2nd person singular) would be /da/, as suggested by the optionality of the elision of the dental. Similarly, *a* < *ad* (3rd person singular) would be /ad/ underlyingly, as indicated by SD in other contexts. Moreover, comparative evidence from other dialects also suggests that the outcome of *de ab* was introduced as a person marker. For example in Campobassano the outcome of *de ab*, which is subject to weakening (*da* > *ra*), only occurs in the 2nd person singular, thus contrasting with *a* in the 3rd person singular: *a ra purtá* ('you will bring'), *a a purtá* ("s/he will bring") (D'Ovidio 1878:183).

10. As argued elsewhere, the synchronic and diachronic dimensions of the Unaccusative Hierarchy (Sorace 2000) suggest that in languages with alternation according to verb class the choice of perfective auxiliaries is determined by semantic factors rather than by syntax (Bentley & Eythórsson 1999).

11. It might be suggested that the mixed paradigm is in some sense to be related to the Silverstein Hierarchy, according to which the 3rd person is more likely to manifest ergative alignment than the 1st and 2nd persons (Silverstein 1976). However, this is not the case in the dialects under consideration here, since they do not show an ergative-absolutive alternation in the 3rd person. In Altamurano "be" and "have" alternate according to verb class in the 3rd person. This alternation, however, is not to be related to the Silverstein Hierarchy. Rather, it may be a manifestation of an active-inactive alignment since "be" occurs with unaccusatives and "have" with unergatives and transitives.

12. We are pleased to note that Loporcaro (2001) has independently reached a similar conclusion on the basis of a synchronic analysis of auxiliary distribution in Italo-Romance.

References

Bentley, Delia & Thórhallur Eythórsson. 1999. "'Have' is not BE: Counterarguments to the decompositional account". Ms., University of Manchester.

Benveniste, Émile. 1946. "Structure des relations de personne dans le verbe". *Bulletin de la societé linguistique de Paris* 43.112.

Cennamo, Michela. 1997. "Unaccusativity in some Old Italian Dialects: A syntacto-semantic account". Paper presented at the University of Manchester, 6 May 1997.

Cennamo, Michela. 1999. "Inaccusatività tardo-latina e suoi riflessi in testi italiani antichi centro-meridionali". *Zeitschrift für romanische Philologie* 115: 2.300–331.

Cennamo, Michela. 2001. "L'inaccusatività in alcune varietà campane: teorie e dati a confronto". *Atti del XXXIII Convegno SLI*, Napoli, 28–30 October 1999 ed. by Rosanna Sornicola et al., 419–444. Roma: Bulzoni.

D'Ovidio, F. 1878. "Fonetica del dialetto di Campobasso". *Archivio Glottologico Italiano* IV.145–184.

Fanciullo, Franco. 1986. "Syntactic Reduplication and the Italian Dialects of the Centre-South". *Journal of Italian Linguistics* 8: 1.67–103.

Giammarco, Ernesto. 1973. "Selezione del verbo ausiliare nei paradigmi dei tempi composti". *Abruzzo* 11.61–87.

Hastings, Robert. 1996. "The Dialects of Abruzzo and Molise". *Quaderni di Ricerca del Centro di Dialettologia e Linguistica Italiana di Manchester* 1.21–38.

Kayne, Richard. 1993. "Toward a Modular Theory of Auxiliary Selection". *Studia Linguistica* 47.3–31.

Kuryłowicz, Jerzy. 1947. "La nature des procès dits analogiques". *Acta Linguistica* 5.17–34.

La Fauci, Nunzio & Michele Loporcaro. 1989. "Passifs, avancements de l'object indirect et formes verbales périphrastiques dans le dialecte d'Altamura (Pouilles)". *Rivista di Linguistica* 1.161–196.

Loporcaro, Michele. 1988a. *Grammatica storica del dialetto di Altamura.* Pisa: Giardini.

Loporcaro, Michele. 1988b. "History and Geography of *Raddoppiamento Fonosintattico*: Remarks on the evolution of a phonological rule". *Certamen Phonologicum* ed. by Pier Marco Bertinetto & Michele Loporcaro, 341–387. Torino: Rosenberg & Sellier.

Loporcaro, Michele. 1999. "Il futuro cantare-habeo nell'Italia meridionale". *Archivio Glottologico Italiano* LXXX. 67–114.

Loporcaro, Michele. 2001. "La selezione dell'ausiliare nei dialetti italiani: dati e teorie. *Atti del XXXIII Convegno SLI*, Napoli, 28–30 October 1999 ed. by Rosanna Sornicola et al. Roma: Bulzoni.

Lorenzetti, Luca. 1995. *Aspetti morfologici e sintattici dei dialetti dei Castelli Romani.* Dottorato di Ricerca in Linguistica, Terza Università di Roma.

Robertson, T. A. & John J. Graham 1991. *Grammar and Usage of the Shetland Dialect.* Lerwick: The Shetland Times.

Rohlfs, Gerhard. 1968. *Grammatica storica della lingua italiana e dei suoi dialetti. Morfologia.* Torino: Einaudi.

Rohlfs, Gerhard. 1969. *Grammatica storica della lingua italiana e dei suoi dialetti. Sintassi e formazione delle parole.* Torino: Einaudi.

Saxon, Leslie. 1999. "Third Person Forms in Paradigms". Paper presented to the Fourteenth International Conference of Historical Linguistics, Vancouver, B. C., August 1999.

Silverstein, Michael. 1976. "Hierarchy of Features and Ergativity". *Grammatical Categories in Australian Languages* ed. by R. M. W. Dixon, 112–176. Canberra: Australian Institute of Aboriginal Languages.

Sorace, Antonella. 1993. "Unaccusativity and Auxiliary Choice in Non-native Grammars of Italian and French: Asymmetries and predictable indeterminacy". *French Language Studies* 3.71–93.

Sorace, Antonella. 2000. "Gradients in Auxiliary Selection with Intransitive Verbs" *Language* 76. 859–890.

Tufi, Stefania. 2000. "Auxiliary Distribution in the Castelli Romani Dialects: The case of Marino". *The Italianist* 20.274–291.

Tuttle, Edward. 1986. "The Spread of *esse* as Universal Auxiliary in Central Italo-Romance". *Medioevo Romanzo* 11.229–287.

Vincent, Nigel. 1982. "The Development of Auxiliaries *habere* and *esse* in Romance". *Studies in the Romance Verb* ed. by Nigel Vincent & Martin Harris, 71–96. London: Croom Helm.

Watkins, Calvert. 1962. *The Indo-European Origins of the Celtic Verb.* Dublin: Institute for Advanced Studies.

On ablaut and aspect in the history of Aramaic

Vit Bubenik
Memorial University of Newfoundland

1. The theory of ablaut

I propose to start my inquiry into the interplay of ablaut and aspect in the history of Aramaic in the context of other Ancient Semitic languages by revisiting the theory of ablaut proposed by J. Kuryłowicz (1961, 1973). When dealing with the rise and role of vowel gradation in Semitic, Kuryłowicz (1973: 32–52) takes pains to emphasize that the widespread conception of the root of the Semitic verb as merely skeleton is erroneous. (In the seventies and eighties this conception was popularized by the templatic approach of autosegmental morphology.) Traditional grammars of Semitic languages tend to treat manifold derivational patterns in isolation and regard them as having an inherent semantic content. Kuryłowicz advocates taking one paradigm whose vocalism (of the second radical) is basic or unpredictable and inferring the rest of the conjugation according "to certain well-defined laws of Semitic apophony". For West Semitic Kuryłowicz suggests that the fundamental paradigm is that of the 'imperfect(ive)'. For instance, in Arabic the paradigms *kataba* "wrote", *yuktabu* "is written", the participle *kātibu* "writing" have a predictable vocalism of R2 and R1. Since the vowel of R2 of the imperfect(ive) is *u* the verbal root is *k(u)tub* and not simply *k-t-b*. "The vocalism of *u* of the 'imperf.' is basic, and undergoes determined changes in the other paradigms of the conjugation", maintains Kuryłowicz (1973: 34).

I agree with Kuryłowicz that word-based morphology (vs. the time honored root-based approach) has considerable merits in the explicating of ablaut alternants expressing various aspectual and diathetic categories in West Semitic. However, the verbal root with the vocalization of the basic imperfective, *-k(u)tub-*, as the derivational base for all the verb forms in other Semitic languages is inadequate. Along the same lines, Schramm (1991) has argued that the derivation of verb forms in Arabic proceeds from a root that generates a base from which the future (=

Kuryłowicz's imperfective) is derived first, then the past. From the point of view of the distribution of ablaut variants in aspectual categories of Semitic languages either proposal is too reductionist and inappropriate for diachronic analysis. I will argue that the verbal root *CCVC is inherited from Proto-Semitic (witness its occurrence in the earliest layers of all Ancient Semitic languages represented by the imperative and subjunctive) and that we are in need of several other derivational bases for other verb forms. This more pluralistic and dynamic conception of Semitic derivational morphology will allow us to describe relationships between derivational bases in terms of qualitative and quantitative ablaut, and will open the possibility for analogical extensions between their derivatives (in sections 2 and 4). We will examine the full-blown aspectual system implemented by ablaut in East Semitic Akkadian, its refunctionalization in a later system represented by Aramaic and its ultimate decay in the system of New Aramaic (in section 3). In the comparative part of the paper (section 4) we will examine the redistribution of apophonic contrasts (most notably from aspectual to diathetic categories) in other Central Semitic languages (Arabic and Hebrew) and South Semitic Gəʕəz.

For the earliest recorded Semitic language, Akkadian, I want to propose the forms with internal vowel sequences {a–i} and {a–u}, appearing in the category of stative, e.g., *damiq* "he is good" and *maruṣ* "he is sick", as suitable derivational bases for finite aspectual categories of intransitive and transitive verbs. This proposal stems from the 'chronogenetic' approach to aspect and tense developed for IE languages by Hewson and Bubenik (1997); it considers verbal adjectives or participles chronogenetically prior to finite forms. In a similar vein Testen (1998) ascribed a central role to the adjective in the formation of ingressive verbs in Akkadian. As shown in (1) the vocalism of statives is identical with that found in primary adjectives such as *dámiq-*, Fem *damíq-tum* "good" and *máruṣ-*, Fem *marúṣ-tum* "sick":

(1)   Primary adjectives   →   Derivational base for finite verb forms (by pronominal clitics)

        damiq- "good"   *damiq* = PRO (stative)   "be good"

                       PRO = *damiq* (fientive)   "become good"

        maruṣ "sick"   *maruṣ* = PRO (stative)   "be sick"

                       PRO = *maruṣ* (fientive)   "fall sick"

These internal vowel sequences, {a–i} and {a–u}, may be called for short 'transfixes' (not to be confused with circumfixes such as the Berber feminine gender morpheme *t–t* in *t-amdakul-t* "girl-friend"). The derivational base with the transfix {a–i} will be of cardinal importance for synchronic derivations of finite verb forms of Aramaic and other Central Semitic languages. Before we examine closely the situation in Aramaic we may glance at derivational processes of Akkadian.

(2) Derivation of finite forms of intransitive verbs from the base *xaliq-* "perish":

	Imperfective	Perfective	Stative
	PRO-*xálliq*	PRO-*xliq*	*xalq*-PRO
3SG	*i-xálliq*	*í-xliq*	*xáliq*

The stative is formed by pronominal enclitics and the fientive imperfective by pronominal proclitics. It is usually assumed that the reduplication of the second radical in the imperfective has to do with the stress falling on the first vocalic radical; the complete reduction of the second vowel in the stative is caused by the stress on the following vowel. Its perfective counterpart, *í-xliq*, differs from the stative and the imperfective by its complete reduction of the first vowel. This complete reduction was labelled 'quantitative apophony' by Kuryłowicz (1973); unlike in the stative, it is caused by the stress on the preceding syllable. Typologically, one may compare this quantitative ablaut involved in the formation of the perfective fientive and the stative in Semitic with a parallel process of the formation of the perfect participle in PIE (where the stress was placed on the following syllable: |bher-tó| > *bhr-tó "carried"):

(3) PS |yá-xaliq| > *í-xliq* "he perished", xaliq-áku > *xalq-áku* "I am destroyed" (Akkadian)

The derivation of fientive forms of ingressive verbs with the internal vowel sequence *a–u*, *i-marruṣ* "he is/will be sick", in (4) is straightforward since here the vocalization of the verbal adjective of the type *maruṣ* "sick" is in common with the stative and the fientive imperfective:

(4) Derivation of finite forms of ingressive verbs from the base (verbal adjective) *maruṣ-* "sick":

Imperfective	Perfective	Stative
PRO+*márruṣ*	PRO+*mruṣ*	*marṣ*=PRO
"is/will be sick"	"fell sick"	"is sick"

In the derivation of transitive verbs in (5) one observes an interplay of two apophonies: quantitative ablaut derives the perfective as in intransitive forms; cf. (2) and (4). In contradistinction, however, one observes effects of qualitative ablaut operating in the second vocalic radical; it is *a* in the imperfective but *u* in the perfective (while in intransitive verbs the second vocalic radical remained either *i* or *u*, the latter with ingressive verbs):

(5) Derivation of finite forms of transitive verbs from the base *paris-* "separate":

Imperfective	Perfective	Stative
PRO=*párras*	PRO=*prus*	*pars*=PRO
"separates"	"separated"	"is separated"

2.   The verb system of Standard Literary Aramaic

In spite of its innovative infinitive *mi-ktab* "to write" (vs. Hebrew *kātōb* and Akkadian *parāsu*) the verb system of Standard Literary Aramaic, whose vocalization system is known to us through the Aramaic portions of the Old Testament (cf. Kaufman 1997:115), is more archaic than that of other Central Semitic languages (Hebrew, Arabic). It is displayed in (6):

(6)   Verb system of Standard Literary Aramaic:

	Imperfective/ Jussive	Preterite	Participles	
			Active	Passive
	yí-ktub	*kətáb*	*kā́tib* ~ *kātéb*	*kətíb*
Factitive	*yə-káttib* ~ *yə-kattéb*	*káttib* *kattéb*	*mə-káttib*	*mə-káttab*
Mediopassive	*yi-t-katíb* ~ *yi-t-katéb*	*hit-katíb*		*mit-katéb*
Mediopassive factitive	*yi-t-káttab*	*hit-káttab*		*mit-káttab*

One notices the absence of the passive marked with the prefix *n-* present in Akkadian and other Central languages; Gordon (1997:110) pinpoints its absence in Eblaite (3rd Mil.), embodying East and West Semitic features (but to others, in Hetzron 1997, Eblaite is East Semitic). To compensate for this loss (?) Middle Aramaic developed an innovative passive formed by cliticizing the suffixes of the preterite to the passive participle of the type *təqíl-tá* "you were weighed". (The term 'preterite' is more appropriate for the suffixal conjugation of Central Semitic languages in view of the absence of the contrast perfect vs. perfective available in Akkadian, cf. Bubenik 1998:51–52).

Let us now ascertain to what extent ablaut is used to implement aspectual contrasts in Aramaic. In the archaic Akkadian system (see 8) qualitative ablaut in V2 (*a* ~ *i*) was used primarily for aspectual purposes to implement the contrast between the imperfective, on the one hand, and the perfect and the perfective aspect in factitive verbs, on the other hand (*u-parras* vs. *u-p-t-arris* and *u-parris*) and their derivatives (mediopassive *u-p-t-arras* vs. *u-p-tat-arris* and *u-p-t-arris*; passive **i-n-parras* vs. **i-n-paris*). In contradistinction to Akkadian, in Aramaic ablaut is used to express diathetic categories in factitive participles: contrast the active form *məkáttib* with its passive counterpart *məkáttab* (Hebrew equivalents display ablaut in both vowels: *məkattéb* vs. *məkuttáb* (**mu-kattib* vs. **mu-kuttab*)). The same type of ablaut (*i* ~ *a*) distinguishes basic factitive forms from their mediopassive counterparts (contrast *yə-káttib* with *yi-t-káttab*); and within the mediopassive category also the nonfactitive verbs from their factitive counterparts (contrast mediopassive *yit̠-kət̠íb̠* with the mediopassive factitive *yit̠-káttab̠*). The function of qualitative ablaut in the Aramaic verb system is sketched in (7); the forms in bold characters are based on the transfix {*a–i*}:

(7) The function of qualitative ablaut in the verb system of Standard Literary Aramaic

	Basic		Mediopassive (prefix *t*-)	
			V_2=i	V_2=a
	V_2=i			
	−factitive	+factitive	−factitive	+factitive
Imperfective	(*yi-k̠tub̠*)	yə-**káttib̠**	*yit̠-kət̠íb̠*	*yit̠-kattab̠*
Perfective	(*kət̠ab̠*)	**káttib̠**	*hit̠-kət̠íb̠*	*hit̠-kattab̠*
Participles		mə-**káttib̠**	**mit̠-kət̠íb̠*	*mit̠-kattab̠*
		mə-**k̠áttab̠** (innovative passive)		

For the sake of comparison, the Akkadian macroparadigm, based on von Soden (1952: 12–13*), is presented in (8). Akkadian forms its diathetic categories by means of the infix -*t*- (mediopassive) and prefix *n*- (passive) without taking recourse to ablaut; thus in the imperfective all the derived forms display *a* as the second vocalic radical: compare *i-parras* and factitive *u-parras*, and their *t*-infixed counterparts (*i-p-t-arras* and *u-p-t-arras*), and the passive *ipparras* (<*i-n-parras). On the other hand, all their quasinominal counterparts (participles) are based on the transfix {*a–i*} (*pā-ris-*, *muparris-*, *muptars-* (<*muptaris), *muptarris-*, and *muppars-* (<**munparis-*)) corresponding to that of primary adjectives in (1). The transfix {*a–i*} is also used in the perfect and the perfective of factitive verbs. As mentioned above, all these forms are related to their imperfective counterparts by qualitative ablaut *a~i* in V2. In addition, all these forms are double-marked vis-à-vis their basic non-factitive counterparts in displaying the vowel *u* after their personal prefixes. In the mediopassive, however, the perfective displays *a* as V2 (*i-p-t-aras* vs. the factitive *u-parris* and the passive *i-n-paris) presumably by analogy with the form of the mediopassive perfect *i-p-tat-ras*; this results in the homophony of the active perfect and the mediopassive perfective, *i-p-t-aras*, the famous 'leak' of the Akkadian grammar. One also observes the homophony of their factitive counterparts (both forms are *u-p-t-arris*). Given the fact that the passive perfective *i-n-paris displays the transfix {*a–i*}, it is somewhat surprising to ascertain that the V2 of the passive perfect is *a*; if, however, it were *i* (i.e., if the qualitative ablaut applied here) the form *i-n-t-apris would be triple-marked. (This is not to say that perfects cannot be triple-marked; e.g., they are triple-marked in Sanskrit and Ancient Greek.) Thus, there is a certain asymmetry in the distribution of the transfix {*a–i*} in the derived forms of transitive verbs; however, it may be observed that the vowel sequences in the basic perfect and perfective are also different. All these matters are surveyed in (8.i):

(8)   i.   The function of qualitative ablaut in the Akkadian verb system: transitive *parāsu* "separate":

	basic		infix -t-		prefix *n*-
	V_2=a	V_2=i	V_2=a	V_2=i	
	−factitive	+factitive	−factitive	+factitive	
Imperfective	*i-parras*	*u-parras*	*i-p-t-arras*	*u-p-t-arras*	**i-n-parras*
Perfect	*i-p-t-aras*	*u-p-t-arris*	*i-p-tat-ras*	*u-p-tat-arris*	**i-n-t-apras*
Perfective	(*i-prus*)	*u-parris*	*i-p-t-aras*	*u-p-t-arris*	**i-n-paris*
Participles	*pāris-*	*mu-parris-*	**mu-p-t-aris-*	*mu-p-t-arris-*	**mu-n-paris-*

The ablaut pattern of intransitive verbs with *i* as V2 is much simpler. Across the board in the perfect, perfective, and participles the internal vowel sequence {*a–i*}, characteristic of primary adjectives in (1), is found; in addition, the imperfective non-factitive are built on the same sequence. The derived (factitive) imperfective forms show the effect of qualitative ablaut in V2: *u-p(-t)-aqqad* vs. *u-p(-t)-aqqid*. This is shown in (8.ii):

(8)   ii.   The function of qualitative ablaut in intransitive verbs with V2 = *i*: *paqādu* "be watchful":

	basic		infix -*t*-		prefix *n*-
	V2 = *i*	V2 = *i*	V2 = *i*	V2 = *i*	V2 = *i*
	−factitive	+factitive	−factitive	+factitive	
Imperfective	*i-paqqid*	*u-paqqad*	*i-p-t-aqqid*	*u-p-t-aqqad*	*i-n-paqqid*
Perfect	*i-p-t-aqid*	*u-p-t-aqqid*	*i-p-tat-qid*	*u-p-tat-aqqid*	*i-n-t-apqid*
Perfective	(*i-pqid*)	*u-paqqid*	*i-p-t-aqid*	*u-p-t-aqqid*	*i-n-paqid*
Participles	*pāqid-*	*mu-paqqid*	**mu-p-t-aqid*	*mu-p-t-aqqid*	*mu-n-paqid*

Contrasted with Akkadian, derivational processes of Aramaic forms are more complex phonologically. As in Akkadian, the factitive forms are derived from the same base of the type *káttib-* by means of finitizing prefixes and suffixes shown in (9):

(9)   Deriving factitive forms in Aramaic:

Imperfective	Preterite	Participle
PRO-*káttib̲*	*káttib̲*-PRO	*mə-káttib̲*

Their mediopassive counterparts are formed by qualitative ablaut operating in the second radical vowel, as was shown in (7). (One notices an occasional absence of ablaut as in *hiṯ-nabbī* ? in [Ezr 5.1] instead of expected **hiṯ-nabbaʔ*, caused perhaps by influence from Hebrew *hiṯ-nabbēʔ*):

(10) *wə-hiṯnabbīʔ*   *Haggay nəḇiyyā*   *ū-Zəḵaryā*   *ḇar*   *ʕiddō* [Ezr 5.1]
       and prophesied Haggai prophet=the and Zechariah son of Iddo
       "Now the prophets Haggai and Zechariah the son of Iddo prophesied"

The derivation of basic forms of intransitive verbs involves quantitative ablaut caused by post- or pretonic vowel reduction. For instance, the imperfective *yíttiḇ* "he is sitting" and the preterite *yəṯíḇ* "he sat" may be derived from the base **yaṯíḇ* as shown in (11):

(11)   Imperfective   Preterite   Participle
       a > Ø / -Σ́   a > ə / -Σ́   a > ā / ⌣
       *yí-yṯiḇ > *yíttiḇ* "is sitting"   *yəṯíḇ* "sat"   *yāṯiḇ* "sitting"

The derivational base **yaṯíḇ* based on the transfix {*a–i*}, with stress on the second vocalic radical, never 'surfaces'; its posttonic *a* is completely reduced in the imperfective, its pretonic *a* is reduced to schwa in the preterite, and its *a* is lengthened under stress.

Mediopassive forms are derived from the derivational base **t-katíḇ* with the same transfix as their intransitive counterpart **yaṯíḇ* in (11). In addition to the pretonic reduction of *a* to schwa, its *i* is lengthened and lowered to *ē* under stress; this is shown in (12):

(12)   Imperfective   Preterite   Participle
       a > ə / -Σ́   a > ə / -Σ́   a > ə / -Σ́
       i > ē / ⌣   i > ē / ⌣
       yi-t-kəṯíḇ   *hi-t-kəṯíḇ*   **mi-t-kəṯíḇ*
       yi-t-kəṯéḇ   *mi-t-kəṯéḇ*

Let us now try to derive the basic aspectual forms of transitive verbs, *yí-ḵtuḇ* and *kəṯáḇ*, and their participles, *káṯiḇ* and *kəṯíḇ*, from the derivational base **katíḇ*, which we used for the derivation of intransitive and mediopassive forms in (11) and (12), respectively. The derivation of the latter three forms in (13) presents no difficulty; in fact, these rules are identical with those we used for the derivation of their intransitive and mediopassive counterparts (notice, however, that V2 of the passive participle is only lengthened but not lowered under stress).

(13)   Preterite   Active Participle   Passive Participle
       ablaut *i ~ a*   metatony
       a > ə / -Σ́   a > ā / ⌣   i > ī / ⌣
       kəṯáḇ   *káṯiḇ*   *kəṯíḇ*

The remaining problem is whether we can derive synchronically the imperfective form *yí-ḵuḇ* from the base **katíḇ* (as we did it in (6) with its intransitive counterpart *yí-ytib*). Its derivation would necessitate quantitative ablaut (or complete post-tonic reduction) of the first vocalic radical and qualitative ablaut of the second vocalic radical *i ~ u*. The question is whether we would be willing to take qualitative ablaut of the second radical *i ~ u* for a synchronic phonological rule of Old Aramaic comparable with reduction and lengthening of vowels adjacent to the stressed vowel. The answer is NO since qualitative ablaut involving two high vowels, *i ~ u*, does not possess much systemic support in the Aramaic morphological system. In fact, it is only used for keeping the transitive and intransitive imperfectives apart. Matters are different in Akkadian; there, ablaut involving two high vowels, *i ~ u*, is crucial in the derivation of the stative of factitive verbs as in the pair *parris ~ parrus*. Furthermore, within the group of intransitive verbs the contrast *u* vs. *i* is used to distinguish between ingressive (*i-rpud* "started running" and non-ingressive verbs *i-pqid* "was watchful"). And finally, the *i ~ u* alternation in the personal prefix was the sole distinguishing mark between the basic and factitive categories in the imperfective aspect of transitive verbs (*i-párras* vs. *u-párras*). Therefore, it would be possible to use qualitative ablaut *i ~ u* in the derivation of the perfective *í-prus* from the base *páris*. (Notice, however, that this proposal would be as reductionist as that advocated by Kuryłowicz).

We may conclude that qualitative ablaut involving high vowels, *i ~ u*, does not play any role in synchronic derivations of Aramaic. As we saw in (2) this language relies on ablaut involving low *a* and high *i* in expressing its diathetic contrasts. Therefore it is better to evaluate the form *yí-ktub* as a form inherited from Proto-Semitic **ya-ktub* which is not relatable to the verbal adjective. As in Akkadian, Aramaic primary adjectives are built on the transfix {*a–i*}, e.g., *šappīr* "beautiful", *ḥakkīm* "wise" (with lengthening of *i* under stress) but not {*a–u*} (unlike Akkadian **maruṣ-*, Fem *maruṣ-tum* 'sick'). Chances for the synchronic derivation of the imperfective (of the Hebrew type *yi-ktōb* and Arabic *ya-ktubu*) from the base **C1aC2uC3* are better in other Central Semitic languages where there is more morphological support for the existence of the ablaut variant *u* seen in primary adjectives such as Hebrew *qārōb* "relative" and the passive participle *kātūb* vs. Aramaic *kətīb*. In Aramaic the derivation of intransitive forms in (11) and medio-passive forms in (12) from derivational bases **yatīb* and **katīb*, respectively, gets support from the existence of the intransitive preterite with *i* as the second vocalic radical, *yətíb* "he sat", and the passive participle *kətīb*. Also some transitive verbs use *i* as the second vocalic radical in the preterite, e.g., *nətín* "he gave".

Since in Standard Literary Aramaic ablaut stopped being a viable strategy for the formation of aspectual categories, it became necessary to rely on morpho-syntactic means in this respect; hence the appearance of analytic formations consisting of the copula and the present participle in Middle Aramaic as shown in (14) taken from Daniel [2.34]:

(14) *ħāzē*   *həwaytā*   *ʕaḏ* *dī* *hitgəzeret*   *ʔeḇen*
look-PART be-PRET-2SG.MASC when REFL cut-MED/PASS+3SG stone

Similar constructions anticipate later developments towards analytic formations of New Aramaic.

3. Elimination of ablaut in New Aramaic

New Aramaic completely rebuilt the ancestral Old Aramaic aspectual system based on the prefixal and suffixal conjugation and ended up with two or three suffixal conjugations based on the active and the passive participle. This rebuilding process is understood as a passive-to-ergative shift sketched in (15):

(15) Passive-to-ergative shift in New Aramaic:

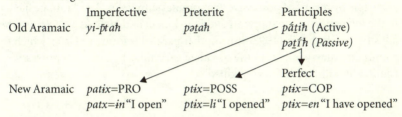

	Imperfective	Preterite	Participles
Old Aramaic	*yi- p̄taħ*	*pətaħ*	*pā́ṭiħ* (Active)
			pəṭíħ (Passive)
			Perfect
New Aramaic	*patix*=PRO	*ptix*=POSS	*ptix*=COP
	patx=in "I open"	*ptix=li* "I opened"	*ptix=en* "I have opened"

To use Hoberman's (1989) data from a Jewish dialect from Iraqi Kurdistan the New Aramaic imperfective is a finitized active participle by direct (nominative) pronominal suffixes, e.g., *patx-in* "I open"; whereas the preterite is based on the passive participle *ptix* (< Old Aramaic *pəṭíħ*) to which the possessive pronominal suffixes accompanied by the preposition *lə* "to" were added, e.g., *ptix-li* "I opened". In the neighboring Azerbaijan one could distinguish even between the preterite and perfect, the latter form displaying the copula (instead of the possessive suffix) cliticized to the possessive participle: contrast *qtíl-li* "I killed" with *qtil-en* "I have killed" (cf. Hopkins 1989:427). At the end of this process the function of ablaut was reduced to keeping apart the derivational base *pátix* for the imperfective aspect (with *a* as V1) vs. the derivational base *ptix* for the preterite and the perfect (with Ø as V1), returning thus, in a sense, to its primordial aspectual function.

A contributing factor in the passive-to-ergative shift were certain dysfunctional forms of the active perfect and the finitized passive participle in Standard Literary Aramaic displaying *i* as the second vocalic radical in the preterite:

(16)

	Active preterite	Finitized passive participle
3SG.MASC	*nəṭín* "he gave"	*nəṭín* "he was given"
3SG.FEM	*nəṭín-at* "she gave"	*nəṭín-aṭ* "she was given"
	~*nəṭḗn-at* ~ *nitn-at*	

One notices that the cardinal distinction of the active and passive was realized solely by the short vs. long vowel or by the mid vs. high front vowel, cf. derivations in (12) and (13). This state of affairs might have precipitated the emergence of an alternative form *niṯnaṯ* "she gave" to *nəṯínaṯ* (or *nəṯén-aṯ*) contrasting clearly with *nəṯín-aṯ* "she was given". These phonological 'infelicities' bordering on homophonic clashes were undoubtedly instrumental in the motivation of the passive-to-ergative shift. An external motivation, suggesting that the Aramaic ergative construction was modelled on the Old Persian ergative construction of the type *manā kartam* lit. of me/for me done "I did [it]", was proposed by Kutscher in 1969. However, as usual in historical linguistics, the internal Semitic motivation should not be underestimated. The finitization of the passive participle by means of direct (nominative) pronominal suffixes in Standard Literary Aramaic is typologically similar to the strategy of forming the stative in Akkadian in (3), and the finitization of the passive participle by means of possessive pronominal suffixes in New Aramaic has a parallel in the formation of the stative in Old Babylonian and New Assyrian from the verbal adjective, cf. Bubenik (1998: 46); another parallel is found in Gəʕəz which forms its conjunctive participle from the so-called gerundive by means of possessive suffixes (*qatīl-o* lit. killing-his "having killed").

4. Redistribution and refunctionalization of ablaut variants in Ancient Semitic languages

In the archaic Akkadian system qualitative ablaut was used primarily for aspectual purposes; as summarized in (17) its salient phenomena are the contrast between the imperfective and perfective aspect in factitive verbs (*u-párras* vs. *u-párris*) with the latter category built on the transfix {*a–i*}; and within the imperfective aspect that between the basic and factitive verbs (*i-párras* vs. *u-párras*) with ablaut involving high vowels *i ~ u* in preradical pretonic position.

(17) North Semitic (Akkadian) qualitative ablaut: prefix *i- ~ u-*; V2 *i ~ a.*

	Basic	Factitive
Perfective		*u-párris*
Imperfective	*i-párras* ~	*u-párras*

In Aramaic the same transfix {*a–i*} was used primarily for the purposes of diathesis as summarized in (18):

(18) Central Semitic (Aramaic) qualitative ablaut: V2 *i ~ a.*

	Basic	Factitive	Participles
Active		*yə-ḵáttiḇ*	*mə-ḵáttiḇ*
Mediopassive	*yi-ṯ-kəṯíḇ* ~	*yi-ṯ-káttaḇ*	*mə-ḵáttaḇ* (innovative)
	(< * *yi-t-katíḇ*)		

Since it is generally assumed that the Akkadian way of forming diathetic categories by means of the infix -*t*- and prefix *n*- without ablaut is representative of the Proto-Semitic state of affairs (cf. Testen 1998) in the extension of ablaut to diathesis we are dealing with an innovation of Aramaic and other Central languages .

In these we encounter further innovations. Arabic and Hebrew exploit the internal vowel sequence for aspectual purposes. In their derived categories the imperfective is built on the transfix {*a–i*}, while its preterite counterparts display qualitative ablaut in V2. Hebrew, in addition, displays intraparadigmatic ablaut whereby the unmarked form of the 3SG.PRET is singled out; contrast *hi-t̲-qattēl* (<*t-qattíl*) "he killed himself" with *hi-t̲-qattal-tā* (2SG.MASC). Consequently, for diathetic purposes, they had to innovate in introducing the ablaut variant *u* in the first vocalic radical. These innovative forms (passive preterite in Hebrew and Arabic, and passive imperfective and participles in Hebrew) are surveyed in (19):

(19)   Central Semitic innovative qualitative ablaut in factitive forms: V1 *i/a* ~ *u*.

	Aramaic	Hebrew	Arabic
Active preterite	*kattib*	*kittab̲-*	*kattab-*
Passive preterite	*(hi-t̲-kattab̲)*	*kuttab̲-*	*kuttib-*
Passive imperfective	*(yi-t̲-kattab̲)*	*yə-k̲uttab̲*	*yu-kattab*
Passive participle	*mə-k̲attab-*	*mə-k̲uttab-*	*mu-kattab*

Given the absence of ablaut in the passive imperfective and the participle in Aramaic and Arabic, the vowel *u* in Hebrew *yə-k̲uttab̲* and *mə-k̲uttab̲* must be considered as arising by extension (analogy) from the preterite.

Biblical Hebrew is unique among Central Semitic languages in exploiting qualitative ablaut involving two high vowels for diathetic purposes; *i* is used as V1 in the factitive and as the prothetic vowel in the causative; their passive counterparts display *u* in the same position.

(20)   Biblical Hebrew qualitative ablaut *i* ~ *u* in derived categories:

	Active	Passive
Factitive	*kittab̲-*	*kuttab̲-*
Causative	*hi-k̲tab̲-*	**hu-ktab- (> ho-k̲tab̲-)*

As is well known, the innovative passive in Arabic uses the internal vowel sequence {*u–i*} in the preterite, and has extended the first vocalic radical *u* even to the preradical vowel in the imperfective, an integral part of the personal prefix. The transfix {*u–i*} results from an interplay of two ablauts: V2 = *a* ~ *i* and V1 = *a* ~ *u*.

(21)   Innovative passive of Classical Arabic exploiting the transfix {*u–i*}:

	Active (preterite)	Passive (preterite)	Passive (imperfective)
Basic	*katab-*	*kutib-*	*(yu-ktab)* ~ *ya-n-katib*
Factitive	*kattab*	*kuttib-*	*yu-kattab*
Causative	*ʔa-ktab-*	*ʔu-ktib-*	*yu-ktab*

One observes homophony of the basic category and the causative in the passive imperfective; in the basic, however, there is also the passive formation with the nasal prefix and the transfix {*a–i*} inherited from Proto-Semitic.

A particularly strong piece of evidence for the central role of the internal vowel sequence {*a–i*} in the morphological make-up of Ancient Semitic languages is supplied by Gəʕəz. It is the only Semitic language which exploits the transfix {*a–i*} in the formation of the causative (imperfective); all the other Semitic languages, Akkadian included, reduce its *a* to zero in post-tonic position:

(22) Ablaut pattern in the causative:

	Akkadian	Aramaic	Gəʕəz
Suffixal conjugation	*ša-prus* (Assyrian)	*h/ʔa-ktib*	*ʔa-ktab-*
Prefixal conjugation	*u-ša-pris*	*yə-ha-ktib* (> *ya-ktib*)	*yā-ktəb* ~ *yā-katəb*

Hebrew and Aramaic do not rely on ablaut in the 2nd vocalic radical (Hebrew *hi-ktīb* vs. *ya-ktīb*) to mark the contrast between the preterite and the imperfective aspect, while other languages do. Akkadian and Aramaic display the original sequence of two prefixes (personal and causative) in the prefixal conjugation; in Aramaic it could be reduced to a portmanteau morpheme *ya-*; the same happened in Gəʕəz with the long vowel *ā* pinpointing to the original state of affairs (**ya-ʔa- > yə-ʔa- > yā-*). The short vowel in the Aramaic prefixal conjugation could be the source of certain ambiguities such as *ʔa-ktib*, 3sg preterite and the 1sg imperfective (the latter from uncontracted **ʔə-ha-ktib*). In Hebrew the preterite and the imperfective are kept apart by ablaut in the preradical vowel (*hi-ktīb* vs. *ya-ktīb*); in Arabic this contrast is accompanied by the contrast in the 2nd vocalic radical (*ʔa-ktab-* vs. *yu-ktib-*); also in Gəʕəz this contrast is double-marked: *ʔa-ktab-* vs. *yā-ktəb*. But the other prefixal form, *yā-katəb*, represents a remarkable innovation of Gəʕəz, consisting of combining the portmanteau morpheme *yā-* with the form based on the transfix {*a–i*}, extended to the causative from the basic imperfective *yə-kattəb* (< **ya-kattib*):

(23)

Basic	Causative	(Gəʕəz)
*ya-kattib	**ya-ʔa-ktib*	
yə-kattəb	*yā-ktəb*	
\	↓	(portmanteau)
(extension)	*yā-katəb*	

5. Further perspectives

As we saw above the ablaut theory allows us to analyze insightfully much of the productive core of Ancient Semitic verbal morphology. In addition it offers new exciting vistas into the intricacies of the development of verb systems in other Afrasian languages. The internal vowel sequences {a–i} and {a–a}, linked by qualitative ablaut in V2, may be reconstructed for Proto-Semitic as exponents of the opposition of perfectivity. Diakonoff (1988: 106) reconstructs the original paradigm of derivative stems in Proto-Semitic as follows:

(24)		Perfective/Jussive	Imperfective
	Factitive	*yu-parris	*yu-parras
	Causative	*yu-ša-p(a)ris	*yu-ša-p(a)ras
	Passive	*ya-n-paris	*ya-n-paras
	Reflexive	*ya-t-paris	*ya-t-paras

The two ablaut varieties of the personal subject marker, u and a, can be linked with transitivity (the factitive and causative $*(y)u$- vs. the passive and reflexive $*(y)a$-).

In Egyptian, as vocalized by Loprieno (1995:77–81), the internal vowel sequences {a–i} vs. {a–a} implemented the contrast between the perfect and the 'general present or aorist' (i.e., imperfective): sḏm.n=f */sa'ḏimn=af/ "he heard" vs. sḏm zȝ=j */saḏam'ziːraj/ "my son listens". The formal connection of the latter form ('imperfective sḏm=f') to the Akkadian imperfective i-parras was established a long time ago. The past perfective (so-called 'indicative sḏm=f') of the Old Kingdom was probably vocalized *CVCCi-, i.e., with V2 = Ø */saḏmi=f/. Here, again we may pinpoint a similarity with the formation of the Proto-Semitic perfective/jussive *yá-prus with V1 = Ø, in that both are based on quantitative ablaut or post/pretonic vowel reduction (as in our derivation of Aramaic forms in (11)). The data of other Afrasian branches which do not possess ancient records are more difficult to explicate. Diakonoff (1988: 86) reconstructed the full vocalism of the imperfective for Proto-Berber with some hesitation: imperfective *ya-g(a)may "he seeks" vs. perfective *ya-gmiy "he sought" with V1 = Ø; nevertheless, he believed that it was very ancient. Data of Cushitic, according to Zaborski (1975), would lend support to Diakonoff's reconstruction as far as the ablaut pattern in V2 is concerned. For Proto-Cushitic Zaborski reconstructs an opposition of the 'instantaneous' (perfective) and the 'continuous' (imperfective) aspect in the form *ya-C1C2iC3 vs. *ya-C1C2aC3. The full vocalism of the imperfective could then be safely reconstructed only for Proto-Semitic-Egyptian(-Berber?); pre-Proto-Cushitic could have it and subsequently lost it, or, more likely, never developed it. The difficult question of whether we can reconstruct a formal opposition of perfectivity in both transitive (*ya-C1C2u/iC3 vs. *yi-C1C2aC3) and intransitive verbs will have to be reserved for another paper.

In conclusion, I want to argue that the ablaut theory can profitably be extended in both space and time beyond the morphosemantics of Semitic into the whole Afrasian phylum. In view of the fundamental importance of the accent pattern in any ablaut theory (the same derivational base C1aC2iC3 produced different results in Akkadian with the accent on the penult vs. Aramaic with the accent on the ultima) we can hope to see further progress in arriving at the overall picture of the function of ablaut only with our improved knowledge of the accentuation of other Afrasian languages.

References

Bubenik, Vit. 1998. "Grammatical and Lexical Aspect in Akkadian and Proto-Semitic". *Historical Linguistics 1997* ed. by Monika Schmid et al., 41–56. Amsterdam & Philadelphia: John Benjamins.

Diakonoff, Igor M. 1988. *Afrasian Languages*. Moscow: Nauka.

Gordon, Cyrus H. 1997. "Amorite and Eblaite". *The Semitic Languages* ed. by Robert Hetzron, 100–113. London: Routledge.

Hetzron, Robert, ed. 1997. *The Semitic Languages*. London: Routledge.

Hewson, John & Vit Bubenik. 1997. *Tense and Aspect in Indo-European Languages: Theory, typology, diachrony*. Amsterdam & Philadelphia: John Benjamins.

Hoberman, Robert D. 1989. *The Syntax and Semantics of Verb Morphology in Modern Aramaic: A Jewish dialect of Iraqi Kurdistan*. American Oriental Society. New Haven, Connecticut.

Hopkins, Simon. 1989. "Neo-Aramaic Dialects and the Formation of the Preterite". *Journal of Semitic Studies* 34.413–432.

Kaufman, Stephen A. 1997. "Aramaic". *The Semitic Languages*. Hetzron 1997. 114–130.

Kuryłowicz, Jerzy. 1962. *L'apophonie en sémitique*. The Hague: Mouton.

Kuryłowicz, Jerzy. 1973. *Studies in Semitic Grammar and Metrics*. London: Curzon Press.

Loprieno, Antonio. 1995. *Ancient Egyptian. A linguistic introduction*. Cambridge: Cambridge University Press.

Schramm, Gene M. 1991. "Semitic Morpheme Structure Typology". *Semitic Studies in Honor of Wolf Leslau* ed. by Alan S. Kaye, 1402–1408. Wiesbaden: Harrassowitz.

von Soden, Wolfram. 1952. *Grundriss der akkadischen Grammatik*. Rome: Pontificium Institutum Biblicum.

Testen, David. 1998. "The Derivational Role of the Semitic N-stem". *Zeitschrift für Assyriologie und vorderasiatische Archäologie* 88.127–145.

Zaborski, Andrzej. 1975. *The Verb in Cushitic*. Warszaw: Uniwersytet Jagieloński.

Language change
and the phonological lexicon of Korean

Young-mee Y. Cho
Rutgers University

1. Introduction

Language contact and subsequent language change often result in lexical stratification in natural languages. Morphemes of different classes not only mirror historical developments but also manifest synchronically real internal variation and alternations that need to be explicated in terms of phonological regularities. In standard generative grammar, lexical stratification was used to motivate certain features associated with phonological rules. In many cases diacritic features such as [+exceptional], [+foreign], [+latinate] were employed to distinguish different lexical domains in which certain rules may or may not apply. In English, for instance, Velar Softening, which accounts for such alternations as *electric/electricity, critical/criticism, medical/medicine*, applies only to Latinate vocabulary; this morphological restriction has been used to motivate the distinction between English and Latinate strata (Chomsky & Halle 1968).

Research into the lexicon over the past thirty years has resulted in a better understanding of stratification and the interrelationship between different strata (Kiparsky 1968; Lightner 1972; Itô & Mester 1995, to name a few). In reaction to the unprincipled use of diacritic features, Kiparsky (1968) proposed the notion of a 'hierarchy of foreignness' whereby the lexicon is organized by different degrees of nativization that govern the application of rules and exceptions, rather than by the division of morphemes in terms of the feature [±foreign]. Such a hierarchy necessarily implies implicational relations where exceptions to one rule are always exceptions to another rule, not vice versa.

Recently, within the framework of Optimality Theory (Prince & Smolensky 1993; McCarthy & Prince 1993, 1995), a new conception of lexical organization was proposed (Itô & Mester 1995, forthc.; Yip 1993); lexical stratification is no longer viewed as an extra-linguistic anomaly but as a legitimate classification that should be characterized straightforwardly as constraint domains. In particular, it is assumed that constraint reranking is the only mechanism that defines the domains. In this context, Itô and Mester (1995, forthc.) propose the 'core/periphery organization' of the lexicon that predicts that constraints holding in a peripheral domain necessarily hold in a core domain, as well, due to the lexical structure given in (1). A hierarchy of implicational relations holds in three domains, A, B, and C. A, being the core of the lexicon, is subject to markedness constraints that are not visible in the other peripheral domains. Similarly, there are constraints that hold only in A and B, to the exclusion of C.

(1)   Core/periphery organization of the lexicon (Itô & Mester 1995)

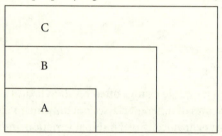

I adopt the core/periphery organization of the lexicon as a general property of any lexicon, and show that Optimality Theory provides an insightful approach for lexical stratification in Korean, following the three assumptions listed in (2).

(2)   Core/Periphery organization
  a.   Ranking Invariance: In the unmarked case there is a single constraint ranking for the whole lexicon.
  b.   Reranking: Lexical stratification is a consequence of constraint (re)ranking.
  c.   Constraint typology and the limits of reranking: The core-periphery organization is a consequence of the fact that, in the typical case, reranking is limited to Faithfulness constraints, within an otherwise invariant constraint system.

2.   The organization of the Korean lexicon

In this paper, I analyze the history of loan word assimilation, in particular liquid adaptation in Korean, and conclude that synchronic stratification is a consequence of lower ranked constraints gaining visibility due to language contact and diachronic change. I propose a lexical stratification which consists of Mimetic, (non-mimetic) Native, Sino-Korean, and Foreign Vocabulary for the Korean lexicon. The lexicon can be stratified in two ways: first, inventories as evidenced by distribution and second, processes exhibiting phonological alternation (Rice 1997).

I propose the following lexical stratification for the Korean lexicon. Although both mimetic and non-mimetic native vocabularies are of native origin as far as their histories can be determined, certain processes such as Vowel Harmony and Consonant Harmony, which had been quite productive throughout the native vocabulary until the 16th century, are restricted to the Mimetic Stratum in the synchronic grammar. Therefore, it is necessary to subdivide the Native Strata into Mimetic and Non-mimetic Native Strata.

(3)   Four strata of the Korean lexicon

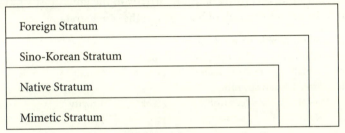

Foreign Stratum

Sino-Korean Stratum

Native Stratum

Mimetic Stratum

The Mimetic Stratum of Korean consists of several thousand sound-imitating and manner-symbolic words which manifest consonantal and vocalic alternations. The consonantal and vocalic qualities of the morphemes correlate with systematic semantic distinctions. Height Harmony (shown below) is one constraint that distinguishes the Mimetic Stratum from all the other outer strata. The crucial distinction in a mimetic pair is the opposition between the lowest vowel in any column in (4) and all higher vowel(s) (Cho & Inkelas 1993; Y. Lee 1993).

(4)   Vocalic alternations

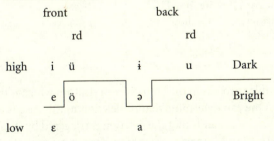

	front		back		
		rd		rd	
high	i	ü	ɨ	u	Dark
	e	ö	ə	o	Bright
low	ɛ		a		

As there are six nonlow vowels in the inventory, each with a low vowel counterpart, we find six possible mimetic alternation types in (5).

(5)   *Dark*   *Bright*   *Gloss*
/i/ – /ɛ/   pisil   pɛsil   "weak"
/e/ – /ɛ/   t'ekul   t'ɛkul   "rolling down"
/ü/ – /ö/   hühü   höhö   "round about"
/ɨ/ – /a/   sɨlc'ək   salc'ak   "secretly"
/ə/ – /a/   əlluk   allok   "motley"
/u/ – /o/   culcul   colcol   "drizzling"

Changes that have taken place over the past 500 years, in particular due to the massive influx of Chinese loan words which do not observe Vowel Harmony, have resulted in restricting this vowel harmony strictly to the innermost stratum of the lexicon. (6) exemplifies the lack of harmony in the other strata.

(6) a. Non-mimetic native stratum
        talamcü   "squirrel"   cinɛ-ə   "to spend"
        minali   "watercress"   kitali-ə   "to wait"
    b. Sino-Korean stratum
        cocəl   "control"   kɨkak   "atrocity"
        kuco   "structure"   yeö   "exception"

A constraint that applies to the native vocabulary (both the Mimetic and the Non-mimetic Strata) is /l/ deletion, as exemplified in (7). /l/ deletes before coronal consonants /n, s, c, t/ across a morpheme boundary.[1]

(7) /l/-deletion before a (plain) coronal consonant (Y-S. Kim 1985; Martin 1992)
     Mimetic
     nal-nal+i   nanali   "day by day"
     tal-tal-i   tatali   "month by month"

     Non-mimetic Native
     sol+namu   sonamu   "pine tree"
     pul +sap   pusap   "fire shovel"
     ssal +cən   ssacən   "rice shop"
     chal+tol   chatol   "pebble"
     t'al+nim   t'anim   "daughter (hon.)"
     mul+com   mucom   "athlete's foot"

Incidently, there is a similar process in the Sino-Korean stratum which is limited to one morpheme, /pul/. One can determine that /l/ deletion in this case is independent from that of (7), on the grounds that the deletion is triggered by /t, c/ but not by /s, n/, as illustrated by (8a). Moreover, other Sino-Korean morphemes that end with /l/ do not exhibit the /l/ ~ Ø alternation, as shown in (8b). According to Alexander Vovin (p.c.), the alternation between /pul/ and /pu/ is not due to any productive phonological process; rather, it reflects a fact about borrowing: the two different morphemes, /pu/ and /pul/ were borrowed as such from the western dialect of Chinese.

(8) a. Sino-Korean /pul/ vs. /pu/ "negative" 不:
      pu-cɔng   "corruption"   pul-kanɨng   "impossibility"
      pu-tong   "immobile"   pul-hwaksil   "uncertainty"
      pu-ci-pul-sik "unwittingly"   pul-nɨng   "inability"
   b. Lack of /l/ deletion in other Sino-Korean morphemes:
      kal-tɨng   "conflict"   kal-cɨng   "thirst"
      kal-mang   "wish"   kal-ku   "pursuit"

In addition, a historical process known as Palatalization is documented to have been sensitive to lexical stratification. The change of /t/ to [c] before the high front vowel and glide started in the late 17th century and the 18th century. In some dialects, velars and /h/ also changed to [c] and [s], respectively. Whereas Palatalization had been well established in the Native Stratum by the end of the 18th century, there was widespread variation in Sino-Korean words until the 19th century, probably due to hypercorrection or spelling pronunciation. Although Palatalization started as a constraint holding in the Native Stratum, Palatalization has gradually extended to the Sino-Korean Stratum. In contemporary Standard Korean, Palatalization of dentals is systematic in the Native and Sino-Korean Strata whereas Palatalization of velars is subject to dialectal variation.

(9) Palatalization in different strata (K.-M. Lee 1980; Choi 1992)
    Native Korean   ti-ta   ci-ta   "to lose"
                  munhɔti-ta   munhɔci-ta   "collapse"
                  tut-ti   tut-ci   "to hear"
    variation in velar/palatal
                  kimcaŋ   ~   cimcaŋ   "kimchee-making"
                  kitali-ta ~   citali-ta   "to wait"
                  hye   ~   sye   "tongue"
    Sino-Korean   tyosyɔn ~   cosɔn   "Chosun"
                  koktyo   ~   kokco   "melody"
                  tyotyɔk ~   tocɔk   "thief"
    variation in velar/palatal
                  kyɔkyaŋ ~   cɔkyaŋ   "excitement"
                  hyuŋak ~   suŋak   "ruthless"

Palatalization, however, is not active in the Foreign Stratum, as shown in (10).

(10) Lack of Palatalizaton in foreign vocabulary
    digital   tijithal
    Tina   thina
    TV   thibi

Originally, Palatalization did not apply to a coronal stop which preceded the diphthong /ɨi/, but the later process of Monophthongization simplified /ɨi/ into [i]. Exceptions to Palatalization are found in the sequences of [ti, thi] as in [canti] (from /cantɨi/) "grass", [thi] (from /thɨi/) "particle", etc. Monophthongization contributes to opacity in the grammar in which the only exceptions to Palatalization are those historically traceable to /tɨi/ or /thɨi/ in the Native Strata.[2]

Rather surprisingly, the Sino-Korean Stratum appears to have undergone a change specific to its stratum in which a coda /t/ was changed to [l], as illustrated in (11). This change did not affect the Native Stratum, as evidenced by such native word as /kot/ "soon" and /mat/ "eldest". According to the organization of the lexicon proposed in (3), whatever processes are applicable to the Sino-Korean Stratum should apply to the innermost stratum. The model excludes constraints holding in Sino-Korean Stratum but not in the Native Strata.

(11)   Lateralization of /t/ in coda in Sino-Korean
        Chinese   Sino-Korean
        wət   wəl   "month" 月
        chət   chəl   "metal" 鐵
        it   il   "one" 一
        sat   sal   "kill" 殺
        put~pul   "Buddha" 佛

Again the answer lies in a proper understanding of loan history. According to Vovin (p.c.), sonorization of the coda /l/ was not a Korean innovation but had started in the northwestern dialect of Chinese from which most of Sino-Korean words originated. In short, there is no lateralizaton of /t/ in the Korean grammar.

Based on the constraints introduced so far, we can motivate a four-level stratification of the Korean lexicon. When we include the syllable constraints (SyllStruc) that hold throughout the entire lexicon, we can show the systematic pattern of the hierarchical organization of the relevant constraints in (12). SyllStruc governs simplification of consonant clusters and vocalic alternations, thus producing the maximal CVVC syllable regardless of the stratal membership of a lexical item.

(12)   Korean lexicon in the 20th century

	SyllStruc	Palatalization	/l/-Deletion	Vowel Harmony
Mimetic	✓	✓	✓	✓
Native	✓	✓	✓	violated
Sino-Korean	✓	✓	violated	violated
Foreign	✓	violated	violated	violated

Prior to the 18th century changes, the lexicon appears to have been much flatter since Vowel Harmony, Palatalization, and /l/-Deletion targeted different strata, as shown in (13).

(13)   Korean lexicon before the 18th century

	SyllStruc	Vowel Harmony /l/ deletion
Native	✓	✓
Sino-Korean	✓	violated

Palatalization, an 18th-century innovation, swept the lexicon before the Foreign Stratum was introduced in the 20th century, while Vowel Harmony began to disintegrate in the Non-mimetic Native Stratum, resulting in a four-level system.

3. Liquid alternation

Among other things, liquid adaptation and subsequent changes best illustrate the ways in which contraint ranking accounts for lexical stratification, and I will devote this section to this topic.

The Sino-Korean Stratum consists of old and well-assimilated loans of a great time-depth. In some cases, etymology and synchronic classification do not match perfectly; there are historically Sino-Korean words which pattern as if they were native. One such example is /caknan/ → [caŋnan] "play, mischief". Prior to the massive influx of Chinese vocabulary into Korean beginning in the 5th century, Korean native vocabulary had morpheme structure constraints prohibiting words beginning with a liquid or a medial cluster of C+liquid (when the first C is not a nasal). The loan vocabulary, however, contained numerous words from Chinese violating these contraints.[3] The nativization process resulted in parsing an offending liquid as [n], rather than as [l] or [r] as in the target language (K.-M. Lee 1972; Martin 1992). On the other hand, loans in the 20th century exhibit a different pattern of nativization, as illustrated in (14c). The last example is of particular interest in that even Chinese loans follow the pattern of adaptation of Western loan words.

(14)   Liquid Adaptation
    a.   Chinese   Korean
            lok   nok   "green"
            latyən   nacən   "Latin"
            lai-il   nayil   "tomorrow"
            lampi   nampi   "pot"
            lyuk   yuk   "six"
            sip-lyuk simnyuk "sixteen"

    b.   English via other languages (before the 20th century)

        lamp   nampho

        Luke   nuka

    c.   All loans in the 20th century

        lamp   ramphi

        Hamlet   hamnit

        Luke   rukhi

        lusin   rusin (in addition to *nosin*) 魯 迅 (Chinese author Lu Xun)

In the initial stage of transcribing the word-initial /l/ from Chinese, there had been some confusion as to how to represent it in the Korean orthography. It is quite clear that Middle Korean has the same distribution of liquid allophones as Modern Standard Korean. According to *Hwunmincengum hapcahay*, "there are two liquid phones (one heavy and the other light) but there is only one liquid phoneme. .... The light liquid can be transcribed as ㄹ̣ and it is produced by a short contact of the tongue with the upper gum", suggesting that it was a tap as in Modern Korean (Huh 1985: 389).[4]

    The liquid in the Native Stratum does not occur in word-initial position, and therefore it was adapted as a nasal (perhaps the closest sonorant consonant) (Iverson & Sohn 1994), but the liquid was sometimes represented as the Korean letter /liɨl/ (which represents [l] syllable-finally and [ɾ] as a word-medial onset). Some examples are shown in (15). Except for this period, the orthography consistently represents the initial liquid as [n] and the post-consonantal liquid as [L], which in most dialects is pronounced [n].

(15)   Orthographic alternation of the initial /l/

      Loŋtam   "joke"   (Sekpo-sangcel 1447 6: 24)

      Lakwi   "donkey"   (Welin-sekpo 1459 21: 75)

      nakwi   "donkey"   (Welin-sekpo 1459 21: 45)

We can see in (16) that the nativization process resulted in parsing an offending liquid as [n] in certain contexts, rather than as [l] or [ɾ] as in the target language.

(16)   Nasalization of liquids[5]

    a.   [n] in initial and postconsonantal positions

        /lak-wən/   [nakwən]   "paradise"

        /lo-in/   [noin]   "old man"

    b.   [r] in intervocalic position

        /khwæ-lak/   [khwæ rak]   "pleasure"

        /co-lo/   [coro]   "premature aging"

Another language change that significantly added to opacity in the lexicon is /n/-deletion in word-initial position. This process is believed to have been preceded by /n/ palatalization before /i, y/. The palatalized /ɲ/ was weakened and started to delete in the 18th century. Not only the underlying /n/ but the [n] derived from the underlying [l] in the Sino-Korean Stratum deleted, as shown in (17). This process swept the entire lexicon to eliminate /ni, ny/ from all the strata. In Contemporary Korean, it remains a robust generalization that the three innermost strata do not allow [r] as an onset, unless it is intervocalic, and also that word-initial [ni, ny] and [ri, ry] are ill-formed. On the other hand, these constraints are inert in the most peripheral part of the lexicon, namely in foreign loans.

(17) /n/ deletion before /i, y/ in word-initial position

niyok	iyok	"mud bath"
nyəca	yəca	"woman"
li	i	"plum"
lyu	yu	"willow"
(cf. lodong	nodong	"labor")
/li-yu/ niyu	[iyu]	"reason"
/nik-myəŋ/	[ik-myəŋ]	"anonymity"
/ɨn-nik/	[ɨnnik]	"hiding"

(18) shows examples from the Native Stratum.

(18) /n/ deletion in native vocabulary (until the early 20th century)

nim	im	"beloved"
niɨn	iɨn	"the letter n" (Ramstedt 1939)
liɨl	iɨl	"the letter l"
Alphabet Template: [CiɨC]		
miɨm		"the letter m"
piɨp		"the letter p"

The names for each consonant in the Korean alphabet, Hangul, are based on the template of the form, /CiɨC/ with the C representing the consonant, as in [niɨn] and [liɨl] (the letters [n] and [l]). Even though it is functionally of great importance to have /n/ and /l/ initially as the names of these consonants, the constraint prohibiting /n/ and /l/ before /i/ was active well into the 20th century. In Contemporary Korean, some prohibited sequences came alive as exceptions to Native Korean (niɨn "the letter n", nim "beloved") and Sino-Korean (rju "family name", ri "family name"), probably due to extra-grammatical reasons. (19) shows a handful of recent innovations where /ni/ and /ri/ unexpectedly surface in strata other than the Foreign Stratum.

(19) Resurrection of underlying /n, l/ before /y, i/
Sino-Korean

ryu	柳	"family name ryu"
ri	李	"family name ri"
Native		
nim		"beloved"
niɨn		"the letter n"
riɨl		"the letter l"

There has been some debate in the literature as to whether word-initial nasalization of /l/ in [nakwon] is a process distinct from postconsonantal nasalization of [kamno] (20) (Kim-Renaud 1974).

(20)   Initial nasalization vs. Postconsonantal nasalization
    a.   *Sino-Korean*
        lak-won   nakwon   "paradise" (initial)
        kam-lo   kamno   "sweet dew" (postconsonantal)
        kwa-lo   kwaro   "excessive labor" (intervocalic)
    b.   *Foreign vocabulary*
        raion   "lion" (initial /l/)
        radio   "radio" (initial /r/)
        hamnit   "Hamlet" (postconsonantally)
        paradaisɨ   "paradise" (intervocalic)

Whereas there is no evidence either way for the Native and Sino-Korean vocabularies, the contrast between the first two examples in (20b) clearly argues for the distinct nature of each of the constraints. In [raion], the underlying /l/ is not nasalized whereas in [hamnit] the postconsonantal lateral surfaces as [n], rather unexpectedly. I believe it is correct to assume that Korean, throughout its entire lexicon, prohibits a liquid (both [l] and [r]) after a consonant. In contrast, word-initial /l/ is realized as [n] in the inner strata whereas it surfaces as [r] in recent loan words. The diverging behavior of recent loans makes it even more implausible to treat /l/-nasalization as an onset strategy as has been argued by McDonough (1995); liquids nasalize only in a consonant cluster.

I propose the constraints in (21) for Korean liquid alternation to account for lexical stratification. **Lat-Licensing** requires that laterality be licensed only in the coda position. It licenses any coda lateral, whether it be a singleton coda or a part of a geminate. The dual association of a geminate lateral has nothing to do with licensing. *CL and *rr are employed to capture the surface-true generalizations in Korean. Geminate *rr*'s are not part of Korean phonology (it may be true universally due to the phonetic impossibility of geminating a tap), and there is no sequence of a consonant followed by a liquid (other than the geminate [ll]).

(21)   Constraints
    Lat-Licensing: laterality is licensed only in the coda position.
    ***C L:** nonnasal sonorant consonants (l, r) are not allowed postconsonantally.
    ***ω[ni:** initial [ni] is prohibited in a prosodic word.
    ***ω[r:** initial [r] is prohibited in a prosodic word.
    ***rr:** geminate [rr] is prohibited.
    Ident-IO: the output correspondent(s) of an input [α F] segment are also [α F]
    (McCarthy & Prince 1995)

The two generalizations, *CL (no postconsonantal liquid) and *ω[r (no word-initial liquid) emerge due to the relative ranking (*CL, ω[r » Faithfulness). In contrast, recent loans, which are of a lesser time-depth, allow massive exceptions to the generalization holding in the core of the lexicon (e.g., /laion/ → [raion], /Hamlit/ → [hamnit]), arguing for the distinctive ranking (*CL » Faithfulness » *ω[r).

(22)   Constraint Ranking in Standard Korean
        Native/Sino-Korean:
            *CL, *rr, Lat-L » *ω[r, *w[ni » Ident-IO
        Foreign:
            *CL, *rr, Lat-L » Ident-IO » *ω[r, *ω[ni

The discussion in Section 2 motivates the following rankings. Mimetic vocabulary and non-mimetic vocabulary can be distinguished by Vowel Harmony that is present only in the Mimetic Stratum synchronically.

(23)   Mimetic Vocabulary: Vowel Harmony » Ident(f)
        Non-mimetic Native, Sino-Korean, Foreign Vocabulary: Ident(f) » Vowel Harmony

Likewise, Native vocabulary and the rest of the lexicon (Sino-Korean, Foreign) have a different constraint ranking with regard to /l/-deletion before a coronal.

(24)   Native Vocabulary: *(/l/+cor) » Max(seg)
        Sino-Korean, Foreign Vocabulary: Max(seg) » *(/l/+cor)

Going back to the discussion of liquid alternation, the tableau in (25) illustrates the surface realization of a liquid in the Native and Sino-Korean Strata. A word-initial liquid surfaces as [n] rather than as [r] due to the active constraint barring the onset [r] initially. Surface [l] is not allowed due to Lat-L. Post-consonantal /l/ is realized as [n], again due to *CL.

(25)   Native/Sino-Korean

/Lak/	*CL	*rr	Lat-L	*ω[r	Ident-Liquid
lak			*!		
rak				*!	
→ nak					*
/kam-Lo/					
kamlo	*!		*		
kamro	*!				
→ kamno					*

In (26), however, with the relative ordering between the faithfulness constraint and *ω[r reversed, there is no reason to map the underlying liquid to a nasal, violating Faith. As a result, [r]-initial words are allowed while [l]-initial words are still prohibited. On the other hand, /l/ still surfaces as [n] in the post-consonantal position due to the higher ranked *CL, as in /Hamlet/ → [hamnit].

(26)   Foreign

"lion"	*CL	*rr	Lat-L	Ident-L	*ω[r
laion			*!		
→ raion					*
naion				*!	
"Hamlet"					
hamlit	*!		*		
hamrit	*!				
→ hamnit					*

We now have a more detailed picture of lexical stratification.

(27)   Standard Korean

	SyllStruc *CL, *rr, Lat-L	Palatalization *ω[r, *ω[ni	/l/-Deletion	Vowel Harmony
Mimetic	✓	✓	✓	✓
Native	✓	✓	✓	violated
Sino-Korean	✓	✓	violated	violated
Foreign	✓	violated	violated	violated

In contrast to the alternations in the Standard dialect, some Northern dialects exhibit a different pattern in the Native/Sino-Korean Strata, as illustrated in (28). This is particularly true in the Yukchin dialect. There is no nasalization of /l/; as in recent loans, syllable-initial laterals surface as a tap. In addition, there is no /n/-deletion either, as shown by [nyəja]. In Phyeangan dialects, it is reported that the preservation of the initial /n/ is accompanied by the deletion of [y] (/nyəca/ → [nəja] "woman").[6]

(28) /l/ and /n/ before /i, y/ (Y.-P. Kim 1997:189ff.)

	Standard Korean	Phyengan (Northwest)	North Korean (Northeast)	
/lyuksip/	yuksip	nuksip	ryuksip	"sixty"
/lyənsɨp/	yənsɨp	nənsɨp	ryənsɨp	"practice"
/nyə-ca/	yəja	nəja	nyəja	"woman"

The ranking in (29) is proposed for North Korean dialects. When we consider liquid alternations and Palatalization in Northern Korean, the distinction between the Foreign Stratum and the rest of the strata seems to be dependent on Palatalization alone.

(29) North Korean Ranking:
    *CL, *rr, Lat-L » Ident-IO » *ω[r, *ω [ni

North Korean Dialects

	SyllStruc *CL, *rr, Lat-L	Palatalization	/l/-Deletion *ω[ni, *ω[r	Vowel Harmony
Mimetic	✓	✓	✓	✓
Native	✓	✓	✓	violated
Sino-Korean	✓	✓	violated	violated
Foreign	✓	violated	violated	violated

An even more intriguing pattern of liquid realization is found in the Yonbyon dialect spoken in Manchuria, as shown by the data in (30).

(30) Yonbyon dialect of Korean (Kang & Han 1999)
    Nasalization /l/ → [r]
    /kyək+lyə/ [kyəŋnyə] [kyəŋryə] "encouragement"
    /kuk+lyək/ [kuŋnyək] [kuŋryək] "national power"

Given these data, it might be necessary to reassess the constraint governing the postconsonantal liquid realization, i.e., *CL which prohibits nonnasal sonorant consonants [l, r] postconsonantally. If nasalization of the post-obstruent liquid is not obligatory, we may have to demote *CL to account for the variable behavior, as in (31).[7]

(31) Yonbyon Ranking
    *rr, Lat-L, *CL, Ident-IO » *ω[r, *ω[ni
    a. *CL » Ident-IO (Nasalization of sonorant)
    b. Ident-IO » *CL (/l/ → [r])

When the two constraints, *CL and Ident-IO, are not ranked with respect to each other, we have outputs that correspond to the two rankings shown in (31a) and (b).

When *CL is higher ranked, the underlying /l/ cannot surface as a liquid; instead nasalization occurs. When the faithfulness constraint (**Ident-IO**) is ranked higher, /l/ is realized as [r] although **Lat-Licensing** prohibits it from surfacing as [l].

4. Conclusion

We have seen that there are reasons to distinguish four strata in Standard Korean as evidenced by the interaction between liquid alternation, /n/-deletion, Palatalization, /l/-deletion, and Vowel Harmony. Such stratification is also motivated for some North Korean dialects where none of the changes concerning liquids and nasals that have affected Standard Korean occurred. In these dialects the adaptation of the initial liquid was not toward the nasal onset but to [r] in parallel to the medial onset. As a result, introduction of foreign loans in the early 20th century did not result in the reranking of the constraints, as the existing ranking was perfectly able to accommodate such words as "Nice", and "radio".

Notes

1. There is another unrelated /l/-deletion that is limited to verbal morphology. The stem-final /l/ deletes before a suffix that begins with /n/, /p/, /s/, as in /al-so/ → [a-so] "to know", /kal-n/ → [kan] "to till", /mul-pnita/ → [mupnita] "to bite". Crucially there is no deletion before a suffix that begins with /t/ or /c/ (e.g., /al-ci/, /kal-ta/).

2. In this sense, Korean Palatalization exhibits the blocking in the derived environment effect. See Kiparksy (1993), Cho (1999), Anttila and Cho (1999) for further discussion.

3. Ramstedt (1939: 12) notes that the lack of initial liquids in Korean parallels the absence of initial liquids in the Tungus and Mongol languages.

4. Ki-Mun Lee (1972) suggests that in pre-Middle Korean there might have been two liquid phonemes (/l/, /r/), which he believes to have merged by the 15th century.

5. It should be noted that the underlying /l/ in some Sino-Korean morphemes is reanalyzed as /n/ and the underlying /n/ is sometimes reanalyzed as /l/ (e.g., /kwan-nyəm/ ~ /kwan-lyəm/ "idea", /lasa/ ~ /nasa/ "screw". [Martin 1992])

6. One informant who speaks the Hwanghae dialect of Nothern Korean allows the postconsonantal /r/ as in /tok-lip/ → [toŋrip] "independence", /coŋ-lo/ → [coŋro] "the Bell street" in contrast to usual pronunciations, [toŋnip] and [coŋno].

7. Kang and Han (1999) propose an account relying on Syllable Contact where the interaction between two constraints, **SyllCon** and **Ident-L** produces the variation observed in (30). SyllCon can be summarized as: when two syllables are in contact, the coda of the first syllable should be more sonorous than or equally sonorous to the onset of the second syllable (Murray & Vennemann 1983).

References

Anttila, Arto & Young-mee Y. Cho. 1998. "Variation and Change in Optimality Theory". *Lingua* 104.31–56.

Anttila, Arto & Young-mee Y. Cho. 1999. "Nonderived-Environment Blocking as a Faithfulness Effect". Paper presented at the Northeast Linguistics Society Meeting, Rutgers University.

Cho, Young-mee Y. 1997. "Liquid Specification in Korean as Geminate Alterability". *Harvard Studies in Korean Linguistics*. 7.78–92.

Cho, Young-mee Y. 1999. "A Historical Perspective on Nonderived Environment Blocking". Ms., Rutgers University.

Cho, Young-mee Y. & Sharon Inkelas. 1993. "A Brief History of Korean Vowels". Paper presented at the Sound Change Workshop, Stanford University.

Choi, Chun-Seung. 1992. *Phonological Processes of the Cholla Dialect in the Late 19th Century and their Diachrony.* [in Korean] Seoul: Hanshin.

Chomsky, Noam & Morris Halle. 1968. *The Sound Pattern of English.* New York: Harper & Row.

Huh, Woong. 1985. *Kwuke Umwunhak* [Korean Phonology]. Seoul: Saymmwunhwasa.

Inkelas Sharon & Young-mee Y. Cho. 1993. "Inalterability as Prespecification". *Language* 69: 3.529–574.

Itô, Junko & Armin Mester. 1995. "The Core/Periphery Structure of the Lexicon and Constraints on Reranking". *Papers in Optimality Theory.* University of Massachusetts Occasional Papers 18.181–209.

Itô, Junko & Armin Mester. Forthcoming. "The Phonological Lexicon". *A Handbook of Japanese Linguistics* ed. by N. Tsujimura. Oxford. Blackwell.

Iverson, Gregory & Hyangsook Sohn. 1994. "Liquid Representation". *Theoretical Issues in Korean Linguistics* ed. by Y. Kim-Renaud, 77–100. Stanford: CSLI.

Kang, Hyunsook & Seo-hwa Han. 1999. "Nasalization Before a Liquid in Yonbyon Dialect of Korean". Japanese/Korean Linguistics Conference, Ohio State University.

Kim, Y.-P. 1997. *Phyengan pangen yenkwu* [A Study of the Phyengan Dialect]. Seoul: Thayhaksa.

Kim, Young-Seok. 1984. *Aspects of Korean Morphology.* Ph.D. Dissertation, University of Texas.

Kim-Renaud, Y.-L. 1974. *Korean Consonantal Phonology.* Ph.D. Dissertation, University of Hawaii.

Kiparsky, Paul. 1968. "How Abstract Is Phonology?" Reprinted in P. Kiparsky. 1982. *Explanation in Phonology.* Dordrecht: Foris.

Kiparsky, Paul. 1993. "Blocking in Nonderived Environments". *Studies in Lexical Phonology* ed. by Sharon Hargus & Ellen Kaisse, 277–313. San Diego: Academic Press.

Lee, Ki-Mun. 1972. *Kuke Umunsa Yenkwu* [A Study of Korean Historical Phonology]. Seoul: Tower Press.

Lee, Ki-Mun. 1980. "19 sekimaluy kwukeey tayhaye" [On Korean of the Late 19th Century]. *Festschrift Dedicated to Nam Kwangwu*, 255–266. Iljokak. Seoul.

Lee, Yongsung. 1993. *Topics in the Vowel Phonology of Korean.* Ph.D. Dissertation, Indiana University.

Lightner, Theodore. 1972. "Some Remarks on Exceptions and on Coexistent Systems in Phonology". *The Slavic Word* ed. by D.S. Worth, 426–442. The Hague: Mouton.

Martin, Samuel. 1954. *Korean Morphophonemics.* Baltimore: Linguistic Society of America.

Martin, Samuel. 1992. *A Reference Grammar of Korean.* Tyoko: Tuttle.

McCarthy, John & Alan Prince. 1993. " Prosodic Morphology". Ms. RuCCS-TR-3.

McCarthy, John & Alan Prince. 1995. "Faithfulness and Reduplicative Identity". *Papers in Optimality Theory.* University of Massachusetts Occasional Papers 18.249–384.

McDonough, Joyce. 1995. "Gemination and the Prosodic Enhancement Strategy". *The Proceedings of the Northeast Linguistics Society Meeting.* 25.347–359.

Murray, Robert & Theo Vennemann 1983. "Sound Change and Syllable Structure in Germanic Phonology". *Language.* 59: 3.514–528.

Prince, Alan & Paul Smolensky. 1993. "Optimality Theory". Ms. RuCCS-TR-2.

Ramstedt, G. J. 1939. *A Korean Grammar.* Helsinki: Suomalais-ugrilaisen Seuran Toimituksia.

Rice, Keren. 1997. "Japanese NC Clusters and the Redundancy of Postnasal Voicing". *Linguistic Inquiry* 28.541–551.

Yip, Moira. 1993. "Chinese Loanword Phonology and Optimality Theory". *Journal of East Asian Linguistics* 2.261–291.

Animals and vegetables, Uto-Aztecan noun derivation, semantic classification, and cultural history*

Karen Dakin
Universidad Nacional Autonoma de Mexico

> "Even if we had a good theory of tendencies and a sense of what is more likely than what to be diffusible (as, despite my strictures above, we sort of do, in a way), the real arena for our contest with history is the individual case. How do we go about sorting the native from the borrowed (and developing, if necessary, a stratification of borrowing) in particular histories?"
>
> Roger Lass, *Historical Linguistics and Language Change* (1997:190)

1. Introduction

In the literature about Mesoamerican linguistic prehistory, a number of linguists, especially Terrence Kaufman, Lyle Campbell, John Justeson, and Will Norman (cf. Kaufman 1971, 1989; Campbell & Kaufman 1976; Justeson et al. 1985) have identified the early diffusion of borrowed terms in unrelated languages in the area that refers to important regional plant and animal names as well as other entities. Terms include, for example, those for the silk-cotton and cork trees, cacao, turkeys, and owls. They have then made initial suggestions as to the directions of the borrowings, suggestions that have wide-reaching implications about the socio-historical relations in the area, including, for example, the probable identification of the Olmecs as speakers of proto-Mixe-Zoquean.

In this paper, the identification of the existence of these early loanwords is not being questioned. However, it is important to note that since the publication of the studies a number of specific queries have been raised that concern the *direction* of the loans. Given the conclusions that the speakers of the lending languages must have either spent more time in the region or held a more important political role than those who spoke the borrowing languages, it would seem necessary to show that the identification of the origin of the terms in question is solid, and that they can be shown to fit well not only into the historical phonological evolution of the lending language, but also into old morphological structure, in particular, old *derivational* processes.

This paper is limited to the domain of plant and animal names because the principal proposal is that in order to argue for the direction of a loan, it is a good idea to look at the structure of each lexical/morphological domain of the languages involved in detail before making a decision, and so there is space to present just one such case. In addition, of course, the specific geographical distribution of flora and fauna can be crucial in determining points of cultural history.

In the Mesoamerican area, along the Gulf corridor where the principal Olmec settlements have been identified, we find representatives of at least seven language families besides Mixe-Zoquean; these include Totonacan, Mayan, and Uto-Aztecan. The archeological paradigm for Mesoamerica that has been widely accepted, at least until recently, is that the Uto-Aztecans who migrated into Mexico and Meso-america were the last peoples to arrive. However, current archeological and linguistic research is changing many of the basic concepts involving the chronology and homeland of Uto-Aztecans as well as of those of some of the other groups mentioned (cf. J. Hill 1999; Dakin & Wichmann 2000). It may be that at least the Eastern branch of the Nahuas, the southernmost Uto-Aztecan group, reached Mesoamerica at a much earlier date than has been believed until now. I should note that the Aztecs were a late group, and I identify it with the separate Western branch of Nahuas. Although it seems clear from Olmec inscriptions which Justeson and Kaufman (1993) identified as proto-Zoquean and which they have deciphered that Mixe-Zoqueans were of great importance during the Olmec period, it will be argued here that the first kind of linguistic evidence used in support of their hypothesis, that of the direction of loanwords, in many cases points to a Nahua presence, since the terms fit much more securely into Uto-Aztecan evolutionary derivational patterns than into Mixe-Zoquean or Totonacan, as they had proposed. Although those earlier identifications do cite phonological hypotheses in some cases, it would seem also that preconceptions about the chronology of migrations based on evidence from other fields and from glottochronology have influenced their analysis more than other systematic linguistic evidence. Justeson et al. (1985) do clarify that for their point of view Nahuatl did contribute many loanwords to Mesoamerica, but they make the qualification that these are *late* loanwords, no earlier than the Terminal Classic. However, in the following discussion it will be argued that many of the early loans they cite are from Nahuatl and thus evidence for earlier contact.

2.   Nomenclature for flora and fauna in Uto-Aztecan languages

It is possible to identify a number of derivational strategies inherited from proto-Uto-Aztecan that are used for but not necessarily limited to creating Nahuatl plant and animal nomenclature. These are listed under (1).

(1) Uto-Aztecan strategies identified in the formation of animal and plant names
   a. Monomorphemic root
   b. *-ka('a) "Agentives/Possesives"
   c. *-ra'a-(wɨ) "Possession of feature"
   d. Suffixes
      *-wɨ   "Augmentative?"
      *-ri   "Diminutive?"
      *-ci   "Diminutive?"
      *-sɨ   "Diminutive?"
   e. Descriptive compounding with nominal roots

The complete list of loanwords whose identification is in question includes terms which can actually be reconstructed in a number of these formations in Uto-Aztecan. In most cases, it seems that names are created by describing features drawn from observation of the specific entity in nature. It appears that at least in the pre-Hispanic period, as a general tendency, Nahuatl speakers preferred creating new terms to borrowing existing ones from speakers of other languages. For example, one compound form that is quite transparent even synchronically is "armadillo" *ayo:to:čin* or "turtle/rabbit", because the armadillo has ears much like a rabbit at the same time that it wears a shell. Although it is not possible to discuss all the creative derivational processes involved in their system, I will present comparative evidence for the strategy mentioned under (1c), a root + *ra'a-wɨ, used in the formation of a great number of words, including four or five found as loanwords in other Mesoamerican languages and previously identified as non-Uto-Aztecan. In most cases, it appears that the *ra'a-wɨ is coupled with a preceding morpheme that identifies a descriptive feature based on observation of the specific entity in nature. It should be noted that in many cases, one finds that the Uto-Aztecan etymologies proposed for the Nahuatl words are corroborated by mythology, cultural traditions, and certain basic semantic concepts that are also associated with the cognates in more northern Uto-Aztecan languages from almost all branches of the family.

Under (2) are found the controversial words that fit into the *ra'awɨ class in proto-Uto-Aztecan (pUA). Included are the Nahuatl (Nah) terms and the same forms as found in some non-related Mesoamerican languages.

(2) Nahuatl words in *-lo:-* (and morphophonemic variants) previously considered borrowings
   a. *počo:-tl* "silk-cotton (kapok) tree, *ceiba*"
      Nah *počo:-tl*
      Totonacan *pú:ču:t* "ceiba tree"

b. *koĉo:-tl* "kind of parrot, papagayo"
    Nah *koĉo:-tl /keĉo(:)l-li*
    Huastecan Nah (Kaufman) *koĉo*
    Huastec *kucu'* (⟨kutxu7⟩ Kaufman 1989: 27)
c. *šolo:-tl* "kind of fish"
    Nah *šo:lo:-tl* "fish species"
    Totonacan *šu:ɫ* "catfish"
    Mayan *šuluk*
    cf. *šolo:tl* "jonote, *Heliocarpus*"
    Nah *šolo:cin, šono:-tl*
    Totonacan *šú:nak*
    Mayan *šunuk*
    Zoque *šunuk* "*jonote* or cork tree"
d. *to:to:-tl* "bird" / *to:tolin* "turkey"
    (Wichmann 1995): proto-Zoque *tu'nuk; proto-Mixe *tu:tuk
    (Campbell & Kaufman 1976: 83): Tzeltal, Tzotzil, Chuj, Jacaltec, and
    Motozintlec *tunik'/tuluk'*

3. Reconstruction

The *-lo:* suffix in the Nahuatl forms (*-tl* is the absolutive), as well as what will be shown to be phonologically conditioned variants *-yo:*, *-ĉo:*, *-so:*, *-no:-*, and *-co:-*, correspond to Cora and Huichol forms in *-ra'a-we*, Guarijío and Tarahumara *-ra*, Tepiman *-da-g*, Hopi *-na-wɨ*, Takic *-na-wV*, and *-na'a-we* in Numic languages such as Southern Paiute and Kawaiisu. These correspondence sets are the basis for reconstructing a pUA *-ra('a) followed by a *wɨ. The *ra('a) morpheme is also associated with inalienable possession in a number of the southern languages; the function of the *-wɨ is not entirely clear, although in many cases it seems to be some sort of augmentative and related to the Uto-Aztecan root for "big". The resulting complex suffix *-ra'a-wɨ is used to form abstract nouns as well as animal names in the southern languages. Except after *a-, the *a'a-we sequence regularly gives *o:* in Nahuatl, while the *-r most commonly corresponds to Nahuatl *-l-*, but goes to *-y-* (or is elided) following a high vowel and before *a*, or goes to *-ĉ, -c-, -s-*, or *-n* by assimilation when preceded by the corresponding coronal consonant. The resulting geminate consonant clusters usually simplify. After a root ending in *-a*, the *a-ra'a-wɨ sequence usually becomes *a:w-*.

pUA *-ra'a-(we) class > Nahuatl *-lo:(-tl), -yo:-, -ĉo:-, -co:-, -so:-, -no:-*

Under (3) are given examples of Nahuatl forms in which *-lo:-* marks inalienable possession and abstract nouns.

(3)   CV + ra'a -
Inalienable possessive (-*lo'* ~ -*yo'*)
a.   Nah *i:-naka-yo* "his flesh (of body)"
b.   Tepiman *-dag
c.   Tarahumara/Guarijío *-rawa
d.   Huichol (Grimes et al. 1981) -*yari* "Specificative"
e.   Cora -*ra'a-n* "3rd person non-reflexive possessive"
f.   Cora -*ra'a* "Specificative"
Abstracts/collective
g.   Nah *kʷal-lo:-tl* "goodness"

The same derivation is found used to form animal and plant names in Uto-Aztecan and the same morphophonemic rules are observable. Because at first sight, some of the correspondences are not clear, under (4) are given the variants found in Nahuatl that reflect these sound changes.

(4)   Morphophonemic variants in Nahuatl *-ra'a-wɨ >
-a:w / a-   *kwa-ra'a-wɨ > *kwa:w-tli* "eagle"
-yo:-/N-[+high]   *ku-ra'a-wɨ > *ko-yo:-tl* "coyote"
-čo:-/ č-   *i:-keč-čo* "his-neck-inalienable"
-co:-/ c-   *tepoc-coh* "back-much" = "hunchback"
-so:-/ s-   *epaso:-tl* "skunkweed"
-lo:-   *wi:lo:-tl* "dove"

The etymologies given for the forms under (5) are based on the hypothesis noted, that the animals must be named for some notable characteristic that they possess inalienably. The derivational class for animal and plant names in Nahuatl appears to be larger than in the other languages, although it may be that the difference is due more to the larger dictionaries and ethnographic sources available for Nahuatl in comparison with those for the other languages.

(5)   Nahuatl animal names in -lo:- with cognates in other languages and etymologies (*r > *n* in Numic, Hopi, Takic; *r > *ḍ*, Ø in Tepiman; *r > *r*, Ø in Cahita; *r > *r*, *y*, Ø in Cora; *r > *l*, *y* in Nahuatl)
a.   *hu-ra'a- "badger" (Miller 1967:18; Iannucci 1973:43; Bright & Hill 1967 *hunwit)
Chemehuevi *hu-n(á)* "badger"
Hopi *hoo-na-w* "bear"
Hopi *ho-na-ni* "badger"
Mayo *hú:-ri* "badger"
Huichol *'ɨ-rá'ave* "wolf"
Cora *háa:-ra'ave* "wolf" Cora ⟨Euràvet⟩; Preuss (1932) ⟨ïrabe, ïràve, ïreabe⟩
b.   *ko "curved" + *sa "hoja seca" = "yellow/brown" + *ma:- "net" (cf. Nah *ma:-tla-tl*) + *ra'a "rainbow" (Miller 1988 ki-07, Bascom 1965:99a, *ki'honari; 99b, *ki'oharai)
Hopi *sa-na-ysokɪti* "for a finger to become infected from pointing at a rainbow"

Mayo *ku-rué-s* "rainbow; kind of snake" (although possibly a borrowing from Spanish *arcoiris*)
Cora (Ortega 1732) *ku'uša-t* ⟨*cùuxat*⟩ "rainbow"
Nah *kosa-ma:-lo:tl* "rainbow" (Mecayapan Nah *a:kosama:lo:'*)

c. *po'o "marked, spotted", *sa (?) "yellow/brown" + *ra'a-wɨ > "ocelote, jaguar" Gila River Pima (Rea 1998:226) *ooša-ḍ* "ocelot" [jaguar] Nah *o:se:-lo:-tl* "ocelot"

d. *wi / mi "seeds, grain" (?) *-ra'a-wɨ
Nah *wi:-lo:-tl* "dove"
Lower Pima *gíig-de-ly* "swallow"

e. *mu- "nose" + *ra'a-wɨ "fly, mosquito"
Huichol *mɨ-rá-ka* "wasp"
Nah *moyo:-tl* "fly, mosquito"

f. *tɨku- "darkness, night" *-ra'awɨ "owl"
Tarahumara (B) *ritúka-ri*
Cora *tuku-rúù* ⟨*tukurú*⟩ (Preuss 1932)
Nah *teko-lo:-tl* "owl"
Miller (1988), no. tu-15:
Northern Paiute *tuhu'u* "burrowing owl"
Tubatulabal *tukluluh* "screech owl"
Hopi *toko-ri* "owl"

g. *kʷa-"tree (?)" *- ra'awɨ "eagle"
Cora *kʷa'a:ra'ave* "eagle"; Ortega (1732) ⟨*quáiravet*⟩ "white-headed eagle"
Tarahumara *korači* "crow"
Tümpisa Shoshone *kʷinaa* "eagle"
Hopi *kwaahu* "eagle" (*-hu* is an epenthetic syllable)

The problem of semantic relatedness of course comes up in some cases. In fact, at times, it is difficult to determine a specific original meaning. In (6) for example, are given cognate forms for *pu-cu-ra'a-wɨ used for animals that in some sense are similar, but have marked differences as well.

(6) Semantic extension
*pucu-ra'awɨ "fat round animal (?)"
Gila River Pima (Rea 1998:177–178) *vošo* "Arizona Cotton Rat, a large edible rodent described as having flesh that tastes like pork"
Nah *pi-c-(c)o:-tl* "pig, peccary"
Cf. Nah *wi-c(c)o:-koyame-tl* "porcupine" (cf. mythical animal who drowned people: *a:-wico:-tl*)

These show the assimilation of *r > *c/c__, and subsequent geminate cluster reduction also found in:

*tɨpocu-ra'a-wɨ
Huastec Nah *tepoco:-tl* "bug species"
Totoguañ Papago *čeepš* "tick"
cf. *tepo-c-tli* "back", *tepoc*[*c*]*oh* "hunchback" = "one who has lots of back"

In some cases, the possessed characteristic may have elements of onomatopaeia, as seems to be the case for the sets under (7). Given the forms in Pima and Nahuatl, it would seem that the pUA word for squirrel probably was based on the "chV" sound the animal makes.

(7)   Onomatopaeic
      Nah *kakalo:tl* "crow"
      Nah *čačalo:tl*
      Gila River Pima *šelik, šelig,* [PL] *šešelik, šešelig* "Round-tailed Ground Squirrel"
      Nah Zacapoaxtlan *čečelo:t* "squirrel"
      CoraMS *čá'a:-ni'i-se* "kind of squirrel"
      Lower Pima *téekely* "cave squirrel"
      Nah *tečalo:tl* "squirrel"
      Gila River Pima *čeekul, čeekol, čirrkul* "rock squirrel"
      Hopi *konàwya (kokonhòoyam)* "little tree squirrel"

Now, to return to the problem of loanwords, but with the proto-Uto-Aztecan lexical classes in mind, in the next section I propose pUA etymologies for the four loanwords mentioned under (2).

4.   Etymologies of Mesoamerican loanwords

(2a) *počo:-tl*
As mentioned earlier, the silk-cotton tree or ceiba is *počo:-tl*. It is a tree of great religious and ceremonial importance in Mesoamerica. Justeson et al. (1985: 27) above attribute this word to Totonac, with no etymology cited, but I would suggest that it is a descriptive term based on the fluffy fruit it produces. The Nahuatl verb *poče:wa* meaning "to card fiber" is a compound form. Since the silk-cotton tree is not found in the area occupied by more northern languages, the term does not exist there. However, one does find cognates for *po- with the sense "fluffy". Voegelin, Voegelin, and Hale (1962: 137, #7) reconstruct *po "body hair, fur"; Lionnet (1985) reconstructs *powa "hair, wool" (cotton?) for Sonoran languages. The *č* in the Nahuatl form probably comes from pUA *ci- that means "twig": *po(wa)-ci + *ra'a-wɨ > *po:č-čo:-tl > *po:čo:-tl*. The Tarahumara forms *kapočí* "*talayote*, wild fruit that is green and cottony on the inside" and *kapočini* "to burst open (pods of the tree)" provide an explanation for the presence of the initial *p* in the Nahuatl form, since it would appear that an initial syllable that protected it during the sound

change by which pUA *p > h > Ø, Vh in Nahuatl was subsequently lost, just as it was in the case of the Nahuatl verb /posteki/ "to break a branch, or something similar", probably from an earlier *tepos-teki "to cut with an axe".

(2b) *koČo:-tl*
Kaufman has suggested that Huastec Nahuatl *koČo* "parrot" is borrowed from Huastec *kuČuʔ*. However, given that there are two variants found in the sixteenth century dictionary of Molina (1571), *koČo-tl* and *keČo(:)lli*, for a kind of parrot, and that the term *kecal-li* apparently originally referred to the long tail feathers of the quetzal, not the bird, it seems probable that *koČo-tl* is derived from *kɨca- + raʔa-we, that is "the one characterized by the [beautiful long green] feathers".

(2c) *Šolo:-tl*
However, perhaps the most interesting loanwords in terms of semantic change and extensions are those which Justeson et al. (1985:41) had suggested as having Totonac origin; they propose that Totonacan *Šú:nak* "jonote" gave Nahua *Šo:no:-tl* "cork tree", an important tree culturally because it is used for paper making, and that Totonacan *Šu:ł* "catfish" was the source of Nahua *Šo:lo:-tl* "fish species". However, both words may be better analyzed as deriving from Nahuatl *Šolo:-tl* which is a word that turns up with multiple extensions of meanings because of mythological connections with duality or halves, canines, and gods. The Nahuatl term has the cognates given under (8) and is derived from pUA *sɨ-raʔa-wɨ "one characterized by being a double". The root *sɨⁿ "double" or "copy" can be isolated in the Ute verb *sɨ-tií* "look like".

Coyote and Big Brother Wolf are well-known characters in North American indigenous mythology, and Coyote is known as "Copycat", for example, among the Utes (T. Givón, p.c. 1994). In Cora mythology, the cognate form *Šuraʔave* (Preuss 1932; Ortega 1732 ⟨xûravet⟩) was the name of Venus, the doubly appearing star, although now its meaning has generalized to "star". Valentín Peralta (p.c. 1998) has noted that another term with the same *Šo-* root, *Šotla*, "to lighten", specifically refers to the way in which a vertical bolt of lightning splits the sky. In Nahuatl mythology, Xolotl is the god who fled from the council where they were creating the sun and the moon because he did not want to die by jumping into the sacred fire. As Xolotl fled, he was transformed successively into twins — twin corn ears, twin maguey plants, and an axolot, a kind of amphibian. As Coyote, the younger brother of the North American group, was the less responsible, Xolo:tl was the naughty one who trailed after Quetzalcoatl, his Big Brother transformed into the Mesoamerican serpent. His canine identify is clear in the iconography and in his name borne today by the Mexican hairless dog *xoloscuintle.*

The borrowings as "catfish" is direct from Nahuatl, apparently through the similarity between the catfish and the *axolot.* In Book XI of the Florentine Codex (Sahagun 1963:59), the ⟨axolomichi⟩, which I am supposing to be the *xolotl* fish, is described: "It is just like an axolotl; it is oily, slick. Its head is much like it, only it is long, thick; and it is very similar in being boneless. Good is its flesh; it is completely flesh".[1]

Although the Nahuatl word for "cork tree" in most dialects contains *šo(:)no(:)-*, often as *šono-k* or *šono-tl*, it seems more likely that the original word was *šolo:-tl* and that it was borrowed into Zoque as *šono-*. The word was then reborrowed, perhaps through the influence of Spanish use of 'jonote', or because the bark fibers were used more by non-Nahuas. The connection between duality and the cork tree would at first seem unlikely, but cork trees in Mexico are well-known because they grow with a trunk formed by many small "trunks". Zoque, which has no lateral, adopted the Nahuatl form by nasalization of the lateral and substitution of the absolutive suffix by Zoquean *-k*. Totonac must have borrowed *šú:nak* "cork tree" from the Zoque form *šunuk*.

(8)   ROOT *si^n*
Ute *sí-tií* V-dat "look like", "resemble"; *siná-ci* "uncle", "mother's younger brother"
Southern Paiute *sin:a-'avi-ˢ* (⟨*cïn:a-'avi-ˢ*⟩) "wolf, dog "; ⟨*cïn:a — ŋwa-vi^n*⟩ "coyote"; *sɔn:ia-ŋwɨ-* (anim. PL) "Great Bear (= Big Dipper)": (the 7 stars of the Big Dipper are believed to be Coyote's daughters who fled him when he tried to rape them)
Kawaaisu *cono'o-* "twin"; *cono'o-vɨ* "Double Mountain";
Comanche *tuhceena'* "wolf ('black-coyote')"
Hopi *sun, sunan* "equal, same"; *súnan-ta* "to be the same"
Cora (Ortega 1732) *šú'ura'ave* [⟨*xûravet*⟩] "Venus" (now just "star");
Nah *šolo:-tl*

(2d) *to:to:-tl*
One of the most important birds in Mesoamerica in terms of ritual significance is the turkey. Campbell and Kaufman (1976: 83) propose that proto-Zoque *tu'nuk* "turkey" is the origin for the term Nahuatl *to:tolin* "turkey hen" which was used for "chicken" as well following Hispanic contact. Their arguments are as follows:

> (26) Turkey: This violates the typical Mayan monosyllabic root structure (the native Mayan form is **'ak'*). The pMi [proto-Mixe] form **tu:tuk* (and **tu:t* to lay eggs) together with pZo form, is probably related to Tequistlatec *-dulu* turkey; Jicaque *tolo*; Huave *tel* female turkey; Zapotec *tou'* turkey; Nahua *totol-* chicken (*toto-tl* bird); and Paya *totoni-* chicken. Since domesticated turkeys appear quite late in Mesoamerica (around A.D. 300; Michael Coe personal communication), it is not certain how these forms are to be interpreted, perhaps as later loans.

The opposite view reconstructs proto-Zoque **tu'nuk* as a borrowing from Nahuatl by various steps. A UA **tɨ-ra'a-wɨ* name, "the one characterized by the stones (eggs)", could have produced an archaic form *to:-lo:-tl; unattested in Nahuatl (except perhaps in Tequitlatec and the proto-Zoque borrowing), subsequent consonant harmony, also reasonably common in Nahuatl, made *to:-lo:-tl become *to:to:-tl, the generic term for "bird"; *to:tolin* is further derived from the older form with the *-li-n* suffix. The Zoque forms could be explained as substituting the *-k* suffix for the Nahuatl absolutive, as they do in a number of cases, as shown by Gutiérrez (1998). So far, unfortunately, no cognates in other UA languages reflecting a *tɨ-ra'a-wɨ have been found; the proto-Zoque form *tu:nu:k would reflect the archaic *tolo:-tl since the *-l-* of Nahuatl is also changed to *-n-* regularly, given that no *-n-/-l-* contrast exists in Zoque, although it does in Nahuatl. The proto-Mixe form would be a later borrowing from the generalized form *to(:)to:-tl.

5. Conclusion

The emphasis in this paper has been on the reconstruction of one of a number of proto-Uto-Aztecan noun classes, and on the derivation of systematic etymologies from it as evidence for the UA origins of certain loanwords in Mesoamerican languages. For all words, it would also be possible to argue that they are loans that were adapted to the lexicon by a regular process for incorporating loans that UA languages developed, much as Amerindian languages in general after European contact invented strategies for regularly incorporating loans from Spanish and English. However, within the Uto-Aztecan family there are differences in the strategies.[2] Law (1961), for example, proposes three chronological stages in the incorporation of Spanish loans in Mecayapan Nahuatl, distinguished by phonological and morphological adaptation. For the latter stages, he points out that the infinitive of Spanish verbs is incorporated as a verb root with an *-o-a* derivative suffix, a procedure found repeated in almost all dialects. A study by Karttunen and Lockhart (1976) examines such processes chronologically in Nahuatl historical documents. In Cora in contrast, as shown by Casad (1988: 115–117), it is the past participle of the Spanish verb that is adapted as the Cora verb root. For the Uto-Aztecan *-ra'a class words, there are not contrasting strategies. The cognates in the different languages show regular sound correspondences and shared morphological structure, indications of an older origin. The plausibility of the etymologies must be given weight as well. To prove a different theory, it would be necessary to show that the words fit better as a group into the development of Mixe-Zoquean, Totonacan, or other Mesoamerican linguistic families. The independent linguistic evidence of UA development is problematic for Mesoamerican cultural history, but the arguments have been given with the idea that detailed reconstruction of lexical classes in all the languages in question may help to answer historical questions still posed by archaeologists and ethnohistorians. In addition, if the UA etymologies proposed are correct, they would indicate that Mesoamerica with its rich conceptual heritage and highly developed society, may be indebted much more than initially apparent to the indigenous groups to the north as well. Academia and official history in Mexico at least have tended to consider the more northern relatives the "poor cousins" so to speak. It would seem to the contrary, that at least some part of the roots of Mesoamerica are to be found in their ancestors' conceptions.

Notes

* The author wishes to express her appreciation for CONACyT grant 25101-H, which provided partial support for the research on this paper, and to my project assistant, José Juan Sánchez, for his patient help; also for very useful criticism, data, and advice that came from the following colleagues: David Beck, Tom Givón, Adriana Hernández, Carmen Herrera, Paulette Levy, Ana Aurora Medina, Mercedes Montes de Oca, Valentín Peralta, Kay Read, Crescencio Buitimea Valenzuela, Thom Smith-Stark, Leopoldo Valiñas, Verónica Vázquez, and two anonymous reviewers, one of whom provided important additional Cora forms for the analysis.

Sources and orthographies: Generally, the orthography has been regularized to standard Amerindian use, although in some cases, the original orthography of the sources has been included between angled parentheses. The following sources have been used for the languages: Chemehuevi (Press 1975); Comanche (Robinson & Armagost 1990); Cora (Ortega 1732, Casad 1985, Preuss 1932); Gila River Pima (Rea 1998); Hopi (Hill et al. 1998); Huastec Nahuatl (Kaufman 1971); Huichol (Grimes et al. 1981); Kawaiisu (Zigmond et al. 1991); Lower Pima (Rea 1998); Mayo (Collard & Collard 1974); Mecayapan Nahuatl (Wolgemuth 1981); Nahuatl Zacapoaxtla (Key & Key 1953); Northern Paiute (Miller 1988); Southern Paiute (Sapir 1931); Tarahumara (Brambila 1980); Totoguañ Papago (Miller 1988); Ute (Southern Ute Tribe 1979); Totonac (Aschmann 1973); Tzeltal and remaining languages (Justeson et al. 1985).

1. "*vel iuhqujn axolotl ic tzotlanj, injc alactic; vel iuhqujn ic ca itzontecon. ieçe ca viac, tomaoac: auh vel iuhqujn injc amo omjo, vel iectli nacatl, vel nacaio*".

2. In the case of Mexican languages, it should be noted that there are also some Spanish borrowings that have been lent to third languages through Nahuatl, which do follow the Nahuatl strategy, as analyzed in studies by Bright (1992) and Casad (1988: 118–119).

References

Aschmann, Herman Pedro. 1973. *Diccionario totonaco de Papantla, Veracruz, Totonaco-español, Español-totonaco.* (= *Serie de vocabularios y diccionarios indígenas "Mariano Silva y Aceves"*, Núm. 16.) Mexico: Instituto Lingüístico de Verano y la Secretaría de Educación Pública.

Bascom, Burton William, Jr. 1965. *Proto-Tepiman (Tepehuan-Piman).* Ph.D. dissertation, University of Washington, Seattle.

Brambila, David. 1980. *Diccionario raramuri-castellano (Tarahumar).* Mexico: Buena Prensa.

Bright, William. 1992. "The Aztec Triangle". *Proceedings of the 18th Annual Meeting of the Berkeley Linguistic Society* ed. by Laura Buszard-Welcher et al., 22–36. Berkeley: Berkeley Linguistic Society.

Bright, William & Jane Hill. 1967. "The Linguistic History of the Cupeño". *Studies in Southwestern Ethnolinguistics* ed. by Dell Hymes, 351–371. The Hague: Mouton.

Campbell, Lyle & Terrence Kaufman. 1976. "A Linguistic Look at the Olmecs". *American Antiquity* 41.80–89.

Casad, Eugene. 1985. "Cora". *Uto-Aztecan Grammatical Studies* ed. by Ronald W. Langacker, vol. iv, 151–459. Dallas: Summer Institute of Linguistics & the University of Texas-Arlington.

Casad, Eugene. 1988. "Post-conquest Influences on Cora (Uto-Aztecan)". *In Honor of Mary Haas, from the Haas Festival Conference on Native American Linguistics* ed. by William Shipley, 77–136. Berlin, New York, & Amsterdam: Mouton de Gruyter.

Collard, Howard & Elisabeth Scott Collard. 1974. *Vocabulario mayo, Castellano-mayo, mayo-castellano.* (= *Serie de vocabularios indígenas "Mariano Silva y Aceves"*, Núm. 6.) Mexico: Instituto Lingüístico de Verano.

Dakin, Karen & Søren Wichmann. 2000. "Cacao and Chocolate: A Uto-Aztecan perspective". *Ancient Mesoamerica* 11.1–21.

Grimes E., José, with Pedro de la Cruz Avila, José Carrillo Vicente, Filiberto Díaz, Román Díaz, Antonio de la Rosa, & Toribio Rentería. 1981. *El huichol, Apuntes sobre el léxico.* Ithaca: Department of Modern Languages and Linguistics, Cornell University.

Gutiérrez Morales, Salomé. 1998. "Préstamos recíprocos entre el náhuatl y el zoqueano del Golfo". *Estudios de cultura náhuatl* 28.399–410.

Hill, Jane. 1999. "El agua en el mundo anciano yuto-aztecano". Paper presented to the Friends of Uto-Aztecan Conference, Taxco, Gro., Mexico, June 17, 1999.

Hill, Kenneth C. et al., eds. 1998. *Hopi Dictionary/Hopìikwa Lavàytutuveni: A Hopi-English dictionary of the Third Mesa dialect with an English-Hopi finder list and a sketch of Hopi grammar.* Hopi Dictionary Project. Tucson: University of Arizona Press.

Iannucci, David Edmund. 1973. *Numic Historical Phonology.* Ph.D. dissertation, Cornell University, Ithaca, NY.

Justeson, John S., William N. Norman, Lyle Campbell, & Terrence Kaufman. 1985. *The Foreign Impact on Lowland Mayan Language and Script.* (= *Middle American Research Institute*, 53.) New Orleans: Tulane University.

Justeson, John S. & Terrence Kaufman. 1993. "A Decipherment of Epi-Olmec Hieroglyphic Writing". *Science* 259.1703–1711.

Karttunen, Frances & James Lockhart. 1976. *Nahuatl in the Middle Years: Language contact phenomena in texts of the colonial period.* (= *University of California Publications in Linguistics*, 85.) Berkeley & Los Angeles: The University of California Press.

Kaufman, Terrence. 1971. "Materiales lingüísticos para el estudio de las relaciones internas y externas de la familia de idiomas mayanos". *Desarrollo cultural de los mayas* ed. by Evon Z. Vogt & Alberto Ruz L., 81–136. Mexico: Universidad Nacional Autónoma de México, Coordinación de Humanidades, Centro de Estudios Mayas.

Kaufman, Terrence. 1989. "Nawa Roots (Huasteca Nawa)". Computer printout.

Key, Harold & Mary Ritchie de Key. 1953. *Vocabulario mejicano de la Sierra de Zacapoaxtla, Puebla.* Mexico: Instituto Lingüístico de Verano y la Secretaría de Educación Pública.

Lass, Roger. 1997. *Historical Linguistics and Language Change.* (= *Cambridge Studies in Linguistics*, 81). Cambridge: Cambridge University Press.

Law, Howard W. 1961. "Linguistic Acculturation in Isthmus Nahuat". *A William Cameron Townsend en el vigésimoquinto aniversario del Instituto Lingüístico de Verano*, 555–562. Mexico.

Lionnet, Andrés. 1985. "Relaciones internas de la rama sonorense". *Amerindia* 10.25–58.

Miller, Wick. R. 1967. *Uto-Aztecan Cognate Sets.* (= *University of California Publications in Linguistics*, 48.) Berkeley: University of California Press.

Miller, Wick R. 1988. *Computerized Data Base for Uto-Aztecan Cognate Sets*. With the assistance of Kevin Jon Hegg, Laurel Anderton, & Cindy High. Salt Lake City: Department of Linguistics, University of Utah.

Molina, Alonso de. 1571. *Vocabulario en lengua castellana y mexicana*. México, D. F. [Facimile edition. México, Porrúa, S. A., 4th edition, 1970].

Ortega, José de. 1732. *Vocabulario en lengua castellana y cora*. México. D. F. [Reprinted in the *Boletín de la Sociedad Mexicana de Geografía y Estadística*, 1ª época, 8: 561–605, 1860; also reprinted in Tepic, 1888].

Press, Margaret L. 1975. *A Grammar of Chemehuevi*. Ph. D. dissertation, University of California, Los Angeles.

Preuss, K. Th. 1932. "Grammatik der Cora-Sprache". *International Journal of American Linguistics* VII.1–2.3–102.

Rea, Amadeo M. 1998. *Folk Mammalogy of the Northern Pimans*. Tucson: The University of Arizona Press.

Robinson, Lila Wistrand & James Armagost. 1990. *Comanche Dictionary and Grammar*. (= *Summer Institute of Linguistics and the University of Texas at Arlington Publications in Linguistics*, 92.) Dallas: Summer Institute of Linguistics & the University of Texas at Arlington.

Sahagún, Bernardino de. 1963. *Florentine Codex. Book 11, Earthly Things*. Translated from the Aztec into English by Charles E. Dibble & Arthur J. O. Anderson. Santa Fe: The School of American Research & the University of Utah.

Sapir, Edward. 1931. "Southern Paiute Dictionary". *Proceedings of the American Academy of Arts and Sciences* 65.537–729.

Southern Ute Tribe. 1979. *Ute Dictionary, Núu — ?apáGa — pi po?wa — ti*. Preliminary edition. Ignacio, CO: Ute Press.

Voegelin, Carl F., Florence M. Voegelin, & Kenneth L. Hale. 1962. *Typological and Comparative Grammar of Uto-Aztecan I (Phonology)*. [= *Indiana University Publications in Anthropology and Linguistics*, Memoir 17 of the *International Journal of American Linguistics*.]

Wichmann, Søren. 1995. *The Relationship among the Mixe-Zoquean Languages of Mexico*. Salt Lake City: University of Utah Press.

Wolgemuth, Carl. 1981. *Gramática náhuatl del municipio de Mecayapan, Veracruz*. (= *Serie Gramáticas de Lenguas Indígenas de México*, 5.) México: Instituto Lingüístico de Verano.

Zigmond, Maurice L., Curtis G. Booth, & Pamela Munro. 1991. *Kawaiisu: A grammar and dictionary with texts*. (= *University of California Publications in Linguistics*, 119.) Berkeley & Los Angeles: University of California Press.

Gradience and linguistic change[*]

David Denison
University of Manchester

1. Introduction

1.1 Syntactic categories

In some traditional grammatical approaches such as that embodied in the National Literacy Strategy for primary schools in England, adjectives are "words which qualify nouns" (anon. 1998: 34). (In fact even the *with*-phrase in *the girl with long hair* is called an Adjective Phrase in the original version of the NLS Glossary, 1998: 85.)[1] It is clear too that a modifying noun is regarded as an adjective. Consider (1), noticed on the side of some Vancouver ambulances:

(1) Advanced Life
     Support Unit

Although (1) seems straight out of Douglas Adams or Steven Spielberg, it isn't the bracketing that is relevant here but the categories. Anyone relying on the original NLS documentation, which has a poor definition of Adjective and little conception of structure, would have to find three adjectives in (1). Now Rodney Huddleston (1984: 93–95, 325–328), for example, shows that this is a wrong-headed analysis which confuses *form class*, to be defined by a basket of properties, with *function*, and ever since I first read his book many years ago I have subscribed to that careful structuralist view: a modifying noun remains a noun. I will return to the distinction between adjectives and nouns. This paper concerns the boundaries between word classes and the consequences for syntactic analysis. I will claim that treatments of word classes, in linguistics as much as in the traditional view, are often inadequate, in particular by showing that certain individual words and constructions defy simple categorisation and analysis. The focus throughout is on recent change in English, and synchronic analysis is harnessed to diachronic explanation.

2.   Some recent approaches

2.1 Chomskyan grammar

By way of introduction, let me now risk caricaturing some respectable and modern linguistics. Much generative grammar assumes that a given sentence has a unique analysis for a given speaker (possibly involving a derivational history, of course), with each of its component words having a unique category: an item either is a noun or it isn't, for instance.[2] An important goal of theorising is to make the overall grammar as economical as possible, usually expressed as a necessity for explaining the miracle of language acquisition, less often to allow for on-line processing. Rather than being directed to the limitations of childhood language learners, this economy drive is perhaps at least as much to do with perceptions of elegance among (mathematically inclined) linguists — a matter of aesthetics.

One development within this tradition, often favoured by those interested in diachrony, allows competing grammars à la Kroch and Pintzuk, recent examples being Henry (1997) and Lightfoot (1999). Variation is handled by allowing that different grammars may co-exist within a society and even within an individual — normally two grammars; most choices remain binary. (Henry allows three in her study of imperatives, but only one per individual.) But *every* variation needs a set of grammars, so that except where different cases of variation can be shown to be related to a single parameter setting, this rapidly becomes an unrealistic model of variation.

2.2 Optimality Theory

An alternative theoretical development is along the route of Optimality Theory, where one aspect of economy is jettisoned, in that the grammars for all human languages and varieties contain the same huge number of rules and differ only in the ordering and salience of the rules, and where one aspect of Procrustean rigour or rigidity is jettisoned by allowing those rules to be violable rather than absolute. However, the underlying representation of any given sentence is typically couched in one of the standard formalisms (for example, a Chomskyan generative syntax or Lexical-Functional Grammar), with unambiguous structural relations and category assignment. All the generative approaches so far mentioned are synchronic approaches at heart, and all concentrate on patterns.

2.3 Economy

If overall economy and maximal efficiency of analysis remain top priorities, certain things follow. The speaker has *a grammar*. All of his or her possible sentences are in principle describable, are predictable, from a single, self-consistent, elegant grammar conforming to Universal Grammar. Any messiness is an essentially uninteresting matter, certainly not part of Internalised-language.

Binarity of parameter settings, of choices between clear Aristotelian categories, and so on, is an understandable move, and a reasonable heuristic. Systems embodying binarity and economy are apparently simpler to describe, and their mathematical properties are easier to state. Questions about the power of the grammar and hence of its falsifiability can be asked and answered. Such approaches started very much as top-down analyses, even if the drive over the last twenty or so years has been increasingly towards modularity by interaction of relatively simple explanatory principles.

However, there is another view of economy which suggests that an individual speaker need not have a wholly consistent grammar. It may be — in my view, it may *well* be — that speakers are capable of routinely using fragments of language which are mutually inconsistent. Speakers may in part organise language at a much more local level. The patterning involved may be less neat but not necessarily more complex. This would be a bottom-up model. The view that an individual's grammar may not be homogeneous is subscribed to by, among others, Harris and Campbell (1995). Croft (2000: 231) quotes a nice line by Bolinger: "I want to suggest that language is a structure, but in some ways a jerry-built structure" (1976: 1).

The idea that the best analysis of a construction comes from a model in which only one derivation is possible always struck me as psychologically implausible. In a paper I wrote some fifteen years ago on Old English word order I suggested the following:

> Rather than a given sentence being the output of some maximally simple, elegant, and maybe unique rule, I regard a sentence as the more likely, the more (potentially conflicting) requirements it satisfies simultaneously, thus the **more** patterns it matches. (Denison 1986: 293)

That rather programmatic statement is somewhat in the spirit of the later Optimality Theory, in which grammaticality derives from the resolution of a large number of possibly conflicting attempts to satisfy particular conditions. It is equally consonant with a theory embracing gradience, regarded as the simultaneous resemblance to different and incompatible prototypes.

2.4 Grammaticalisation

Yet another approach which commands widespread recognition is Grammaticalisation Theory. Here we have a rather different point of view: essentially diachronic, essentially gradualist, and in its synchronic consequences involving co-existence of more and less grammaticalised variants in the same variety. Grammaticalisation typically concerns itself with individual lexical items, at least at the input stage, and with transitions from major lexical word classes to more functional elements (though there are exceptions to the latter, as in Werner Abraham's and Paolo Ramat's contributions to 14ICHL). In this paper I will try to stick to examples of gradience which would not normally be regarded as either grammaticalisation or degrammaticalisation, as I am interested in exploring the question of gradience as a more widespread phenomenon in language.

2.5 Notional grammar

John Anderson's Notional Grammar (1997 and earlier papers) appears to embody gradience, in that a scale of categories runs from complete N (Referentiality, nominality of proper name) to complete P (Predicability, finite verbality), with as many intermediate points between N and P as are thought necessary. But any given category — for instance, the gerund, the adjective, whatever — is assigned a fixed point on this scale, which can be represented in effect as a particular numeric proportion of N to P. I want here to explore gradience between categories which are not necessarily adjacent on Anderson's scale, and also to consider the idea that a given item doesn't always have a fixed place on that single scale.

3. A project on gradience

3.1 Context of this paper

There is no room here for a properly extensive discussion of linguistic theory. What I have attempted above is the merest sketch of some salient characteristics of different approaches, in order to provide a context for what follows: a preliminary survey of some gradient phenomena in grammar. This is a return to a topic which I looked at unsystematically in the 1980s and which I hope to develop with Bas Aarts of University College London as a major research project. It takes two ideas as its starting-points:

– that language routinely exhibits gradient boundaries in the synchronic state
– that linguistic change may proceed by means of, perhaps even because of, gradient stages

The first point is noted by many writers, for example — with increasing degrees of emphasis — Huddleston (1984:72), Quirk et al. (1985:90), and Langacker (1987:18).

As for the second, gradience in change does not necessarily mean gradualness chronologically. Lightfoot (1999) and others have argued that apparent gradualness of change in the historical record may be compatible with sudden grammatical change at the level of the individual speaker. At present I am working on the assumption that gradience in a certain historical change means that the change occurs by means of a number of small steps, but I do *not* assume that progress through a series of steps must be prolonged in time, so this is potentially the exact opposite of Lightfoot's approach.

In the proceedings of a conference like ICHL with no E in the acronym, I must ask forgiveness for appearing to assume, like the worst kind of 1960s synchronic transformational grammar, that the business of linguistics can be conducted solely on the basis of English data. I don't for one moment think that, but my examples here *are* all from the recent history of English.

3.2 Taxonomy of gradience

A taxonomy which Bas Aarts has been developing now simply distinguishes gradience within a form class and gradience between form classes. The first is almost uncontroversial. Thus it is a truth more or less universally acknowledged within linguistics that the form class 'Adjective' is defined by a cluster of distributional properties, and that adjectives which satisfy all of them — *wide, happy,* etc. — are more prototypical members of the class in English than items like *mere, potential, dead, ill* which satisfy some but not all of the properties. Nevertheless, those marginal members of the class are still universally recognised as being adjectives: no other form class seems appropriate. If it is conceded that there are degrees of closeness to the prototype, then we have gradience within a single form class, what Aarts calls 'subsective gradience'.

Gradience between two form classes he calls 'intersective gradience', but Aarts adopts the working assumption that most claimed examples of intersective gradience between category A and category B in synchronic linguistics are unnecessary complications of the grammar which, by more careful or delicate analysis, can be decided as either A or B but not both. Diachronically, however, the possibility of intersective gradience between form classes seems to me still worth considering, and it often co-occurs with intersective gradience between constructions. Here a given sentence type manifests behaviour which suggests two different structures at the same time.

I think it is fair to say that subsective gradience is quite widely acknowledged (not under that name, of course), in the sense that most scholars would subscribe to it, even though it is rarely built into theories. Intersective gradience between categories has been looked at by a few scholars, and between constructions is not generally acknowledged at all. Where gradience has been dealt with in the literature it has mostly involved placing *different* items along a gradient. I move on now to discussion of possible gradience on the basis of real data. Sometimes I illustrate gradience by assigning different positions on a gradient to different occurrences of the *same* word or syntactic pattern.

4. Subsective gradience

Given that subsective gradience is relatively familiar, I will add just two further examples.

4.1 Modal membership

Some modals are less central than others. This is much-visited territory. So, for instance, CAN and WILL were the last modals to become wholly grammaticalised in the early Modern English (EModE) period — see here Warner's (1990) account — while in Present-day English (PDE), OUGHT is more marginal than the prototypical modals. Recently MAY has been showing signs of obsolescence, and its form *may* is losing paradigm modal properties like present tense distribution and clitic negation (Denison 1998: 177–178, 197). Within the category Modal, then, there has always been subsective gradience.

4.2 less (cf. more)

See Quirk et al. (1985: 262–64) for some discussion of quantifiers like *more* and *less*. Here, I will suggest, we find a kind of gradience. If this is gradience wholly within a category, presumably we must call it subsective, but if so, it is subsective gradience of a problematic kind. First, it is a moot point precisely *which* category to use for *less*: Quantifier, Post-determiner, or Determiner, in increasing order of generality?[3] Second, there is no obvious prototypical core — unless we take an item like *the* as the prototypical Determiner, in which case Post-determiner and Quantifier would already have to be consigned to the periphery — so that a definition of subsective gradience which depends on distance from a prototype would be difficult to apply.

Now consider the following material, adapted from my recent survey of late ModE syntax (Denison 1998: 124):

(2)   *Noncount nouns*   *Count nouns*
      more work   (mo) → more students
      less work   fewer → less students

The quantifiers show some changes of usage over time. Already with the loss of *mo* in the EModE period, *more* had come to be used both with noncount and count nouns. *Less* has a strong tendency to behave similarly, and in fact did so between Old English and the sixteenth century. Usages like *less raindrops* then became stigmatised, and in standard English a distinction has until recently been made between *less* and *fewer*: *less work*, but *fewer students*. Now probably most younger speakers would say *less students*. *OED* already has a few nineteenth-century citations of *less Ns*. Within the last generation or so, the usage has become increasingly frequent, and the current revival seems inexorable, given the strong pressure of analogy.[4] So what about the following example?

> (3)　Capt. Goldsmith, a young Surrey officer, came with me for the first couple of hours, with a party of 19 mounted police — for honour you understand, not for safety. I could have done with *less* but in spite of them all the ride over the desert green with aromatic plants was delicious. (1918 Bell, *Letters* II.451 (28 Mar.))

When I first discussed example (3) (Denison 1998), I wrote that the modern reader is likely to interpret *less* as "less policemen", whereas the highly educated Gertrude Bell more probably understood something like "less honour" or "a smaller party". But perhaps not, since *less* is not directly followed by a plural noun. Such environments have long been somewhat more acceptable for *less* in the sense "fewer", e.g.,

> (4)　(no) less than twenty students

> (5)　groups of twenty students or less

This looks, therefore, like a case of (re-)introduction of an innovation through the least salient point. *Less* in very conservative varieties is a quantifier like *much* which collocates with noncount head nouns only; in more advanced varieties it is like *more* and collocates with both count and noncount head nouns. (That is a recurrent distinction within the Determiner category; see Quirk et al. 1985: 377–385, Tables 6.45, 6.48, 6.49, 6.53.) But moderately conservative usage (e.g., my own) — which allows (4) and maybe (5) but not *less students* — shows fairly stable subsective gradience in the usage of *less*, part-way between the *much* type and the *more* type.

5.　Intersective gradience between categories

5.1　Gerund

The classic example of a mixed category is the gerund, which blurs the distinction between N and V, and used to do so even more than is now normal. Despite distributional changes in the last two centuries, there are still examples where nominal behaviour (modification by a determiner) coexists with verbal behaviour (complementation by objects, etc.):

> (6)　The days had been very full: the psychiatrist, the obstacle courses, *the throwing herself from the hold of a slowly chugging plane*. (1998 Sebastian Faulks, *Charlotte Gray* [Vintage, 1999] x.111)

The gerund is much-analysed topic, too big to go into here; for some historical discussion see Denison (1998: 268–272) and references given there. I now turn to some further instances of intersective gradience.

5.2   N ~ A

The distributions of A(djective) and N(oun) are different. Within the NP — the choice between a DP and NP analysis is not germane in this rather "surfacey" account — the usual descriptive statement is that the possible items are as follows:

(7)   D A^{1-n} N^{1-n} N_{head} Postmodifiers^{1-n}

That is to say, there is a single D(eterminer) slot (ignoring for now pre- and post-determiners), an iterative slot for modifying adjectives, an iterative slot for modify-ing nouns, and then the head noun; after that come any postmodifying elements. Crucially, all premodifying adjectives precede all premodifying nouns:

(8)   a.   National Literacy Strategy
       b.   *Literacy National Strategy

5.3   N → A

Are there words which have moved from noun to adjective over time? I should point out that the "bible" of English word formation doesn't recognise such a process: "No transposed substantive can be called an adjective unless it has received a categorial marker" (Marchand 1969: 361), that is, a derivational suffix or other explicit change of form. Other writers do, however, at least in a limited way. Huddleston writes (1984: 328):

> There will then be very little occasion to postulate conversion from noun to adjective. Where we can add degree adverbs as dependents, as — for some speakers at least — in *a very fun party, an extremely Oxbridge accent*, we will certainly regard the degree of adjectivalisation such as to justify a conversion analysis, but there are not many examples of this kind.

For noun → adjective conversion — as opposed to the "partial conversion" (in fact, non-conversion) shown in *the wealthy* and similar phrases — Quirk et al. have relatively few examples, most of them words for materials like *brick, stone* (1985: 1562), thus objective, non-evaluative modifiers. I show now that there are others of more subjective, evaluative semantics and thus potentially "better" adjectives.

5.3.1 *Powerhouse*

(9)   Raves coming thick and fast for George Auld's *new powerhouse band* now at the Arcadia Ballroom, N. Y. (1942 [*OED*])

(10) The *powerhouse new bestseller* from ELIZABETH GEORGE (1996 Bantam Press advertisement, *The Guardian* p. 1 (3 Feb.))

Example (10) shows that the former noun modifier of (9) has now (at least once) been used as an adjective, but the word *powerhouse* as modifier is too rare for me to detect gradience in the transition.[5]

5.3.2 *Fun*

This is a more common word, already noted in this connection by previous scholars, and a range of examples can be found:[6]

(11) Painting is *more fun* and less soul-work than writing. (1927 [*OED*])

(12) It was *such fun.*

Fun is clearly a noun in (11) and (12). Like all nouns, *fun* can be used as a noun modifier:

(13) I was remembering Marianne and *the fun times* we have had. (1968 [*OED*])

This kind of usage neutralises the N ~ A distinction.

In (14) *fun* looks somewhat more adjectival:

(14) She's so completely lovely and *fun* and joyful. (W1B-003 #73:1 [ICE-GB])

Here it occurs in a coordinated sequence of what are otherwise clear adjectives (but without becoming itself an unequivocal adjective, cf. *It's lovely but a mess*).

In (15)–(18), however, *fun* shows distinctively adjectival behaviour:

(15) We have the Osborns, the Beals, the Hartungs, the Falmers, and us. Now let's think of *someone fun.* (1971 [*OED*])

(16) … perhaps send for that book you never bought earlier and have *a really fun time* with the wealth of designs from Iris Bishop or Wendy Phillips or whoever you like best. (CA2 553 [BNC])

(17) It may not be *as fun* to watch it up close (A17–113 [Frown])

(18) It was *so fun.* (1999 att. DD)

In (15) it postmodifies an indefinite pronoun; in (16)–(18) it is premodified by an intensifier or conjunction which typically co-occurs with adjectives rather than nouns. The contrasting examples (12) and (18) represent normal usage in different generations of my family. Leech and Li (1995: 187) also mention "the adjectival use of *fun* both predicatively and attributively (as in *The event was fun* and *It was a fun event*)", which takes to "its fullest form" what they identify as "the tendency for

Noun Phrase complements to gravitate towards adjectival use".

A superlative — sign of full morphological adjectivehood — appears in the following journalistic parody:

(19)   Valspeak is... the *funnest*, most totally radical language, I guess, like in the whole mega gnarly city of Los Angeles. (1982 [*OED Online*])

5.3.3 *Key*

This word shows similar behaviour. It can of course be a noun — indeed normally is so. There is a longstanding use as noun modifier, as in:

(20)   Occupants of *key offices* such as the Presidency or the Attorney-Generalship. (1926 [*OED*])

Interestingly, *OED* labels this usage as follows (s.v. *key* n.[1] 17.b):

Passing into *adj.* in the sense of 'dominant', 'controlling', 'chief', 'essential'; esp. designating some person or thing that is of crucial importance to others.

Here is another example, where the near-synonymy of *key* with the adjective *crucial* is explicit:

(21)   *The key verse* in this first section is verse 4; it is a crucial one. (1959LLOY.H9 [ARCHER])

However, on the Huddleston analysis the modifier *key* in (20)–(21) would still be a noun, since until quite recently *key* did not show criterial properties of adjectives other than occurrence in premodifier position, which is available for nouns too.

In some cases there is a subtle further development in usage:

(22)   Another source said that the interview with Jaafar's family did not provide any helpful leads and indicated that Jaafar did not play *any key role* in the case. (1989LAT1.N0 [ARCHER])

This and other examples show that *key* is losing the sense of uniqueness, which may eventually lead to semantic gradability.[7] Word order too is suggestive:

(23)   a.   But the *key foreign and defense* portfolios remained unchanged. (1982CHI2.N0[ARCHER])
       b.   two *key Southern* states (S2B-006 #9:1:B [ICE-GB])

(24)   More emotional weight is carried in the *key domestic* scenes in which ... (C01 103[FLOB])

Use before adjectives may not be wholly convincing evidence of adjectivehood, despite (7) and (8), since *foreign portfolio, defense portfolio,* and *Southern states* are institutionalised phrases. What would be happening in (23) would then be that the ordering of subjective/evaluative modifiers before modifiers expressing provenance and so on (a matter of semantics, pragmatics, or discourse) is overriding the ordering of categories, of A before N (a matter of syntax). But even if so, this is gradience, and (24) is better evidence of a category change, since *domestic scenes* is not obviously a set phrase.

A further development is illustrated in (25):

(25) a. "Claudia brings an unforgettable quality of joy to all her work that is *key* to Revlon's view of beauty". (FBM 759 [BNC])
b. The agreement of a mutually acceptable reserve price is *key*. (HJ5 1349 [BNC])
c. Noting that such incidents are not marginal but *key* to Edgeworth's plots, ... (1992 M. Butler, "Introduction", p. 41, Maria Edgeworth, *Castle Rackrent* and *Ennui*, Penguin)

Now *key* is being used without a determiner, very much like *fun*, and in (25c) is coordinated with an adjective.

Finally, we see a significant further step:

(26) There are a number of reasons why people lose their hair, stress is a *very key* factor. (HVE 174 [BNC])

(27) we are fast approaching a *very key* point er in that process erm [...] and *the key point, which really is* arises out of what we're discussing tonight, the key point is what regulatory framework should the P I A place on intermediaries and on er life assurance companies, pension funds, financial advisors generally (JSG 337 [BNC])

Now *key* is being used with *very*: this must be an adjective. (Notice too the anacoluthic clause *which really is* in (27), which also implies gradability.) A syntactic superlative appears in:

(28) Meirion Rowlands, one of the Ashleys' *most key* appointments of this time, was well known as the local prizewinning sheep shearer; he met Bernard over a pint in the pub. (GU9 7[BNC])

And yet the same speakers who might use (28) would still (I believe) accept as another instance of the same word:

(29) Fear is the key.

(30) Fear and ambition are the respective keys to their characters.

Reviewing the examples of *key* in this section, we appear to have nouns — (20), (29), (30), etc. — adjectives — (26)–(28), etc. — and several intermediate types all current in the language. My point is that there is no simple switch from N to A, rather a graded series of transitions. If that is so, then we have demonstrated synchronic gradience.

5.3.4 *Designer*

A similar process is happening with *designer*. For brevity I cite some NPs to illustrate its use before an institutionalised A+N (N-bar) phrase:

(31)   The designer Italian menu (ECU 2974); so it's finally happened — designer industrial action (ANY 2084); Designer interior decoration (BMD 1695); from under the designer fitted units (CB8 3479 [BNC])

On West 10th Avenue in Vancouver you can see a shop-front which says:

(32)   Designer Direct Sofas

In (31) and (32) the modifier *designer*, originally a noun, is occurring before adjective modifiers, albeit adjectives which form set phrases with their head noun. This could be the beginning of a gradient for *designer* which might take it towards being a true adjective itself.

Many of my students say they would find the following quite normal:

(33)   Those sunglasses are very designer.

(34)   Those sunglasses look designer.

For them it has taken another step towards adjectivehood.

5.4   A → N

Going the other way is not (obviously) a matter of gradience. "There is no very productive pattern of adjective → noun conversion" (Quirk et al. 1985: 1560). "Miscellaneous examples" given by the Quirk team include *bitter, daily, final*, where derivation involves ellipsis of a noun head from well-established A + N = NP phrases. Another straightforward example can be constructed from citations for the word *elastic* in *OED*:

(35)   Elastic Bitumen..is of a brown color, has no lustre, and is *very elastic*. (1794)

(36)   Cavallo in *Phil. Trans.* LXXI. 519 Common vitriolic ether..could not affect *elastic gum*. (1781)

(37)   With the *elastics* supplied by the ladies, for a halter..the young dog passed from the shores of time. (1847)

(38)   Adèle had been enquiring for *a piece of elastic* for her hat. (1863)

In (35)–(36) *elastic* is an adjective; in (37)–(38) it is being used as a noun. I am content to regard this as an abrupt change. Note that once again Marchand (1969: 361) doesn't recognise any synchronic relationship here:

Some of these elliptic expressions [*sc. hopeful* < *hopeful candidate*] have gained complete independence from their original full syntagma basis, as is the case with *musical.* The word is no longer thought of as a shortening of *musical comedy*, but has become a sb in its own right. The final result is an unmotivated new moneme […] Unmotivated signs, however, do not belong in word-formation.

5.5 Intersective gradience between N and A?

Among the basket of properties normally used for defining Noun is the possibility of plural marking: this is to be contrasted with Adjective, which lacks it. Both classes share the distributional property of occurring as premodifiers of nouns — in that position the distinction between them is partially neutralised — but it is interesting that a noun premodifying another noun is typically not plural:

(39) a.   trouser-press, child support
      b.   *trousers-press, *children support

Quirk et al. note that plural marking is absent here even for what they call "summation plurals" like *trousers* which otherwise do not occur without a plural inflection (1985: 301).

Here, then, an adjective-like position is associated with one aspect of adjective-like morphology. Furthermore, a noun in that position won't have a determiner of its own, and even when used elsewhere and acting as a head may be a noncount noun (*fun*, for example) and so potentially without determiner even then. Potential for use with a determiner helps to distinguish Noun from Adjective, so the N ~ A distinction is further blurred. Again, Leech and Li (1995: 186) mention in a different context — complement NPs — "a tendency to omit the article initiating an NP, a characteristic which … gives the NP a more adjectival quality". The conclusion I am driven to is that the traditional usage reflected in the National Literacy Strategy which I mentioned and mocked at the start — "noun used as adjective" is a common version — may not be entirely wrong-headed: we can see from the kinds of fact discussed here why it has seemed reasonable to so many people.

What is interesting about the trading relationship between Noun and Adjective is that there seems to be some directionality. So far I haven't come across examples of category shift which move in opposite directions along exactly the same gradient. There are different routes from one category to the other.

5.6 A ~ P: Transitive adjectives

A notorious case of uncertain categorial status is the 'transitive adjectives' *like*, *worth*, and *near*. Consider PDE examples complemented by an NP:

(40) a. like a man
      b. worth a lot of money
      c. near the river

The structures in (40) bear considerable resemblance both to AP and to PP, so the category of the head is correspondingly uncertain: A(djective) or P(reposition)? This might be one case of what Ross (1972, 1973) calls a 'squish'. Maling (1983) categorises the first two items as prepositions, the third as an adjective, and Anderson (1997:74–82) places them along a gradient between adjective and preposition in the order *near, like, worth,* whereas Quirk et al. treat *all* of them as prepositions but with greatest hesitation over *like* (1985:661–663, 1064 n.[c]). I will not repeat the distributional evidence in detail, but it is clear that these words pose some problem for the categorisation of PDE lexemes.

When considered historically, such words generally become *less* problematic over time, revealing a sharpening of categories. We might add *(un)becoming, (un)worthy, next,* which fell nearer to the P ~ A border earlier in the late ModE period:

(41) a. and any such feeling on her part was mean, ignoble, and *unbecoming the spirit* with which she wished to think that she was endowed. (1860–1861 Trollope, *Framley* xxxv.343)
      b. to make the subject *well worthy the attention* of all who have occasion to treat diabetes mellitus. (1868PINK.M7 [ARCHER])
      c. The end of the piece which was *next the now detached pipe,* is called the nose. (1880 [*OED*])

It is noticeable that *(un)becoming, (un)worthy,* and *next* have virtually lost all prepositional character and become wholly adjectival.[8] There were, arguably, many more transitive adjectives in Old English, but all have lost their NP-governing character.

Conversely, *like* has lost some adjectival properties:

(42) a. A nation means *a like body* of men, because of that likeness capable of acting together. (1872 [*OED*])
      b. It was *very like* and very laughable, but hardly caricatured. (1854 [*OED*])
      c. The two or three places I am *like to have* business relations with. (1886 [*OED*])

The patterns of (42) are pretty much obsolete. The main uses now of *like* are as preposition (or 'quasi-prepositional adverb', as *OED* would have it) and increasingly as conjunction/complementiser, a pairing which in some analyses is a single category anyway (for example, Emonds 1976; Huddleston & Pullum in prep.):

(43) a. He entered *like a whirlwind.* (cf. He died *before his time.*) [+NP]
      b. He acted *like there was no tomorrow.* (cf. He left *before it finished.*) [+clause]

As for *worth*, use without a dependent NP or clause — and therefore as pure adjective — has been obsolete for centuries: *OED*'s last citation is dated a1450 (s.v., 4.a) or possibly 1535 (s.v., 6).

All of the words just discussed have thus been moving away from peripheral joint membership of the two categories P and A and towards membership of a single category (even if they have not all yet attained prototypical membership). The particular direction each one has taken gives some support to Maling's analysis of their PDE distributions. Only *near* obstinately keeps a foot in both adjectival and prepositional camps.[9] So we may be able to conclude that (intersective) 'squish' or something like it is necessary in linguistic categorisation, but also that items can lose some of their squishiness over time.

I don't know if there is a tendency for intersective gradience to be unstable, though I suspect so. It would fit plausibly with Warner's suggestion of a tendency for category distinctions which are 'basic' in the Roschian sense to be sharpened over time:[10] "[O]nce an opposition becomes basic its internal coherency and external distinctiveness should tend to increase, if opportunity offers." (1990:550). But then we face the problem that confronts every proponent of a historical account in which some structure or other is said to be disfavoured: if it is so low-valued, how come it ever arose in the first place?

6.   Intersective gradience between constructions

Given that this type of gradience is perhaps least familiar, I discuss a number of possible examples.

6.1 Partitives, **kind of**

It is possible to analyse an NP (again, I am not taking it as a DP) like *a majority of students* in two ways:

(44) a.   head noun *majority*, premodified by determiner *a* and postmodified by the
       prepositional phrase *of students* (cf. *a steak in breadcrumbs*)
   b.   head noun *students*, premodified by complex determiner *a majority of* (cf. *a
       few students*)

For conflicting views see Huddleston (1984:236–239), Quirk et al. (1985:264, 764–765). Analysis (44a) corresponds to the syntactic origin of the pattern, while there is some semantic support for (44b), in that *a majority of students* is notionally more likely to be a partitive of *students* than a kind of *majority*. The most obvious test of structure is verbal concord: with singular *majority* or with plural *students*? For quite a number of phrases, the historical development has been a classic process of replacement: first analysis a alone, then a and b in variation, and finally b alone. The older structure is shown in:

(45)   The progress of phonetics has been so great ... that *the great bulk of the observations* already made on living languages *is* next to useless. (1873–1874 Sweet, "On Danish Pronunciation", *TPhS* 94)

The newer structure appears in:

(46)   *a crowd of people were* arguing with and even shoving the Guards, ... (1906 Nesbit, *Amulet* xi.206)

Both variants exist today in:

(47)

A group of students $\left\{ \begin{array}{c} \text{is} \\ \text{are} \end{array} \right\}$ waiting outside.

With the *majority* example already discussed, the singular variant is now somewhat pedantic and is probably obsolescent. And with *a lot of* the singular construction has disappeared entirely (and of course was never found with the plural variant *lots of*). Informal English even permits concord between a plural (notional) head noun and a central determiner which, historically speaking, should be the modifier of a singular noun and thus singular in form:

(48)   a.   *These* sort of ideas (1788 Betsy Sheridan, *Journal* 42 p. 131)
        b.   *those* sort of jokes (1949 Streatfeild, *Painted Garden* xxiii.256)

Such examples — Quirk et al. have a similar one with *kind of* (1985: 764) — give additional support to analysis (44b) over and above verbal concord, with *sort of* functioning syntactically as a kind of postdeterminer.

Nonpartitives like *a tiny stifling box of a place* (1917 Bell, *Letters* II.405) and *a/one hell of a party* (cf. also the common spelling *helluva*) may show a rather similar shift from head to part of premodifier; see here Aarts (1998), *OED* s.v. *of* prep. 24.

What is the nature of the diachronic shift from one analysis to another, and of the synchronic variation between analyses? Timberlake (1977), for instance, assumes that a diachronic process of reanalysis requires some contexts which are structurally ambiguous. Reanalysis in such contexts is followed by a gradual process of actualisation in which the reanalysed variant extends its distribution. It is implicit in his account that there are only two possible analyses — what we might call 'before' and 'after' — and that any one speaker at any one time assigns only one of these analyses to a given string. Some generative accounts of phenomena like the prepositional passive have built reanalysis into *synchronic* derivations, so that a speaker could have different structural analyses at different stages of a sentence's derivation; for some references and discussion see Denison (1993: 151–152), Haspelmath (1998). Even in a synchronic reanalysis account, though, there is in effect a 'before' and an 'after' (not to be interpreted temporally, of course) and nothing in between. *Prima facie*, however, I believe that we can make a case for intersective gradience diachronically and probably synchronically too. The argument runs as follows.

Within the partitive construction type in Present-day English there are a range of particular constructions, from those where the analysis of (44a) is plausible to those which can only be analysed like (44b). Between the extremes are constructions which give evidence of both analyses. We can plausibly identify not one but *several* intermediate types which vary in their degree of closeness to analysis (44b). If we are prepared to recognise the possibility of intersective gradience between morphosyntactic categories, i.e., word classes, then the consequence seems to be that we must recognise intersective gradience between syntactic constructions. A given string may have for a given speaker an analysis in some sense intermediate between the conventional 'before' and 'after' analyses. The theoretical status of such intermediate structures remains unclear at the moment.

6.2 Pronoun case and verb concord

I have argued (Denison 1996) that there is a person hierarchy in certain case changes. In recent history — the last hundred or so years — there has been a narrowing of the distribution of the subjective case in case-marked pronouns, with objective increasingly the unmarked form. But the loss of subjective case has been uneven. To take a single context as an example:

(49)   a.   "Not *he*", said Robert sleepily. (1906 Nesbit, *Amulet* ix.175)
        b.   "Not *she*", said the Psammead a little less crossly. (ibid. viii.146)
        c.   "Not *they*", cried the Princess joyously. (1907 Nesbit, *Enchanted Castle* i.28)

(50)   a.   "Not *me*!" was Gerald's unhesitating rejoinder. (ibid. i.26)
        b.   "Not *us*!" said Mabel. (ibid. xi.221)

We find that first person had changed to use of objective case in disjunctive position, (50), by the turn of the twentieth century, while third person was unaffected even in nonstandard usage for several decades longer: cf. (49). Similar changes lasting over longer stretches of the ModE period have begun to remove subjective pronouns from certain other syntactic contexts in most varieties:

(51)   a.   It is *I/me.
        b.   He is taller than *I/me.

Person no longer appears to be a conditioning factor in any of these contexts, but in the past it was. Whether this is gradience depends on how pronoun case is to be analysed. If (as one referee suggests) pronouns are taken to be collections of features, then we merely have (as another referee suggests) grammatically conditioned variation. But differing case choices in a given variety may reflect a structural difference during the period of variation, as is particularly plausible for the (51b) type: *than me* analysed as PP, *than I* certainly not. On that view they can be regarded as exhibiting intersective gradience. I have speculated that the shrinking distribution of the explicitly case-marked subjective pronouns and the increasing numbers of invariant verbs may be interconnected processes (Denison 1996: 294–296, 1998: 206–212), in effect the gradual loss of subject-verb concord, but that is to stray towards grammaticalisation and so will not be developed here.

6.3 Pseudo-imperatives (conditionals)

Compare two different sentence patterns: the imperative and the conditional protasis. I will suggest that there is a gradient between them.

The prototypical imperative has the force of a directive:

(52)   Give me some money.

It can occur with *please* and with tag questions, can co-occur with the subject pronoun when negative, and cannot be used with a VP that is unselfcontrollable:

(53)   a.   *Give* me some money, *please.*
       b.   *Give* me some money, *will you?*
       c.   *Don't you give* me any money.
       d.   **Be tall.*

Conditional protases may be marked in a number of ways: by a subordinating conjunction, most commonly *if;* by subject-auxiliary inversion; perhaps by the use of a subjunctive verb; in certain circumstances by the imperative. The last-named is of course the relevant option here:

(54)   a.   "... *Stir* a whisker, Lungri, and I ram the Red Flower [*sc.* fire] down thy
            Gullet!" (1894 Kipling, *Jungle Book*, "Mowgli's brothers" [Macmillan, 1895] 28)
       b.   *Try* to be nice and people walk all over you.

This pattern is semantically similar to a conditional (*If you stir a whisker ...*) and can be called a pseudo-imperative. The verb form is clearly imperative, morphologically the base form of the verb and identical to the present subjunctive, but examples like (54) behave conversely to true imperatives with respect to the properties exemplified in (53).

An intermediate type retains some directive force and all the properties of (53) as well as approximating to a conditional protasis:

(55)   Give me some money and I'll let you go.

The conjunction *or* is similarly used to imply a negative condition, as in:

(56) a. Give me some money or I'll shoot.

    b. and do for goodness' sake try and realize that you're a pestilential scourge, or you'll find yourself in a most awful fix. (1898 Grahame, *The Reluctant Dragon* 19)

See McCawley (1988: II 708, 737–739), Quirk et al. (1985: 931–934), (Davies 1986: 161–228). The gradience here runs from true imperatives like (52) to pseudo-imperatives which are mere conditional protases, (54), via an intermediate type, (55)–(56), which has most of the properties of true imperatives combined with the conditional sense. This is certainly semantic gradience. In distributional terms it should count as syntactic gradience too, though whether this is intersective gradience depends on the analysis offered for pseudo-imperatives.

6.4 Prepositional verbs

Quirk et al. (1985: 1156, 1163–1156) and others have argued that two complementary analyses for prepositional verb structures may each capture aspects of the syntax:

(57)   [$_V$ rely] [$_{PP}$ on a friend]

and

(58)   [$_V$ rely on] [$_{NP}$ a friend]

They do not, however, appear to argue directly for gradience between the two structures.[11] Huddleston (1984: 200–203) tries to demonstrate that only (57) can be sustained, though if he is right it is clear at least that lexical and semantic structure would be at odds with the syntax for some prepositional verbs. There is in any case great variation among prepositional verbs in the degree of closeness between V and P, as shown by Quirk et al.'s (1985: 1166, Fig. 16.15). I will look at one special type.

6.5 Object to V

There are a number of verbs where the *to* which was formerly a marker of the following infinitive has now been reanalysed as belonging with the higher verb. Here is the older syntax:

(59) a. ... hatred against anything which might *contribute to bring on* the disease of which he died. (1858 PEO2.N6 [ARCHER])

    b. I have *taken to write* a little in a penny paper called the *Star*. (1856 [*OED*])

    c. *look forward to be disinherited; had been reduced to learn; I will not submit to be ruined* (1867/1867/1838–1839 [cited in Denison 1998: 266])

Normal usage for (59) since the second half of the nineteenth century would be complementation by *to* + *Ving*, with a period of variation for each verb:

(60) a. … that Celia *objected to go* (1871–1872 Eliot, *Middlemarch* x.87)
      b. but the signs she made of this were such as only Lydgate *was used to inter-pret*. (ibid. lxxviii.777)

(61) a. what he *objects to giving*, is a little return on rent-days to help a tenant to buy stock. (ibid. xxxviii.383)
      b. but she had *been* little *used to imagining* other people's states of mind. (ibid. lxxviii.777)

Such cases differ from routine alternation between complementation by *to*-infinitive and complementation by *Ving* (e.g., *prefer to V* ~ *prefer Ving*), since here the *to* is sufficiently important semantically and syntactically to be retained even with *Ving*.

I wrote in Denison (1998:266) that the change in complementation reflects two long-term changes. One is the rise of the prepositional verb, as OBJECT and *to* come to form a unit (and likewise the other cases exemplified in (59)). The other is the drift of the English infinitive from a somewhat more nominal to a verbal character, now virtually complete, and the concomitant dissociation of the infinitive marker *to* from the homonymous preposition. (In fact it is doubtful whether the English *to*-infinitive ever was a PP or its verbal formative ever wholly nominal; see now Los 1999: Ch. 11.) Consider the effect of these changes on *to depart*:

(62) a. Max objected to departure.
      b. Max objected to depart.
      c. Max objected to departing.

The former parallelism between (62a) and (62b) lost its force, and (62c) became necessary, since the gerund was the only form capable of combining the distribution of an NP with the possibility of its own verbal adjuncts and complements (e.g., *departing surreptitiously*).

There is another point of view. In (59), (60) and (62b) the *to* is perhaps simultaneously a preposition and an infinitival particle, since all the verbs concerned were used in exactly the same sense either with a *to*-PP or with a *to*-infinitive. Compare (62b) with (62a) and (63), respectively, which represent the two straightforward categorial possibilities:

(63) Max refused to depart.

If *to* in (62b) is partly prepositional,[12] there is intersective gradience. And the gradience has been resolved by the loss of that construction. This, therefore, can be regarded as another indication of the instability/markedness of intersective gradience.

6.6 I'm going Adverbial and V

I conclude this data survey with some examples which will, I predict, be very surprising to all British and some north American speakers:

(64) a. I'*m going* back there *and ask* her to marry me. (1906 [*OED*])
      b. "I'*m going* back *and tell* Terry and Gottlieb they can go to the devil ..."
          (1925 S. Lewis, *Arrowsmith* (Grossett & Dunlap) xxvii.300)
      c. I'*m going* out *and get* a girl for my picture. (1933 *King Kong* [movie], dir.
          Merian C. Cooper)
      d. I'*m going* in *and ask* him. (1934 *It Happened One Night* [movie], dir. Frank
          Capra)
      e. I'*m going* outside *and see* what fresh air smells like. (1939 *Destry Rides Again*
          [movie], dir. George Marshall)
      f. "I'*m going* over *and saddle* The Pi [a racehorse] now." (1944 *National Velvet*
          [movie], dir. Clarence Brown)
      g. I'*m going* home *and see* my wife and family. (1947 *It's a Wonderful Life*
          [movie], dir. Frank Capra)
      h. "You'*re going* right back into that office *and explain* to them ... (1949 *I Was
          a Male War Bride* [movie], dir. Howard Hawks)
      i. I'*m going* back to business *and make* myself a little dough. (1955 [*OED*])
      j. I'*m going* down below *and see* what I can [unintelligible] (1964 *Dr. Strange-
          love* ... [movie], dir. Stanley Kubrick)
      k. Sherry and I *are going* to Florida *and get* into the seashell business. (1991 G.
          Keillor, *Radio Romance* (Faber, 1992) 361)

A similar pattern occurs without *and*:

(65) a. I'*m going* back in a coupl'a' years ...*open* up a dress shop. (1997 *L.A. Confi-
          dential* [movie, set in early 1950s], dir. Curtis Hanson])
      b. I'*m going* up again next weekend. *Give* it another whirl. (1965 [*OED*])

Generally speaking, the phenomenon of 'pseudo-coordination' (Quirk et al.
1985: 978–979) in standard PDE disallows morphologically different verbs on either
side of *and*:

(66) a. *Try and behave.*
      b. We will *try and behave.*
      c. *He's *trying and behave.*

In my data (64)–(65), the second verb is a base form, as is normal in pseudo-
coordination, but the first verb is an *-ing* form, which is not. Notice that the first
verb is never directly adjacent to *and* (or to the second verb in the case of asyndetic
coordination), which suggests that the saliency of coordination must be reduced if
this construction is to be permitted. It is very tempting to regard the strange
construction above as dependent on a grammaticalisation gradient made familiar
by Hopper and Traugott (1993), which runs between the extremes of (67) and (68):

(67) I'm going$_1$ to the market.   [literal verb of motion + PP]

(68) I'm going$_2$ to/gonna solve this problem. [auxiliary of future incorporating *to*]

Since both usages co-exist in PDE, could our construction be a blend involving a reduction operation? Thus, for example,

(64a)   I'm going$_1$ back there and I'm going$_2$ to ask her to marry me →
         I'm going$_{1+2}$ back there and ask her to marry me

If so, the construction's origin is dependent on the existence of that synchronic gradience. The construction has sporadically been extended further:

(69)   I'*m coming* over there *and drag* you out myself. (1934 *It Happened One Night* [movie], dir. Frank Capra)

(70)   I'*m taking* him to the Sheriff *and make sure* he's destroyed. (1939 *Wizard of Oz* [movie], dir. Victor Fleming)

(71)   I'*ll be turning* the key *and see* if it works. (1997 Margaret McPhee, telephone, attested DD (10 Jan.))

I assume that (69)–(71) are in some way based on the I'*m going* Adverbial *and* V construction and do not in themselves involve gradience.

7.   Conclusion

I have looked at a selection of possible cases of gradience in recent English, including those where the gradience lies in the degree of category membership, i.e., closeness to the prototype — subsective gradience, and the logically similar case where subsective gradience within two adjacent categories can lead to gradience between categories — intersective gradience. Intersective gradience between categories will often involve the soft boundary between syntactic analyses, that is, intersective gradience between constructions. The data I have covered seem to me *prima facie* awkward for generative models of syntax. I am aware that some but not all could be handled under Grammaticalisation, some but not all could be taken as support for Construction Grammar.

Bas Aarts and I are beginning a collaboration in which we will take both horizontal and vertical snapshots of English — synchronic PDE, and recent and current change — using corpora. Possible outcomes of our research project range all the way from finding that gradience is entirely unnecessary or at least insignificant, through deciding that it is a marginal phenomenon which must be grafted on to some standard model of language at appropriate points, to claiming that it is so pervasive as to damage standard models beyond repair. I can't prejudge the outcome. What I have been doing here is more like an investigating magistrate, trying to decide whether there is a case to answer at a full-scale trial. I won't be at all surprised if some of the examples I have given don't stand up to scrutiny, but I think the weight of evidence is sufficient to justify further work. And so I want to suggest that historical linguists should certainly be alive to the possible existence of gradience in their data; and if it is there, they should work to find theoretical approaches which reflect that reality — and convince synchronic linguists of their value.

Notes

* I had a period of Research Leave in 1996–1997 for my work on a pronoun hierarchy in syntactic change (mentioned below). During that time I had the opportunity to read and reflect on several of the ideas discussed here, and I am grateful to the British Academy for their contribution to that period of leave. Revision of this paper has been greatly aided by helpful comments received from Bas Aarts, Dick Hudson, Alison Cort, and two anonymous referees, though of course the usual disclaimers apply.

1. This revolution in primary school teaching of English language was launched in 1997–1998. After protests by a few linguists who saw the original glossary which had been issued to schools (one of the appendices in Section 3 of anon. 1998), a revised and extended glossary was commissioned in collaboration between them and the Department for Education and Employment and published on the web in 2000, now at http://www.standards.dfee.gov.uk/literacy/publications/

2. Aarts (2000) notes a few recent attempts to consider fuzzy categories within formal syntax.

3. For the quantifiers *much* and *few* Hudson finds evidence for categorisation as both Adjective and Noun (1990:307–308), which threatens to pull this case into the arena of intersective gradience. Aarts (2000) makes the following point: "It is important to see that the existence and extent of pervasiveness of I[ntersective] G[radience] are a function of the categories of the adopted taxonomic framework. Thus, for example, if it is claimed that there is boundary fluidity between two categories α and β, then it must first be established that α and β actually exist as form classes, i.e., that they are 'grammatically real'."

4. I note that in a paper first published in 1944, Sapir says without comment: "*More* and *less* apply to both count and measure" (1949:131).

5. An anonymous reviewer points out that *powerhouse* is less easy to imagine as a predicative adjective than as an attributive one. If true — and certainly I have no examples of predicative adjectival *powerhouse* — example (10) would still be sufficient to classify the word as an adjective.

6. I am grateful to Bas Aarts for access to examples from the International Corpus of English (Great Britain) (ICE-GB) and British National Corpus (BNC), and to Douglas Biber and Edward Finegan for the use of A Representative Corpus of Historical English Registers (ARCHER). For other data sources see the list of references.

7. Scholars disagree on whether semantic gradability can be found in nouns. Gnutzmann, for example, argues as follows (1975:421): "Though gradability belongs to the province of semantics, it is nevertheless not completely detached from grammar: in opposition to Sapir [1949] we would like to claim that only adjectives and adverbs admit gradation."

8. A referee rightly points out that definitions of the category Adjective in earlier English could not include an inability to take NP complements, so that examples like (41) would not in themselves demonstrate prepositional character *at the time of their writing*. In that case, though, what they might demonstrate is that the whole categories A and P have since become better differentiated: most complement-taking adjectives have either lost that property or now take PP rather than NP complements.

9. Newmeyer (1998:201–202) would claim that it can be *either* P *or* A but not both simultaneously.

10. For an introduction to Eleanor Rosch's psychological work on categories, see for instance Rosch (1978), Taylor (1995).

11. Elsewhere in the verb complementation system they argue for intersective gradience between certain infinitival structures (1985:1216–1220).

12. Syntactic proof is difficult to find. Stranding of prepositions (*That's what she objected to*) is not the same as ellipsis after infinitival *to* (*And she refused to*), which in any case is only found sporadically from the late eighteenth century and is rare before mid-nineteenth century (Denison 1998:201–202). Coordination of an infinitive with a nominal after *to* is very rare; a fifteenth-century example in Denison (1993:189) repeats *to* before NP and before verb. For Old English see Los (1999:242).

References

Data sources

ARCHER = A Representative Corpus of Historical English Registers; see footnote 6.
BNC = British National Corpus; published on the web by Oxford University Computing Services.
FLOB = The Freiburg-LOB Corpus of British English; published on The New ICAME Corpus Collection on CD-ROM.
Frown = The Freiburg-Brown Corpus of American English; published by ICAME.
ICE-GB = International Corpus of English (Great Britain); published by the Survey of English Usage; see footnote 6.
OED = Simpson, J. A. & E. S. C. Weiner. 1992. *The Oxford English Dictionary: CD-ROM version*, 2nd ed. Oxford: Oxford University Press.
OED Online = *The Oxford English dictionary*, 2nd ed. And 3rd ed. in progress; published on the web by Oxford University Press. [searched Sept. 2000]

Other individual examples as noted in text.

Secondary works

Aarts, Bas. 1998. "Binominal Noun Phrases in English". *Transactions of the Philological Society* 96.117–158.
Aarts, Bas. 2000. Modelling Gradience. MS., University College London.
Anderson, John M. 1997. *A Notional Theory of Syntactic Categories*. (= *Cambridge Studies in Linguistics*, 82.) Cambridge: Cambridge University Press.
anon. 1998. *The National Literacy Strategy: Framework for teaching*. 2nd edn. Sudbury: DfEE Publications.
Bolinger, Dwight. 1976. "Meaning and Memory". *Forum Linguisticum* 1.1–14.
Croft, William. 2000. *Explaining Language Change: An evolutionary approach*. (= *Longman Linguistics Library*.) London: Longman.
Davies, Eirlys. 1986. *The English Imperative*. London: Croom Helm.
Denison, David. 1986. "On Word Order in Old English". *Dutch Quarterly Review* 16.277–295.
Denison, David. 1993. *English Historical Syntax: Verbal constructions*. (= *Longman Linguistics Library*.) London & New York: Longman.

Denison, David. 1996. "The Case of the Unmarked Pronoun". *English Historical Linguistics 1994: Papers from the 8th International Conference on English Historical Linguistics (8.ICEHL, Edinburgh, 19–23 September 1994).* (= Current Issues in Linguistic Theory, 135.) ed. by Derek Britton, 287–299. Amsterdam & Philadelphia: John Benjamins.

Denison, David. 1998. "Syntax". *The Cambridge History of the English Language,* vol. 4, *1776–1997,* ed. by Suzanne Romaine, 92–329. Cambridge: Cambridge University Press.

Emonds, Joseph. 1976. *A Transformational Approach to English Syntax.* New York: Academic Press.

Gnutzmann, Claus. 1975. "Some Aspects of Grading". *English Studies* 75.421–433.

Harris, Alice C. & Lyle Campbell. 1995. *Historical Syntax in Cross-Linguistic Perspective.* (= Cambridge Studies in Linguistics, 74.) Cambridge: Cambridge University Press.

Haspelmath, Martin. 1998. "Does Grammaticalization Need Reanalysis?". *Studies in Language* 22.315–351.

Henry, Alison. 1997. "Viewing Change in Progress: The loss of V2 in Hiberno-English imperatives". *Parameters of Morphosyntactic Change* ed. by Ans van Kemenade & Nigel Vincent, 273–296. Cambridge: Cambridge University Press.

Hopper, Paul J. & Elizabeth Closs Traugott. 1993. *Grammaticalization.* (= Cambridge Textbooks in Linguistics.) Cambridge: Cambridge University Press.

Huddleston, Rodney. 1984. *Introduction to the Grammar of English.* (= Cambridge Textbooks in Linguistics.) Cambridge: Cambridge University Press.

Huddleston, Rodney & Geoffrey K. Pullum (in prep.) *The Cambridge Grammar of English.* Cambridge: Cambridge University Press.

Hudson, R. A. 1990. *English Word Grammar.* Oxford: Basil Blackwell.

Langacker, Ronald W. 1987. *Foundations of Cognitive Grammar,* vol 1. Stanford: Stanford University Press.

Leech, Geoffrey & Lu Li. 1995. "Indeterminacy Between Noun Phrases and Adjective Phrases as Complements of the English Verb". *The Verb in Contemporary English: Theory and description* ed. by Bas Aarts & Charles F. Meyer, 183–202. Cambridge: Cambridge University Press.

Lightfoot, David. 1999. *The Development of Language: Acquisition, change, and evolution.* (= Blackwell/Maryland Lectures in Language and Cognition, 1.) Malden, MA & Oxford: Blackwell.

Los, Bettelou. 1999. *Infinitival Complementation in Old and Middle English.* The Hague: Thesus. [Ph. D. dissertation, Vrije Universiteit, Amsterdam, 2000]

Maling, Joan M. 1983. "Transitive Adjectives: A case of categorial reanalysis". *Linguistic Categories: Auxiliaries and related puzzles* ed. by Frank Heny & Barry Richards (= Synthese Language Library, 19.), vol 1, 253–289. Dordrecht: Reidel.

Marchand, Hans. 1969. *The Categories and Types of Present-Day English Word-Formation: A synchronic-diachronic approach.* 2nd ed. Munich: Beck'sche Verlags Buchhandlung.

McCawley, James D. 1988. *The Syntactic Phenomena of English.* 2 vols. Chicago: University of Chicago Press.

Newmeyer, Frederick J. 1998. *Language Form and Language Function.* (= Language, Speech and Communication.) Cambridge, MA & London: MIT Press.

Quirk, Randolph et al. 1985. *A Comprehensive Grammar of the English Language.* London & New York: Longman.

Rosch, Eleanor. 1978. "Principles of Categorization". *Cognition and Categorization* ed. by Eleanor Rosch & B. B. Lloyd, 27–48. Hillsdale, NJ: Lawrence Erlbaum.

Ross, John Robert. 1972. "The Category Squish: Endstation Hauptwort". *Papers from the 8th Regional Meeting of the Chicago Linguistic Society* ed. by Paul Peranteau et al., 316–328. Chicago: CLS.

Ross, John Robert. 1973. "A Fake NP Squish". *New Ways of Analyzing Variation in English* ed. by Charles-James N. Bailey & Roger W. Shuy, 96–140. Washington, D.C.: Georgetown University Press.

Sapir, Edward. 1949. "Grading: A study in semantics." *Selected Writings of Edward Sapir: Language, culture, and personality.* ed. by David G. Mandelbaum, 122–149. Berkeley & Los Angeles: University of California Press/London: Cambridge University Press.

Taylor, John R. 1995. *Linguistic Categorization: Prototypes in linguistic theory.* 2nd ed. Oxford: Clarendon Press.

Timberlake, Alan. 1977. "Reanalysis and Actualization in Syntactic Change". *Mechanisms of Syntactic Change* ed. by Charles N. Li, 141–177. Austin, TX & London: University of Texas Press.

Warner, A. R. 1990. "Reworking the History of English Auxiliaries". *Papers from the 5th International Conference on English Historical Linguistics: Cambridge, 6–9 April 1987.* (= *Current Issues in Linguistic Theory,* 65) ed. by Sylvia Adamson et al., 537–558. Amsterdam & Philadelphia: John Benjamins.

Distinctive vowel length in Old French
Evidence and Implications

Randall Gess
University of Utah

1. Introduction

This paper addresses the question of whether or not distinctive vowel length arose in Old French (OF) as the result of the deletion of syllable-final consonants.[1] Of the syllable-final consonants that were lost (see Gess' (1998a) full treatment of this process), I look specifically at the deletion of /S/ (/S/ = [s] or [z]), shown in (1), where a colon indicates vowel length.

(1) Loss of syllable-final /S/ in OF
    isle "island" [izlə] > [iːlə]
    feste "feast" [fɛstə] > [fɛːtə]

I focus on /S/-deletion for two reasons. First, the type of evidence I use (rhymes in poetry) cannot be used with the loss of other consonants, due to vowel quality (rather than quantity) changes which accompanied their deletion (e.g., nasality on vowels with nasal consonant deletion ([antə] (*ante* "aunt") > [ãːtə]); the absorption of syllable-final /l/ into the nucleus, resulting in a diphthong ([albə] (*albe* "dawn") > [awbə])).[2] Second, there is widespread agreement on the dating of syllable-final /S/-deletion (from the 11th to the middle of the 13th century), due to strong textual evidence for it. Datings for the other changes have been controversial (Gess 1999).

Most traditional scholarship on OF assumes that compensatory lengthening (CL) accompanied syllable-final /S/ deletion. However, empirical evidence previously provided for CL in OF has been scant at best, and its reality has been questioned in more recent work. I begin, then, by discussing some of the traditional scholarship and the recent challenges to it, in §2. In §3, I provide the results from a detailed analysis of textual data which reveals that the deletion of syllable-final /S/ was indeed accompanied by CL. The findings also suggest that the length distinction introduced by CL was lost in the 16th century, thus shedding new light on the controversial question of whether there was distinctive vowel length at this later period. In §4, I turn to the more theoretical implications of my findings, relating to the notions of structure preservation and quantity sensitivity.

2.   Previous scholarship

Most often cited as evidence for the traditionally-held view that CL accompanied syllable-final /S/-deletion are remarks made by 16th-century grammarians, such as the ones shown in (2), taken from Pope (1952: 206).

(2)   Statements on lengthening by 16th-century grammarians

    a.   "… when *s* is elided before a consonant, as in *est*, they sound a double or triple sound *eee*" (Erasmus 1528)

    b.   "*Afin qu'il gemist* … the interpolation of this letter *s* shows that this letter *i* is to be pronounced differently from the way it is pronounced in the present tense *il gemit*" (Estienne 1582)

    c.   "Every *s* mute before a consonant … lengthens the preceding vowel" (Bèze 1584)

    d.   "Nothing can offend the ear more than the lengthening of the short vowel and the shortening of the long …" (Bèze 1584)

Indeed, mention by grammarians of vowel length in this context continues into the 17th century (Hindret 1687; La Touche 1696). However, the issue of vowel length in general appears to have been a matter of some debate at that time (Bullock 1997: 26, 31–32; Monferran 1999: 71). The issue of phonological vowel length in the 16th and 17th centuries continues to be a vexed question for today's scholars (see, for example, Bullock 1997; Morin 2000).[3]

When the traditional view has been challenged, the argument generally made against CL has been that remarks made by 16th and 17th-century grammarians, as well as by prosodists, were due not to a true long/short distinction in French, but solely to a desire to force the French language into the "superior" Latin mold (Bickakjian 1986; Monferran 1999). Bichakjian (1986: 18) makes the important comment that "since prosodists also admonished poets not to couple in rhyme words with 'short' and 'long' vowels it could safely be concluded that even the learned natives had not developed such a fine feeling for vowel length".

In fact, Bichakjian does not deny that vowel lengthening accompanied the loss of syllable-final /S/, but he claims that it was non-distinctive. His claim is, then, that the lengthened vowels were purely phonetic, and not phonemic. This suggests that the lengthening of vowels would be unavailable for exploitation by poets, as unavailability to poetic schemes is one of the defining characteristics of purely phonetic rules (P2 postlexical rules according to Kaisse's 1990 typology). Bichakjian points to the remark made by Pope that "No direct evidence of differentiation of quantity in vowels is afforded by the rhymes in Old or Middle French. Fifteenth-century poets like Villon couple together freely in rhyme words like *abbēsse*: *mĕsse*, *honnēstes*: *fillĕtes*, *maistre*: *mĕtre* ..." (Pope 1952: 205). Although Pope claims that there was CL following the deletion of *s*, she states here (falsely, as we will see) that there is no direct evidence for it from Old and Middle French poetry, and relies instead solely on the words of 16th-century grammarians.

What I want to do in the following section is to challenge the assertion that Old and Middle French poetry offers no direct evidence for CL. But first let me say that it is extremely problematic to rely in this matter solely on statements made by 16th and 17th-century grammarians, considering that by then, at least two and a half centuries had transpired since the loss of syllable-final /S/. It is impossible to conclude, on the basis of these statements, that poets did or did not feel the distinction between long and short vowels in the intervening period. In fact, I suspect that Bichakjian (1986) and Monferran (1999) might be correct with respect to the motivation of the grammarians and prosodists in their insistence on a vowel length distinction, but I would like to suggest that this is not because there never were contrastive length distinctions from the latter half of the 13th century through the 15th century, but precisely because these distinctions were beginning to disappear in the 16th century.

3.   Data analysis

I looked at 116,755 lines of poetry from the 12th century to the end of the 16th century (see the appendix for details). Before going to my findings, let me briefly discuss the types of rhymes that I considered. In looking for CL following the deletion of syllable-final /S/, one immediately thinks to look for the rhyme types shown in (3), where V stands for any vowel and C for any consonant. The sub-scripted variables mean, of course, that in the rhyming pairs, the vowels and consonants have to match each other.

(3)   Relevant rhyme types for showing CL
   a.   Evidence for CL: orthographic rhyme matches
      $V_iC_j : V_iC_j$
      $V_isC_j : V_isC_j$ (*s* orthographic only)
      $V_iC_je : V_iC_je$ (*e* orthographic, here schwa ([ə]))
      $V_isC_je : V_isC_je$ (*s* orthographic only; *e* orthographic, here schwa ([ə]))
   b.   Evidence against CL: orthographic rhyme mismatches
      $V_iC_j : V_isC_j$ (*s* orthographic only)
      $V_iC_je : V_isC_je$ (*s* orthographic only; *e* orthographic, here schwa ([ə]))

A final syllable with schwa as its peak does not count on its own in rhyming schemes. That is, it cannot simply rhyme with another schwa. Rather, such syllables are entirely dependent on the quality of the preceding syllable for participation in rhyming pairs. Furthermore, a syllable followed by schwa must rhyme with a syllable likewise followed by schwa.

Following the deletion of /S/, an overwhelming number of matches (3a) would indicate that CL did occur, in which case orthographic *s* might be taken as an orthographic indicator of the resultant length (see Morin 1991:51). An overwhelming number of mismatches (3b) would indicate that CL did not occur (or was no longer present, depending on the date of the poem being considered), in which case *s* would be nothing more than an etymological remnant.

The problem with looking for rhymes of these types is that, before syllable-final /S/, or along with the post-/S/-deletion lengthening of vowels, most vowels underwent an important change in quality (/a/ → [a]; /e/ → [ɛ]; /ɔ/ → [o]). Given these qualitative changes, the orthographic rhyme types shown in (4) must be ruled out, because a preference for them may indicate not a grouping based on common length, but on quality alone. (It is worth pointing out here that the consonant in all rhyme types is, by far, most frequently /t/.)

(4)   Orthographic rhyme types ruled out[4]

    a $aC_j(e) : aC_j(e)$ (may rhyme because both short, or because both [a])
        $asC_j(e) : asC_j(e)$ (may rhyme because both long, or because both [a])
    e $eC_j(e) : eC_j(e)$ (may rhyme because both short, or because both [e])
        $esC_j(e) : esC_j(e)$ (may rhyme because both long, or because both [ɛ])
    o $oC_j(e) : oC_j(e)$ (may rhyme because both short, or because both [ɔ])
        $osC_j(e) : osC_j(e)$ (may rhyme because both long, or because both [o])

This leaves the high vowels /i/ and /u/, as well as the high diphthong /ui/. No differentiation of quality occurred with the high vowels, as pointed out by Bichakjian (1986:19–20), and generally agreed upon by Romance scholars. So the rhyme types that were included in this study are listed in (5).

(5)   Orthographic rhyme types included
    a. Evidence for CL: orthographic rhyme matches
        i $iC_j(e) : iC_j(e)$ $isC_j(e) : isC_j(e)$
        u $uC_j(e) : uC_j(e)$ $usC_j(e) : usC_j(e)$
        ui $uiC_j(e) : uiC_j(e)$ $uisC_j(e) : uisC_j(e)$
    b. Evidence against CL: orthographic rhyme mismatches
        i $iC_j(e) : isC_j(e)$
        u $uC_j(e) : usC_j(e)$
        ui $uiC_j(e) : uisC_j(e)$

The percentage of relevant rhyme matches (any of the types shown in (5a)) from the works consulted is displayed in the graph in Figure 1.

The periods shown are by century, with the 13th century divided between the first half (grouped with the 12th century), when /S/ is still possibly intact, and the

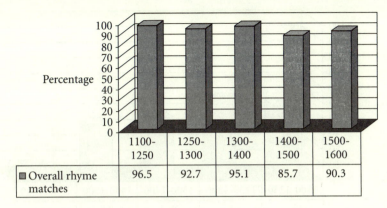

Percentage	1100-1250	1250-1300	1300-1400	1400-1500	1500-1600
■ Overall rhyme matches	96.5	92.7	95.1	85.7	90.3

Figure 1. Overall orthographic rhyme matches by period

second half (grouped on its own), when /S/ had been deleted from pronunciation (but was still orthographically present). These periods, properly containing the interval surrounding the loss of /S/, are the crucial OF periods. The other periods are included to determine the effect of /S/-loss (if any) into Middle and Renaissance French.

What we see in Figure 1 is a remarkably level rate of orthographic rhyme matches through all periods (including the interval surrounding the loss of /S/). Although there is a slight dip in the number of orthographic rhyme matches in the 15th century, the percentage of matches for all periods shown is quite similar, and is very high, significantly above chance. It appears, then, that the loss of /S/ had no impact on rhyming schemes, suggesting that some trace of it (presumably its timing slot) remained.

Following the slight dip in the 15th century, there is a rise again in the 16th century. Is the 15th-century dip a fluke due to the arbitrary selection of texts? In fact, I do not think it is. We will see, below, that the 16th-century rise is an illusion, due to a dramatic fall in the use of any forms with orthographic s in the relevant rhyme types, so that the vast majority of rhyme types were those with a vowel followed by a consonant, with or without a following schwa, but with no s.

Figure 2 charts the percentages of forms with s in the relevant rhyme types through the same periods. Here I believe the increase in forms with s in the relevant rhyme types in the latter half of the 13th century is purely coincidental. In two of the texts from this period, between 30% and 35% of the forms in the relevant rhyme types were with s, which fits in approximately with the period before and the two periods after. But in the two other texts from the latter half of the 13th century, there was an unusually high number of forms with s, 74.2% in one and 62.9% in the other. Notice that the use of forms with s in the 16th century is dramatically lower than during any other period.

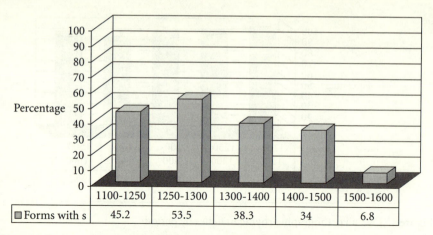

Figure 2. Forms with *s* in relevant rhyme types, by period

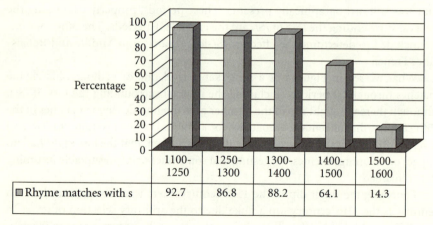

Figure 3. Orthographic rhyme matches in rhymes with *s*, by period

Figure 3 shows the percentages of rhyme matches in only those rhymes involving at least one form with *s*.

Here we see that the level of matches, again very high and significantly above chance, is relatively stable through the 14th century. In the 15th century, we see a rather large dropping off, which suggests that length was becoming unstable during this period. It should be noted that the earliest text analyzed from this century is dated between 1430 and 1440, and in that first text the level of matches is 94.4%, so that the instability could be a development in the second half of the century, when the other two texts were written. These texts had percentages of 58.4% and 50%. We notice again that the 16th century saw a dramatic decrease in matches in rhymes involving *s*.

My interpretation of the data in Figures 1–3 is that the lengthening that accompanied the deletion of syllable-final /S/ was distinctive through at least the 14th century, a century and a half after the deletion occurred. The evidence is very strong that from the middle of the 13th century through the 14th century, poets consciously segregated rhymes with orthographic s, an orthographic marker of length (see also Morin 1991:51),[5] from those without it. Again, in the 15th century, or at least in the latter half of the 15th century, we see an instability in the perception of length. This instability is followed by an obvious, cataclysmic loss of distinctive vowel length in the following century.

What we have seen shows that the periods shown in Figure 4 are linguistically significant with respect to syllable-final /S/ and distinctive vowel length.

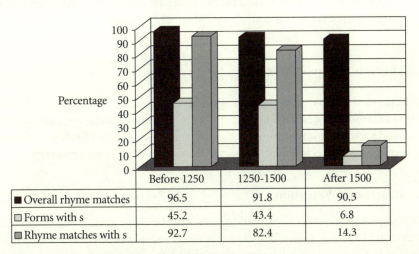

	Before 1250	1250-1500	After 1500
■ Overall rhyme matches	96.5	91.8	90.3
☐ Forms with s	45.2	43.4	6.8
▨ Rhyme matches with s	92.7	82.4	14.3

Figure 4. Linguistically significant periods

When the data are grouped this way, we see that Period I (prior to 1250), before the deletion of syllable-final /S/, is remarkably similar to Period II (from 1250 to 1500) and following the deletion of /S/. Period III (the 16th century) is altogether different with respect to the treatment of forms and rhymes with orthographic s.

To summarize, we have seen that the traditionally-held view that CL accompanied the loss of syllable-final /S/ is correct. Indeed, we have seen that not only did lengthening occur, but that it was distinctive. Pope's statement that rhymes from Old and Middle French poetry do not provide evidence for the lengthening is incorrect. We have seen that poets consciously segregated rhymes with orthographic s, a marker of length, from those without it. Claims that 16th-century grammarians' remarks were due to a desire to imitate Latin may well be true. However, this is not because there never was vowel length between the 13th and 16th centuries, as Bichakjian (1986) claims, but because the distinctive length that did result from the loss of syllable-final /S/ was lost in the 16th century.

These findings thus shed important new light on the controversial question of whether there was contrastive vowel length in the 16th and 17th centuries (Bullock 1997; Morin 2000). I can only interpret the data presented here as suggesting, contra Morin (2000), an answer in the negative. Why else would poets have ceased so dramatically, in the 16th century, to segregate the rhyme types in question?[6] Further, why would the orthographic marking of etymological s have fallen off so sharply at the same time? A disappearance of distinctive length also provides a reasonable explanation for this fact, since orthographic s had been, since the mid-13th century, simply a marker of length. Finally, if there were truly a phonological vowel length contrast in the language in the 16th and 17th centuries, what is the explanation for the fact that it was a matter of debate among grammarians? This is totally unexpected for a truly distinctive feature of a language.

4.   Theoretical implications

As mentioned at the outset, the findings presented here have implications for the notion of structure preservation, as it applies to phonological change. I discuss this next, and then some implications of the findings for our understanding of the OF metrical system, especially with respect to the notion of quantity sensitivity.

4.1 Structure preservation

With respect to structure preservation, consider the claim made by de Chene and Anderson (1979:508), that "the existence of an independently-motivated length contrast in the language is a necessary condition for compensatory lengthening", i.e., "no language INTRODUCES distinctions of length into its phonological system through compensatory lengthening alone". In other words, de Chene and Anderson claim that CL is structure preserving. In order to defend that position in the case of OF, they have to claim that there was phonemic vowel length in OF before the CL discussed in the previous sections. Indeed, they make precisely this claim. Specifically, de Chene and Anderson (1979:523) make the claim that "distinctive length was introduced in French, primarily during the course of the 10th and 11th centuries after the deletion of intervocalic t and d". They provide several examples in support of their claim, such as OF *baailler* "yawn" < Latin *bataculare* and OF *seel* "seal" < Latin *sigillum*, all of which Gess (1998b) shows in OF poetry. Gess (1997) provides many more of the same type. However, in each of the examples, the relevant sequence was clearly counted as constituting two separate syllables and not as one syllable with a long vowel. Such examples are abundant, and I have to date found no counter-examples through the middle of the thirteenth century. That I have found no counter-examples is surprising in itself, given the high degree of variation found in other aspects of OF poetry.

So the fact that CL did accompany the loss of syllable-final consonant deletion, as I have shown (at least with respect to /S/), together with the fact that there was no pre-existing vowel length in OF (contra de Chene & Anderson 1979), seriously calls into question the validity of structure preservation as a theoretical principle relevant to phonological change. However, Gess (1998b) provides further support, together with Lin (1997), for Hayes' (1989) suggestion that CL is mora conserving. I suggest that mora conservation, the most trivial possible interpretation of structure preservation, falls out from two fundamental aspects of Optimality Theory: faithfulness and the principle of minimal violation. There is no independent principle of structure preservation operating on phonological change; rather, its effects are derived from the more general principles of faithfulness and minimal violation.

4.2 OF stress and quantity sensitivity

'Quantity sensitivity' is generally construed as defining systems in which certain segments, marked with a mora, are prosodically active (Hayes 1995: 52). The term is most often used with respect to stress assignment, in which case it is thought of as a parameter, but according to Hayes, prosodic activity may also include participation in "weight-based segmental rules, minimal word requirements, [and] quantitative meter" (1995: 53). Not surprisingly, then, mora conservation is often considered a property of quantity sensitive systems. The question then arises as to whether OF was quantity sensitive, since as we have seen, it was definitely mora conserving with respect to /S/-deletion.

The problem with defining OF as a quantity-sensitive language is that reference to quantity is not necessary in defining the stress pattern of the language, in which the final syllable is stressed unless it contains a schwa, in which case the penultimate syllable is stressed. Since OF was, then, quantity insensitive in its assignment of stress, perhaps we must rethink mora conservation as a phenomenon particular to quantity sensitive systems. However, while it is true that reference to quantity is never necessary in defining the stress pattern of the language, there is at least one other property of OF besides mora conservation that is characteristic of quantity sensitive languages, at least according to Hayes (1995): namely, vowel reduction in weak position. Diphthongization under stress (presumably preceded by lengthening), a very salient property of OF, might also be construed as a property of quantity sensitive systems.[7]

The upshot of this discussion is that if we describe the OF metrical system as quantity sensitive, then mora conservation and the other quantity sensitivity effects are expected, but the fact that its quantity sensitivity was irrelevant to stress assignment needs explanation. If, on the other hand, we describe OF as quantity insensitive, then stress assignment requires no explanation, but the quantity sensitivity effects do.

An obvious suggestion to make here is that we rethink the notion of quantity sensitivity. This has already been addressed in a somewhat different context by Alber (1997). She suggests "that the concept of quantity sensitivity is neither adequate nor necessary" as a theoretical construct. I agree, as it is clear that we must allow both for a type of quantity sensitivity that determines stress, and for a type that induces mora and rhythm-based effects. It seems inappropriate to attribute the two types of behavior to the same theoretical construct.

Appendix

Text	Date	Author	Lang. represented in ms.
Enéas	2nd half 12th	unknown	Norman
Le Livre des Manières	1174–1178	de Fougères	western zone of Langued'Oïl
Le Roman de Tristan	last ¼ 12th	Béroul	eastern Norman
Le Roman de la Rose	1225–30	de Lorris	Champenois
Escanor (I)	1280	d'Amiens (G.)	Franco-Picard
Fou (Dixième Conte…)	2nd half 13th	unknown	few Champenois traits
Les Oeuvres Complètes	2nd half 13th	Rutebeuf	Français
Du Bouchier d'Abevile	13th	d'Amiens (E.)	Picard/Franco-Picard
Oeuvres (I, II)	1340–60	de Machaut	Champenois
La Prison Amoureuse; Le Paradis d'Amour; L'Orloge Amoureus	1361–73	Froissart	Picard
Griselidis	1395	Unknown	Français (some Picard)
Oeuvres Complètes (I, II)	14th/15th	Deschamps	Champenois
Cycle de Mystères	1430–40	Unknown	Français
Myst. de la Résurrection (I)	1456	Unknown	Français
Le Lais; Le Testament	1456–61	Villon	Français
Recueil de Repues Franches	1480	Unknown	Français
Les Amours d'Aymée	2nd half 16th	de Brach	no dialectal traits
Les Eglogues et Aultres…	1555–65	Bereau	author Poitevin
Les Oeuvres Poétiques (III)	1578	de Nuysement	no mention

Notes

1. The question, brought up by an anonymous reviewer, of whether lengthening in fact preceded the deletion of syllable-final consonants in OF (as Hajek (1997) suggests, at least for the deletion of syllable-final nasal consonants) is not addressed here. My principal goal is to ascertain whether

there was distinctive length in OF following the loss of syllable-final consonants. Even if allophonic lengthening preceded consonant loss, length could only be distinctive once the consonants (i.e., the conditioning environment) were lost. For the purposes of this paper, I follow traditional terminology in referring to the lengthening in question as 'compensatory lengthening' (CL).

2. Indeed, as we will see, this same concern holds for an important subset of rhymes with syllable-final /S/ as well.

3. Morin (2000) claims to have found evidence for a phonological vowel length distinction in the 16th-century 'vers mesurés' of Jean-Antoine de Baïf. Bullock (1997) reaches the opposite conclusion on the basis of the same works (a conclusion supported by the results of this study, as we will see).

4. In (4) and (5), the parenthetical *es* (schwas) are to be interpreted as either both present or both absent.

5. The data that Morin discusses here, from a biblical glossary written in Hebrew characters, provides additional evidence for compensatory lengthening. The Hebrew character *aleph* is used in place of etymological *s*.

6. One reviewer suggests the possibility of a rhyming convention based purely on orthography. This begs the question, however, of why an orthographically-based convention specifically targeting this segment would have come into being at this particular time, as there is no evidence for a wholesale switch to orthographically-based rhyming schemes during this period.

7. Hayes (1995:84) notes that in quantity insensitive languages which manifest lengthening, "it is typically (though not always) phonetic in character, falling short of the duration given to true phonological long vowels". I assume that this shorter duration would not easily give rise to diphthongization.

References

Alber, Birgit. 1997. "Quantity Sensitivity as the Result of Constraint Interaction". *Phonology in Progress — Progress in Phonology. HIL Phonology Papers* III ed. by Geert Booij & Jeroen van de Weijen, 1–45.

Bèze, Théodore de. 1584. *De Francicae linguae recta pronuntiatione*. Geneva. [Reprinted in 1868. Berlin: Tobler.]

Bichakjian, Bernard. 1986. "When Do Lengthened Vowels Become Long?". *Studies in Compensatory Lengthening* ed. by Leo Wetzels & Engin Sezer, 11–36. Foris: Dordrecht.

Bullock, Barbara. 1997. "Quantitative Verse in a Quantity-Insensitive Language: Baïf's vers mesurés". *Journal of French Language Studies* 7.23–45.

de Chene, Brent & Stephen R. Anderson. 1979. "Compensatory Lengthening". *Language* 55.505–535.

Erasmus. 1528. *De recta latini graecique sermonis pronunciatione*.

Estienne, H. 1582. *Traicté de la conformité du langage françois auec le grec*. [Reprinted in 1853. L. Feugère.]

Gess, Randall. 1997. "Compensatory Lengthening and Structure Preservation Revisited". Paper presented at the Annual Meeting of the Linguistic Society of America, Chicago, Illinois, January 2–5.

Gess, Randall. 1998a. "Old French NoCoda Effects From Constraint Interaction". *Probus* 10.207–218.

Gess, Randall. 1998b. "Compensatory Lengthening and Structure Preservation Revisited". *Phonology* 15.353–366.

Gess, Randall. 1999. "Rethinking the Dating of Old French Syllable-Final Consonant Loss". *Diachronica* 16.261–296.

Hajek, John. 1997. *Universals of Sound Change in Nasalization*. Oxford & Boston: Blackwell.

Hayes, Bruce. 1989. "Compensatory Lengthening in Moraic Phonology". *Linguistic Inquiry* 20.253–306.

Hayes, Bruce. 1995. *Metrical Stress Theory. Principles and case studies*. Chicago: University of Chicago Press.

Hindret, Jean. 1687. *L'art de bien prononcer et de bien parler la langue françoise*. Paris: d'Houry. [Reprinted in 1973. Geneva: Slatkine Reprints.]

Kaisse, Ellen M. 1990. "Toward a Typology of Postlexical Rules". *The Phonology-Syntax Connection* ed. by Sharon Inkelas & Draga Zec, 127–143. Chicago: University of Chicago Press.

La Touche, Pierre de. 1696. *L'art de bien parler français*. Amsterdam. [Reprinted in 1973. Geneva: Slatkine Reprints.]

Lin, Yen-Hwei. 1997. "Syllabic and Moraic Structures in Piro". *Phonology* 14.403–436.

Monferran, Jean-Charles. 1999. "Le Dialogue de l'Ortografe e Prononciacion Françoęse de Jacques Peletier du Mans: De l'oeil, de l'oreille et de l'esprit". *Nouvelle Revue du Seizième Siècle* 17.67–83.

Morin, Yves-Charles. 1991. "Old French Stress Patterns and Closed Syllable Adjustment". *New Analyses in Romance Linguistics* ed. by Dieter Wanner & Douglas A. Kibbee, 49–76. Amsterdam & Philadelphia: John Benjamins.

Morin, Yves-Charles. 2000. "La prononciation et la prosodie du français du XVIe siècle selon le témoignage de Jean-Antoine de Baïf". *Langue Française* 126.9–28.

Pope, Mildred K. 1952. *From Latin to Modern French with Especial Consideration of Anglo-Norman*. 2nd ed. Manchester: Manchester University Press.

Remains of a submerged continent

Preaspiration in the languages of Northwest Europe[*]

Gunnar Ólafur Hansson
University of Chicago

1. Introduction

Preaspiration can be defined pretheoretically as the development of a period of voicelessness — seemingly 'out of thin air' — preceding a consonant, typically a voiceless stop, where this aspiration acts phonologically as if it were an integral part of that consonant. Icelandic is probably the best known example of a language with preaspiration; some examples are shown in (1). Note that preaspiration has two manifestations: 'preaspiration proper' as in (1a) and 'sonorant devoicing' as in (1b), whereby a sonorant becomes voiceless before a [+spread glottis] ('fortis') stop. Throughout this paper, the unmodified term 'preaspiration' will be used in this broader sense.

(1) Examples from Modern Icelandic:
  a. Preaspiration proper:
    hattur "hat" = [hahtʏr] ([ha̤tʏr])   cf. *hatur* "hate" = [haːtʏr]
    opna "open (v)" = [ɔhpna] ([ɔ̤pna])   cf. *ofna* "oven (GPL)" = [ɔpna]
  b. Sonorant devoicing:
    valt "rolled (3SG)" = [val̥t]   cf. *vald* "power" = [valt]
    lampi "lamp" = [lam̥pɪ]   cf. *lambi* "lamb (DSG)" = [lampɪ]

Preaspiration seems to be rare cross-linguistically, at least in the Old World. However, it appears in a cluster of languages spoken in a mostly contiguous area in Northwest (NW) Europe. The languages involved belong to three families: Germanic (Scandinavian), Celtic (Gaelic) and Uralic (Saami).

  This paper outlines a unified historical explanation for this seemingly areal distribution of preaspiration in NW Europe, whereby Gaelic and Saami preaspiration are taken to be due to contact with Scandinavian. Such a hypothesis crucially hinges on the claim that preaspiration within Scandinavian goes back at least to the Viking Age, and this discussion will focus almost exclusively on this point. On the basis of various sources of evidence, I argue that preaspiration should be reconstructed for Late Proto-Scandinavian. Some of the claims have been made before (see, e.g., Liberman 1982; Salmons 1992; Page 1997), but the range of evidence examined here — and more so in Hansson (1997) — goes well beyond what previous scholars have adduced. Furthermore, the reconstruction I suggest also differs in important ways from earlier proposals.

2.   Preaspiration in Scandinavian: A peripheral archaism

The strongest support for the hypothesis that Scandinavian preaspiration is an archaism comes from a convergence of evidence. In this section, I argue that the geographic distribution of preaspiration, as well as its phonological distribution within individual dialects, constitutes a pattern of retention rather than innovation. Note that in both cases we are dealing with preaspiration in the broad sense, i.e., including sonorant devoicing. Furthermore, there is tentative textual evidence for the existence of preaspiration as early as the 13th–14th centuries.

2.1 The geographic distribution

On the whole, preaspiration is more characteristic of West Scandinavian (Icelandic, Faroese, Norwegian) than of East Scandinavian (Swedish, Danish). Nevertheless, preaspiration proper has been attested in Swedish dialects, and an analogous phenomenon is found dialectally in Danish as well (see Section 3). Sonorant devoicing is also found in West and East Scandinavian alike, though it has a more extensive distribution in the western part of the area. The following survey gives an overview first of preaspiration proper, then of sonorant devoicing.

2.1.1 *Preaspiration proper*
Preaspiration proper is found in all dialects of the Insular Scandinavian languages (Icelandic and Faroese). There is also reason to believe that it existed in Shetland Norn, the extinct language once spoken on the Shetland islands, judging from transcriptions in Jakobsen (1921). It should be emphasized, however, that Jakobsen is not describing Norn as such, but the etymologically Norse vocabulary of the 19th century local dialect of Scots *English*. Since it is unlikely that these words had an entirely unique phonetic character, preaspiration (including sonorant devoicing) must have been a general feature of 19th century Shetland English. The crucial question is then whether this was in fact a direct carryover from Norn, or simply 'imported' to the islands as a feature of Scots English itself. (Many Scots dialects

have preaspiration as a Gaelic substratum feature.) Which explanation is more plausible remains a matter of further investigation.

Moving to the Scandinavian mainland, we find preaspiration proper well attested in several Norwegian dialect areas, all indicated on Map 1. Two of these are Jæren in the southwest and North Gudbrandsdal. A third area comprises most of Härjedalen and the two northwesternmost parishes of Dalecarlia: Särna and Idre. This area, along with the province of Jämtland, has been Swedish territory since 1645, but linguistically it is best seen as part of the East Norwegian dialect continuum. Finally, preaspiration is attested on the island of Senja. Aside from these four well-defined areas, stray examples of preaspirated stops can also be found in transcribed texts from various dialects close to the Härjedal and/or North Gudbrandsdal areas. For example, Reitan (1930:73) makes vague reference to preaspirated geminates in Røros, just across the Norwegian border from Härjedalen. This may indicate that North Gudbrandsdal and Härjedalen are best seen as belonging to the same macro-area with respect to preaspiration.

In Swedish, preaspiration has been found in a few dialect areas, also shown on Map 1. One of these is northeastern Uppland, where it is best attested on Gräsö, but also on the adjacent mainland (Valö, Hållnäs, Forsmark).[1] Preaspiration was also characteristic of the peculiar dialect once spoken on Kökar, the most isolated of the Åland islands, as well as some nearby dialects (Kumlinge, Korpo, Hitis, Finnby). In the Estonian Swedish dialect on Ormsö, Tiberg (1962:64) cites the form *vaihpp* 'blanket' (Old Norse *veipa*), but notes that such phonotactic sequences are otherwise unattested in Estonian Swedish. One isolated example has little empirical weight, and it must remain unclear whether preaspiration was ever a regular feature of Estonian Swedish.[2] Two dialects spoken in the Lapland parts of Västerbotten (Vilhelmina) and Norrbotten (Arjeplog), respectively, have also been reported to have preaspiration. These are very young settlements (two centuries old or less), and a certain degree of dialect mixture must have occurred in their formation. More importantly, these dialects are spoken within the Saami language area. The settlers had extensive contact with Saami speakers over a long period, at times with widespread bilingualism. This, and the fact that preaspiration is pervasive in Saami phonology (see Section 5), makes it plausible that the preaspiration found here is of secondary origin, i.e., due to contact with Saami. Finally, preaspiration is occasionally claimed to exist in Stockholm Swedish. Statements to this effect (e.g., in Liberman 1982) are usually based on antiquated phonetic studies whose interpretation is by no means straightforward. For example, what Rositzke (1940) describes is hardly related to preaspiration at all (a point made also by Page 1997). Nevertheless, it should be pointed out that Helgason (1999) has found preaspiration to occur in spoken corpus data from Central Standard Swedish. I shall address the potential implications of these findings in Section 4 below.

Map 1 shows the areas where preaspiration proper is attested in Norwegian and

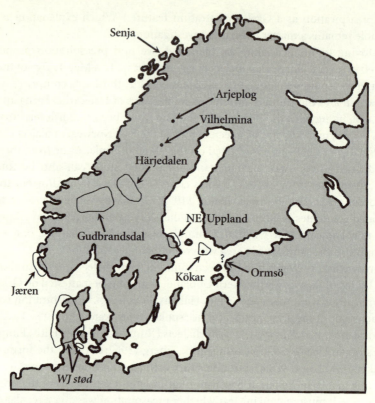

Map 1. Geographic distribution of preaspiration proper in Norwegian and Swedish dialects, and West Jutlandic stød in Danish dialects

Swedish dialects, as well as the extent of West Jutlandic preglottalization (see Section 3). Recall that beyond the territory shown on the map, preaspiration proper is also found in all dialects of Icelandic and Faroese.

Several of the dialects in which preaspiration has been found have either become extinct or have lost all traces of preaspiration. Furthermore, existing descriptions, even those of living dialects, are at times inaccurate, vague, or incomplete, especially as regards fine-grained phonetic detail (e.g., the relative duration of vowel vs. aspiration vs. stop closure). This makes it difficult to analyze the phonological status of preaspiration in many cases. It is safe to say that only in Icelandic have the properties of preaspiration been studied well enough to warrant extensive phonological analysis — as witnessed by the proliferation of such analyses in the theoretical phonological literature over the last two decades, starting with Thráinsson (1978). On the other hand, the less well-known durational aspects of Faroese and Jæren Norwegian preaspiration seem to suggest that the situation in

Icelandic is in fact not representative at all, and may in part be due to secondary phonological restructuring. I will return to this issue in Section 4.

Even though descriptions are often lacking in phonetic detail, they usually contain enough data to give a good picture of the distribution of preaspiration across phonological environments. The range of environments in which preaspiration occurs can be divided into the following classes:

(2)   A: Original geminate /pp, tt, kk/
      A2: Secondary geminate /pp, tt, kk/ (from lengthened /p, t, k/)
      B: /p, t, k/ + sonorant (nasal or /l/, sometimes also /r/)
      C: /p, t, k/ + obstruent (/pt/, /ks/, etc.)
      D: Singleton /p, t, k/

Not all of the above classes are relevant for every dialect. For example, A2 is relevant only for dialects which have secondary lengthening of /p, t, k/; this automatically excludes Icelandic, Faroese, and the Norwegian dialects of Jæren and Gudbrands-dal. Furthermore, C is irrelevant for Icelandic, where stops usually spirantize before another obstruent (/pt/ → [ft], etc.). The distribution across environments for each preaspirating dialect is as follows (N = Norwegian, S = Swedish):

(3)   Icelandic: A, B   (A2, C irrelevant)
      Faroese: A, B, C, D   (A2 irrelevant)
      Jæren (N):   A, B, C, D   (A2 irrelevant)
      Gudbrandsdal (N):   A, B, C   (A2 irrelevant)
      Härjedalen (N):   A, B   in most archaic dialect (Vemdal)
                                       A, A2, B   in surrounding dialects
      Senja (N):   A, ...?   (description incomplete)
      NE Uppland (S):   A, A2, ..., D   (description incomplete)
      Kökar & surroundings (S):   A, C, D   on Kökar (oldest generation)
                                       A, A2, C, D   on Kökar (middle-aged speakers)
                                       + evidence for B in nearby dialects
      Arjeplog, Vilhelmina (S):   A, ..., D   (description incomplete)

Note that several dialects have preaspiration in environment D, i.e., on singleton /p, t, k/ (in V__V or V__#), a fact which is not well-known and often ignored in the literature. In the dialects of Jæren and Kökar, this is clearly secondary, because the only words that have /p, t, k/ in such environments in the first place are loanwords (including dialect borrowings). The situation is less clear for Faroese and the NE Uppland (Gräsö) dialects: here there is no a priori reason to assume that pre-aspiration of singleton /p, t, k/ is secondary. However, the dialect and age-group differences observed in Härjedalen and on Kökar suggest that, if singleton /p, t, k/ were originally preaspirated, they had lost their aspiration in these dialects by the time of the secondary lengthening of /p, t, k/.[3]

2.1.2 *Sonorant devoicing*

The brief survey in the preceding section is based on facts that are relatively well documented, and other detailed overviews of the distribution of preaspiration proper can be found elsewhere — most notably in Liberman (1971a, 1982 et passim; but cf. Hansson 1997 for a more critical approach). It is quite remarkable how little attention has been paid to the full geographic extent of sonorant devoicing in relation to the origin and development of preaspiration proper, considering how intimately related the two are, phonetically and phonologically. Virtually all dialects with preaspiration proper also have preaspiration in the form of sonorant devoicing, but the fact is that the latter is much more widespread in Scandinavian than the former.

No comprehensive study of the extent of sonorant devoicing in Swedish or Norwegian dialects appears to exist. Hansson (1997) attempts to give a concise yet thorough survey of the dialectal distribution, but based on somewhat limited data resources. The overview given here is entirely based on that survey. As for the reliability of the sources, descriptions of individual dialects often contain gaps when it comes to allophonic phenomena such as sonorant devoicing. For example, one source may describe devoicing of /l/ but fail to even mention /r/, when another source on the same dialect explicitly states that devoicing applies to /l/ and /r/ alike. Furthermore, some gaps are inevitable due to the fact that no adequate (phonetic) dialect descriptions exist for certain parts of the Scandinavian language area. As a final caveat, it should be noted that a historically oriented overview such as this one is bound to be somewhat anachronistic — in the sense that the descriptions consulted may be as far as a century apart. Since the goal is to shed light on the past, the older (and more detailed) a source is, the greater its value. The upshot of this methodology is that the full picture, as presented in Map 2, does not depict the *current* geographic distribution, nor the complete distribution at any specific point in the past. Rather, it is intended to give a tentative idea of the 'minimum extent' of sonorant devoicing one or two centuries ago.

As it turns out, the environments in which devoicing occurs form a hierarchy, in that certain clusters seem more prone to show devoicing (or less prone to give way to voicing!) than others. In general, devoicing of /r/ is the most common, and devoicing of nasals the least common:

(4)   A.   /r/ + /p, t, k/   (frequently [ɻ] > [ʂ], merging with /rs/)
      B.   /l/ + /t/   (/l/ often palatal [ʎ])
      C.   /l/ + /p, k/   (often 'thick *l*', i.e., velarized [lˠ] or flap [ɽ])
      D.   nasal + /p, t, k/
      E.   sonorant + voiceless fricative (e.g., /s/)

The difference between classes B and C is most probably due to a widespread distinction — at least allophonic, if not phonemic — between two types of /l/:

'clear' vs. 'dark' /l/ (whatever the actual phonetic distinction was originally). As for class E, it is best understood as an extension of the devoicing pattern to all [+spread glottis] segments, rather than those that are [+spread glottis, -continuant].

Using the classification in (4), virtually all the dialects can in fact be arranged into a typological hierarchy, going from no devoicing whatsoever to devoicing in one or more of the above environments, where each class of environments presupposes the ones above it on the list:

(5) Type 0: No devoicing
     Type 1: Devoicing in A
     Type 2: Devoicing in A, B
     Type 3: Devoicing in A, B, C
     Type 4: Devoicing in A, B, C, D
     Type 5: Devoicing in A, B, C, D, E

Faroese is the only language exhibiting a Type 5 system (and possibly Shetland Norn as well). Icelandic has a Type 4 system throughout most of the country, but Type 2 is found in a limited and receding area in the northeast, with Type 3 occurring mostly in the transition area between the two.[4] If we turn our attention to the geographic distribution of the above types on the Scandinavian mainland, as shown on Map 2, the resulting picture is quite interesting.

The devoicing dialects form a very large, mostly contiguous area along the Scandinavian periphery. Within this area, dialects with more extensive sonorant devoicing emerge as areal pockets, contained within regions of less extensive devoicing; also, devoicing becomes more limited around important cities of commerce (Bergen in Norway, Vasa in Finland). Furthermore, a comparison of Maps 1 and 2 reveals the strong geographic correlation between preaspiration proper and the more extensive patterns of sonorant devoicing (Types 3, 4). Both tend to be found in languages and dialects that are relatively isolated — not on major trading routes — and/or notorious for being linguistically conservative. The overall peripheral orientation, the 'nested-islands' pattern, the correlation with isolated and/or conservative areas, are all hallmarks of a pattern of *retention*, not innovation.

2.2 The phonological distribution

Just as the geographic distribution suggests retention rather than innovation, so does the phonological distribution — especially of preaspiration proper — in many modern dialects. Preaspiration has often come to support a phonological contrast, but only as an indirect consequence of various independent sound changes which would otherwise have resulted in merger were it not for the presence of preaspiration. Such changes, most of which are listed in (6), can thus be said to have increased the 'functional load' of preaspiration, changing it from redundant to contrastive.[5]

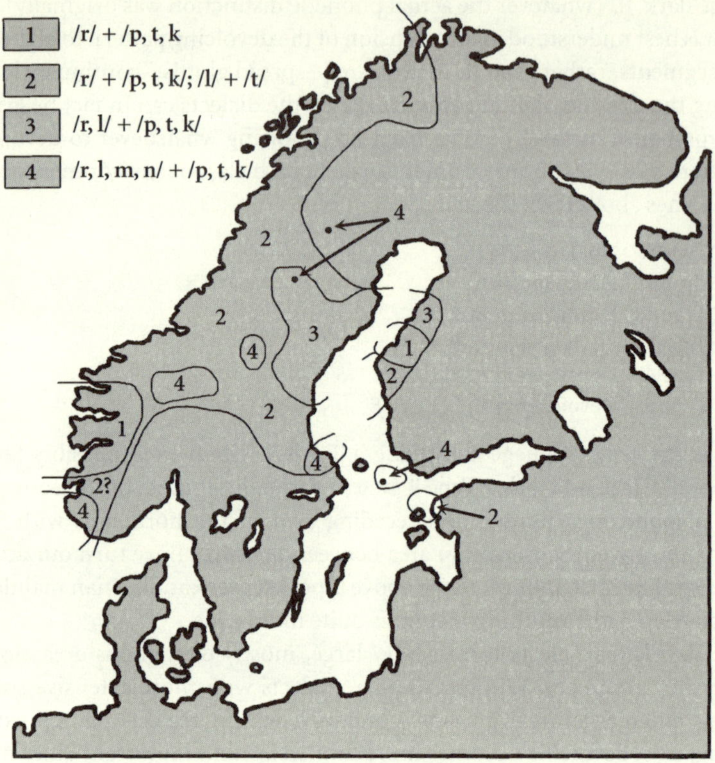

1	/r/ + /p, t, k
2	/r/ + /p, t, k/; /l/ + /t/
3	/r, l/ + /p, t, k/
4	/r, l, m, n/ + /p, t, k/

Map 2. Geographic distribution of sonorant devoicing in Norwegian and Swedish dialects

(6)   Additional functional load on preaspiration (all examples from Modern Icelandic):

    a.   Devoicing of /b(b), d(d), g(g)/
        [Icelandic, Faroese, Jæren, Gudbrandsdal, Uppland]
        henda "throw" [hɛnta]; *vagga* "cradle (n)" [vakːa]; *bera* "carry" [pɛːra]
    combined with:

    b.   Hardening of voiced fricatives (esp. [β], [ɣ]) to stops before /l, n/
        [mainly Icelandic, Faroese, W. Norway (including Jæren)]
        sofna "fall asleep" [sɔpna]; *afl* "strength" [apɬ]; *hegna* "punish" [hɛkna]

    c.   Hardening of voiced fricatives (esp. [ð], [ɣ]) to stops after /l, r/
        [Icelandic, Faroese, most Norwegian dialects, Härjedalen (Vemdal),
        Uppland, some Northern Swedish dialects]
        valdi "chose (3sɢ)" [valtɪ] (< Old Norse *valði*); *mergur* "marrow" [mɛrkʏr]

    d.   /nn, rn/ > /dn/, /ll, rl/ > /dl/
        [Icelandic, Faroese, Shetland Norn, W. Norway (including Jæren), Uppland]
        seinna "later" [seitna]; *barn* "child" [patn̥]; *hella* "pour" [hɛtla]

I suggest that preaspiration shows the distribution it does precisely because it has been *retained* in those environments where it has become contrastive. It is far less plausible that each individual dialect would have chosen to invent preaspiration — out of all conceivable alternative 'strategies' — as a means of avoiding merger (but see Section 4 for a subtle reinterpretation of this alternative).

2.3 Textual and other evidence

In addition to the geographic and phonological arguments, the hypothesis that preaspiration is an archaic feature receives further support from philological evidence. In various Icelandic, Norwegian, and Swedish manuscripts, forms can be found where /tt/, or even /t/, is unexpectedly represented as ⟨ct⟩, ⟨pt⟩ or ⟨ft⟩ (presumably reflecting [xt], [ft]). One possible explanation is that these represent a reinterpretation of the [h] portion of a preaspirated stop as a buccal fricative.

(7)   Forms in manuscripts with unexpected ⟨c⟩, ⟨p⟩, ⟨f⟩ ([x], [f]):
⟨doctir⟩, ⟨doctur⟩ = *dóttir, dóttur* (Sweden, 14th c.)
⟨aktag⟩ = *áttak*, ⟨freckt⟩ = *frétt* (Iceland, early 15th c.)
⟨recta⟩ = *rétta*, ⟨gect⟩ = *gæt*, ⟨lyrictar⟩, ⟨lyriftar⟩ = *lýrittar* (various Icelandic mss.)
⟨Suictun⟩, ⟨Sviptun⟩ = *Svittun* < OE *Swithun* (Iceland, Norway, 14–15th cc.)

These are paralleled by various attested dialectal forms which actually contain an unexpected /ft/ or /kt/ (possibly = [xt]), often in dialects that are not traditionally described as preaspirating.

(8)   Examples of dialectal words with unexpected /kt/, /ft/:
okta, ofta = ON *ótta*; *ogte* = ON *ótti*   (Trøndelag, Norway)
lægt = ON *hlátr*   (Hallingdal, Norway)
flykkta = ModSw *flytta*; *stikkt* = ON *stétt* (Dalecarlia, Sweden)

There is one additional piece of potential textual evidence, a 13th century runic inscription, consisting of a single word, found on a small wooden object unearthed in a 1985 excavation in Trondheim in what was probably a carpenter's workshop. The object seems to be a template for a particular piece of a string instrument, and inscribed on it is the term for that piece. The runic spelling of the word on the inscription contains an unexpected ⟨ht⟩ (for /tt/ or /t/):

(9)   Early 13th century runic inscription (Trondheim, Norway):
ruhta 'part of string instrument'
(word found in various continental European mss. as *rotta, rutta, rute*, etc.)
cf. 'phonetic' spelling of foreign words and names, common in other runic material:
santibisetur   = Lat. *sanctificetur*, where ⟨b⟩ = [β]
pendihta   = *Benedicta*, where ⟨ht⟩ = [xt] (1248)

The forms in (7)–(9) would hardly constitute persuasive evidence on their own. Combined with the evidence adduced in the previous sections, however, they lend further support to the hypothesis that preaspiration was present in Scandinavian at least as early as the 12th–13th centuries.

3.   Preaspiration and West Jutlandic stød

Various Danish dialects spoken on Jutland and Northern Funen display a glottalization phenomenon referred to as West Jutlandic (WJ) stød (Ringgaard 1960; cf. Page 1997). WJ stød is phonetically distinct from the better-known Common Danish (CD) stød, in that it consistently involves full glottal closure. More importantly, the two occur in radically different environments: WJ stød is found only before reflexes of Old Norse /p, t, k/, where CD stød can *never* occur. It appears that, at least historically, WJ stød is best seen as preglottalization of stops, rather than a 'prosodic' element like CD stød (and its cognate pitch accents in Swedish and Norwegian).

The phonological distribution of WJ stød corresponds quite closely to that of preaspiration (including sonorant devoicing) in Modern Icelandic. There is one important difference, however: WJ stød occurs only in those forms that were *polysyllabic* in Old Norse — i.e., those that carried the pitch accent referred to as 'Accent 2'. In the modern dialects, minimal pairs exist, because the so-called Jutlandic apocope has rendered many polysyllabic forms monosyllabic. WJ stød is thus contrastive: [stærk] "strong (sɢ)" vs. [stærʔk] "strong (ᴘʟ)" (cf. Old Norse *sterkr* vs. *sterkir*).

The traditional historical explanation has been to interpret WJ stød as triggered by the apocope, a compensatory effect to avoid the merger of many original polysyllables with original monosyllables.[6] There is an alternative interpretation, however, namely that the conditioning by syllable count — or pitch accent, or apocope — is a secondary development (Hansson 1997). On this view, /p, t, k/ were originally preglottalized in *all* positions, regardless of syllable count or pitch accents. Preglottalization (i.e., [ʔ]) was subsequently lost under one of the two pitch contour patterns, Accent 1 (that of monosyllables), but it was preserved under the Accent 2 pattern (that of polysyllables). The Accent 1 vs. Accent 2 opposition has since been replaced by CD stød vs. no CD stød, just as it has elsewhere in Danish.

The crucial evidence for this hypothesis comes from the archaic dialects spoken on the island Als (off the SE coast of Jutland), where the pitch accent opposition is still preserved as such (Jensen 1961). The dialect of the most remote and isolated villages on Als *also* has WJ stød — which thus coexists with true pitch accents, rather than with a CD-stød contrast as in all other dialects. As it turns out, this dialect has WJ stød on original monosyllables and polysyllables alike, i.e., cooccuring with *both*

Accent 1 and 2. It is hard to interpret this as anything but an archaism. We can thus conclude that WJ stød is cognate with preaspiration elsewhere in Scandinavian. The phonological distribution is virtually identical (note that this includes sonorant devoicing: Icelandic [n̥t] = West Jutlandic [nʔt]). Also, WJ stød is geographically *peripheral*, and its distribution fits quite nicely into the pan-Scandinavian preaspiration map, bolstering the archaism argument.

4. The origin and nature of Proto-Scandinavian preaspiration

If preaspiration — or perhaps preglottalization — existed already in Late Proto-Scandinavian, what was the range of its phonological distribution? The answer to this question may depend on what the ultimate origin of Scandinavian pre-aspiration is assumed to be. Marstrander (1932) proposed that preaspiration of /pp, tt, kk/ was the result of an incomplete assimilation of Proto-Scandinavian *mp, *nt, *nk, and *xt clusters into /pp, tt, kk/ (cf. also Page 1997).[7]

(10)   *mp > [m̥p] > [hp], *nt > [n̥t] > [ht], *nk > [ŋ̊k] > [hk]; *xt > [ht]

The assimilations thus remained incomplete in certain parts of Scandinavia. As for preexisting /pp, tt, kk/ from other sources, it is necessary to assume that pre-aspiration was generalized to these by 'phonetic analogy'. Page (1997) argues for the scenario in (10), but assumes that other /pp, tt, kk/ were already phonetically preaspirated at the time it took place (p. 177). One advantage of this view is that the clusters in (10) can be assumed to have been reinterpreted as a phonotactic configuration already present in the language. However, this paradoxically entails that (10) is in fact *not* a hypothesis about the origin of preaspiration any more; rather, it constitutes a diachronic path along which *additional* tokens of pre-aspirated stops entered the lexicon.

Neither Marstrander (1932) nor Page (1997) appears to be aware of the existence of preaspirated singleton /p, t, k/, e.g., in Faroese or in NE Uppland dialects. If (10) represents the origin of preaspirated stops, then preaspiration on any non-geminate stops must be secondary. This is less problematic on Page's reinterpretation, but, on the other hand, he is not very explicit about the distribution of preaspiration at the stage *preceding* (10). Were /p, t, k/ preaspirated only as geminates, only in coda position, or perhaps only in heterosyllabic clusters?

The scenario I propose is somewhat similar to the one Page (1997) suggests, but different in that /p, t, k/ are here explicitly assumed to have been phonetically preaspirated in *all* non-initial positions in Late Proto-Scandinavian (Hansson 1997). This pattern may well have applied throughout the language area. A crucial assumption is that preaspiration did originally *not* have full segmental duration (unlike its Modern Icelandic descendant), but was a subsegmental feature, entirely analogous to word-initial *post*aspiration. The /pp, tt, kk/ vs. /p, t, k/ distinction was thus realized in terms of closure duration alone — i.e., a true length contrast. In other words, both geminates and singletons were preaspirated: [^{h}tː] : [^{h}t]. (Note that this entails that after a sonorant, preaspiration was, in effect, partial sonorant devoicing: [r̥k], [n̥t], etc.) Preaspiration has generally been on the retreat throughout Scandinavia ever since. Preaspiration proper on singleton /p, t, k/ is very rarely retained, possibly because these did not contrast with other stops, voiced or otherwise. In other words, preaspiration was redundant in postvocalic onset position: Old Norse had *saka* [sa^{h}ka] "accuse", but *[saka] and *[saga] were impossible (*saga* "tale" was phonetically [saɣa]).

The [^{h}tː] : [^{h}t] pattern reconstructed for Late Proto-Scandinavian is in fact identical to what is found phonetically in Faroese and in Jæren Norwegian today. This pattern stands in sharp contrast with the better-known Modern Icelandic one, where preaspiration is always a full-blown (moraic) segment [h], the following stop closure is of relatively short duration (comparable to that found in CC clusters), and singleton postvocalic /p, t, k/ are never preaspirated. I propose that the Icelandic pattern be interpreted as a *secondary* development. This may well have been ultimately triggered by the general devoicing of /b, d, g/ (far less consistent or pervasive in Faroese than in Icelandic). The development may have been as outlined in (11), which can be interpreted as a chain-like constellation of sound changes. The three components of the 'chain' are presented here as sequential steps, but they could equally well be interpreted as orthogonal factors operating in tandem (yielding the change [gː] : [^{h}kː] : [^{h}k] > [kː] : [hk] : [k] in one leap, as it were).[8]

(11) A conjectural history of Icelandic preaspiration (velars used as an example):
  a. Devoicing of /g(g)/, [gː] > [kː]. As a consequence, /gg/ : /kk/ = [kː] : [^{h}kː].
  b. Polarization of /gg/ : /kk/ contrast: preaspiration of /kk/ is *segmentalized*, [^{h}kː] > [hk]. As a consequence, /kk/ : /k/ = [hk] : [^{h}k].
  c. Polarization of /kk/ : /k/ contrast: redundant preaspiration of /k/ is dropped, [^{h}k] > [k]. As a consequence, /kk/ : /k/ = [hk] : [k].

The hypothesis that preaspiration existed as a subsegmental property of stops already in Proto-Scandinavian does of course not constitute an explanation for how and when it *arose*. There seems to be no conclusive evidence for any relation between preaspiration and the Swedish-Norwegian pitch accents or Common Danish stød (*pace* Liberman 1982; Salmons 1992). A certain interaction between preaspiration and pitch accents is found (e.g., in the Flekkefjord case cited by Liberman 1982:66–67; cf. also the above discussion of WJ stød), but this is hardly surprising, given the shared physiological mechanism: pitch contours and laryngeal gestures/segments frequently interact. However, interaction alone does not constitute evidence of common historical origin.

Kortlandt (1988, 1996) suggests that preaspiration, as well as the cognate WJ stød, are direct reflexes of Proto-Indo-European 'glottalic' stops (as reconstructed by proponents of the Glottalic Theory). In effect, this explains away the development of preaspiration by pushing its roots even further back in time, into PIE. Kortlandt's arguments are quite subtle, and a detailed discussion of his ideas goes well beyond the scope of this short paper. Although plausible in principle, the hypothesis of course hinges on the validity of the Glottalic Theory as such, as well as Kortlandt's idea that PIE ejectives changed into preglottalized voiced stops (sic!) on the way to Proto-Germanic.

The question of the ultimate origins of Scandinavian preaspiration does not have a straightforward answer. Since the main claim of this paper is simply that preaspiration goes *at least* as far back as Late Proto-Scandinavian, I will take a rather agnostic position on this issue, and simply propose that Proto-Scandinavian /p, t, k/ *became* either preaspirated or preglottalized through a simple sound change. That change itself can be characterized as a slight misalignment of articulatory gestures, (laryngeal vs. oral). As for the relationship between WJ stød and preaspiration, I will assume (with Page 1997) that preglottalization developed out of preaspiration, rather than the other way around, although nothing that has been said here crucially hinges on that assumption.[9]

Finally, we must briefly address the issue of the precise phonological status of preaspiration in Proto-Scandinavian. I have already argued that it was subsegmental, not a full-fledged segment [h]. But does this necessarily mean that the subsegmental 'gestural misalignment' had become *phonologized*, i.e., incorporated into the phonological norm? Or could it be that the preaspiration reconstructed for Proto-Scandinavian was merely a characteristic tendency toward a particular pattern of gestural timing — i.e., an aspect of phonetic realization rather than phonological structure? There is some evidence that such low-level articulatory strategies may display areal distribution and variation. Gobl and Ní Chasaide (1988) found a tendency towards early glottal abduction before 'fortis' stops in most of their Swedish speakers, and some of their English ones, as opposed to the tighter synchronization of glottal and oral gestures observed for French speakers. Helgason (1999) found the same tendency in speakers of Central Standard Swedish. This preaspiration, which is non-normative (but nonetheless articulatorily planned), varies with speech rate, sentential focus, etc. It stands in sharp contrast with the normative preaspiration found in Uppland dialects (Gräsö) or Icelandic.[10] Finally, similar non-normative preaspiration has been reported in Norwegian outside of traditionally preaspirating areas (see, e.g., van Dommelen 1999).

Was the preaspiration reconstructed for Proto-Scandinavian normative (i.e., phonologized), or could normative preaspiration — in Iceland, the Faroes, Jæren, Uppland, etc. — have developed later and independently in the individual dialects, perhaps in part as a response to sound changes of the type listed in (6)? The evidence is hard to interpret on this point, but the full geographic distribution of sonorant devoicing suggests, if anything, a relatively early phonologization, i.e., that devoicing of a preceding sonorant was full and categorical already at an early stage. The development of WJ stød may also be harder to reconcile with the notion of a late normativization.

5.   Prespiration outside Scandinavian

Due to space limitations, this topic can only be touched upon extremely briefly here. An in-depth discussion, including a detailed survey of relevant literature, is provided in Hansson (1997), where it is argued at length that preaspiration in both Gaelic and Saami is most likely due to contact with Scandinavian (following Borgstrøm 1974 and Posti 1954, respectively).

The theory that preaspiration in Gaelic is due to Norse influence (Marstrander 1932; Borgstrøm 1974) remains the most convincing explanation to date. According to this theory, preaspiration was a feature of Late Proto-Scandinavian at the time when Norse settlers first came to Scotland and Ireland. The geographical distribution of preaspiration in Scottish Gaelic matches this settlement history quite nicely. As pointed out by Borgstrøm (1974), the counterargument that preaspiration is 'strongest' (phonetically [xp, xt, xk]) in areas further away from the main Scandinavian settlements is misguided. It is highly unlikely that preaspiration would have arisen directly as preaffrication ([xp], etc.), and that the [ʰp] realization found in the Hebrides (e.g., on Lewis) is the result of subsequent lenition of [x]. Moreover, severe problems of relative chronology appear to result from this view (cf. Hansson 1997): the cluster /xk/ (from earlier /xt/) is retained as [xk] in all dialects, even ones where preaspirated /t(t), k(k)/ is [ʰt], [ʰk] and not [xt], [xk].

The particular mechanism of contact-induced change would in this case have been interference through language shift (from Norse to Gaelic). This is fairly unremarkable, given that preaspiration is frequently carried over from one language to another as an interference feature, e.g., from Gaelic into Scots English, from Saami into Norwegian, from Saami into Finnish, and as a characteristic feature of an Icelandic 'accent' in various foreign languages (cf. Thráinsson 1978).

As for the origins of preaspiration in Saami (a.k.a. Lapp, or Lappish), a popular opinion has been that it is inextricably tied to the development of so-called consonant gradation (cf. Ravila 1956; Liberman 1971b), a pervasive system of alternations — once quantitative, now mostly qualitative — which was originally conditioned by the weight of the following syllable. One of the many instantiations of gradation is an alternation between preaspirated and unaspirated stops (North Saami [johkɑ] "river", GSG [jokɑ]). The idea is, then, that preaspiration plays such an important role in Saami morphophonology that it cannot possibly be a contact phenomenon. However, this is a non sequitur: there is no inherent link between consonant gradation and preaspiration. What plays a central role in Saami grammar is not preaspiration as such but simply gradation itself, i.e., systematic *quantity* alternations. Since only geminates became preaspirated in Saami, geminate vs. singleton alternations (/pp/ vs. /p/) are realized in the modern dialects as alternations between preaspirates and non-preaspirates (/hp/ vs. /p/). Finally, the theory that Saami preaspiration is due to contact (Posti 1954) has an important advantage over the alternative account. The contact theory can, at least potentially, explain the fact that preaspiration gets less pervasive in terms of its phonological distribution towards northeast, i.e., in the direction away from Scandinavian-speaking areas.

6. Conclusions

Preaspiration in the Scandinavian languages is a feature whose geographic distribution, and phonological patterning suggests that it constitutes an archaism, preserved on the (mostly western and northern) periphery of the language area, and in notoriously conservative dialects. I have argued on the basis of this and other evidence that preaspiration should be reconstructed for Late Proto-Scandinavian. Furthermore, the preglottalization referred to as West Jutlandic stød is clearly cognate with the preaspiration found elsewhere, and most likely developed out of the latter. However, it is still unclear whether preaspiration was already *phonologized* at that stage, or whether it was merely an (areal) pattern of low-level gestural timing, i.e., of phonetic implementation. Either way, the situation in Modern Icelandic is clearly secondary, the result of a phonological restructuring, possibly triggered by other independent sound changes. I have also suggested that distributional restrictions in terms of syllable count or pitch accent (e.g., for WJ stød) are secondary, and do not indicate that the preaspiration or preglottalization in question had a 'prosodic' function at any time. Finally, I briefly argued that the preaspiration found in Gaelic and Saami is most convincingly accounted for as due to contact with Scandinavian.

Notes

* During the extensive work on which this short paper is based, I benefitted greatly from discussion with more people than I could possibly enumerate. Höskuldur Thráinsson, Pétur Helgason, and Jan Ragnar Hagland deserve special thanks. Thanks also to the two anonymous referees for helpful comments. All errors are of course my own.

1. As for the possible existence of preaspiration further north than Uppland, Posti (1954: 204, fn. 1) quotes Manne Eriksson as having claimed that "remnants of this phenomenon are found in Gästrikland and Hälsingland". Given the context of the quote, it seems likely that this refers

specifically to preaspiration proper, and not simply to sonorant devoicing (which is most certainly found in these provinces, cf. Map 2).

2. Other references to the existence of preaspiration proper in Estonian Swedish (e.g., in Liberman 1982) are apparently based on a misinterpretation of descriptions in the dialectological literature having to do with the development of the clusters /ft/ and /kt/ (often pronounced [xt] or even [ht]) in these dialects.

3. One reviewer suggests that this lengthening may be itself the direct reflection of a lost glottal element. However, the fact remains that in Härjedalen, only the more *innovative* dialects (as opposed to that of Vemdal) preaspirate these secondary geminates, and on Kökar, only *younger* speakers preaspirate them. Both are obvious cases of later generalization; thus, preaspiration in environment A2 is clearly more recent than the lengthening itself.

4. In fact, the northeastern Type 2 dialects seem to have had even more limited devoicing within class B in earlier times, with *heteromorphemic* sequences of /l/ + /t/ showing no devoicing. It seems best to interpret this as an innovation — even though it is 'archaic' nowadays, in that it is disappearing — namely a paradigmatic levelling of the voiced [l]. This levelling has a parallel in certain Swedish Type 2 dialects with 'thick' vs. 'clear' /l/, where the 'thick l' of, say, *gul* "yellow (masc.)" can spread to the neuter form *gult*, thus escaping devoicing.

5. One reviewer suggests that devoicing and hardening may never have taken place, i.e., that what happened was *voicing* and *frication* elsewhere. This is an intriguing idea, but hardening most certainly did take place in the documented history of Icelandic (e.g., [lð] > [ld]; [rð, βð, γð] > [rd, vd, γd] and [βð, γð] > [pð, kð] dialectally).

6. Ringgaard (1960), who instead assumes that /p, t, k/ became preglottalized already in Old Danish, attempts to explain the poly- vs. monosyllabic divergence by assuming that preglottalization arose only in *medial* position, not word-finally. Page (1997:185) takes a similar view: "[T]he laryngeal feature associated with the medial stop had acquired a prosodic function by the time of [WJ] apocope. Therefore, WJ stød is absent from monosyllables".

7. Curiously, Page (1997) consistently attributes this theory to Chapman (1962), even though it is clear that the latter is merely recapitulating Marstrander (1932). In fact, preaspiration is a mere side issue for Chapman, whose central thesis is that certain shared innovations in 14th -15th century Icelandic and Norwegian are due to contact.

8. It is quite possible that the Quantity Shift (which included closed-syllable shortening: -VVC.CV- > -VC.CV-) played a role in the segmentalization of Icelandic preaspiration. In Modern Icelandic -VC.C- contexts, the coda C appears to carry the 'quantitative peak' of the syllable; in preaspirated stops, this peak thus falls on the [h] portion, potentially increasing its duration. If /b, d, g/ were already voiceless in Proto-Scandinavian, as suggested by one reviewer, then perhaps the *Quantity Shift* might be listed instead of (11a–b) as providing the 'impetus' for (11c).

9. If glottalization of /p, t, k/ in English is related to preaspiration and WJ stød (Ringgaard 1960), this view may need to be revised. One reviewer suggests that preaspiration "can easily have arisen from preglottalization by lenition". It is true that [ʔ] > [h] is quite common, but so is [h] > [ʔ], and besides, this use of the term 'lenition' is reminiscent of pencil-and-paper phonetics. There is no 'weakening', or target undershoot, involved in going from a glottal *constricting* gesture to the glottal *spreading* gesture required to articulate [h].

10. Notice that in the Gräsö case, preaspiration is still of subsegmental duration (unlike its Icelandic counterpart), even though it has nevertheless been phonologized and is now part of the pronunciation norm.

References

Borgstrøm, Carl Hj. 1974. "On the Influence of Norse on Scottish Gaelic. Preaspiration of stops and pitch patterns". *Lochlann. A Review of Celtic Studies* 6.91–103.

Chapman, Kenneth G. 1962. *Icelandic-Norwegian Linguistic Relationships.* (= *Nordisk Tidskrift for Sprogvidenskap,* Suppl. Vol. 7.) Oslo: Universitetsforlaget.

Gobl, C. & A. Ní Chasaide. 1988. "The Effects of Adjacent Voiced/Voiceless Consonants on the Vowel Voice Source: A cross language study". *Speech Transmission Laboratory-Quarterly Progress and Status Report* 2–3.23–59 Stockholm: Royal Institute of Technology.

Hansson, Gunnar Ólafur. 1997. *Aldur og útbreiðsla aðblásturs í tungumálum Norðvestur-Evrópu.* M. A. thesis, University of Iceland. [To appear, Institute of Linguistics, Univ. of Iceland.]

Helgason, Pétur. 1999. "Phonetic Preconditions for the Development of Normative Preaspiration". Ohala et al. 1999.1851–1854.

Jakobsen, Jakob. 1921. *Etymologisk ordbog over det norrøne sprog på Shetland.* Copenhagen.

Jensen, Ella. 1961. "'Vestjysk' stød med musikalsk accent". *Danske Folkemaal* 18.14–24.

Kortlandt, Frederik. 1988. "Proto-Germanic Obstruents". *Amsterdamer Beiträge zur älteren Germanistik* 27.3–10.

Kortlandt, Frederik. 1996. "The High German Consonant Shift". *Amsterdamer Beiträge zur älteren Germanistik* 46.53–57.

Liberman, Anatoly S. 1971a. *Islandskaja prosodika.* Leningrad: Nauka.

Liberman, Anatoly S. 1971b. "The Voiceless Vowel in Lapp Again". *Soviet Fenno-Ugric Studies* 7.269–276.

Liberman, Anatoly S. 1982. *Germanic Accentology. Vol. 1: The Scandinavian Languages.* Minneapolis: University of Minnesota Press.

Marstrander, Carl J. S. 1932. "Okklusiver og substrater". *Norsk Tidskrift for Sprogvidenskap* 5.258–314.

Ohala, John J., Yoko Hasegawa, Manjari Ohala, Daniel Granville, & Ashlee C. Bailey, eds. 1999. *Proceedings of the XIVth International Congress of Phonetic Sciences.* Department of Linguistics, University of California, Berkeley.

Page, B. Richard. 1997. "On the Origin of Preaspiration in Scandinavian". *American Journal of Germanic Linguistics & Literatures* 9: 2.167–190.

Posti, Lauri. 1954. "On the Origin of the Voiceless Vowel in Lapp". *Svenska landsmål och svenskt folkliv* 76–77.199–209.

Ravila, Paavo. 1956. "Der sog. stimmlose Vokal im Lappischen". *Ural-Altaische Jahrbücher* 28.184–185.

Reitan, Jørgen. 1930. *Vemdalsmålet, med oplysninger om andre Herjedalske mål.* Oslo: Det Norske Videnskaps-Akademi.

Ringgaard, K. 1960. *Vestjysk stød.* Aarhus: Universitetsforlaget.

Rositzke, Harry A. 1940. "Epenthetic Consonants in Swedish". *Journal of English and Germanic Philology* 39.473–485.

Salmons, Joseph C. 1992. *Accentual Change and Language Contact. Comparative Survey and a Case Study of Early Northern Europe.* London: Routledge.

Thráinsson, Höskuldur. 1978. "On the Phonology of Icelandic Preaspiration". *Nordic Journal of Linguistics* 1.3–54.

Tiberg, Nils. 1962. *Estlandssvenska språkbidrag.* (= *Estlandssvenskarnas folkliga kultur* 6. Acta Academiae Regiae Gustavi Adolphi, 38.) Uppsala: Lundequist.

van Dommelen, Wim A. 1999. "Preaspiration in Intervocalic /k/ vs. /g/ in Norwegian". Ohala et al. 1999.2037–2040.

Rapid change among expletive polarity items

Jacob Hoeksema
University of Groningen

1. Minimizers

Modern Dutch, like many other languages, has a large number of indefinite negative polarity items intended to strengthen negation by making the statement more emphatic. Among these, there is a large group referred to in the literature (e.g., Bolinger 1972; Horn 1989) as 'minimizers' denoting scalar endpoints. This group includes superlatives meaning "the slightest" or "the least", cf. English *Fred did not have the faintest idea* or *The inspector did not have the slightest inkling* but also expressions denoting minimal units of measurement, cf. English *Fred did not doubt it for a moment* or *The police gave instructions not to pay a dime to the kidnappers*. Included in this group are various idioms denoting things considered small or negligible on some scale:

(1)   *een rooie cent*   "a red cent"
      een gebenedijd woord "a blessed word" (Southern Dutch)
      een haarbreed   "a hair's width"

In older stages of Dutch, the set of expressions used as minimizers was very large and varied (see De Jager 1858), and in many cases, they had a distinctly pejorative character:

(2)   *een sikkepit*   "a goat's dropping"
      een mijt   "a mite"
      een verrotte mispel   "a rotten medlar"
      een zier   "a maggot"

Many of these idioms not only denoted something small, but indeed something worthless or distasteful. Hence they could be used as minimal endpoints for scales of *size* as well as scales of *value*. In particular for evaluative statements, pejorative elements are obviously useful. For modern readers, the pejorative character of some of these items may not be all that obvious. In judging a Middle Dutch example such as

(3)   *En   prise mijn lijf niet twee peeren*
      NEG prize my   life not two pears
      "I don't give two pears for my chances of survival."
      (from: Karel ende Elegast, 13th century)

one should consider that pears, and fruit in general, were not considered valuable, or even healthy food in the Middle Ages.

The use of minimizers to strengthen negation is robustly attested in the European languages (cf. Pott 1833; Jespersen 1917). Making new minimizers is a productive process. New ones are added constantly, and old ones are being replaced. Of the dozens of Middle Dutch minimizers, only a couple are in use today, like the word for "hair", *haar*.

2.   Taboo terms as minimizers

What appears to be a later development is the rise of *taboo terms* as reinforcers of negation (cf. Postma 2001). Beginning in the 19th century, we see a steady rise of indefinite taboo terms in the same kinds of negative contexts where previously minimizers were in use. These taboo terms can be divided into several subsets. The first to appear on the scene is a group of religious origin, or if you like, originating in folklore superstition, attested from the early 19th century onward.[1] Then there is a somewhat larger group of sexual or scatological taboo terms, the first of which are attested in the late 19th century. Finally there is a set of expressions denoting various contagious or lethal diseases, attested from the early 20th century onward. The religious taboo terms are all designations of the devil, or of thunder/lightning:

(4)   *een drommel*   "a devil"
      een duvel   "a devil"
      een verdommenis   "a damnation"
      een donder   "a thunder"
      een bliksem   "a lightning"
      een deksel   "a lid" (but used as euphemism for devil)

      Dat gaat je   geen drommel / duvel / verdommenis / donder / bliksem / deksel aan.
      that goes you no   devil   / devil / damnation   / thunder / lightning / lid   on
      "That does not concern you one bit."

Note that names for God, Jesus, or the saints are absent, although they are omnipresent, so to speak, in swear words and curses. Only negative religious terms are used, presumably because only they are inherently pejorative. What is interesting about this group of expressions is that they show up in a number of emphatic constructions, not just polarity contexts, but also as degree adverbs and as evaluative adjectives:

(5) *drommels mooi*   "devilishly pretty"
     duvels moeilijk   "devilishly difficult"
     verdomd lastig   "damned hard"
     donders goed   "thunderishly good = very well"
     bliksems aardig   "lightning-like nice = damned nice"
     deksels knap   "fiendishly clever"

(6) *een drommelse/duvelse/verdomde/donderse/bliksemse/dekselse idioot*
     "a damned idiot"

and in adverbial constructions denoting speed:

(7) *Ga als de drommel/duvel/(gesmeerde) bliksem   hier weg!*
     go as the devil   /devil / greased   lightning here away
     "Get the hell out of here"

Sexual and scatological taboo terms begin to occur toward the end of the 19th century in Dutch texts. Just how old they are in spoken Dutch is difficult to tell precisely, but it is safe to suppose that they are not of ancient origin. In the farces and popular literature of the 17th century they are not to be found, and there can be no doubt that they would have shown up there, had they been around at the time. In the 19th century, we must, of course, consider Victorian attitudes toward sex and bodily functions in general as factors which may explain the absence of taboo words in the written language. However, already in the late 19th century, we see a general lifting of these taboos in certain genres, particularly naturalistic novels and plays, where there is a serious attempt at capturing then-current spoken language. Almost immediately, we see sexual taboo terms being used as negative polarity items. Some examples are given in (8):

(8) a.   *'t kan ze   geen bal verdommen*[2]
          it can them no   ball care
          "they don't give a damn."
     b.   *verder ontlopen jullie mekaar   geen flikker*[3]
          further differ   you-all each-other no   faggot
          "Otherwise you differ not at all."

A list of sexual and scatological taboo terms currently in use, is given in (9):

(9) *bal*   "ball, testicle"   *kloot*   "testicle"
     barst   "crack"   *kut*   "cunt"
     drol   "turd"   *laars*   "boot" (euphemism
     flikker "faggot"   for *aars* "arse")
     fluit   "flute, penis"   *reet*   "asshole"
     fuck   "fuck" (recent loan)   *sodemieter* "sodomite"
     hol   "hole"   *zak*   "sack, scrotum"

These terms vary widely in usage. Some are used quite generally, like *bal*, and are considered acceptable in polite language, some are widely known, but considered rude, yet others are restricted to small subsections of the population.

Rather more limited, and also more typically Dutch, it appears, is a set of taboo terms denoting contagious or lethal diseases:

(10) *kanker*   "cancer"   *pokken*   "smallpox"
      pest   "plague"   *tering*   "tuberculosis"
      pleuris "pleuritis"   *tyfus*   "typhus"

With the exception of *pest*, which gained a broad popularity in the 1960s and 1970s, the use of disease terms as polarity items appears to be limited to the Rotterdam area. It should be noted that the same items are also in use as pejorative noun modifiers. The two uses, noun modifier and polarity item, are both illustrated by example (11):

(11) *FEYENOORD KAMPIOEN en   daar kunnen die   kanker nepperds van PSV*
      Feyenoord   champion and there can   those cancer phonies of PSV
      geen kanker aan   doen!!!!![4]
      no   cancer about do
      "Feyenoord is champion and those fucking phonies of PSV can't do a fuck about it!"

As the English translation is meant to suggest, it is not uncommon in English either that pejorative noun modifiers and polarity-sensitive minimizers are tapped from the same well.

3.   Minimizers and predicates

In contemporary Dutch, I have counted 170 terms which are being used as minimizers. It would be inconceivable that a language would support such a large set of items unless they were diversified along a number of dimensions. I have already mentioned the fact that there is variation in politeness and social acceptability as well as regional variation. But it is not this type of variation that I want to discuss here. Another dimension of variation concerns the predicates with which the various minimizers combine. As it turns out, some items combine rather freely with predicates of all sort, whereas others show a remarkable fastidiousness in their choice of predicates.[5]

Now some of these combinatory constraints are entirely unremarkable. When minimizers have a transparent etymology, and a use which is transparently related to their etymology, we may see the effects of ordinary selection restrictions. Consider, for a moment, the use of the English transparent minimizer *a word*:

(12)   a.   The count did not say a word.
       b.   The police don't believe a word of it.
       c.   Fred doesn't speak a word of French.
       d.   #Ed didn't have a word.
       e.   #Edna didn't do a word all evening.
       f.   #Alex didn't care a word for his colleagues.

Being a linguistic unit, *word* may be combined with predicates of linguistic units, especially verbs of communication, like *say, speak, utter*, but also cognitive verbs such as *believe*. While it is literally speaking impossible to believe a word, objects of belief are linguistic in the sense that they can be expressed in words. Hence linguistic minimizers such as *word, syllable*, or *iota* combine with cognitive predicates such as *believe, understand*, or *mean*. The semantically deviant examples in (12) contain predicates whose objects are not readily understood as linguistic in nature.

With many other minimizers, however, the etymological word meaning plays no role whatsoever. This is obvious with words whose etymology is no longer transparent, or where the original word meaning is plainly irrelevant, as is the case with taboo minimizers. The question is whether such terms are used interchangeably, with only stylistic or idiolectal differences, or whether they too show semantic specialization.

The main hypothesis of this paper is the following: When a nontransparent minimizer is first used, it does not show semantic specialization. Since its basic or original meaning is irrelevant, and hence does not constrain the combinatory potential of the minimizer, it may be used with a wide variety of predicates. However, due to fierce competition within the set of minimizers, such general-purpose minimizers easily become obsolete. The next generation of speakers may replace them by other equally general expressions which may sound more forceful because they are newer. But instead of dropping out, expressions may also specialize in some semantic domains. When this happens, stable collocation relations may get established between predicate and minimizer which help prevent early obsolescence.

As evidence for this diachronic tendency toward semantic specialization, I will discuss of number of Dutch minimizers which have undergone just such a process of specialization in this century. Based on a corpus of about 7500 natural occurrences of minimizers, mostly from the 20th century, I have looked at the type of predicate and tracked developments over time for some of the more frequent items. Because the evidence is statistical in nature, it is not possible to test the hypothesis on all minimizers. Many are just too infrequent, or only frequent in one period, so that any observable change in patterning might be due to mere chance. The items for which I will present some striking findings are listed in (13):

(13) *snars*   (origin unclear, probably it denoted a fast, abrupt movement)
      zier   (originally: maggot; but this original meaning is lost)
      steek   (sting or stab)
      spat   (spatter)

I have divided the 20th century data into three periods: 1900–1950, 1950–1990, and 1990–2000 and cross-classified it according to predicate type. Here I distinguish nouns, comparatives, verbs of cognition, such as *geloven, begrijpen, snappen, verstaan* "believe, understand", verbs of indifference, which denote indifference in combination with negation, such as *kunnen schelen, interesseren, geven om* "care, interest, give a damn", and a category of remaining verbs. The division into periods may seem uneven, but has to do with the fact that it is far easier to find relevant data for the 1990s (from CD-ROMs, Internet, electronic corpora, etc.) than it is for earlier periods. I note that certain minimizers are mainly or often used as modifiers of nouns, such as for instance *shred* in English, which is typically found in combinations like *without a shred of evidence, not a shred of truth,* and the like. The same is true for Dutch.

In (14), an overview is given for those minimizers which do not have selection restrictions based on their etymological meaning. Note that the set of predicates is not equally divided over the three periods.

(14)   Minimizers and their predicates (NB: temporal, financial, linguistic or spatial minimizers are not included, as these tend to attract different predicates)

	1900–1950 N = 524	1950–1990 N = 1328	1990–2000 N = 1546
noun	19%	9%	6%
comparative	6%	6%	10%
verb of cognition	19%	18%	18%
verb of indifference	23%	39%	35%
other	32%	28%	31%

With this in mind, let's now take a look at *snars*. The developments surrounding this item are summarized in (15):

(15)   SNARS: developments throughout the 20th century

	1900–1950 N = 35	1950–1990 N = 75	1990–2000 N = 107
verbs of cognition	43%	56%	66%
verbs of indifference	26%	28%	16%
other	31%	19%	21%

We see an early preference for verbs of cognition which gains strength in the course of time, at the cost mainly of the class of verbs of indifference. The category "other" remains fairly stable, it appears, but the limited amount of data does not allow us to analyze possible developments in this category.

In the case of *zier*, we see similar developments, this time favoring the class of verbs of indifference. Again we see how a small early preference for one type of predicate gets stronger over time. Note that here the "other" category seems to decrease monotonically:

(16)   ZIER: developments throughout the 20th century

	1900–1950 N = 65	1950–1990 N = 72	1990–2000 N = 74
verbs of cognition	5%	7%	3%
verbs of indifference	38%	69%	84%
other	57%	24%	13%

When we consider the position of *snars* and *zier* relative to their favorite semantic domains, a striking difference emerges:[6]

(17)

	1900–1950	% snars	1950–1990	% snars	1990–2000	% snars
verbs of cognition	130	11	290	14	327	21
		% zier		% zier		% zier
verbs of indifference	95	20	462	10	478	13

While *snars* shows a steady increase within the domain of cognition predicates, *zier* remains stable at best within the domain of indifference predicates. Hence the steady increase of verbs of indifference to be noted in (16) is due merely to the fact that all other contexts are slowly disappearing. The increase of verbs of cognition in (15), on the other hand, is not just due to all other contexts withering away, but also due to a growing preference of verbs of cognition for the item *snars*.

The next item to be considered is *steek*, the word meaning "sting, stab":

(18)   STEEK: developments throughout the 20th century

	1900–1950 N = 50	1950–1990 N = 77	1990–2000 N = 104
verbs of cognition	38%	18%	2%
verbs of indifference	30%	26%	5%
comparatives	6%	23%	46%
verbs of change	2%	11%	33%
zien "to see"	2%	9%	8%
other	28%	13%	6%

Here, there is a growing association with comparatives and verbs of change which have a comparative-like meaning. Foremost among these verbs are expressions like *vooruitgaan* "go forward, improve" and *veranderen* "change". These verbs form a natural class with comparatives. Evidence for this claim comes from certain adverbials, such as Dutch *een stuk* ("a lot"), which only combine with verbs of change and comparatives (cf. 19 below), but not with positive adjectives or verbs which do not denote change (cf. Klein 1998: 80 ff.):

(19)   *een stuk groter*   "a lot bigger"
        een stuk sneller   "a lot faster"
      * *een stuk groot*   "a lot big"
      * *een stuk snel*   "a lot fast"
        een stuk vooruitgaan   "improve a lot"
        een stuk veranderen   "change a lot"
        een stuk versnellen   "accelerate a lot"
      * *een stuk werken*   "work a lot"
      * *een stuk haten*   "hate a lot"

Semantically, this makes sense, of course. If we add the notion of time to a comparative, we get predicates of change (cf. Kamp 1980): e.g., to improve is to become or make better, to change is to become different. I note here that within the group of comparatives and comparative-like expressions, the importance of *steek* rose continually throughout the 20th century, from 10% in the first half of the century to 37% of all combinations with minimizers in the last decade.

Before moving on to the next minimizer, there is a problem with *steek* that I need to address. The table in (18) is compatible with my general claim that non-transparent minimizers show increasing semantic specialization, or become obsolete. However, if we look beyond the 20th century, the picture looks rather different. According to the WNT, the large scientific dictionary of the Dutch language, *steek* was used in the early Modern Dutch period as a minimizer, but solely in combination with the verb *zien* "to see". From the 19th century onward, however, it is used with a much wider set of predicates. This, then, looks like a perfect counter-example to my claim of unidirectional specialization. However, the WNT also suggests a way out of this problem. It suggests that the original minimizer *steek* does not come from the noun meaning "sting, stab", but from a homophonous word meaning "stitch". This makes sense because stitches are precisely the kind of small things which are difficult to see, unlike stabs. The latter, much wider usage would then be due to the emergence of a separate minimizer, this time meaning "sting, stab", which belongs to a group of minimizers denoting quick, abrupt movements, listed in (20) below:

(20) *klap* "slap"   *snars* "sip, also: snatch"
     ruk   "jerk"   *steek* "stab, sting"
     slag "slap, hit"

The final minimizer to be considered here is *spat* "speck". Unfortunately, there are not very many data points for this item, which is fairly rare, but whatever little I could find is summarized in (21):

(21) SPAT: developments throughout the 20th century

	1900–1950 N = 12	1950–1990 N = 38	1990–2000 N = 72
verbs of cognition	16%	6%	3%
verbs of indifference	8%	8%	4%
comparatives	33%	21%	14%
verbs of change	8%	6%	39%
nouns	17%	18%	21%
other	16%	41%	19%

Just as with *steek*, the most robust change appears to be a general increase of comparatives and verbs of change. This time, however, verbs of change are the more important category. Unlike *steek*, *spat* is also frequently combined with nouns. An example of such a combination is given in (22):

(22) *Er   zat geen spat   muziek in zijn body*[7]
      there sat no   speck music in his body
      "There wasn't a speck of music in his body"

4. Adverbial modifiers

Minimizers have much in common with adverbial modifiers. Just like minimizers, adverbial modifiers can be used to lend emphasis to a statement, and just like minimizers, they often show signs of semantic specialization, leading to increasingly limited distributions.[8] I have already pointed out that some adverbial modifiers may originate from the same source as minimizers, and mentioned the various modifiers derived from terms for the devil or thunder and lightning as a case in point (cf. 5 above). In (23), I have listed the verbs which combine with adverbial expressions consisting of one of these modifiers + the word *goed* "good, well", with a number indicating the frequency of the combinations in my material:

(23)   *donders/deksels/drommels goed*
"thunder+s/lid+s/devilish+s good"

+	*weten*	"know"	62
	begrijpen	"understand"	8
	beseffen	"realize"	2
	zien[9]	"see"	2
	herinneren	"remember"	1
	opletten	"look out"	1
	snappen	"understand"	1
	op de hoogte	"in the know"	1
	in de gaten hebben	"be aware of"	1
	uitleggen	"explain"	1
	kennen	"know"	1

A very similar pattern of collocations is associated with the English adverbial expression *full well* (data from newspapers on CD-ROM: *The Guardian* and *The Observer*, 1995, *The Washington Times*, 1992–1993).

(24)   *full well* + verb:

know	98
understand	3
realize	1
expect	1
suspect	1

What emerges from this list is the same set of verbs that combine readily with *snars*, the ones I have termed verbs of cognition. So adverbial phrases may select for the same semantic classes as minimizers, showing a cross-categorial similarity between these types of degree expressions.

5.   Conclusions

I have argued that expletive minimizers are highly sensitive to the lexical semantics of the predicates they combine with. Various semantic classes are preferred by the Dutch minimizers studied in this paper, e.g., some pick out verbs of change, while others pick out verbs of cognition, or predicates of indifference. Similar classes of predicates are selected by various adverbial expressions in Dutch and English. The selectional restrictions of expletive minimizers are not stable, as they do not rest on the basic meaning of the word, but may rapidly develop, within the time span of one century. I have given evidence that minimizers show increasing semantic specialization, hence narrowing of their distribution, and not widening.[10] So far, this claim appears to be supported by the available evidence, but more work on more languages is needed to tell whether we are really dealing here with universally unidirectional developments of the kind outlined in grammaticalization theory (cf., e.g., Traugott & Heine 1991). In this connection, it is interesting to note that Hopper and Traugott (1993:98) claim that narrowing of meaning appears to be absent in grammaticalization. Whether we want to view the developing collocational restrictions of minimizers as narrowing of meaning is questionable, but worth considering when we view lexical meaning not as an isolated property of individual words, but as contextual in nature.

With the advent of large-scale online corpora, the study of collocation relations is rapidly advancing. At the moment, very little is known about the ways in which these collocations come about and develop over time. This paper is a small contribution toward a better understanding of this phenomenon.

Notes

1. Other European languages show parallel developments, cf. e.g. Horn (2001) for a discussion of current English minimizers of taboo origin.

2. From A. M. de Jong, *Notities van een landstormman*, 1917.

3. From H. Heijermans, *Kamertjeszonde*, 1894.

4. From the homepage of the Feyenoord Fanatics, a group of supporters of the Rotterdam soccer team Feyenoord.

5. Postma (1995) claims that verbs with true agentive subjects cannot combine with polarity items. In this connection, he notes a difference between the verbs *horen, zien* "hear, see" and their agentive counterparts *luisteren naar, kijken naar* "listen to, look at". While the former verbs allow minimizers, the latter do not: *geen bal zien/horen* "no ball hear/see = hear/see not a thing" versus **luisteren naar/kijken naar geen bal* "listen to/look at not a thing". While it is true that there are severe restrictions on the predicates which combine with minimizers, it is not so clear how to characterize them as a set in general terms. Postma's suggestion is too general, in that it would incorrectly block combinations of minimizers/taboo terms with predicates such as *praten met* "talk to":

Ik heb op het feestje met geen hond gesproken.
I have at the party with no dog spoken
"I have not spoken to anyone at the party"

6. The numbers of the different verb classes are larger than those that can be inferred from table (14), because this time all occurrences of predicates were counted, including those combining with the types of minimizers explicitly excluded from table (14).

7. From L.-F. Céline, *Reis naar het einde van de nacht*, translation of *Voyage au bout de la nuit*, Amsterdam, 1968.

8. See Hoeksema and Klein (1995) for a discussion of distributional similarities among non-minimizing polarity-sensitive indefinites, and the adverbial phrase *as yet*.

9. The verb *zien* is used in the two examples as a verb of cognition, meaning "to understand", comparable to the use of English *see* in *I see your point*, and not as a verb of perception.

10. Widening of distribution may be found with nonexpletive minimizers, when the etymological meaning is lost through semantic bleaching. A case in point is French *ne ... pas*, which developed from an idiom meaning "not a step", restricted to verbs of motion, to the general marker of negation in French.

References

Bolinger, Dwight. 1972. *Degree Words*. The Hague: Mouton.

Hoeksema, Jack, Hotze Rullmann, Víctor Sánchez-Valencía, & Ton van der Wouden, eds. 2001. *Perspectives on Negation and Polarity Items*. Amsterdam & Philadelphia: John Benjamins.

Hoeksema, Jack & Henny Klein. 1995. "Negative Predicates and their Arguments". *Linguistic Analysis* 25: 3–4.146–180.

Hopper, Paul J. & Elizabeth Closs Traugott. 1993. *Grammaticalization*. Cambridge: Cambridge University Press.

Horn, Laurence R. 1989. *A Natural History of Negation*. Chicago: University of Chicago Press.

Horn, Laurence R. 2001. "Flaubert Triggers, Squatitive Negation, and Other Quirks of Grammar". Hoeksema et al. 2001. 175–202.

Jager, A. de. 1858. "De versterkte ontkenning in onze taal, vooral bij de middelnederlandsche schrijvers". *Latere verscheidenheden uit het gebied der Nederduitsche taalkunde*, 59–154. Deventer: A. ter Gunne.

Jespersen, Otto. 1917. *Negation in English and Other Languages*. Copenhagen: A. F. Høst.

Kamp, Hans. 1980. "Some Remarks on the Logic of Change". *Time, Tense and Quantifiers* ed. by C. Rohrer, 135–179. Tübingen: Max Niemeyer Verlag.

Klein, Henny. 1998. *Adverbs of Degree in Dutch and Related Languages*. Amsterdam & Philadelphia: John Benjamins.

Pott, August F. 1833. *Etymologische Forschungen auf dem Gebiete der Indo-Germanischen Sprachen*, vol. 1. Lemgo: Meyer.

Postma, Gertjan. 1995. *Zero Semantics. A Study of the Syntactic Conception of Quantificational Meaning*. Dissertation, University of Leiden.

Postma, Gertjan. 2001. "The Syntax of Taboo". Hoeksema et al. 2001. 285–332.

Traugott, Elizabeth Closs & Bernd Heine, eds. 1991. *Approaches to Grammaticalization*. (= *Typological Studies in Language*, 19.) Amsterdam & Philadelphia: John Benjamins.

WNT = *Woordenboek der Nederlandsche Taal*, 1882–1998. 's Gravenhage, Leiden: Nijhoff and Sijthoff, 's Gravenhage: SDU.

The conversational factor in language change

From prenominal to postnominal demonstratives

Maria M. Manoliu
University of California, Davis

1. Introduction

Generally speaking, the changes undergone by demonstratives from Latin to Romance are a favorite domain for emphasizing the importance of the role played by talk-interaction signals in accounting for different types of grammaticalization. The particular case analyzed in this contribution deals with the shift in the position of Romanian demonstratives and the functional split between prenominal and postnominal adjectives. The theoretical interest of the evolution of Romanian deictics is two-fold. On the one hand, it shows how the interplay between two contradictory typological patterns determines particular changes.[1] On the other hand, it shows how diachronic discourse patterns can be reconstructed on the basis of attested synchronic variants co-occurring in a period of language instability. These variants provide some of the missing links in the series of bleaching and/or remotivation of the deictic value.

1.1 The Balkan hypothesis

In current histories of Romance and Romanian, the Balkan hypothesis has been the preferred explanation for the postposition of both the definite article and the demonstratives, because the languages in the area under consideration prefer the order Noun +Adjective. However, the origins of this preferential word order differ from one family to another. In Bulgarian as well as in several Russian dialects, postposition is the result of a general tendency for enclisis characterizing common Old Slavic idioms. In Albanian and Romanian, the preference for postnominal demonstratives (including the definite article) is attributed to the Thraco-Illyrian substratum (see Rosetti 1968:235–236). According to this explanation, in an utterance such as (1), the prenominal *ille* would have moved after the noun to conform to the preferred position of any adjective. Consequently, Romanian chose to continue the order displayed in (2), whereas the rest of the Romance languages continued the order Demonstrative + N. Compare Latin (1) with presumed preferred spoken Balkan Latin (2):[2]

(1)   *ille homo bonus*
      that man good
      "that good man"

(2)   *homo ille bonus*
      man that good
      "that good man"

and Italian (1'a) or Spanish (1'b) with Romanian (2'a,b):

(1')   It.   a.   *quel uomo*
                   that man
       Sp.   b.   *aquel hombre*
                   that   man

(2')   Rom.   a.   *acel om*
                   that man
                   "that man"
              b.   *omul   acela*
                   man-the that
                   "that man"

The Balkan hypothesis alone is incapable of explaining the following facts:

1.   The epithet may very well follow the noun in any other Romance language, and in Spanish the demonstrative may also follow the head-noun when expressing contempt or disdain in familiar registers, but the article still precedes the noun (see (3)):

(3)   *la   muerta de hambre esa*
      the dead   of hunger this
      "that despicable [girl]"
      (Telenovela *Preciosa*, June 1999, Univision)

2.   The prenominal demonstratives can occur even when the noun is followed by an adjective in both Old (4) and Contemporary Romanian (5):

(4)   *această apă   limpede*
      this   water limpid
      "this limpid and purifying water" (CI, 5)

(5)   *acest copil nevinovat*
      this   child innocent
      "this innocent child"

3.   In 16th century texts, cases in which the postnominal demonstrative is followed by an adjective or/and any other definite description are extremely rare, and the definite article may also precede the noun (6), so the substratum influence could hardly be invoked as being still active.

(6)   *lui   proroc   David*
      the.GEN prophet David
      "of the prophet David"   (CC1: 54 in Densusianu 1961.2:112)

1.2   The hypothesis of cyclic bleaching

In my opinion, the proliferation and the distribution of Romanian demonstratives is explicable if a variety of factors are considered.

a.   *The typological factor.* On the one hand, Romanian belongs to the Romance pattern favoring prepositional markers; on the other, it is located within the European area favoring postpositions. Thanks to these two tendencies, Romanian could develop both prenominal and postnominal case markers, articles, and demonstratives.

b.   *The predominance of the oral register.* In the Balkan area, to the north and south of the Danube, during the medieval period, the socio-historical conditions favored the oral rather than the written registers of the Romance variety. The first Romanian text available is a private letter of June 1521 by the boyar Neacşu from Câmpulung (Muntenia).[3] The oral character favored the extensive use of discourse-coherence devices and markers of talk-interaction such as demonstratives. It may be worth recalling here that recent discourse and pragmatic theoretical developments have underscored the fact that demonstratives are means of enabling the addressee to identify the referent. As such, they function as talk-interaction clues, which explains their overuse in conversation and the faster bleaching of their deictic value.[4]

As will become clear in what follows, in Romanian there are more variants originating in the Latin demonstratives than anywhere else in the Romance-speaking world. In my opinion, we are faced with a cyclic phenomenon, in which each demonstrative goes through similar stages, even if the final result is different. These stages may be described briefly as follows:

a.   The starting point is represented by the use of the demonstrative as a conversation marker (providing supplementary information for retrieving the referent).
b.   It then becomes a foregrounding marker (upgrading the discourse salience of the following description (either restrictive or not).[5]
c.   It ends by losing its foregrounding value.

Consequently, another variant of the demonstrative is used for the same purpose and undergoes the same cycle of progressive bleaching of its indexical value.

Due to the lack of attestation until the 16th c., the evolution of Romanian demonstratives requires discourse reconstruction. Fortunately, such a reconstruction is possible thanks to the fact that, starting with Old Romanian texts in the 16th c., the stages of this cycle are present in one or another variant originating in Latin demonstratives. In what follows we shall propose a model of these cycles on the basis of the attested forms from the 16th c. onward.

2.   From pronouns to articles

2.1   Cycle 1: The definite article

As in Latin, in Romanian (unattested period) the demonstratives followed by a definite description must have had the role of providing supplementary information with the purpose of ensuring the correct identification of the referent. On the basis of the attributive and dative constructions found in Old Romanian (compare (6) and (7)), the following reconstructions are possible: (1) Dem + N (*lŭ împăratu* "of/to that emperor") and (2) N + Dem (*împăratu lŭ* "emperor that one") — see Densusianu 1961.2:112–113).

(7)   N   Pro-GEN/DAT Att
      împăratŭ- lui   leşescŭ
      emperor   that-GEN/DAT Polish
      "of/to the Polish emperor"

In Old Romanian the postnominal distal deictic -*lu*(*i*) is already specialized as a definite article, as a means of signaling only that the referent belongs to the co-textually or contextually activated knowledge, and also as a case marker. As I hope to have demonstrated elsewhere (Manoliu 1985), the postposition of the definite article must have been related to the preservation of case markers in the first declension for the genitive/dative singular. This unique phenomenon in the Romance domain is probably due to the fact that Romanian is situated in the larger European geographical area that preserved case inflection, regardless of language family (Romance, Slavic, Greek, Germanic, Finno-Ugric). The definite article became a new case marker, and the postposed variant was preferred in order to conform to the morphological pattern already in place (see Manoliu 1985, 1995b; Renzi 1992). For readers unfamiliar with Romanian I provide two examples characterizing the most productive Romanian declensions, namely the feminine declension originating in the Latin first declension (e.g., *doamnă* "queen, mistress") and the masculine declension based mainly on the Latin second declension (*domn* "king, lord, master"). The feminine declension has preserved the opposition between nominative/accusative (Lat. -*a*(*m*) > Rom. *ă*) on the one hand, and the genitive/dative (Lat. *ae* > Rom. *e*) on the other (see (8)). The arrows in (8) and (9) below indicate the spread of the original nominative/accusative forms to the genitive/dative.

(8) Lat. *domina* "mistress"

		V. Latin		Romanian		
SG	NOM/ACC	*domina*		*doamnă*	with article	*doamna*
	GEN/DAT	*dominae*		*doamne*		*doamnei*
PL	NOM/ACC	*dominae*	↓	*doamne*	↓	*doamnele*
	GEN/DAT	*dominae*		*doamne*		*doamnelor*

Thanks to the definite article, even nouns originating in other declensions acquired a postposed bound morpheme:

(9) Lat. *dominu-* — Rom. *domn* "master"

	SG				PL		
NOM/ACC	*domn*			*domnul domni*			*domnii*
GEN/DAT	*domn*	↓ with article	*domnului domni*		↓ with article	*domnilor*

A supporting proof for the hypothesis of case marking is constituted by the following phenomena present in 16th c. texts:

1. Both variants of the definite article (that is *lui* <Lat.*illui and *lu* <Lat. *illu-*) can be found in either prenominal or postnominal position. Proper nouns preferred prenominal case markers (see Rosetti 1986:599). Even in contemporary oral registers, *lu* is the preferred variant of the genitive-dative case marker before proper nouns and nouns denoting unique family members, regardless of their grammatical gender (e.g., *lu tata* "of/to my father", *lu mama* "of/to [my] mother"). This preference was interpreted as a way of encoding "personal gender".[6]

2. But even masculine proper nouns ending in -*a* (like feminine nouns continuing the Latin first declension) may take an enclitic article as the genitive/dative marker (10).

(10) *lu   Marco şi   Lucăei*
      the-MASC.GEN Marc and Luca-the.FEM/GEN
      "Marc's and Luca's" (CI: 2)

In my opinion, this reinterpretation of the prenominal article as a marker of both case and personal gender is a result of the interplay between the two typological patterns determining the changes undergone by Romanian as a whole.[7]

2.2 Cycle 2: The reinforced demonstratives: *cestŭ* (< **ecce-istu-*) and *celŭ* (< **ecce-illu-*)

As a consequence of the cliticization and the bleaching of the deictic value of the definite article, a second postnominal demonstrative (followed or not by a definite description) may be used to fulfill the same conversational function of providing supplementary information. It is very likely that the second pronouns that occurred in the appositive construction were the variants *cestŭ* and *celŭ*, reinforced by *ecce* "here is", since they seem to be the first reinforced demonstratives that lost their capacity of functioning as independent pronouns. In 16th c. texts they already require the presence of either a noun or a definite description. In Old Romanian, the appositive structure illustrated by (7), namely N-Art+Adj (+Art) changes to the one shown in (11):

(11) a. N-Art   Pro Adj-Art
          vițelulŭ celŭ hrănitu
          calf-the that fed
          "the fat calf " (CI: 31)
      b. N-Art   Pro Adj-Art
          letopisețul   cestŭ moldovenescŭ
          chronicle-the this Moldavian
          "this Moldavian Chronicle" (Ur: 83)

The function of introducing an appositive description may be found in all periods of attested Romanian.[8] Their transformation into means of foregrounding is obvious in the contexts in which they introduce an attribute that could constitute a definite description by itself, even in the absence of the demonstrative (see below *Act de hotărnicie*, 1636).

(12) *Într-aceaea preuții și bătrînii orașului, mic și mare, văzîndu cum au mutat Sava*
      piatra cea den luncă, *care au fost pusă de Radul-Voievod cu 12 boiari, și le-au*
      împresurat moșiile fără direptate, venit-au popa Borcea [...] și Iane [...] și Costea
      [...] cu preoții și cu toți oroșanii, de la mic pînă la mare, înaintea Domniii meale,
      la divan, de au dat știre și se-au plînsu de Sava, cum au mutat **hotarul cel den**
      luncă *de le-au împresurat Sava moșiile ...* (CLRV: 200).
      "For this reason the priests and the old men of the town, of all categories, seeing
      that Sava moved **that stone in the meadow** [lit. stone-the that in meadow],
      which has been set there by King Radu together with 12 boyars, and took their
      lands unjustly, Father Borcea and Ian [..], and Costea [...] together with the
      priests and all the townsmen, of all categories, came before me, at the council, to
      inform me and to complain about Sava, how he moved **that border in the mead-**
      ow [lit. border-the **that** from the meadow] and took their land."

It is clear that "the border stone in the meadow" is the key-factor in the complaint to the King and the reason for the King to issue the act in question reinstating the former borders.

Even in 16th-17th centuries, *celŭ/cestŭ* behave as semi-bound morphemes because they can co-occur only before a noun (13–14) or before a definite descrip-tion (15). Later *cel* becomes an "adjectival article" and part of the marker of the relative superlative in standard varieties (16).

(13)   *den   ceastă evanghelie*
       from this   Gospel
       "from this Gospel" (CI: 11)

(14)   *celŭ feciorŭ mai   micŭ*
       that son   more young
       "the youngest son" (CI: 20)

(15)   *celŭ fără de   păcate*
       that without sins
       "the one without sins" (CI: 33)

(16)   *cel mai   bun   sfat*
       the more good advice
       "the best advice"

2.3 Cycle 3: The two-way reinforced deictics: *cesta* and *cela*

As mentioned above, in 16th c. texts, the variants *cesta* "this" (*ecce+iste+a*) and *cela* "that" (*ecce+illu+a*) may be found as pronominal demonstratives (17), or as intensifiers (18). *Cela* "that" is the preferred intensifier introducing an attribute (see Table 1).

(17)   *cesta al mieu, cesta al tău*
       this of mine, this of yours
       "this one [is] mine, this one [is] yours"
       (*Regulamentul vieții monahale*, 1626 in CLRV: 188)

(18)   *locul   cela strîmtul   ce   știi   și   Domnia   Ta*
       place-the that narrow-the that knows also Highness Your
       "that narrow place that Your Highness also knows"
       (Neacșu, in CLRV: 51)

In current histories of the Romanian language this enclitic *-a* is considered a morpheme that reinforces the deictic function. In my opinion, it is very probably based on locative adverbial deictics such as Lat. *hac* "in this place, on this side, here" or *illac* "on that side, there". At first, the adverbial *hac* could very well follow the proximity deictic when pronominal in colloquial registers: e.g., *iste hac* "this one, in here" (Cf. Ar. *aestu*(< *istu-*)-*aoa* "this one", where *aoa* is also an adverb "here"; It. *questo qua* "this one, in here"; cf. also Sp. *aca*, and OFr. *ça* < Lat. *ecce-hac* "here it is"). The distal adverb *illac* "there" could follow the distal deictic: e.g., *illu-illac* (cf. Ar. *ațelu* (< *ecce-ille*)-*aclo* "that [one]", *aclo* can function also as an adverb "there"; It. *là*, OFr. *la* < Lat. *illac* "through/in there").[9]

   Like *cel*, when functioning as a foregrounding device, the doubly reinforced distal deictic *cela* may be used even when the following attribute has no restrictive value:

(19)   *și   voi blăstăma cu   mâna   mea ceaea înralta*
and will curse   with hand-the mine that   high-the
"and I shall curse with my high hand" (CS: 239)

As a pronoun, *cela* has to be followed by a definite description:

(20)   *ajutoriulŭ celuia   de   susŭ*
help-the   that.GEN from above
"the help of the one above" (i.e. "in heaven") (CI: 16)

Table 1.   The distribution of cel[a] in 16th and 17th century texts

	demonstrative	total	Pro	Dem +/Adj/PN	Dem+N (+Adj/PN)	Dem+S	N+Dem+ Adj/PN/S
Coresi	cela	73	43	5	0	38	30
		100%	60%	7%		52%	41%
	cel	17	7	4	9	3	1
		100%	41%	24%	53%	18%	6%
	cest	7	0	0	7	0	0
		100%			100%		
Costin	cela	4	1	0	0	1	3
		100%	25%			25%	75%
	cel	17	4	4	1	0	12
		100%	24%	24%	6%		71%
Ureche	cela	9	8	0	0	8	1
		100%	89%			89%	11%
	cel	38	0	10	0	0	28
		100%		19%			74%
	cest	4	0	0	1	0	3
		100%			25%		75%
Neculce	cela	5	2	0	3	0	0
		100%	4%		6%		
	cel	22	3	3	0	3	13
		100%	14%	14%		14%	59%

3. Postnominal versus prenominal demonstratives

3.1 Cycle 4: The three-way reinforced deictics: *acest(a)* "this" – *acel(a)* "that"

The previous cycles are supporting evidence for the ways in which the three-way reinforced demonstratives (that is *ad* "to" + *eccu-* "here is"+ *iste/ille* + *a*) acquired the present distribution for the periods in which there are no written texts available. The hypothesis of a pronominal origin of the postnominal demonstrative is favored also by the fact that the three-way reinforced deictic has been used first and foremost as a pronoun in 16th-c. texts: 84% of the total number of forms ending in *-a* are pronouns and only 16% occur after a noun (see Table 2).

In 16th- and 17th-century texts (especially in sermons and chronicles, which make ample use of oral devices), the longest postnominal demonstratives frequently occur as means of foregrounding the characteristics expressed by the following attribute. As such, they replace the other variants, which started to undergo a bleaching of their foregrounding value, as shown by their transformation into semi-cliticized morphemes before attributes (this is the case with the adjectival article *cel*) or remained only as regional variants (*cesta/cela*).

The fact that the postnominal demonstratives are no longer full pronouns but first and foremost means of foregrounding is proved by the following distributional properties:

1. Due to its focalizing function, the demonstrative can co-occur even after a personal pronoun:

(21)   *Elŭ acesta* [...] *vru   să se întrupească*
      he this   wanted that REFL embodies
      "He (this one) wanted to take human form". (CI: 2)

2. The demonstrative may co-occur with a noun followed by a definite description that could be sufficient for retrieving the referent:

(22)   *domniia aceea a   lui   Simion vodă*
      reign-the that that the-GEN Simion King
      "King Simion's reign" (Costin: 72)

As (22) shows, the attribute (*lui Simion vodă*) would have represented a restrictive, definite description by itself. The addition of the demonstrative has the role of upgrading the discourse salience of the whole NP.

3. The postnominal demonstrative expresses a *contrastive focus*. In (23) "this brother of yours" is opposed to the addressee, the older brother, who remained at home, but the prodigal son is absent when the father is talking (there are only two brothers).

Table 2. The distribution of demonstratives in 16th–17th century texts

	Demon-strative	total	Pro	Adj	Dem +N	Dem-a +N	N+ Dem-a	N+Dem
Coresi	acest[a]	106	56	50	31	1	18	0
		100%	53%	47%	29%	1%	17%	
	acel[a]	65	53	12	5	4	3	0
		100%	82%	18%	8%	6%	6%	
Costin	acest[a]	48	9	39	31	4	3	1
		100%	19%	81%	65%	8%	6%	2%
	acel[a]	43	9	34	18	14	2	0
		100%	21%	79%	42%	33%	5%	
Ureche	acest[a]	29	4	25	23	1	1	0
		100%	15%	85%	63%	12%	12%	
	acel[a]	41	10	31	21	9	1	0
		100%	24%	76%	51%	22%	2%	
Neculce	acest[a]	20	5	15	14	0	1	0
		100%	25%	75%	70%		5%	
	acel[a]	35	6	29	23	5	1	0
		100%	17%	83%	66%	14%	3%	
Texts	demonstrat-ives	387	152	235	166	38	30	1
		100%	39%	61%	43%	10%	8%	0.3%

(23) *că   fratele   tău acesta* mortŭ era …
because brother-the your this   dead was
"because this brother of yours was dead …" (CI: 33)

As the unmarked term of the discourse opposition [± Foregrounded], the pre-nominal adjective functioning mostly as an endophor still represents the majority of occurrences: Comp. Dem + N: 167+38 out of 236 occurrences, i.e. 86%; N + Dem: 31 out of 236, i.e. 13% (see Table 2).

3.2 Final stage of the fourth cycle: Modern Romanian (19th–20th centuries)

Recent studies of Romanian demonstratives have pointed to several phenomena belonging to various language levels, such as morphemic diversification (Iordan et al. 1967:140–141), syntactic constraints (Giusti 1995:111–114), and pragmatic/discourse functions (Iliescu 1988; Tasmowski-De Ryck 1990; Manoliu 2000). As I hope to have demonstrated elsewhere (Manoliu 2000), the conditions governing the use of demonstratives in contemporary Romanian transgress the syntactic constraints. After examining previous discourse and pragmatic explanations of the present distribution of Romanian demonstratives, I concluded that the following dimensions could define the main differences between the postnominal and prenominal demonstratives:

1. *the speaker's hypothesis on the origin of information necessary for the retrieval of the referent; (a) the co-text or (b) the addressee's general active knowledge.*
2. *the relation between the story-world and the enunciation world* (consisting in speakers and space/time dimensions): the two worlds may be presented as merging or being different.
3. *the stage distance*: this accounts for the difference in the choice of the distal or the proximity deictic. The speaker intends to make the addressee see the events as happening in front of him (*close-ups*) or as happening at a certain spatial or temporal distance (*remote perspective*).

Within the framework of an instructional type of semantics, the difference between pre- and post-nominal demonstratives may be described as follows: (1) the prenominal demonstrative could be assimilated to a directive such as: "you know the referent I am talking about because we talked about it"; (2) the postnominal demonstrative gives a different directive, namely: "you know the referent, don't you?!".

3.2.1 *The prenominal demonstratives as endophors*

Being neutral as to expressive function, the prenominal demonstratives are used primarily as an anaphoric device (see Table 3). In other words, the prenominal demonstratives take the text as the point of origin when giving instructions for the retrieval of the referent. They carry the conventional implicature of 'the separation between the world of enunciation and the story-world'. The distal prenominal endophor strongly activates the implicature of the difference between these two worlds, whereas the proximity endophor tends to blur it. In (24), for example, *acest împărat* "this emperor" refers back to the newly introduced topic *un împărat bogat și puternic* "a rich and powerful emperor":

(24)　A　fost　odată　un împărat　foarte bogat și　puternic.
　　　　has been once　an emperor very　rich　and powerful.

　　　Acest împărat avea　　　*un fecior și*　*o fată*
　　　this　emperor had-IMPERF a　son　and a daughter
　　　"Once upon a time there was a very rich and powerful emperor. **This emperor** had a son and a daughter". (Ispirescu: 307)

The distal demonstrative also refers to the story-world for the retrieval of the referent but overtly marks the existing distance (non-identity) between the story-world and the speaker's world. Compare (25) with (24) above:

(25)   *A fost odată un împărat. Acel împărat mare şi puternic bătuse pe toţi împăraţii de*
      prinpregiurul lui ...
      "Once upon a time there was an emperor. That great and powerful emperor
      had defeated all the neighboring emperors". (Ispirescu: 12)

3.2.2 *The postnominal demonstratives as actualisers*

The postposed demonstrative undergoes a certain degree of bleaching and can no
longer function as a marker of foregrounding. From its deictic value it preserves the
capacity of referring to the enunciation. As such, it functions as a marker carrying the
conventional implicature that presents the story-world as merging with the enunciation world even when it is not followed by an attribute.[10] This hypothesis predicts
the fact that the postnominal demonstratives are used as indexicals par excellence
(see Table 3).

1.   *Exophoric use.* In the segment of dialogue reproduced in (26), for example, the
referent is included in the space of the enunciation; both the speaker and the
addressee are present.

(26)   *–Văz că tu eşti voinică, fata mea, şi bine ai făcut de ţi-ai luat **calul ăsta**, căci fără*
      dînsul te-ai fi întors şi tu ca şi surorile tale.
      "I see that you are courageous, dear girl, and you made the right decision when
      you took this horse [lit. **horse-the this**], because, without it, you would have
      gone back as your sisters did." (Ispirescu: 19)

2.   *Deixis ad phantasma.* As Bühler (1982: 12) emphasizes, in this mode of pointing, the index finger as the natural tool of *demonstratio ad oculos* is replaced by
other deictic aids.[11] When orienting the addressee these deictics take as the point of
origin an enunciator in the domain of grown-up *memories* and of the constructive
imagination. According to Iliescu (1988: 17), the postposed demonstrative *acela*
"that" may occur even at the beginning of a story, because the narrator wants to
attract the reader into his/her intimate world. This is the case with the temporal
phrase in (27).

(27)   *Până în **clipa aceea**, mă plictisisem. Şi cum nu sunt obişnuit să aştept subtilităţi de*
      gândire din partea d-lui Roman, eram gata să închid televizorul, ca să mă scutesc de
      alte platitudini.
      "Until that moment [lit. **moment that**], I had been bored. And, since I am not
      accustomed to expect any subtleties in Mr. Roman's thoughts, I was about to
      switch off the television set, so I could escape other platitudes." (*Luceafărul*
      românesc, 8. 89 (1998): 1)

3.   *Endophoric use.* When used as an endophor, the demonstrative overtly anchors
the story-world into the speaker's hypothesis about the addressee's knowledge. In
(28) *flăcăul acesta* "this fellow" refers to the previously introduced referent and also
establishes a relation between the story-world and the enunciation-world:

Table 3. The distribution of demonstratives in 20th century texts

Texts	Demonstrative Adj		Dem + N	N + Dem	N+Dem+Att
Adameşteanu	acest[a]	29/100%	1/3%	22/76%	6/21%
	acel[a]	11/100%	0	6/55%	5/45%
Tănase	acest[a]	62/100%	3/5%	45/73%	14/23%
	acel[a]	19/100%	1/5%	10/53%	8/42%
Academia Caţavencu	ăsta/asta	24/100%	6/25%	12/50%	6/25%
	ăla/aia	13/100%	0	6/46%	7/54%
România Mare	ăsta	118/100%	40/34%	47/38%	31/26%
	ăla	34/100%	8/24%	3/9%	23/68%
total	demonstrative	290/100%	59/20%	131/45%	100/34%

(28) Bag de seamă nu era   aşa de căscăund flăcăul   acesta [...]
      I realize   not was.IMPERF SO   dumb   fellow-the this
      "I realize that this fellow was not so dumb" (Ispirescu: 200)

4. The fifth cycle: The oral variants as means of foregrounding

It seems that a parallel development occurs in the variants preferred by oral registers, namely ăl[a]/ăst[a], from the very beginning of Romanian history. According to Ivănescu (1980: 148–149), these short variants continue directly Latin non-reinforced forms such as iste "this" and ille "that". They are found mainly in Muntenia and in some Southern Danubian dialects, such as Aromanian (see Caragiu et al. 1977; see Table 4).

Table 4. The variants of demonstratives according to the social register

Register	Literary				Oral			
Type	proximal		distal		proximal		distal	
Gender	MASC	FEM	MASC	FEM	MASC	FEM	MASC	FEM
SG	acesta	aceasta	acela	aceea	ăsta	asta	ăla	aia
PL	aceştia	acestea	aceia	acelea	ăştia	ăstea	ăia	alea

4.1   Pragmatic values of oral variants

As mentioned earlier (see 3.2.1 above), the postnominal demonstratives carry the conventional implicature of the merger between the story-world and the enunciation-world, serve to visualize the events, or at least to bring them into the actuality of enunciation. Thanks both to this conventional implicature and to their reduced phonetic form, the shorter postposed demonstratives are preferred in familiar conversation. When not activated, the value of physical (spatial/temporal) distance can be reinterpreted as an affective detachment activating positive or negative connotations of the attribute. In (29), the story teller describes the beauty of the king's daughter and makes ample use of postposed demonstratives for expressing his admiration:

(29)   *ochii   ăia   marii,   frumoşi   şi   vioi,*
eyes-the those big-the beautiful and lively

de   te   bagă în   boale
that you-ACC drive into illnesses

mânuşiţa   aia micuţă şi   picioruşul   ca de zână
hand-little-the that tiny   and leg-little-the as of fairy
"those beautiful, big and so lively eyes that drive you crazy, that tiny hand and the little leg like [the leg] of a fairy, ..." (Ispirescu: 20)

As happened with the older variants, in contemporary written registers imitating the spoken varieties, these shorter postnominal demonstratives may serve to foreground the following description. The pragmatic exploitation of short forms in written registers — usually favoring a derogatory connotation — rests mainly on the difference between spoken and written variants in particular and on the low social status of the regional variety in general.[12] The fact that most of the time the distal rather than the proximity demonstrative expresses the speaker's psychological detachment is due to the perspective of remoteness, which conflicts with the implicature of merging worlds.

(30)   *Mai tunde-te, ceafă groasă [...]: şi cu floacele alea-n obraji, ce-i?!... Un'te crezi!*
"Have a haircut, big head [...]: and what about that tuft [lit. **tufts-the those**] on your cheeks. Where do you think [you are]?!" (ST: 13)

The proximity postnominal demonstrative can convert its feature of 'physical proximity' to the enunciator into psychological involvement and express a derogatory attitude (31):

(31)   *Cine ne scapă de   prostul   ăsta fudul   [...]?*
who us deliver from dummy-the this arrogant
"Who is going to deliver us from **this arrogant dummy** [...]?"
(*România Mare.* 408, May 8: 2)

4.2 The pro-utterance *asta* "this"

In spite of the socially low status of oral registers, the pro-form *asta* "this" (original-ly a regional variant from Muntenia) has lost its familiar character and occurs frequently in written registers (in newspapers, for example), when carrying the information of a whole utterance.

(32)   *Europa s-a oferit să ne ajute cu bani și oameni și să ne integreze. Pentru România de astăzi asta înseamnă, pur și simplu, viața.* (*Adevărul* 26/1/2000).
   "Europe has offered to help us with money and people and to integrate us. For today Romania this (neuter) means, purely and simply, life."

5. Conclusions

As has been pointed out above, the theoretical interest of the history of Romanian demonstratives is two-fold:

1.   It shows how two conflicting typological tendencies served to remotivate the differences between preposed markers (favored by the preferences of the Romance type) and postposed markers (favored by the areal typological tendencies). The enclitic demonstrative became both a definite article and a case marker. The preposed demonstrative became a marker of both case and personal gender. The preposed *al* and the postnominal *cel* became semi-independent pronouns in the sense that they cannot occur alone but require the presence of a definite description (an attribute). However, their function is different: *al* serves as a genitive-possessive marker, whereas *cel* became an intensifier. The preposed demonstratives *acest/acel* specialized as anaphors referring exclusively to the co-textual information. The postnominal demonstratives *acesta/acela* serve to present the text-world as merging with the enunciation world. The shorter spoken variants are preferred in post-nominal position and are extensively used as pragmatic markers.

2.   The evolution of Romanian demonstratives provides interesting evidence for diachronic discourse reconstruction on the basis of attested synchronic variants. In the case under discussion, the co-occurrence of synchronic variants of demonstratives serves to advance a hypothesis of a more general diachronic sequencing of bleaching stages:

Stage 1: appositive demonstratives used as *conversation markers*: they provide supplementary information for retrieving the referent.

Stage 2: demonstratives used as *discourse (foregrounding) markers* and/or *pragmatic markers*.

Stage 3: *specialization of demonstratives according to their distribution* (see above).

3. Statistical data also support the hypothesis of cyclic bleaching of the deictic value. For example, in Old Romanian (16th-17th cs.), the occurrence of *cel* before a noun is in continuous decline: from 53% in Coresi, it falls to 0% in Costin, Ureche, and Neculce. This decline is in agreement with the specialization of *cel* as a foregrounding device before an adjectival attribute. In its turn, *acel*, which will become the standard prenominal variant, presents an increasing number of occurrences (Coresi: 8%, Costin: 42%, Ureche: 51%, Neculce: 66%). When functioning as foregrounding devices in the structure N + Dem + Att, the frequency of *cel* and *cela* is also revealing for the cyclic development: *cela* (which will be marginalized as a regional variant) occurs frequently in Coresi (41%), then its occurrence diminishes considerably (Ureche: 11%, Costin and Neculce: 0%), whereas the frequency of *cel* increases dramatically (Coresi: 6%, Costin 71%, Ureche: 78%), which explains the fact that *cel* will remain a foregrounding device even in the 19th c. In 16th- and 17th-c. texts, the three-way reinforced deictic *acela* (which will become the standard postnominal and pronominal demonstrative) hardly ever occurs before an attribute (Coresi: 1, i.e., 0.9%, Costin 1, i.e., 2%, Ureche: 2, i.e., 2%, Neculce: 1, i.e., 3%).

Notes

1. For details on these two conflicting tendencies see Manoliu (1995b).

2. See, for example, the same construction in a translation of the Bible: *cito perferte mihi stolam illam primam et induite illum* (Luca. 15, 22, in Mihăescu 1960:163) "bring right away my ceremonial garment that first [one] and put [it] on him". Renzi (1992:173) also thinks that this construction was already used in Latin for the purpose of introducing an apposition.

3. Earlier written texts used either Latin or Slavonic.

4. See Bühler (1982). According to Kleiber (1992), "Si un locuteur utilise une expression indexicale, c-est-à dire une expression qui déclenche une procédure de répérage spatio-temporel, c'est qu'il juge que son interlocuteur n'a pas encore le référent à l'esprit (cas du référent nouveau) ou qu'il entend le lui faire découvrir sous un aspect nouveau (dans l'hypothèse où le référent est déjà connu)."

5. The concept of 'foregrounding' is used here in the sense given by Chafe (1976:287), namely "a process by which a particular referent is established in the foreground of consciousness while other discourse elements remain in the background" (see also Brown & Yule 1986:135).

6. For more details see Rosetti (1986:599).

7. Because of space limitations, I shall not elaborate here on the evolution of the semi-clitic *al*, another variant originating in *ille*, which became a possessive article introducing a secondary description (expressed by a possessive NP). A detailed description of its evolution may be found in Manoliu (1995a).

8. Iordan et al. (1967:178) pointed to the fact that this use is still frequent in the 18th and 19th centuries: e.g., *oile cele rătăcite* "the sheep those [which are] lost" (Ivireanul: 126), *Și eu eram vesel ca vremea cea bună* "and I was joyful as the weather [the one which is] beautiful" (Creangă: 33).

9. According to Rohlfs (1969:247–248), in Southern Italian dialects *qua* (<*eccum-hac*) and *là* (*alla, lla,* etc. < *illac*) are predominant as local adverbials. For *-a* in *acela* see Puşcariu (1905) and Candrea & Densusianu (1907). Once it became a clitic intensifier, *-a* could be attached to all kinds of deictics, pronominal or adverbial: *acesta* "this one", *acela* "that one", *acuma* "now" (cf. *acum*), *aicea* "here" (cf. *aici*), and even *atuncea* "then" (cf. *atunci*). The cliticization of the adverbial deictic (*hac* or *illac*) constitutes another phenomenon pointing to the importance of the conversational factor in morphological change.

10. For Grice (1975), conventional implicatures are non-truth conditional inferences that are not derived from superordinate pragmatic principles as maxims are, but are simply attached by convention to particular lexical items or expressions: this is the case with expressions serving to deny expectations: e.g., *but* (vs. *and*); *even* (*if*), *however, although,* etc.

11. As Bühler (1982:23) underscores: "It is not the case at all that the natural deictic aids, upon which the *demonstratio ad oculos* is based, are *completely* missing in the *deixis ad phantasma*. Rather, it is such that speaker and listener in a vivid description of something absent dispose of the devices and means which permit an *actor* on stage to make the absent present, and which permit the *spectator* of the play to interpret that which is present on stage, as a mimesis of the absent."

12. According to Iordan et al. (1967:140–141), in contemporary spoken Romanian the literary forms have a somewhat official/formal, almost pedantic character. In what follows their contemporary use is illustrated by a few newspapers of a polemic character such as *Academia Caţavencu* and *România mare* (see Table 3).

References

Corpora

Caţavencu: Academia Caţavencu, Săptămînal de moravuri grele, Bucharest.

CI: Diaconul Coresi, *Carte cu învăţătură* (1581), publicată de Sextil Puşcariu şi Alexie Procopovici, 1. Textul, Bucharest: Socec and Co., 1914.

CLRV: *Crestomaţia Limbii române vechi.*1 (1521–1639), ed. by Alexandru Mareş, Bucharest: Editura Academiei Române, 1994.

Creangă: Ion Creangă, *Opere,* ediţie îngrijită, prefaţă şi glosar de G. Călinescu [Clasicii români], Bucharest: Editura de stat pentru literatură şi artă, 1953.

CS: *Codex Sturdzanu.* Studiu filologic, studiu lingvistic, ediţie de text şi indice de cuvinte de Gheorghe Chivu, Bucharest: Editura Academiei Române, 1993.

CV: *Codicele Voroneţean,* ediţie critică, studiu filologic şi studiu lingvistic de Mariana Costinescu, Bucharest: Minerva, 1981 [15th c.–16th c.].

GA: Adameşteanu, Gabriela, *Dimineaţa pierdută.* Bucharest: Editura Albatros, 1991.

Ispirescu: Petre Ispirescu, *Legende sau basmele românilor* ed. by Aristiţa Avramescu. Prefaţă de Iorgu Iordan, Bucharest: Editura pentru Literatură, 1968.

Ivireanul: Ivireanul, Antim. *Predici.* Ediţie critică, studiu introductiv şi glosar de G. Ştempel, Bucharest: Editura Academiei, 1962 [18th c.].

MC: Miron Costin. *Opere alese. Letopiseţul Ţării Moldovei. De neamul moldovenilor, Viaţa lumii.* Texte stabilite, studiu introductiv, note şi glosar de Liviu Onu, Bucharest: Editura Ştiinţifică, 1967 [16th c.].

Nec: Ion Neculce, *Opere. Letopiseţul Ţării Moldovei şi O samă de cuvinte,* ediţie critică şi studiu introductiv de Gabriel Ştrempel. Bucharest: Minerva, 1982 [18th c.].

Rugă: *Cărticică de Rugăciune*, Sibiu, Progresul, 1942.
ST: Stelian Tănase, *Corpuri de iluminat*. Roman. Bucharest: Cartea românească, 1990.
Ur: Grigore Ureche, *Letopisețul Țării Moldovei*. Texte stabilite, studiu introductiv și glosar de Liviu Onu, Bucharest: Editura Științifică, 1967 [16th c].

Secondary Sources

Brown, Gillian & George Yule. 1986. *Discourse Analysis*. Cambridge: Cambridge University Press.

Bühler, Karl. 1982. "The Deictic Field of Language and Deictic Words". *Speech, Place, and Action: Studies of deixis and gesture* ed. by Robert J. Jarvella & Wolfgang Klein, 9–30. Chichester (West Sussex) & New York: John Wiley & Sons Ltd.

Candrea, Ion A. & Ovidiu Densusianu. 1907–1914. *Dicționarul etimologic al limbii române. Elemente latine (A-Putea)*. Bucharest: Socec.

Caragiu-Marioțeanu, Matilda, Ștefan Giosu, Liliana Ionescu-Ruxăndoiu, & Romulus Todoran, eds. 1977. *Dialectologie română*. Bucharest: Editura Didactică și Pedagogică.

Chafe, Wallace L. 1976. "Giveness, Contrastiveness, Definiteness, Subjects, Topics, and Point of View". *Subject and Topic* ed. by Charles N. Li, 25–55. New York: Academic Press.

Densusianu, Ovidiu. 1961 (1938[1]). *Istoria limbii române. 1 (Originile) — 2 (Secolul al 16-lea)* ed. by Jack Byck. Bucharest: Editura Științifică.

Giusti, Giuliana. 1995. "Heads and Modifiers among Determiners: Evidence from Rumanian". *Advances in Roumanian Linguistics* ed. by Gugliemo Cinque & Giuliana Giusti, 103–125. Amsterdam & Philadelphia: Benjamins.

Grice, Peter H. 1975. "Logic and conversation". *Syntax and Semantics. 3. Speech Acts* ed. by Peter Cole, & Jerry L. Morgan. 41–58. New York & London: Academic Press.

Iliescu, Maria. 1988. "La pragmatica degli aggettivi dimostrativi rumeni". *Linguistica* 28.15–33.

Iordan, Iorgu, Valeria Guțu-Romalo, & Alexandru Niculescu. 1967. *Structura morfologică a limbii române contemporane*. Bucharest: Editura Științifică.

Ivănescu, Gheorghe. 1980. *Istoria limbii române*. Iași: Junimea.

Kleiber, Georges. 1992. "Anaphore-Deixis: deux approaches concurrentes". *La deixis. Colloque en Sorbonne (8–9 juin 1990) (= Linguistique nouvelle)* ed. by Mary-Annick Morel & Laurent Danon-Boileau, 613–623. Paris: Presses Universitaires de France.

Manoliu, Maria. 1985. "Genetic Type versus Areal Coherence: Rumanian Case Markers and the Definite Articles". *Mélanges linguistiques dédiés à la mémoire de Petar Skok (1881–1956)*, 301–308. Zagreb: Académie Yougoslave des Sciences et des Arts.

Manoliu, Maria. 1995a. "Genetic Congruence Versus Areal Convergence: The misfortune of Latin *ad* in Romanian". *Historical Linguistics 1993* ed. by Henning Andersen, 269–281. Amsterdam & Philadelphia: Benjamins.

Manoliu, Maria. 1995b. "Underground Typological Tendencies: Danubian Latin at the crossroads of contrary linguistic types". *Rask* 3.3–35.

Manoliu, Maria. 2000. "Demonstratives, Story-World, and Talk-Interaction". *Traiani Augusti Vestigia Pressa Sequamur. Studia Linguistica in Honorem Liliane Tasmowski de Rick* ed. by Martine Coene, Walter De Mulder, Patrick Dendale, & Yves D'Hulst, 583–600. Padova: Unipress.

Mihăescu, Haralambie. 1960. *Limba latină în provinciile dunărene ale Imperiului Roman*. Bucharest: Editura Academiei Române.

Pușcariu, Sextil. 1905. *Etymologisches Wörterbuch der rumänischen Sprache.1 Lateinisches Element, mit Berücksichtigung aller romanischen Sprachen*. Heidelberg: K. Winter.

Renzi, Lorenzo. 1992. "Le développement de l'article en roman". *Revue Roumaine de Linguistique* 37.2–3.161–176.

Rohlfs, Gerhard (1969). *Grammatica storica della lingua italiana e dei suoi dialetti. Sintassi e formazione delle parole* trans. by Temistocle Francescho e Maria Caciagli Fancelli. Torino: Einaudi.

Rosetti, Alexandru. 1986. *Istoria limbii române. De la origini pînă la începutul secolului al XVII-lea.* Ediție definitivă. Bucharest: Editura Științifică și Enciclopedică.

Rusu, Valeriu, ed. 1984. *Tratat de dialectologie românească.* Institutul de Cercetări Etnologice și Dialectologice. Craiova: Scrisul Românesc.

Tasmowski-De Ryck, Liliane. 1990. "Les démonstratifs français et roumain dans la phrase et dans le texte". *Langages. Aux confins de la grammaire: l'anaphore* ed. by Pierre Cadiot & Anne Zribi-Hertz 25: 93.82–99. Paris: Larousse.

On the origin of the Portuguese inflected infinitive

A new perspective on an enduring debate*

Ana Maria Martins
University of Lisbon

1. Traits of the uninflected infinitive and theses on its origin

The Modern Portuguese inflected infinitive shares some properties with both finite and uninflected infinitival forms of the verb. This is apparent in its syntactic behavior as well as in its morphophonological pattern.

Like finite clauses, inflected infinitival clauses take lexical subjects Case-marked as nominative and show overt subject-verb agreement morphology. Compare the inflected infinitival clause in (1) to the finite clause in (2); in addition, contrast the inflected infinitival clause in (1) to the uninflected infinitival clause in (3) which does not allow for a lexical subject Case-marked as nominative.

(1) Vi [eles prenderem o ladrão]
     saw-1SG they catch-INFL.INFIN-3PL the thief
     "I saw them catch the thief"

(2) Vi [que eles prenderam o ladrão]
     saw-1SG that they caught-3PL the thief
     "I saw that they caught the thief"

(3) *Vi [eles prender o ladrão]
     saw-1SG they catch-INFIN the thief
     "I saw them catch the thief"

Contrary to finite clauses, however, uninflected infinitival clauses do not occur as independent clauses, but are restricted to embedded domains. This is why sentence (5), in opposition to (4), is ungrammatical.

(4) Eles prenderam o ladrão
     they caught-3PL the thief

(5) *Eles prenderem   o   ladrão
    they catch-INFL.INFIN-3PL the thief

In this respect, inflected infinitival clauses are just like uninflected infinitival clauses. Also like uninflected infinitival clauses and in opposition to finite clauses, they are incompatible with the complementizer *que* "that". The relevant contrast is displayed by sentences (6) versus (7).

(6) Vi   que eles prenderam o   ladrão
    saw-1SG that they caught-3PL the thief
    "I saw that they caught the thief"

(7) *Vi   que eles prenderem   o   ladrão
    saw-1SG that they catch-INFL.INFIN-3PL the thief

On the morphophonological level the inflected infinitival forms of the verb are made up of a verbal root (VR), a thematic vowel (TV), the infinitival morpheme, -r(e)- (which I take as a tense morpheme (T) — cf. footnote (4) in Section 2), and the subject-agreement (suffixal) morphemes, encoding person and number (P/N). For the purpose of exemplification, I take the verb *prender* "to catch" (a second conjugation verb with e as its thematic vowel). The same person/number suffixes appear in the inflected infinitive and in most finite paradigms of the verb (-ø, -s, -ø, -mos, -des/-is, -m) and are absent from the simple infinitive. In (8), the paradigm of the inflected infinitive is compared to the one-form paradigm of the uninflected infinitive and to the paradigms of the present and the pluperfect indicative.

(8)

	inflected infn.	uninflected infn.	present indc.	pluperfect indc.
	VR-TV-T-P/N	VR-TV-T	VR-TV-P/N	VR-TV-T-P/N
1SG	prend-e-r	prend-e-r	prend-o	prend-e-ra
2SG	prend-e-re-s		prend-e-s	prend-e-ra-s
3SG	prend-e-r		prend-e	prend-e-ra
1pl	prend-e-r-mos		prend-e-mos	prend-e-ra-mos
2pl	prend-e-r-des		prend-e-is	prend-e-re-is
3pl	prend-e-re-m		prend-e-m	prend-e-ra-m

With respect to the origin of the Portuguese inflected infinitive, two theses have been put forward. Some authors view the simple infinitive as the source of the inflected infinitive: Otto (1889), Michäelis de Vasconcelos (1891), Vasconcelos (1900), Bourciez (1930), Martin (1960), Maurer (1968), Gondar (1978), Maia (1986), Vincent (2000). Others trace the origin of the inflected infinitive back to the imperfect subjunctive of Latin: Wernecke (1885), Gamillscheg (1913), Rodrigues (1914), Michäelis de Vasconcelos (1918), Piel (1944), Meier (1950), Sten (1952), Lausberg (1962–1963), Osborne (1982), Wireback (1994).

None of the proposals faces problems with respect to deriving the phonetic forms of the inflected infinitive. Either a regular morphological process would be at stake, consisting of adding regular person/number affixes to the regular infinitival form of the verb, or a regular phonetic change from Latin to Portuguese would have given rise to the Portuguese inflected infinitival forms of the verb as straightforward phonetic outcomes of the Latin imperfect subjunctive verbal forms. According to the latter hypothesis, finite subordinate clauses without a conjunction and with the verb in the imperfect subjunctive would have been equated to infinitival subordinate clauses. Two sets of data helped to enforce this equation: in most syntactic contexts, by the third century A. D., the pluperfect subjunctive of Latin had replaced the imperfect subjunctive; the imperfect subjunctive, which continued to survive in purpose and result clauses, was similar in form to an infinitive plus person/number suffixes. The relevant correspondences between Latin and Portuguese verbal paradigms are represented under (9), considering again the verb *prender* "to catch".

(9)	Latin		Portuguese
	pluperfect subjunctive		imperfect subjunctive
1SG	prendissem		prendesse
2SG	prendisses		prendesses
3SG	prendisset	→	prendesse
1PL	prendissemus		prendessemos
2PL	prendissetis		prendesseis
3PL	prendissent		prendessem
	imperfect subjunctive		inflected infinitive
1SG	prenderem		prender
2SG	prenderes		prenderes
3SG	prenderet	→	prender
1PL	prenderemus		prendermos
2PL	prenderetis		prenderdes
3PL	prenderent		prenderem

The Romance-based approach to the origin of the Portuguese inflected infinitive has been far more popular in the last decades than the Latin-based approach. Since the seminal work of Theodoro Maurer, Jr. (1968) on the Portuguese inflected infinitive, there has been a broad consensus among scholars on this matter (Osborne 1982 and Wireback 1994 are exceptions). Arguments in favor of the origin of the inflected infinitive internal to Romance are: (1) the occurrence of gerunds and participles with verbal inflection (for person and number), in addition to inflected infinitives, in Old Neapolitan (see Loporcaro 1986 and Vincent 1996, 1998); (2) the existence of an inflected gerund in some Portuguese and Galician dialects[1] (see (10) below); (3) the possibility of nominative subjects in certain uninflected infinitival clauses of different Romance languages (see (11) below and Ledgeway 1998:3ff.); (4) the uncertainty about the persistence of the imperfect subjunctive in the Vulgar Latin of the Northwest of Iberia (see Maurer 1968:15ff.; but cf. Wireback 1994:549ff. for a different view).[2]

(10) *Em chegandos/-em   lá,   telefona/-em*
      in   arriving-2sg/2pl there call-imp.2sg.2pl
      "When you (2sg/2pl) arrive there, call (2sg/2pl) me"
      (*Alentejo* Portuguese dialect)

(11) *Para celebrar   Rita su cumpleaños, se.fue   de viaje al   Caribe*
      for   celebrate-infin Rita her birthday   went-3sg on a-trip to-the Caribbean
      "In order for Rita to celebrate her birthday, she went on a trip to the Caribbean"
      (Taken from Torrego 1998:209)

In this paper I will compare the syntax of the Old Portuguese inflected infinitive to the syntax of the Modern Portuguese inflected infinitive and I will show that the Latin-based approach to the origin of the Portuguese inflected infinitive, taken up by eminent scholars in the first half of this century, deserves some further consideration. The remainder of the paper is organized into three parts. First I will present the analysis of the syntax of the Modern Portuguese inflected infinitive put forth by Eduardo Raposo in 1987. Then I will compare Old Portuguese and Modern Portuguese and I will account for the changes observed with respect to the syntax of the inflected infinitive; I will argue for the hypothesis that the Infl(ection) of inflected infinitives changed from having an active [assign Case] feature to being inert with respect to Case assignment, therefore losing the possibility of assigning nominative Case unless in a local relation to an external Case assigner. Finally I will consider the implications of this hypothesis for the debate on the origin of the Portuguese inflected infinitive, with the aim of rescuing the nowadays-unpopular thesis which traces the origin of the Portuguese inflected infinitive back to the imperfect subjunctive of Latin.

2. Raposo's account of the syntax of the Portuguese inflected infinitive

In an influential article published in 1987, Eduardo Raposo assumes the Principles and Parameters framework of Chomsky and builds up an analysis of the syntax of the Portuguese inflected infinitive based on the crucial idea that in inflected infinitival clauses the functional category Infl (specifically, Agr(eement) in Infl, assuming Pollock's Split-IP hypothesis) can assign nominative Case to the subject only if it is itself assigned Case. The reasoning behind this hypothesis is that in null subject languages, like Portuguese, the functional category Agr is nominal in nature and therefore must be Case-marked. In finite clauses, Agr is Case-marked by T(ense). On the assumption that infinitives do not have Tense, Raposo states that infinitival Agr must 'look for' an external Case assigner. Thus, inflected infinitival clauses are expected to be able to occur only in Case-marked positions. This line of reasoning, together with considerations on selectional requirements of different types of predicates, straightforwardly derives the distribution of inflected infinitival clauses. It also derives certain facts concerning the internal word order of inflected infinitival clauses, a matter which I will leave out of the scope of this paper.

At this point I will summarize some relevant empirical facts in order to see how Raposo's proposal deals with them.

Inflected infinitival clauses occur as subject clauses (see (12) below), as adjunct clauses introduced by a preposition (see (13) below), and as complement clauses subcategorized by different types of predicates, such as the factive in (14) or the perception verb in (15).[3]

(12) *Prenderem*   *o   ladrão será   difícil*
      catch-INFL.INFIN.3SG the thief   will-be difficult
      "They will have difficulty in catching the thief"

(13) *Regressámos   sem   terem   prendido o   ladrão*
      came-back-1PL without have-INFL.INFIN-3PL caught   the thief
      "We came back before they could catch the thief"

(14) *Surpreendeu-me terem   prendido o   ladrão*
      surprised-3SG me have-INFL.INFIN-3PL caught   the thief
      "It surprised me that they could catch the thief"

(15) *Vi   os ladrões fugirem*
      saw-1SG the thieves run-away-INFL.INFIN-3PL
      "I saw the thieves run/running away"

In all these positions the inflected infinitival clauses are in a local enough relation to an external Case assigner, namely, the Infl-head of the matrix clause, in the example of the subject clauses, the preposition, in the example of the adjunct clauses, and the main verb, in the example of the complement clauses. These external Case assigners are thus able to govern and assign Case to the infinitival Agr which then assigns nominative Case to the infinitival subject.

Inflected infinitival clauses, on the other hand, are not allowed as complement clauses of volitional predicates (see (16) below), as embedded relative clauses (see (17)), or as independent clauses (see (18)–(19)).

(16) **Desejavam terem   prendido o   ladrão*
      wished-3PL have-INFL.INFIN-3PL caught   the thief
      "They wished that they could have caught the thief"

(17) **Os polícias não sabiam   quem prenderem*
      the policemen not knew-3PL who catch-INFL.INFIN-3PL
      "The policemen didn't know whom they should catch"

(18) *Os polícias   voltarem   sem   terem   prendido
     the policemen left-INFL.INFIN-3PL without have-INFL.INFIN-3PL caught
     o   ladrão
     the thief

(19) *Os polícias   prenderem   o ladrão
     the policemen catch-INFL.INFIN-3PL the thief

Raposo (1987) derives the fact that inflected infinitives cannot occur as complements of volitional predicates from selectional properties of those predicates. As for
relative clauses, the infinitival Agr is much too deeply embedded to be accessible to
an external Case assigner. With respect to independent clauses, there is no possible
Case assigner for Agr. Thus, since Agr is not assigned Case, it cannot itself assign
Case to the subject of the infinitival clause.

In the next section, I will look at inflected infinitival clauses in Old Portuguese
in the light of Raposo's proposal, which I adopt in its essentials. I will nevertheless
recast it in the terms of the Minimalist framework of Chomsky (1995), and in line
with recent literature on the structure of infinitival clauses.

As for Case-theory, I will follow Bobaljik and Thráinsson (1998) on the
assumption that Case is checked under the local relations of head-specifier, head-
complement, and head-head (the configuration of adjoined heads). Note that
Bobaljik and Thráinsson (1998) depart somewhat from Chomsky in taking all local
relations to a head, thus including the head-complement relation, as potential
checking relations with that head.

Furthermore, I adopt a principle of Economy of Representations in terms of
Bošković (1996). Bošković formulates *The Minimal Structure Principle* (MSP) as
shown under (20):

(20)   Provided that lexical requirements of relevant elements are satisfied, if two repre-
        sentations have the same lexical structure, and serve the same functions, then *the
        representation that has fewer projections is to be chosen as the* syntactic representa-
        tion serving that function.

According to the MSP, infinitival clauses will be C(omplementizer)P(hrase)s only
if their CP status is imposed by lexical requirements (e.g., *wh*-infinitival clauses).
Otherwise, since infinitival clauses are not introduced by a complementizer, CP will
not be projected. The IP status of infinitival clauses follows (see Bošković 1996 and
Martins 1995). Assuming a clause structure with Infl split into Agr and T (again
following Bobalijk & Thráinsson 1998), Agr dominating T, I take inflected infinitival clauses in general to be AgrPs — which are often embedded in a P(reposit-
ional)P(hrase).

In the generative literature it has been argued, both on syntactic and semantic
grounds, that infinitival clauses do have Tense. I will adhere to this view although
space considerations preclude me from going into the arguments which support it.[4]

The idea that infinitival clauses have Tense, however, apparently constitutes a problem for Raposo's analysis. If it is the case that infinitival clauses do have Tense, why doesn't Tense act as a Case checker for the Agr head of inflected infinitives, as is the case in finite clauses? Based on two quite different approaches, both Chomsky (1995) and Hornstein (1999) develop the idea that infinitival T is defective, being unable to assign/check nominative Case. Without going into the specifics of their proposals, I will assume this is the reason why a local relation to a Case assigner is still needed. Figure 1 below shows how checking relations between infinitival Agr and different external Case assigners obtain. Recall that the external Case assigners are the matrix Infl, with respect to subject clauses, the matrix V, with respect to complement clauses, and the preposition, with respect to adjunct clauses. Note moreover that the features of a projection are those of its head, and since the maximal projection AgrP is in a Case-checking position, its head, Agr, is in a Case-checking position as well.

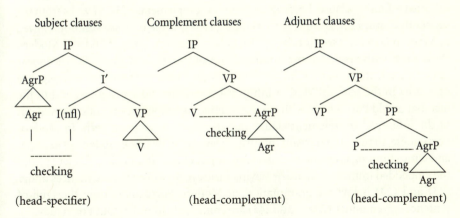

Figure 1.

3. Old Portuguese versus Modern Portuguese

With respect to the syntax of the inflected infinitive, Old Portuguese differs from Modern Portuguese in two ways. Old Portuguese, contrary to Modern Portuguese, does not allow inflected infinitival clauses as complements of causative and perception verbs, that is, the class of *Exceptional Case Marking* (ECM) verbs — see Maurer (1968:58). On the other hand, in Old Portuguese the inflected infinitive is found in a certain kind of independent clause which is not allowed in Modern Portuguese. I claim that the latter fact reveals a change in the syntax of inflected infinitival clauses, the former being mainly a function of a change in the selectional properties of ECM verbs (but see footnote 10 in Section 4).

3.1 Inflected infinitival clauses as complements of causative and perception verbs

In Modern Portuguese, both simple infinitives and inflected infinitives can be embedded under causative and perception verbs, as examples (21) and (22) below show.

(21) *Mandei/Vi os polícias prender   o ladrão*
       sent/saw   the cops   arrest-INFIN the thief
       "I sent/saw the cops (to) arrest the thief"

(22) *Mandei/Vi os polícias prenderem   o ladrão*
       sent/saw   the cops   arrest-INFL.INFIN-3PL the thief
       "I sent/saw the cops (to) arrest the thief"

Sentences such as (22), however, are not attested in the early (Galician-)Portuguese texts[5] and are barely attested in the fourteenth and fifteenth century. In Portuguese, inflected infinitival clauses become common as complements of ECM verbs from the sixteenth century on, according to Maurer (1968), while they are still not allowed in Modern Galician (see Gondar 1978). Other divergent traits of Old and Modern Portuguese with respect to the infinitival complements of ECM predicates appear to correlate with the ban on inflected infinitives. I refer to the absence of negative operators in the relevant kind of infinitival clauses in Old Portuguese, and to the fact that in Old Portuguese, with few exceptions, embedded object clitics moved out of the infinitival complement clause and cliticized to the main verb. In Modern Portuguese, in turn, the relevant infinitival clauses can be (independently) negated, and clitic climbing is optional, embedded object clitics either being extracted from the embedded infinitival clause or staying inside it. So while all the sentences under (23) and (24) below are grammatical in Modern Portuguese, only the type of sentences given under (23a) and (24a) are commonly found in Old Portuguese.

(23) a. *O médico mandou-o   beber muita água*
          the doctor sent-him-ACC drink much water
          "the doctor sent him to drink plenty of water"
       b. *O médico mandou-o   não beber vinho*
          the doctor sent-him-ACC not drink wine
          "the doctor sent him to not drink wine"

(24) a. *Mandou-lho   entregar*
          sent-3SG-him-DAT-it-ACC give
          "He/she sent to give it to him"
       b. *Mandou entregar-lho*
          sent-3SG give-him-DAT-it-ACC
          "He/she sent to give it to him"

This set of facts can be straightforwardly accounted for if we analyze the Old Portuguese infinitival complements of ECM verbs as having a reduced structure. In earlier work on clitic climbing, I take such reduced clauses as being TPs. Elizabeth Pearce (1990), who observed a similar set of facts in Old French, analyzes the reduced infinitival complement clauses of the verbs under consideration as VPs. Regardless of whether the correct structure is a VP or a TP, ECM verbs selecting infinitival complements would have a more auxiliary-like character in Old Romance than in Modern Romance and, in general, would not support complement structures containing agreement, negation, or a position for 'syntactic' cliticization.

3.2 Non-dependent inflected infinitival clauses

In Modern European Portuguese, aside from some marked or fossilized expressions, the inflected infinitive occurs only in embedded clauses, being excluded from independent or matrix clauses.[6] In Old Portuguese, however, the inflected infinitive is commonly found in unembedded domains. The relevant clauses have an imperative import and are either independent clauses or the matrix part of a conditional construction. These 'stipulative' infinitival clauses are attested in legal documents from the late twelfth century[7] up to the sixteenth century, being more frequent during the first half of this period (see Maia 1986 and Martins 1994). Sentences (25) to (28) below are relevant examples, showing that unembedded infinitival clauses alternate with subjunctive clauses in Old Portuguese. Note that the sentences of the pairs (25)–(26), on the one hand, and (27)–(28), on the other, diverge minimally, making clear that the alternation between inflected infinitive and subjunctive is not context-dependent. In Modern Portuguese this alternation is lost and so sentences (25) and (27) below would be ungrammatical, only (26) and (28) being admitted.

(25) *e   se achassem   que Moor Eanes siia no   plazo   con seu*
      and if find-IMPERF-SUBJ-3PL that Moor Eanes was in-the contract with her
      marido   ualerlj   seu plazo
      husband hold-INFL.INFIN-3SG-her her contract
      "and if they found that Moor Eanes and her husband actually had a contract, the contract should hold (to her advantage)" (year 1273)
      (Taken from Martins 1994, Vol. 2, p. 9)

(26) *e   se achassem   que non siia no   plazo   (...) que lhe*
      and if find-IMPERF-SUBJ-3PL that not was in-the contract   that her
      fezesse   o   Abade plazo
      make-IMPERF-SUBJ-3SG the Abbot contract
      "and if they found that Moor Eanes did not have a contract, the Abbot should make a contract with her" (year 1273)
      (*Ibidem*)

(27) E   ffazerem   a   dita   cassa e   Reffazerem
      and build-INFL.INFIN-3PL the mentioned house and rebuild-INFL.INFIN-3PL
      de   todo casso fortoyto
      from any event accidental
      "and they will build and rebuild the house after any accidental bad event"
      (year 1407)
      (Taken from Martins 1994, Vol. 2, p. 460)

(28) E   a faca   e   refaca   de   todo caso
      and it build-PRES-SUBJ-3SG and rebuild-PRES-SUBJ-3SG from any event
      furtuyto
      accidental
      "and he will build and rebuild the house after any accidental bad event"
      (year 1414)
      (Taken from Martins 1994, Vol. 2, p. 467)

A possible analysis for the 'imperative' inflected infinitives of Old Portuguese, in the vein of Kayne (1992) and Zanuttini (1997), naturally comes to mind. We might posit the existence of a phonetically unrealized modal or causative verb which would select an infinitive as its complement (on a descriptive level a proposal of this sort is put forth by Maia 1986). The empty modal, or causative, would be in turn licensed by a directive operator in Comp encoding the 'imperative' illocutionary force. There are several problems with this hypothesis, however. The first problem is that crosslinguistic evidence points against identifying the directive operator as an appropriate licenser for the hypothesized empty modal or causative verb. In all the Romance varieties observed by Kayne (1992) and Zanuttini (1997), an infinitival suppletive imperative is only possible in negative clauses. This fact leads both Kayne and Zanuttini to the conclusion that it is the negative marker which licenses the empty modal or causative. The second problem is that modals do not take inflected infinitival clauses as complements in Old Portuguese; as we have seen before, causatives do not do so either. Moreover, uninflected infinitival clauses are never found in the kinds of Old Portuguese sentences under examination, although modal and causative verbs select precisely uninflected infinitival clauses as complements. Note on the other hand that uninflected infinitives are the only kind of infinitives that show up in the suppletive negative imperatives studied by Kayne and Zanuttini. The third problem is that the empty auxiliary analysis cannot explain the fact that in Old Portuguese inflected infinitives are occasionally attested in embedded relative clauses, as shown in (29):

(29) Mas a esto nom minguava quem rresponder   muitas rrazões
      but to this not lessened who answer-INFL.INFIN-3SG many reasons
      culpandoo
      accusing-him
      "But there were many people who advanced reasons to consider him guilty"
      (Fernão Lopes; 15th century. Taken from Maurer 1968: 16)

As an alternative analysis, I will advance the hypothesis that in Old Portuguese the inflected infinitival T was just like finite T in having an [assign nominative Case] feature which checked the Case feature of both Agr and the subject NP. This would be obtained by T adjoining to Agr and therefore coming to be in a checking relation with both Agr and its specifier position (or else the subject NP could be checked in the specifier position of T with T adjoining to Agr afterwards). Note that according to Chomsky (1995:279ff.), multiple checking by the same [assign Case] feature is permitted.

As for the change which took place in the history of Portuguese, I hypothesize that the [assign Case] feature of the inflected infinitival T came to be inert for Case checking, although under the appropriate conditions it can still be activated. Let us assume that the inert [assign Case] feature of T is still attracted by the Case feature of Agr. T will thus raise adjoining to Agr. If in this position T can enter into a local relation with an external head bearing an active [assign Case] feature, the correspondent feature of T will be activated and checking of the [+Case] features of the NP subject and of Agr will proceed as stated above. Otherwise, the derivation will crash because the inert [assign Case] feature of T will not be able to perform the checking operation. We can think of the activation process as follows: take categories which assign Case as being those and only those specified as [−N] (in accordance with Chomsky 1981); this includes Verbs, [+V, −N], Prepositions, [−V, −N], and, I suggest, categories like T which are part of the extended projection of the Verb; furthermore, take inflected infinitival T as being positively specified with respect to its V feature but underspecified with respect to its N feature; being so it does not qualify by itself as a Case assigner. If it enters into a local relation to a head of the intended type, however, an 'agreement'-type relation will be established which will lead to the 'filling in' of the N feature value of T (cf. Martins 2000). Since the external Case assigner will be inherently specified as [−N], the attribution of a negative specification to the N feature of infinitival T follows. Becoming specified as [+V, −N] the inflected infinitival T will concomitantly have its [assign nominative Case] feature activated.[8]

We can now explain why the Old Portuguese 'imperative' infinitival clauses (illustrated in (25) and (27) above) are ungrammatical in Modern Portuguese: there is no external Case assigner which can activate the inert [assign Case] feature of T. Therefore, neither the [+Case] Agr nor the nominative subject can be 'licensed'.

On the other hand, the relative clause in (29) above is possible in Old Portuguese, contrary to Modern Portuguese, because the inflected infinitival T has an active [assign Case] feature and therefore can perform by itself the necessary Case-checking operation.

A question is in order at this point. If Old Portuguese inflected infinitives can independently check nominative Case, why don't they unrestrictively occur as independent clauses? The answer is to be found in the dependent character of the infinitival T(ense), a trait which is shared with subjunctive T(ense). In the vein of Picallo (1985), we may think of subjunctive and infinitive as conveying an anaphoric tense, or along the lines of Tsoulas (1995), we may view subjunctive and infinitive as amounting to temporal indefiniteness in the clausal domain. In any case, subjunctive and infinitival Tenses will have a dependent character needing to be anchored in a non-dependent Tense (the Tense of the embedding clause) or licensed by certain operators (such as an imperative operator).

We may now ask, however, what it is that in Old Portuguese distinguishes the inflected infinitive from the subjunctive. On the empirical level, we can answer that while embedded subjunctive clauses (and finites in general) take an overt complementizer (the complementizer *que* "that"), inflected infinitival clauses do not; moreover, subjunctives and inflected infinitives are not subcategorized by the same set of main predicates. On the conceptual level, there are grounds for thinking, following a proposal by Zanuttini (1997:127), that, differently from subjunctives, infinitives (as well as main verb true imperatives) lack a specification for mood. If we further assume that the overt complementizer generally found in subordinate finite clauses has a [+mood] feature, we derive the fact that it is incompatible with infinitives (and true imperatives).[9]

4.   Consequences of the proposed approach to the debate on the origin of the Portuguese inflected infinitive

In this paper I have proposed that certain differences between Old Portuguese and Modern Portuguese can be accounted for if we admit that Old Portuguese inflected infinitives, contrary to Modern Portuguese inflected infinitives, shared nominative Case assigning properties with finite clauses, whilst diverging from finite clauses in having a dependent Tense. If this analysis proves to be on the right track, it will have consequences with respect to the debate on the origin of the Portuguese inflected infinitive. On the assumption that Old Portuguese inflected infinitives were in a way more finite-like than they are in Modern Portuguese, we find support for the hypothesis that traces its origin back to a Latin finite form of the verb, namely the imperfect subjunctive. In contrast, this analysis does not seem to be compatible with the hypothesis according to which the inflected infinitive developed from the simple infinitive.

The change from Old Portuguese to Modern Portuguese can be viewed as a movement of the inflected infinitive, born from the imperfect subjunctive, in the direction of the simple infinitive.[10] This would be motivated by the presumably marked character of an infinitive having an active [assign nominative Case] feature.

Since the debate on the origin of the Portuguese inflected infinitive doesn't appear to be settled, the arguments on both sides being in my view mostly inconclusive, I believe the empirical evidence and the conceptual approach I have put on the table might bring some 'fresh air' into an old debate. Although the possibility of nominative subjects in certain uninflected infinitival clauses of different Romance languages has been taken as an argument in favor of the thesis that personal desinences grew onto the simple infinitive, there hasn't been, as far as I am aware of, any in-depth work comparing the Portuguese and Galician inflected infinitive to the uninflected infinitives with nominative subjects of the other Romance languages, taking into account especially their older stages.[11] Research in this trend would certainly bring new insights to the debate on the origin of the Portuguese inflected infinitive. I leave the gathering and the analysis of those data for future research.[12]

Notes

* I am grateful to Delia Bentley, Ellen Thompson, Gary Miller, Nigel Vincent, and an anonymous reviewer, who, in different ways, helped me with revising a former version of this work. Nigel Vincent in particular, having "diametrically opposed views" from my own on the topic under discussion in this article, greatly contributed to improving it. The *Instituto Camões* and the *Fundação para a Ciência e a Tecnologia* (through *Programa Lusitânia*) provided the financial support which enabled me to attend ICHL XIV, where this paper was first delivered.

1. It should be noted, however, that the inflected gerund has not been attested in Old Portuguese and Old Galician. Thus, the inflected gerund appears to be a modern development in the relevant dialects. In Old Neapolitan inflected infinitives are attested earlier than inflected gerunds; verbally inflected participles are not only later but very rare.

2. Maurer (1968) also objects to the imperfect subjunctive thesis — as formulated by Gamillsheg (1913) — that volitional constructions, where *ut* could be omitted in Latin, did not use the inflected infinitive in Old Portuguese. The Latin-based approach to the origin of the inflected infinitive would therefore fail with respect to locating the reanalysis process in a syntactic context that permits the inflected infinitive in Old Portuguese. Wireback (1994), however, claims that the imperfect subjunctive survived in Vulgar Latin in result and purpose clauses at a time when it had already been replaced by the pluperfect subjunctive in other syntactic contexts. A relevant example can be found in the *Peregrinatio Egeriae ad Loca Sancta* — a Western Vulgar Latin text written at the close of the fourth century A.D.: *Iter sic fuit ut per medium transversaremus caput ipsius vallis et sic plecaremus nos ad montem Dei* "The journey was made in such a way that we crossed through the middle of the head of that valley and thus arrived at the mountain of God" (taken from Wireback 1994: 550). Wireback then suggests that the emergence of the inflected infinitive is to be traced mainly to purpose clauses, where '*ut* + impf. subj.' competed with infinitives, rather than to volitional clauses.

3. With respect to perception verbs, a construction which does not permit the inflected infinitive is also found in Portuguese (as well as in other Romance languages); namely, a restructuring construction where the subject follows the uninflected infinitive. In this construction, the perception verb and the infinitive form a complex predicate.

4. For arguments and further references, see Stowell (1982), Hornstein (1990), Peres (1992), Bošković (1997), Ambar (1998).

5. The earliest documents date from the late 12th century and early 13th century, at a time when the Galician-Portuguese linguistic domain had not yet split into Galician and Portuguese.

6. Some Portuguese dialects allow an independent bare inflected infinitive with imperative meaning: *andarem*, go-INFL.INFIN.3PL, "go (away)". A similar situation arises with respect to the simple infinitive and the gerund, which can also be used in bare verb 'imperative' sentences. In Standard Portuguese, an independent inflected infinitive is possible in exclamative sentences such as: *Fazeres uma coisa dessas!*, do-INFL.INFIN.2SG one thing of-that-(sort), "I can't believe you did that!"

7. *Et quando ipsa uinea dederit vᵉ Modios de uino, dares inde quarta tu* (year 1189), and when that vineyard give-FUT.SUBJ.3SG five *modios* of wine, give-INFL.INFIN.2SG of-it the-fourth-part you, "And when that vineyard produces five *modios* of wine, you should give the fourth part of it (in payment to the landlord)" (*Arquivo Nacional da Torre do Tombo, Mosteiro de Tarouquela, maço 4,* 33).

8. Raposo (1987) had to stipulate that Agr had a special filtering effect on Case, converting whatever Case it was licensed with (i.e., accusative, nominative, or oblique) into nominative.

9. Using the features [±mood] and [±T(ense)-dependent], we obtain the following four-way distinction: subjunctive: [+mood, +Tdependent]; indicative: [+mood, −Tdependent]; imperative: [−mood, −Tdependent]; infinitive: [−mood, +Tdependent].

10. Note that the inflected infinitive is scarcely attested in the infinitival complements of ECM predicates (see 3.1) during the time that it is attested in independent clauses with imperative import (see 3.2). Thus, the inflected infinitive expands to a domain earlier reserved for the simple infinitive only when it moves in the direction of the latter. This spreading of the inflected infinitive to a new syntactic context must have happened concomitantly with a change in the selection properties of ECM predicates (which came to take AgrP complements).

11. If we compare the Modern Portuguese inflected infinitive with the Modern Spanish uninflected 'nominative' infinitive, the syntactic contexts and the syntactic conditions that permit each kind of infinitive are not the same (see Torrego 1998). Yet this partial dissimilarity could be the result of divergent change from an unified initial state. On the other hand, we cannot discard without previous consideration an hypothesis which reverses the rationale behind the Romance-based approach: the 'Romance simple infinitive with nominative properties' might have developed from a Proto-Romance inflected infinitive. That the inflected infinitive can lose its morphological inflection while keeping its former syntactic properties is shown by the variety of colloquial Brazilian Portuguese represented in the following sentence: *O Pedro chegou sem a Maria e eu saber,* the Pedro arrived without the Maria and I know-INFIN, "Pedro arrived without Maria and I knowing"(Taken from Pires 2000).

12. Piel (1944:399) registers the inflected infinitive in a Portuguese legal document, in Latin, of the year 1004. This is the oldest attestation of the inflected infinitive in the Galicien-Portuguese area which I am aware of: *Et intrarunt in placito testimoniale pro in tertio die darent testes,* "and they began the hearing in order to, on the third day, provide [give-INFL.INFIN.3PL] witnesses".

References

Ambar, Manuela. 1998. "Infinitives vs. Participles". *Semantic Issues in Romance Syntax* ed. by Esthela Treviño & José Lema, 1–20. Amsterdam & Philadelphia: John Benjamins.

Bobalijk, Jonathan D. & Höskuldur Thráinsson. 1998. "Two Heads Aren't Always Better Than One". *Syntax* 1.37–71.

Bošković, Željko. 1996. "Selection and the Categorial Status of Infinitival Complements". *Natural Language and Linguistic Theory* 14.269–304.

Bošković, Željko. 1997. *The Syntax of Nonfinite Complementation: An economy approach.* Cambridge, MA: MIT Press.

Bourciez, Éduard. 1930. *Éléments de Linguistique Romane.* Paris: Klincksieck.

Chomsky, Noam. 1981. *Lectures on Government and Binding.* Dordrecht: Foris.

Chomsky, Noam. 1995. *The Minimalist Program.* Cambridge, MA: MIT Press.

Gamillscheg, Ernst. 1913. *Studien zur Vorgeschichte einer romanischen Tempuslehre.* Wien. [= *Sitzungsberichte der Kaiserlichen Akademie der Wissenscaften in Wien (Philosophish-Historische Klasse)* 172]. Reprinted in 1970: Gamillscheg, Ernst. *Studien zur Vorgeschichte einer romanischen Tempuslehre.* 2nd ed. Tübingen: Tübingen Beiträge zur Linguistik.

Gondar, Francisco G. 1978. *O Infinitivo Conxugado en Galego.* (= *Verba, Anejo 13.*) Santiago de Compostela: Universidad de Santiago de Compostela.

Hornstein, Norbert. 1990. *As Time Goes By.* Cambridge, MA: MIT Press.

Hornstein, Norbert. 1999. "Movement and Control". *Linguistic Inquiry* 30.69–96.

Kayne, Richard. 1992. "Italian Negative Infinitival Imperatives and Clitic Climbing". *Hommages à Nicolas Ruwet* ed. by L. Tasmowsky & Anne Zribi-Hertz, 300–312. Gent: Communication and Cognition.

Lausberg, Heinrich. 1962–1963. *Romanische Sprachwissenschaft.* Berlin: Walter de Gruyter.

Ledgeway, Adam. 1998. "Variation in the Romance Infinitive: The case of the Southern Calabrian inflected infinitive". *Transactions of the Philological Society* 96.1–61.

Loporcaro, Michele. 1986. "L'infinito coniugato nell'Italia centro-meridionale: ipotesi genetica e ricostruzione storica". *L'Italia Dialettale* 49.173–240.

Maia, Clarinda de Azevedo. 1986. *História do Galego-Português: Estado linguístico da Galiza e do Noroeste de Portugal desde o século XIII ao século XVI.* Coimbra: INIC.

Martin, John W. 1960. "Remarks on the Origin of the Portuguese Inflected Infinitive". *Word* 16.337–343.

Martins, Ana Maria. 1994. *Clíticos na História do Português.* Ph.D. dissertation, University of Lisbon. [2 volumes]

Martins, Ana Maria. 1995. "A Minimalist Approach to Clitic Climbing". *CLS 31. Papers from the 31st Regional Meeting of the Chicago Linguistic Society.* Volume 2: *The Parasession on Clitics* ed. by Audra Dainora et al., 215–233. Chigago: CLS.

Martins, Ana Maria. 2000. "Polarity Items in Romance: Underspecification and lexical change". Pintzuk et al. 2000. 191–219.

Maurer Jr., Theodoro H. 1968. *O Infinito Flexionado Português (estudo histórico-descritivo).* São Paulo: Companhia Editora Nacional.

Meier, Harri. 1950. "A génese do infinito flexionado português". *Miscelânea de Filologia, Literatura e História Cultural à memória de Francisco Adolfo Coelho (1847–1919).* Vol. II, 115–132. Lisboa.

Michäelis de Vasconcelos, Carolina. 1891. "Der portugiesische Infinitiv". *Romanische Forschungen* 7.49–122.

Michäelis de Vasconcelos, Carolina. 1918. "O Imperfeito do conjuntivo e o infinito pessoal no Português". *Boletim da Segunda Classe da Academia das Ciências de Lisboa* 12.312–331.

Osborne, Bruce. 1982. "On the Origin of the Portuguese Inflected Infinitive". *Papers from the 5th International Conference on Historical Linguistics* ed. by Anders Ahlqvist, 243–248. Amsterdam & Philadelphia: John Benjamins.

Otto, Richard. 1889. "Der portugiesische Infinitiv bei Camoes". *Romanische Forschungen* 6.299–398.

Pearce, Elizabeth. 1990. *Parameters in Old French Syntax: Infinitival complements*. Dordrecht: Kluwer.

Peres, João. 1992. "Toward an Integrated View of the Expression of Time in Portuguese". *Cadernos de Semântica*. Lisboa: Universidade de Lisboa.

Picallo, M. Carmen. 1985. *Opaque Domains*. Ph.D. dissertation, CUNY.

Piel, Joseph-Maria. 1944. "A flexão verbal do português: Estudo de morfologia histórica". *Biblos* 20.359–404.

Pintzuk, Susan, George Tsoulas, & Anthony Warner, eds. 2000. *Diachronic Syntax: Models and mechanisms*. Oxford: Oxford University Press.

Pires, Acrísio. 2000. "Infinitives, Control as Movement and the Loss of Inflection in Portuguese". Paper delivered at *DIGS VI*. University of Maryland at College Park.

Pollock, Jean-Yves. 1989. "Verb Movement, Universal Grammar, and the Structure of IP". *Linguistic Inquiry* 20.365–424.

Raposo, Eduardo. 1987. "Case Theory and Infl-to-Comp: The inflected infinitive in European Portuguese". *Linguistic Inquiry* 18.85–109.

Rodrigues, José M. 1914. "O Imperfeito do conjuntivo e o infinito pessoal no Português". *Boletim da Segunda Classe da Academia das Ciências de Lisboa*. 8.72–93.

Sten, Holger. 1952. "L'infinitivo impessoal et l'infinitivo pessoal en portugais moderne". *Boletim de Filologia* 13.83–142, 201–256.

Stowell, Timothy. 1982. "The Tense of Infinitives". *Linguistic Inquiry* 13.561–570.

Torrego, Esther. 1998. "Nominative Subjects and Pro-drop Infl". *Syntax* 1.206–219.

Tsoulas, George. 1995. "Indefinite Clauses: Some notes on the syntax and semantics of subjunctives and infinitives". *Proceedings of the 13th West Coast Conference on Formal Linguistic* ed. by Raul Aranovich et al., 515–530. Stanford: CSLI.

Vasconcelos, J. Leite de. 1900. *Estudos de Philologia Mirandesa*. Lisboa: Imprensa Nacional.

Vincent, Nigel. 1996. "Appunti sulla sintassi dell'infinito coniugato in un testo napoletano del '300". *Italiano e Dialetti nel tempo: Saggi di Grammatica per G. Lepschy* ed. by Paola Benincá et al., 387–406. Roma: Bulzoni.

Vincent, Nigel. 1998. "On the Grammar of Inflected Non-finite Forms (with special reference to Old Neapolitan)". *Clause Combining and Text Structure* ed. by Iøra Korzen & Michael Herslund, 135–158. Copenhagen: Samfundslitteratur.

Vincent, Nigel. 2000. "Competition and Correspondence in Syntactic Change: Null arguments in Latin and Romance". Pintzuk et al. 2000. 25–50.

Zanuttini, Rafaela. 1997. *Negation and Clausal Structure: A Comparative study of romance languages*. New York & Oxford: Oxford University Press.

Wernecke, H. 1885. *Zur Syntax des portugiesischen Verbs*. Weimar (Programm des Realgymnasiums in Weimar).

Wireback, Kenneth J. 1994. "The Origin of the Portuguese Inflected Infinitive". *Hispania* 77.544–552.

Innovation of the indirect reflexive in Old French*

D. Gary Miller
University of Florida

1. Introduction

The typical Modern French (MF) indirect reflexive type *il se lave les mains* [he washes himself the hands] "he_i washes his_i hands" did not exist in early Old French (OF), but the type *il lui lave les mains* [he washes to.him (DAT) the hands] "he_i washes his_i hands" was well entrenched. Prior to 1150,[1] the former was expressed *il lave ses mains* "he_i washes his_i hands" (ungrammatical in MF). This paper argues that a change which allowed *se* to adjoin to the verb entailed changes in reflexive and causative structures. Specifically, *se*-incorporation predicted four seemingly unrelated syntactic changes: (1) indirect reflexives; (2) adjunction of *se* to the lower verb; (3) accusative (as opposed to prepositional) causees; and (4) binding of *se* with the causee, rather than the higher subject. It is also shown that several constructions served as cues for the indirect reflexive, others for *se* with no case, and others for incorporation. The optimal solution was incorporation, which provided for *se* without case and the indirect reflexive.

2. The indirect reflexive in Modern French

The constraints on the use of the indirect reflexive (IR) in MF have been described by Hatcher (1944) and Bro (1993);[2] for a partial formalization, see Vergnaud and Zubizarreta (1992). The main condition is that the object must be inalienable. Contrast (1a) and (1b).

(1) Possessed NPs and the IR (MF)
    a.   IR with Inalienable Object
        i.   *il se lave les mains*   "he washes his hands"
        ii. **il lave ses mains*

    b.   POSS with Alienable Object
       i.   *il se lave la chemise   "he washes his shirt"
      ii.   il lave sa chemise

The object must be affected (in the traditional sense), as in (1a); if the object is not affected, the possessive construction (POSS) is triggered (2b).

(2) POSS with Non-Affected Object
    a.   i.   *il se lève la/*sa main   "he raises his hand"
       ii. *il se tourne la/*sa tête "he turns his head"
    b.   i.   il lève sa/la main   "he raises his hand"
       ii. il tourne sa/la tête   "he lifts his head"

That affectedness is at issue is clear from (3a). Moreover, (3b) shows that physical exertion can also trigger IR.[3]

(3) IR, Affectedness, and Effort
    a.   il s'est tourné (foulé) la cheville
       "he sprained his ankle"
    b.   malgré l'extrême douleur, en la prenant à deux mains, il a réussi à se tourner la tête vers moi
       "despite the extreme pain, taking it with both hands, he has managed to turn his head toward me"

Socially conventionalized acts are especially important when performed on another. These trigger the dative construction (DAT) in (4a), in contrast to the non-conventionalized acts with POSS in (4b).

(4) a.   DAT with Stereotypical Acts
       i.   il lui prit la main (qu'il baisa)
          "he took her hand (which he kissed)"
       ii. je lui serre la main
          "I shake his/her hand" (in a conventional way)
      iii. je lui baise les lèvres
          "I kiss his/her lips"
    b.   POSS with Non-Stereotypical Acts
       i.   le docteur prit sa main (et la tapota)
          "the doctor took his/her hand (and tapped it)"
       ii. il avait pris ses mains (et il les serrait, tressaillant)
          "he had taken his/her hands (and squeezed them, trembling)"
      iii. elle rougit et serra sa main
          "she blushed and squeezed his/her hand"
      iv. il baisa sauvagement ses lèvres
          "he savagely kissed her lips"

(4b-i) focuses on the hand rather than the gesture. (4a-i) is polite. (4b-iii) involves her own hand or someone else's that she was holding, in contrast to the handshake in (4a-ii). A precise description of the differences in nuance in these contrasts is a task for future scholarship. Our purpose here is to isolate the structural conditions that provided for the innovation of the IR.

The main constraints on DAT and POSS occur with inalienable objects. (5) shows that different dative constructions must be distinguished. The DAT of inalienable possession cannot cooccur with POSS (5a), while the indirect object dative can (5b), as can the dative of (dis)advantage (5c). (5d) is an ordinary construction of alienable possession.

(5)   Constraints on DAT and POSS
    a. *il lui   embrassa sa main
        he to.her kissed   her hand
        "he kissed her hand"
    b. je te   rendrai   ton argent demain
        I to.you payback.FUT your money tomorrow
        "I'll pay you back your money tomorrow"
    c. il lui   a pris son épée
        he to.him has taken his sword
        "he$_i$ took his$_j$ sword away from him$_j$"
    d. il a pris son épée
        "he$_i$ picked up his$_j$ sword"

Another contrast between IR and POSS is linked to figurative and literal interpretations, as in (6a) and (6b), respectively.

(6)   a. une tuile m'est tombée sur la tête
        "bad luck fell on my head"
    b. ?une tuile est tombé sur ma tête
        "a tile fell on my head" (literal interpretation only)

(6a) can be interpreted as another instance of the stereotypical, in contrast to the non-conventionalized/non-stereotypical in (6b). The contrasts in (7) and (8) are illuminating for the interaction of [±affected], [±stereotypical], and foregrounding/backgrounding of the possessor.[4]

(7)   a. i.   il se rogne la barbe
           "he trims his beard"
      ii. elle s'essuya les yeux
           "she wiped (tears from) her eyes" (possessor backgrounded)
    b. i.   il rogne sa barbe
           "he trims his beard" (down to virtually nothing)
      ii. elle essuya ses yeux
           "she wiped (tears from) her eyes" (possessor foregrounded)
(8)   a. il se tire la barbe
    b. *il tire sa barbe
        "he pulls his beard"

While the *use* (or non-use) of IR is highly idiosyncratic, involving a number of semantic and pragmatic conditioning factors, it has been argued (e.g., Miller 1993:§11.11) that IR requires the structural condition that *se* (and other relevant clitics) not need case in order to be so used to begin with.

3.   Possessed D/NPs in Old French

The *Chanson de Roland* has only type (9a); contrast the MF counterpart in (8a). The other *Roland* examples (9b–d) are the same in MF; cf. (2) above.

(9)   Possessed NPs (Old French)
   a.   *tiret sa barbe* (R 2414)
        "(he) pulls his beard"
   b.   *turnat sa teste vers la paiene gent* (R 2360)
        "(he) turned his head to(ward) the heathen folk"
   c.   *lievet sa main, fait sa b[en]eïçun* (R 2194)
        "(he) lifts his hand, makes his benediction"
   d.   *sun cheval broche(t)* (R 1125, 1197)
        "he spurs his horse"

(10a) is from the 13th c. *Roman de Renart* investigated by Bro (1993), who empha-sizes the contrast between the OF and its MF counterpart (10b), and notes that even that very lengthy and more recent text has no examples of the typical MF IR construction. Some dialects, however, have earlier IRs.

(10)   a.   *Renart l'oi … si met ses piez en une seille* (*Renart* 169f.)
           "R. hears it … and puts his feet in a bucket"
       b.   *il se met les pieds dans un seau* (MF)
           "he puts his feet in a bucket"

By sharp contrast, the DAT construction of MF (11) is well attested in OF texts (cf. Herslund 1980:152ff.), including *Roland* (12).

(11)   The DAT Construction (MF)
       a.   *il lui a baisé le pied* [he to.him/her has kissed the foot]
           "he$_i$ kissed her/his$_j$ foot"
       b.   *il lui lave les mains* [he to.him/her washes the hands]
           "he$_i$ washes her/his$_j$ hands"
(12)   Type (11) in *Roland*
       a.   *brisier* "to crush, shatter"
           i.   *trenchet le piz, si li briset les os* (R 1200)
               "he$_i$ cuts the breast and to-him$_j$ shatters the bones"
               (i.e., "he slices his chest and breaks his bones")

    ii.   *en dous meitiez li ad brisét le col*   (R 1205)
        "in two halves to-him$_j$ he$_i$ has broken the neck"
  b. *liier/li̇ër* "to tie, bind"
    i.   *les mains li li̇ent a curreies de cerf* (R 3738)
      "his hands they bind with deer(skin) straps"
    ii. *puis si li li̇ent e les piez e les mains* (R 3965)[5]
      "and then they bind his feet and hands"
  c. *fraindre* "to break", *desclore* "to break open", *fendre* "to split"
    i.   *l'escut li freint e l'osberc li desclot*   (R 1199; R 1619f [1576f])
      "his shield he shatters and his hauberk he breaks open"
    ii. *desur la teste li ad frait e fendut* (R 3604)
      "upon his head has shattered and split"
  d. *trenchier* "to cut"
    i.   *si li trenchat les oilz e la faiture* (R 1328)
      "and cuts his eyes and face"

Since the DAT type *il lui tire la barbe* "he$_i$ pulls his$_j$ beard" was available in OF, the fact that the IR *il se tire la barbe* "he$_i$ pulls his$_i$ beard" was obligatorily expressed with POSS *il tire sa barbe* "he$_i$ pulls his$_i$ beard", suggests that *se* could not accommodate a dative-shift-type structure.

4. The IR innovation in later Old French

One traditional account derives IR from the Vulgar Latin/Proto-Romance case syncretism of DAT *sibi* and ACC *sē* (etc.). But there was no continuity because the oldest OF texts, prior to 1150, contain no such examples (Hatcher 1944:159; Stéfanini 1962:267, 318ff., 321). The first author to use rampant IRs is Chrétien de Troyes (Champenois dialect); cf. (13).[6]

(13) Sample of IRs in Chrétien de Troyes
  a. *ne plus qu'il se tranchast la gole* (L 1306K/1312P)
    "he would as soon cut his own throat"
    (*autant que de ne pas se trancher la gorge*)
  b. *que je crien qu'il se brit la cuisse* (L 1622K/1628P)
    "I fear that he [my horse] would break his leg"
    (*sans crainte qu'il ne se brise la cuisse*)
  c. *et de l'autre doi se trancha/la premerainne jointe tote* (L 4642f.K/4650f.P)
    "and of the other finger he severed the whole first joint"
    (*et qu'il se trancha complètement la première articulation du doigt voisin*)
  d. *mains et genolz et piez se blece* (L 3112K/3118P)
    "wounds his hands, knees, and feet"
    (*il se blesse aux mains, aux genoux, aux pieds*)

e.   *mialz li vandroit que il s'eüst/les ialz treiz ou le col brisié* (L 5554f.K/5564f.P)
"he'd prefer to have his eyes put out or his neck broken"
(*il vaudrait mieux pour lui s'être arraché les yeux ou cassé le cou*)

Most of Chrétien's examples are the same in MF (as is clear from Poirion's translations). There is also general agreement between L and the MF use of POSS, as shown in (14).

(14)   POSS in Chrétien de Troyes and MF
a.   *peçoie sa lance* (L 2223K/2229P)
"split his lance"
(*brise sa lance*)
b.   *que ses piez desarme et ses mains* (L 3097K/3103P)
that his feet disarm and his hands
"by removing the armor from his feet and hands"
(*car il dégarnit ses pieds et ses mains de leur armure*)
c.   il met sa main devant sa face (L 3124K/3130P)
"he raised his hand before his face"
(*il met sa main devant son visage*)
d.   *de mostrer tote sa proesce* (L 5921K/5931P)
"to demonstrate all his skill"
(*de montrer toute sa prouesse*)
e.   *que nus ne puet ses ialz retreire/de lui esgarder, ou qu'il soit*
(L 5624f.K/5634f.P)
"that no one could take his eyes from him [Lancelot], wherever he might be"
(*que personne ne peut détacher ses yeux de lui, où qu'il soit*)
f.   *por ce reisons anferme et lie/son fol cuer et son fol pansé* (L 6846f.K/6856f.P)
"thus Reason encompassed and bound her foolish heart and thoughts"
(*c'est pourquoi elle enferme et retient son coeur insensé et ses idées folles*)

Not surprising, Chrétien uses the older and the newer construction with some competition; for the older construction, cf. (15).

(15)   *et ses chevols a detirer;/ses mains detuent et ront ses dras* (Yv 1156f.)
"(she began) to tear her hair; her hands she strikes, and she tears her clothes"
(*(elle se mettait) à s'arracher les cheveux et à déchirer ses vêtements*)

In the first line of (15), MF requires IR instead of POSS. It is impossible to determine, of course, whether or not Chrétien could have used IR with a different nuance here.

To conclude this section, the MF distribution of IR and POSS was in the process of being established in the second half of the 12th c., primarily in the works of Chrétien de Troyes. But the question of the source of IR remains.

5.   Partitive apposition

The source of IR is disputed. One incorrect account, as mentioned above, sees it as a continuation from Vulgar Latin. Realizing the lack of any such continuity, Hatcher (1944: 159) mentions that the DAT type is older than IR and accounts for the innovation of IR by analogy with the DAT type. That, of course, cannot explain the distributional facts. The account that is perhaps most cited in this context is the double object construction in a part-whole relation, which I will call *partitive apposition* (PA), following several articles by Hahn (1953, 1964).[7] While the syntactic distribution of PA is quite different in some respects from that of IR, there are certain shared properties that make it likely that PA is one source ("cue") for the innovation of IR.

Gamillscheg (1957: 348) cites (16a) from *Aïol* (A), Francian dialect [1150–75],[8] and (16b) in the passive with two (conjoined) objects.

(16)   a.   *si la baisa le pié* (A 443)
             "and kissed her (on) the foot"
       b.   *chascuns fu liés...les mains et les pies* (*Octavian* 4992)
             "everyone was bound hands and feet."

Gamillscheg labels (16) *accusative of respect*, typical of Greek and Vulgar Latin, and not uncommon in OF (Herslund 1980: 154–158). The importance of (16a) is that it has two of the three main properties of the target MF structure: (i) inalienability and (ii) effort. The third property (affected object) appears in (16b). We have, then, a possible source for the MF structure, except that the equivalent to (16a) must be rendered with a dative (11a).

The IR *il se lave les mains* "he$_i$ washes his$_i$ hands" appears to derive from the PA, except that the accusative was replaced by the dative — *except* with a reflexive clitic, and that suggests some change in the case system. What is important in terms of cue-theory (e.g., Lightfoot 1998, 1999) is that (i) the second object cannot receive case from the verb, and (ii) the construction motivates the quirks of the Modern French IR.

6.   Case and reflexive clitics: More cues

Reflexive clitics (*se*, for short) in certain contexts apparently did not require case. For instance, as a telic change of state marker, *se* had no obvious source of case with intransitive verbs (17).

(17)   Intransitive Change of State Verbs (*Roland*)
    a.   *gesir* "to lie" (intr./atelic) : *se gesir* "to lie down" (telic)
       i.   *sur l'erbe verte veit gesir sun nevuld* (R 2876)
          "on the green grass (he) sees his nephew lie/lying"
      ii.   *li quens Rollant se jut desuz un pin* (R 2375)
          "the count Roland lay down beneath a pine" (telic)
    b.   *pasmer* (< *(s)pasmāre*) "to faint; be passed out"; refl. "to pass out"
       i.   *Carles se pasmet, ne s'en pout astenir* (R 2891)
          "Charles passes out; he can't help himself"
      ii.   *a icest mot sur sun cheval se pasmet* (R 1988)
          "at this word, on his horse (he) passes out"

Intransitive verbs assimilated to the contrast between telic with *se* (17a-ii) and atelic without *se* (17a-i). For *pasmer* (17b) note also the telic change of state with *se*. As the first contexts in which *se* could not receive case, these constitute an important cue for other contexts in which *se* did not need case.

Consider next the raising verbs with *se* in (18).

(18)   Raising Verbs (OF)
    a.   *plus se fait fiers que lëon ne leupart* (R 1111)
         "(he) becomes more fierce (NOM.SG.MASC) than lions or leopards"
    b.   *pur Pinabel se cuntienent plus quei* (R 3797)
         "on account of Pinabel they keep (themselves) more quiet"

Se faire has two constructions. When *se* is an argument of the verb (anaphor), it means "make oneself x" and the predicate adjective requires ACC concord (Moignet 1984:91). With NOM concord, *se faire* is a raising verb "become" (cf. Stéfanini 1962:326; Moignet 1984:91). (18a), as shown by the case of *fiers* "fierce" (NOM.SG.MASC), illustrates the latter, in which *se* is not an argument of the verb (anaphor). In other words, the argument-type was reanalyzed as a raising verb, as in Old Icelandic (Miller 1993:212–213). In (18b) the NOM *quei(t)* "quiet" shows that *se* is not an argument in syntax. Accompanying an ergative verb, *se* has no syntactic argument status (Miller 1993:234ff.), from which case-concord could be transmitted.

OF also had an 'ethical dative' inherited from Latin, frequently in the first and second persons (de Kok 1985:550ff.), but also involving *se* (Stéfanini 1962:266ff.), as in (19). This use doubtless derived from case syncretism of ACC and DAT.

(19)   a.   *li quens Rollant nel se doüst penser* (R 355)
         "the count Roland should not have conjured this up"
         ("le comte Roland n'eût jamais dû y songer" trans. Short)
    b.   *se je onques le me pensai!* (L 4869K/4879P)
         "if I ever even conceived of such!"
         (*si j'en ai eu seulement la pensé*)

Nel in (19a) is contracted for *ne l(o)* "not it"; assuming that *l(o)* receives structural object case, there is no source of structural case for *se* which, as an old ethical dative, has the same real-world referent as the IR, and shares with the IR the impossibility of receiving/checking structural object case.

In terms of Lightfoot's cue-theory of language change, the reflex of the ethical dative has the proper real-world referent and lack of structural case. The old PA has the other core properties of the IR: inalienability, effort, affectedness. Together, these two structures served as important cues for the innovation of the IR. The other contexts in which *se* did not need (or could not get) case increased the likelihood of the main structural condition necessary for the IR – incorporation.[9]

'Incorporation' is defined as X^0 adjunction to a c-commanding X^0-level category (Baker 1988, 1995). Since incorporated elements do not need case (Baker), incorporated reflexives frequently allow dative shift phenomena because they do not exhaust the verb's structural (object) case (Miller 1993: §§ 8.10 Quechua; §§ 9.3, 9.9 Old Icelandic; § 9.16 Swedish; § 11.11 French; etc.). Incorporation was, in the case of French, facilitated by a morphological change in pronouns and anaphors during the 12th c.: the demise of the non-clitic forms. Chrétien de Troyes was one of the last poets to use non-clitic forms (e.g., *soi*) with infinitives (Stéfanini 1962: 254, 264), and the MSS are divided.

7. Evidence from causatives

To show that OF *se* had mostly clitic status and was not yet incorporated (relevant only when it was an argument), examples can be adduced from causative structures, e.g., (20a), from *Le roman de Rou de Wace* (Rou) [ca.1150–1175].[10] The intersection of (20a) and (20b), from *Eustache* [ca.1200–1225], another poem with Norman features, confirms that *se fist* is the relevant constituent, i.e., that *se* accompanies *faire* in Infl (brackets delineate constituents). These and other examples are cited by Pearce (1990: 199).

(20) OF *se* as (non-incorporated) Clitic: Causative Structures
a. *et {a ses anemis} {se fist} forment douter* (Rou 2.1513)
"and (he$_i$) made his enemies$_j$ fear him$_i$ greatly"
b. *amer {se fist} tant {a la gent}* (*Eustache* 738)
"(he$_i$) caused the people$_j$ to love him$_i$ so much"

Note *a* (= *à* "to"), required of the causee in MF only when the lower object needs case. In (21a), *les* "them" needs case. Therefore, since *faire* + *Verb* has only one structural object case to discharge (see Miller 1993: Ch. 11), *enfants* cannot receive case, and consequently needs a preposition. In (21b), *se* does not need case. Therefore, *enfants* can receive structural object case and the P is not needed (*aux* is ungrammatical). This makes sense if *se* is incorporated, which also explains its position in (21b). As thematic object of *laver, se* adjoins to it and therefore does not accompany *faire* in Infl, as it does in (20), parallel to the position of *les* in (21a–d).

(21)   Modern French Causatives
   a.   *Jean les fait laver aux (*les) enfants*
        "Jean makes the kids wash them"
   b.   *Jean fait se laver les (*aux) enfants*
        "Jean makes the kids wash themselves"[11]
   c.   *Jean fait enterrer les documents (à Bruno)*
        "Jean makes someone (Bruno) bury the documents"
   d.   *Jean les fait enterrer (à Bruno)*
        "Jean has someone (Bruno) bury them"

The (partial) analysis in (22) also explains the binding of *se* to *les enfants* in (21b). As VP-internal subject (argument), *les enfants* can serve as local binder to *se* (discussion in Miller 1993:262–274). By contrast, the preposition *a* in (20a–b) shows that *se* in OF still checked structural case in this context.

(22)   Skeletal Diagram of (21b)

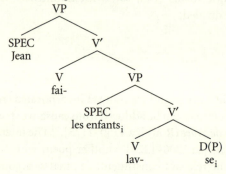

The tree in (22) represents the essential part of the lower portion of the total structure. The main reason for assuming a complex VP is that *faire* + *Verb* has at most one structural object case to assign, as opposed to *laisser* "let; cause" for which a multiple clause structure is more readily defensible because both *laisser* and the lower verb have separate object case to assign (details in Miller 1993). I assume that *Jean* moves into the highest case-checking position in Infl and *fai-* to T/M; that *se* incorporates with *lav-* and that unit moves into one of the independent functional phrases, probably its own VoiceP (see Kratzer 1996).

As to (20b), the lower VP subject must be PRO because *se* must receive case, which precludes any other lexical DP from getting case. Since incorporated X^0s typically do not need case (Baker 1988; Miller 1993), several properties of French *se* are explained simultaneously: (1) the linearization of *se* adjoined to the lower verb, versus OF where *se* cliticized to *faire* in Infl; (2) the case requirement (in many contexts) of OF *se* vs. its modern counterpart which does not need case; and (3) the appearance of long distance binding in OF: in (20b), the causee *a la gent* "(to) the people", as adjunct rather than argument, is not an appropriate binder. Moreover, since *se* does not incorporate with the lower verb, local binding with the subject of *faire* is expected. The appropriate point of comparison is type (21c–d), where *à Bruno* is an optional adjunct (Miller 1993: § 11.8). Since OF *se* needed case in many contexts, like MF *le, la, les,* it is to be expected that OF *se* should behave like MF *le(s)* rather than like MF *se*. Since *se* did not incorporate with the verb in OF, it was free to cliticize to the higher verb in Infl (*fist,* in (20)). This account has the advantage of not requiring any change in 'restructuring' (in the sense of Wurmbrand 1998) for causatives between OF and MF. The same monoclausal structure accommodates both constructions.

Older causatives of the type (20) are attested as late as the 17th c. (Stéfanini 1962: 658; Pearce 1990: 199), but already prose writers of the 13th c. allow *se* to incorporate, entailing the newer binding relations (see below).

8. Evidence from non-causatives

There is a well-known change that began around the end of the 12th c. which I analyze as incorporation of a clitic to the verb. Stéfanini (1962: 658 ff.) schematizes the change as that from (23a) to (23b); Pearce (1990: 225), as that from (24a) to (24b); cf. also de Kok (1985: 260 ff.).

(23) a. *il se peut défendre*
       b. *il peut se défendre*
          "he can defend himself"

(24) a. *Charles me veut bien voir*
       b. *Charles veut bien me voir*
          "Charles indeed wants to see me"

This change was widespread and did not just affect modal verbs. Since the older situation is well documented in Stéfanini (1962), de Kok (1985), and Pearce (1990: Ch. 6), I will focus on some early examples of the innovated types in (25), all cited by de Kok and/or Pearce. In the innovated examples, the pronoun or anaphor forms a constituent with the infinitive. In each case, the pronoun or anaphor in the earlier corresponding type formed a constituent in Infl with the higher verb.

(25) a. *or penst li dus de sei deffendre* (Rou 3.10856)
          "now let the duke think of defending himself" (Pearce, p. 233)
       b. *toute jor entendirent a eus logier* (M Artu 108.8)
          "nevertheless they undertook to lodge themselves" (de Kok, p. 265)

c.   *d'euls desarmer ne s'oublia* (Clari 2265)
"he did not forget to disarm them (Pearce, p. 237)

In (25b), *eus* is a common OF replacement of reflexive *se* in the plural (Brandt 1944; Moignet 1965: 102 ff.). What is important is that it precedes the infinitive rather than *entendirent*, as it would have in earlier OF.[12] (25a) from Wace is important because he was a contemporary of Chrétien de Troyes. (25b–c) are important, though from the 13th c., because they represent prose texts.[13] (25c) belongs to a special type in which both the higher verb and the infinitive have an object-type pronoun. According to de Kok (1985: 243 ff.), OF never stacked the pronouns in Infl in this case. Type (25c) then represents another cue for incorporation of the lower object with the infinitive.

The evidence is strong that incorporation of a pronoun or anaphor to the infinitive began in the second half of the 12th c., as did IR. Chrétien de Troyes, who has many IRs, uses the older type (26) rather than (25).

(26)   a.   *mialz se voloit il mahaignier* (L 3107K/3113P)
"he would rather maim himself"
(*il préférait se mutiler*)

b.   *ou Morz qui ne me vialt ocirre* (L 4332K/4340 P)
"or Death, who refuses to take me!"
(*ou la Mort qui ne veut pas m'ocirre!*)

c.   *que s'il vers toi se puet desfandre* (L 3270K/3276P)
"that if he can defend himself against you"
(*c'est que s'il peut te résister*)

d.   *et de desore armer se rueve / aus vaslez que devant soi trueve*
(L 6765f.K/6775f.P)
"and from there he$_i$ asked to arm him$_i$ (*se*) the valets$_j$ whom he found in front of him$_i$" (*soi*) (my trans.)

It seems to be the case that the IRs in (13) provided yet one final cue for the incorporation of a pronoun or anaphor to the lower (or only) verb. It was then the possibility of incorporation to the infinitive that provided for the innovated structures in (25).

9.   Conclusion

The appearance of historical continuity of the IR from Latin to MF is a mirage. It was not until long after the changes in the Vulgar Latin case system that the typical French IR became possible. This paper has identified five cues that prompted innovation of IR:

1. Contexts in which *se* did not need case
   a. Raising verbs (§6)

      plus se fait fiers (R 1111)
      "he becomes more fierce (NOM.SG.MASC)"

   b. *Se* as change of state marker with intransitive verbs (§6)

      Carles se pasmet (R 2891)
      "Charles passes out"

2. DAT (§3)

   si li briset les os (R 1200)
   "and (he$_i$) breaks his$_j$ bones"

3. Partitive Apposition (§5)

   si la baisa le pié (A 443)
   "and (he) kissed her (on) the foot"

4. *Se* (etc.) as ethical dative (§6)

   Rollant nel se doüst penser (R 355)
   "Roland should not have conjured this up (to himself)"

5. Non-stacking: each clitic appears with its own verb (§8)

   d'euls desarmer ne s'oublia (Clari 2265)
   "to disarm them he did not forget"

6. IR (§4)

   qu'il se brit la cuisse (L 1622K/1628P)
   "that he$_i$ would break his$_i$ leg"

7. *Se*-incorporation to infinitive
   a. Non-causative type (§8)

      i. *il se peut défendre*
      ii. *il peut se défendre*
      "he can defend himself"

   b. Causative type (§7)

      i. *il se fait laver aux enfants*
          "he$_i$ makes the kids wash him$_i$"
      ii. *il fait se laver les enfants*
          "he makes the kids wash themselves"

The first four cues were inherited; (5) was either inherited from Vulgar Latin or innovated in pre-OF. Cue (1) suggested a use of *se* without case. Cues (3) and (4) suggested a use of *se* parallel to DAT (cue 2). Cue (3) suggested the quirks of the MF IR. Cue (5) suggested object incorporation (X^0 adjunction).[14] Incorporation provided the optimal solution by allowing for dative shift and no case simultaneously. It is significant that in the examples of IR in (13) *se* is adjacent to the verb, a remarkably fixed pattern for OF, suggesting adjunction, i.e., incorporation (in Baker's sense).

Once incorporation was introduced, it could be exploited elsewhere as a means of capturing local dependencies in multiple verb structures, hence the innovations in the (b)-sentences of (7). In terms of cues, (5) and (6) 'conspired' to make (7) more probable. In overall terms of the grammar, selection of anaphor-incorporation is a change in parameter setting, which in turn predicted/entailed four seemingly unrelated syntactic changes: (1) IRs; (2) adjunction of anaphors to the lower verb; (3) argument (as opposed to adjunct) causees; and (4) binding of *se* with the causee rather than the higher subject. Initially based on an analysis of MF, our task was to go back in history to the time when anaphor-incorporation was first innovated and to account for that innovation. To this end, we have identified a number of structural cues that triggered the innovation ca. 1150.

Notes

* For insightful discussion on the draft presented at ICHL XIV, I wish to thank especially Nigel Vincent, Lene Schøsler, Vit Bubenik, Werner Abraham, and two anonymous referees. My colleague George Diller is heartily thanked for critiquing an early draft of this paper and supplying several references and improvements. For their fine judgments on the Modern French (MF) data, I am indebted to John and Danielle Bro. Starred examples from MF, of course, relate to the 'standard' dialect.

1. Two main periods of literary OF are traditionally assumed: early [ca. 850–1100] and later OF [1100–1300] (cf. Machonis 1990:21f.). The main break seems rather to have been ca.1150. The text culled for the older period is the *Chanson de Roland*, an early [ca. 1100–1125] heroic poem of over 4000 lines with Norman dialect features. Accidental gaps in the *Roland* text are supplied by examples from other texts. For Roland, I have used mainly the Oxford MS (ed. Mortier 1940 and Short 1990). Occasional variants from other MSS are so indicated; e.g., the French MS IV of the Library of St. Mark at Venice (Mortier, Vol.2) is marked V^4. Useful diacritics, e.g., *culchét* "lain" (vs. *culchet* "lies") are supplied from Short's edition. Only substantive differences in reading or line numbering between Mortier's and Short's editions are noted.

2. Some of Hatcher's assumed contrasts seem to be inaccurate, but since she doesn't translate any of her examples, a thorough critique is impossible. For convenience, this section repeats many of her examples, but with glosses and commentary provided by John and Danielle Bro.

3. The act must be socially conventionalized; any deviation may trigger POSS even when the object is affected, as in (i-b). Still, (i-a) and (i-b) differ in focus.

(i)   POSS with Non-Conventionalized Acts and Effort
  a.   *elle se reconstruisit le visage*
       "she recomposed her expression" (focus on the subsequent act)
  b.   *elle reconstruisit son visage*
       1.   "she recomposed her expression" (focus on her effort to recompose)
       2.   "she reconstructed her face" (plastic surgery)

c.   *elle s'est fait reconstruire le visage*
     "she had reconstructive surgery done on her face"

(i-b.2) is, of course, a purely grammatical interpretation that is valid only if one can perform plastic surgery on one's own face. Normally, one has it done, as in (i-c). What is important in (i-a/b) is that both are grammatical; Hatcher implies that (i-a) is ungrammatical.

4. For a contrast between POSS and IR, cf. (i).

(i)   a.   *je me tire les oreilles*
      b.   **je tire mes oreilles*
           "I pull my ears"
      c.   *il a tiré mes oreilles*
           "he pulled my ears" (what teachers do to pupils, hence "stern reprimand")

5. The assonance of the line is questionable, but conjectures for emendation generally retain the syntax and metathesize the hemistichs. In any event, the syntax is precisely what one expects and the textual tradition apparently agreed.

6. The main text culled for this section is *Lancelot*, or *Le Chevalier de la Charrete* "The Knight of the Cart" [ca.1176–1181] (Poirion 1994:1238). Editions used are those of Kibler (K) (1981), with English translation, and Poirion (P) (1994), with MF translation. Although the text of *Lancelot* (L) differs minimally in the two editions, the line numbering differs slightly, so both are cited for convenience. Also, P is useful for comparison of the corresponding structures in L and MF. P's MF translations are cited in parentheses. English translations are K's, unless otherwise noted. L contains 7122 lines in P's edition; I have used the entire text, but most of my citations precede line 6142, the imprisonment of Lancelot, the approximate point at which the poem was continued/completed by Godefroi de Lagny.
     Also used are *Yvain* (Yv), or *Le Chevalier au Lion* [1177–1181] (ed. Uitti & Walter 1994); and *Érec et Énide* (E) [ca.1170] (ed. Dembowski 1994).

7. The layered specifier analysis providing for multiple case (here ACC) checking (Chomsky 1995:286) will not work here because the second object gets case by apposition (coindexing) rather than from the verb.

8. The corresponding expression in *Roland* (i-a) uses a preposition, but the construction otherwise occurs, as in (i-b); cf. Moignet (1984:96).

(i)   a.   *par amistiét l'en baisat en la buche* (R 1530 [1487]; cf. 601, 626, 633)
           "for friendship then kissed him on the mouth"
      b.   *cascun le fiert .IIII. [quatre] colps de son puign* (R 1824 Mortier)
           "each strikes him four blows with the fist"

9. An anonymous referee notes that the development of the IR is also related to the development of the definite article around the same time. That there is a correlation is undeniable. Despite the referee's claim that "the definite article is a fundamental part of the construction under consideration", I would maintain that the article is neither a sufficient nor a necessary condition for the innovation of the IR. In Chrétien de Troyes, for instance, there are IRs without the article (e.g., 13d).

10. Wace, from Jersey, wrote in the variety of Norman French spoken on the Channel Islands. Rou was the Duke Rollo, who gained possession of Normandy in 911 (Price 1985:208f.).

11. A more recent change in French has rendered (21b) marginal for many speakers; it was, however, the formal successor to the OF type in (20), which is all that concerns us here.

12. In fact, M Artu (*La Mort le roi Artu*) [ca. 1230] has considerable variation, as documented by Moignet (1970) and Pearce (1990); cf. (i).

(i) a. *car moult le desir a savoir* (M Artu 74.33)
"for I greatly wish to know it" (Pearce, p. 229)
   b. *car moult les amoit a veoir pres de lui* (M Artu 36.89)
"for he very much liked to see them near him" (Pearce, p. 235)

Variation continues in the 14th c. (see de Kok 1985: 327 ff.) and in the 15th c., e.g., in Arnould Greban, *Mystère de la Passion* (Stéfanini 1962: 311).

13. Robert de Clari wrote *La Conquête de Constantinople* [ca. 1216] in Picard dialect.

14. De Kok (1985: 350 ff.) shows that most preinfinitival pronouns in OF were atonic, and places that change in the 15th c. That, however, was the period of productivity and diffusion. It seems clear that the change began ca. 1150.

References

Baker, Mark C. 1988. *Incorporation: A theory of grammatical function changing*. Chicago: University of Chicago Press.

Baker, Mark C. 1995. *The Polysynthesis Parameter*. Oxford: Oxford University Press.

Brandt, Gustaf. 1944. *La concurrence entre* soi *et* lui, eux, elle(s): *Étude de syntaxe historique française*. Lund: Gleerup & Copenhagen: Ejnar Munksgaard.

Bro, John. 1993. "Possessive Reflexives in French and English". Ms., University of Florida, Gainesville.

Cennamo, Michela. 1993. *The Reanalysis of Reflexives: A diachronic perspective*. Naples: Liguori Editore.

Chomsky, Noam. 1995. *The Minimalist Program*. Cambridge, MA: MIT Press.

Dembowski, Peter F., ed. & trans. 1994. *Érec et Énide*. Poirion 1994.1–169, 1053–1114.

Donaldson, W. 1973. *French Reflexive Verbs*. Paris: Mouton.

Flobert, Pierre. 1975. *Les verbes déponents Latins des origines à Charlemagne*. Paris: Société d'Éditions «Les belles lettres».

Gamillscheg, Ernst. 1957. *Historische französische Syntax*. Tübingen: Max Niemeyer.

Hahn, E. Adelaide. 1953. "Vestiges of Partitive Apposition in Latin Syntax". *Transactions and Proceedings of the American Philological Association* 84.92–123.

Hahn, E. Adelaide. 1964. "Partitive Apposition". *Proceedings of the 9th International Congress of Linguists, Cambridge, MA 8/27–8/31, 1962* ed. by Horace G. Lunt, 784–794. The Hague: Mouton.

Hatcher, Anna Granville. 1942. *Reflexive Verbs: Latin, Old French, Modern French*. Baltimore: Johns Hopkins University Press.

Hatcher, Anna Granville. 1944. "Il me prend le bras *vs.* il prend mon bras". *Romanic Review* 35.156–164.

Herslund, Michael. 1980. *Problèmes de syntaxe de l'ancien français: Compléments datifs et génitifs*. (= *Études romanes de l'Université de Copenhague, Revue Romane*, numéro spécial 21.) Copenhagen: Akademisk Forlag.

Kibler, William W., ed. & trans. 1981. *Chrétien de Troyes: Lancelot or, The Knight of the Cart (Le Chevalier de la Charrete)*. New York: Garland.

Kok, Ans de. 1985. *La place du pronom personnel régime conjoint en français: Une étude diachronique*. Amsterdam: Rodopi.

Kratzer, Angelika. 1996. "Severing the External Argument from Its Verb". *Phrase Structure and the Lexicon* (= *Studies in Natural Language and Linguistic Theory*, 33) ed. by Johan Rooryck & Laurie Zaring, 109–137. Dordrecht & Boston: Kluwer.

Lightfoot, David W. 1991. *How to Set Parameters: Arguments from Language Change*. Cambridge, MA: MIT Press.

Lightfoot, David W. 1998. "The Development of Grammars". *Glot International* 3.3–8.

Lightfoot, David W. 1999. *The Development of Language: Acquisition, change, and evolution*. Malden, MA & Oxford: Blackwell.

Machonis, Peter A. 1990. *Historie de la langue: Du latin à l'ancien français*. Lanham, MD: University Press of America.

Miller, D. Gary. 1993. *Complex Verb Formation*. Amsterdam & Philadelphia: John Benjamins.

Moignet, Gérard. 1965. *Le pronom personnel français: Essai de psycho-systématique historique*. Paris: Klincksieck.

Moignet, Gérard. 1970. "Le pronom personnel avec l'infinitif dans la 'Mort le Roi Artu'". *Mélanges de langue et de littérature du moyen âge et de la renaissance offerts à Jean Frappier* 2.831–844. Geneva: Droz.

Moignet, Gérard. 1984. *Grammaire de l'ancien français: Morphologie — syntaxe*. 2nd ed. Paris: Klincksieck.

Mortier, Raoul, ed. 1940. *Les textes de la chanson de Roland*. Vol. 1. *La version d'Oxford*. Paris: La Geste Francor.

Pearce, Elizabeth. 1990. *Parameters in Old French Syntax: Infinitival complements*. Dordrecht: Foris.

Poirion, Daniel, ed. & trans. 1994. *Chrétien de Troyes: Oeuvres complètes*. Paris: Éditions Gallimard.

Price, Glanville. 1985. *The Languages of Britain*. London: Edward Arnold.

Short, Ian. 1990. *La Chanson de Roland: Édition critique et traduction de Ian Short*. Paris: Librairie Générale Française.

Stéfanini, Jean. 1962. *La voix pronominale en ancien et en moyen français*. Aix-en-Provence: Éditions Ophrys.

Uitti, Karl D. & Philippe Walter, eds. & trans. 1994. *Yvain ou Le Chevalier Au Lion*. Poirion 1994.337–503, 1170–1234.

Vergnaud, Jean-Roger & Maria Luisa Zubizarreta. 1992. "The Definite Determiner in French and English". *Linguistic Inquiry* 23.595–652.

Wurmbrand, Susanne. 1998. *Infinitives*. Ph.D. dissertation, MIT, Cambridge, MA.

Lexical forces shaping the evolution of grammar*

Marianne Mithun
University of California, Santa Barbara

A feature commonly noted in typological descriptions of languages from early times to the present has been their degree of synthesis, their average number of morphemes per word. At one extreme of the synthesis continuum are analytic constructions, in which most words consist of a single morpheme. An analytic structure is in (1) from Engenni, a Kwa language of Nigeria.

(1) Analytic construction from Engenni (Thomas 1978:121)
á   ta na wa ōmu
one go to seek house
"Let's go look for the house."

At the other extreme are polysynthetic constructions, in which words typically consist of large numbers of morphemes. An example of a more polysynthetic structure can be seen in (2) from Mohawk, an Iroquoian language of Quebec, Ontario, and New York State.[1]

(2) Polysynthetic construction from Mohawk
teninonhsihsákha
te-ni-nonhs-ihsak-ha
1.INCL.AGENT.DUAL-house-seek-ANDATIVE
"Let's go look for the house."

One might wonder whether a construction like that in (2) is really a single word. There are numerous formal indications that it is, including the position of primary stress, the operation of various phonological processes, and its morphological structure, but of special significance are the judgments of Mohawk speakers. Whether or not they have ever given much conscious thought to their language or seen it written, they immediately recognize (2) as a single word. They cannot usually identify its components in isolation. Asked the meaning of *-ni-* or *-nonhs-* for example, even the best speakers are at a loss (unless trained as linguists), nor are they be able to isolate which elements mean "look for" or "go and". The contrast in structure between (1) and (2) raises an obvious question: does it matter how much information is packaged in a word?

There is evidence that it does. Languages with polysynthetic constructions generally offer their speakers analytic constructions as well. Each of the elements of the Mohawk word in (2) could have been expressed with a separate word. The language contains an independent first person pronoun *i:'i*, an independent numeral *tékeni* "two", an independent nominal *kanónhsote'* "house", and a full verb root *-e-* "go". Such options would not coexist so systematically alongside of the bound morphemes of (2) if they were functionally equivalent to them. The alternatives do indeed serve different functions. Synthetic constructions are used by Mohawk speakers to package together elements of what is treated as a single idea or concept. Separate words, by contrast, are used to focus special attention on their individual content, such as to introduce significant new information, add emphasis, or highlight a contrast. Similarly when English speakers use the synthetic form *eggbeater*, they are likely to visualize a familiar tool, rather than first imagining eggs that have been broken, then the action of beating them, then various objects that could be used for the action. The *-er* suffix is also used in English to derive agentive nominals, but in this case it is the instrument that springs to mind rather than a person hitting eggs with his fists or another tool, because we immediately recognize the word as a lexicalized unit. We might, on the other hand, first introduce an unfamiliar, complex idea with a phrase, such as a "device for registering the serial numbers of bills". Here we will see that the phenomenon of lexicalization can affect not just language use but language change as well.

In the Northern Iroquoian languages of northeastern North America, just three lexical categories have traditionally been recognized: nouns, verbs, and particles. Qualities expressed by adjectives in other languages are predicated by verbs. The early stages of development of a distinct attributive adjective category can now be discerned, however. The nature of this evolution demonstrates the potentially powerful role of lexicalization in certain processes of grammatical change.

1.   Lexical categories

Words in Northern Iroquoian languages fall into three classes on the basis of their internal morphological structure: particles, nouns, and verbs. Particles are by definition morphologically unanalyzable. Examples here are Mohawk, but the structures are the same in the related languages.

(3)   Morphological particles
    wáhi'   *kí:ken*
    "Isn't that so?"   "this"

Nouns consist of a prefix indicating the gender of the referent or its possessor, a noun stem, and a noun suffix, which contributes no meaning but identifies the word as a formal noun.

(4) Morphological nouns
 ora'wísta'   *akera'wísta'*
 o-ra'wist-a'   *ake-ra'wist-a'*
 NEUT.II-pancake-NOUN.SUFFIX   1.SG.POSS-pancake-NOUN.SUFFIX
 "pancake"   "my pancake"

Nominals may also be followed by various word-level suffixes, including locatives, residentials, a characterizer, a distributive, an augmentative, a diminutive, and a decessive.

(5) *kahnawa'kehronon'kénha'*
 ka-hnaw-a'-ke-hronon'-kenha'
 NEUT.I-rapids-NOUN.SUFFIX-LOC-RESIDENTIAL-DECESSIVE
 "the former (or late) residents of the place at the rapids"

Verbs consist minimally of a pronominal prefix specifying the core arguments of the clause, a verb stem, and an aspect suffix.

(6) Morphological verb
 Rikétskwas
 ri-ketskwa-s
 1.SG.AGENT/MASC.SG.PATIENT-raise-IMPERF
 "I wake him up."

They may also contain a number of other affixes. In addition to the obligatory pronominal prefix, there may be coincident, contrastive, partitive, negative, translocative, factual, duplicative, future, optative, cislocative, repetitive, reflexive/reciprocal, and/or middle prefixes. In addition to the aspect suffixes (perfective, imperfective, or stative), there may be inchoative, reversive, causative, instrumental applicative, benefactive applicative, distributive, andative, faciliative, purposive, continuative, and/or various past tense suffixes.

(7) More complex verbs
 a. *Tontahshako'nikonhrotakwenhákie'*
  t-on-ta-hshako-'nikonhr-ot-akw-en-hatie'
  DUP-FACT-CISLOCATIVE-he/her-mind-stand-REVERSIVE-STATIVE-PROGRESSIVE
  "He changes her mind at every turn" = "He rules over her (mentally)."
 b. *Enkatatekhónnien*
  en-k-atate-khw-onni-en-'
  FUTURE-I-REFL-food-make-BENEFACTIVE-PERF
  "I'll cook for myself."

Verbs may also contain incorporated noun stems, like -'*nikonhr*- "mind" in (7a) and -*khw*- "food" in (7b). Only the noun stem is incorporated: the full noun for "food" is *ká-khw-a'*, with neuter prefix and noun suffix, but only the stem -*khw*- appears in the compound verb stem -*khw-onni* "food-make" = "cook". The incorporated noun does not function as a syntactic argument. The core arguments of (7a), for example, are "he" and "her", not "he" and "mind", as can be seen in the pronominal prefixes. Verbs formed with noun incorporation in Mohawk may be transitive, intransitive, or ambivalent. They are formed for a purpose, as labels for nameworthy concepts. Once lexicalized, they are stored, accessed, and learned by other speakers as single units.

Qualities expressed by adjectives in other languages are usually predicated in Northern Iroquoian languages by stative verbs. Like all verbs, they show morphological marking for aspect, tense, negation, and other typical verbal distinctions. Many appear with incorporated nouns.

(8)   Mohawk statives with typical verbal morphology
   a.   *kakowá:nen*
        ka-kowan-en
        NEUT.I-be.big-STATIVE
        "It is big."
   b.   *Kahentowanèn:ne*
        ka-hent-owan-en-hne
        NEUT.I-field-be.big-STATIVE-PAST
        "It was a big field."
   c.   *Iah tekanatowá:nen*
        iah te-ka-nat-owan-en
        not NEG-NEUT.I-town-be.big-STATIVE
        "It's not a big town."

The syntactic functions served by words in each lexical category are to some extent as might be expected. Morphological particles serve as demonstratives, numerals, question words, adverbials, conjunctions, discourse markers, etc. Morphological nouns function syntactically as arguments of clauses. Morphological verbs function syntactically as predicates. Verbs can also serve other functions. Since they contain pronominal prefixes specifying their core arguments, they can function as complete grammatical sentences in their own right, as can be seen in many of the preceding examples. Verbs can also be used as descriptive labels for entities.

(9)   Morphological verbs as lexical nominals
   a.   *iera'wistakarhathóhstha'*
        ie-ra'wist-a-karhatho-hst-ha'
        INDEF.AGENT-pancake-EPENTHETIC-turn.over-INSTR-IMPERF
        "one flips pancakes with it" = "spatula"

b. *atekhwà:ra*
(zero)-*ate-khw-hra*
(NEUT.AGENT)-MIDDLE-food-set.on
"food is set on it" = "table"

c. *kà:sere*
ka-'ser-e'
NEUT.AGENT-drag-IMPERF
"it drags" = "wagon" > "vehicle, car"

Verbal nominals like these can function syntactically as arguments of clauses, without any overt marking of their status as nominals. A great many have been lexicalized as nominals, names of entities, much like English *eggbeater*. Their verbal origin can still be detected in their morphological behavior, however. Only formal noun stems can be incorporated into verbs. If verbal nominals are incorporated, they must be overtly nominalized with a suffix. The choice of nominalizer is a lexical matter. That for "table" is -*'tsher*-, and that for "car" is -*ht*.

(10) *wa'ke'serehtahní:non*
wa'-k-'sere-ht-a-hninon-'
FACT-1SG.AGENT-drag-<u>NOMINALIZER</u>-EPENTHETIC-buy-PERF
"I bought a car."

2. Lexicalization, headedness reversal, and decategorialization

The lexicalization of morphological verbs as names of entities has set the stage for a significant grammatical development. The head of an endocentric construction is usually taken to be that element which determines grammatical properties of the whole. The head of a noun-verb compound like -*khw-onni* "food-make" = "cook" is the verb root -*onni* "make", since the resulting stem is a verb. The incorporated noun root serves as a modifier, describing a kind of preparation.

Certain stative verbs with incorporated nouns are evolving in an interesting direction. The verbs -*iio* "be good" and -*aksen* "be bad" can be seen in their basic predicative function in (11).

(11) Mohawk statives as predicates: Awenhrathen Deer, speaker
ótia'ke kanahskwí:io
ótia'ke ka-nahskw-iio
some NEUT.I-domestic.animal-be.good.STATIVE

ótia'ke ni'   *kanahskwáksen*
ótia'ke ni'   *ka-nahskw-aks-en*
some CONTRAST NEUT.I-domestic.animal-be.bad-STATIVE
"Some were good animals, some were bad animals."

The same morphological construction, based on the same verb roots, shows a reversal of headedness in some contexts. The last word in (12) below shows the internal morphological structure of a verb, with the literal translation "it is a good thing". It is used syntactically as a nominal, however, and its free translation is "good will". The incorporated noun -rihw- "matter, affair, idea, thing" has become the head of the word, and the original verb -iio "be good" serves simply as a modifier "good".

(12)   Headedness reversal: statives as modifiers Warisose Karierithon, speaker
  ratihá:wi'   *ne   raoneriáhsakon*
  rati-hawi-'   *ne   raon-eriahs-ak-on*
  MASC.PL.AGENT-carry-IMPERF   the MASC.PL.POSS-heart-be.in-STATIVE

  ne   skén:nen' tánon' ne   karihwí:io.
  ne   skén:ne' tánon' ne   ka-rihw-iio
  the peace   and   the NEUT.I-matter-be.good.STATIVE
  "They had hearts full of peace and good will."

As noted earlier, both verbs and nouns contain prefixes distinguishing gender and number. Those on verbs are pronominal prefixes that refer to the core arguments of the clause. They distinguish two grammatical relations based on semantic role. One paradigm of prefixes (Paradigm I) generally represents grammatical agents (*ka-tákhe'* "it is running"), a second paradigm (Paradigm II) represents grammatical patients (*ió-ta's* "it is sleeping"), and a third paradigm (transitive) represents combinations of agents and patients (*tahshakóhsere'* "he was chasing them"). Arguments of inherent states are generally represented by Paradigm I prefixes (*ka-kowá:nen* "it is big"), while participants affected by resultant states are generally represented by Paradigm II prefixes (*io-'taríhen* "it is hot"). Perfects are classified grammatically as resultant states (*ió:kon* "it has eaten").

The prefixes on nouns simply indicate gender and, for humans, number. The vast majority of nouns are neuter, because the majority of nouns refer to objects. There are two paradigms of noun prefixes, but unlike the pronominal prefixes on verbs they do not distinguish grammatical role. The choice of prefix paradigm is simply lexicalized with each noun: *ka-nákta'* "bed" (neuter, Paradigm I), *o-'nó:wa'* "guitar" (neuter, Paradigm II). The choice is invariant for each noun, unrelated to the syntactic role of the noun in the clause. As can be seen in (13), the noun for "mouse" always appears with a Paradigm II prefix (*o-*), whether the coreferent pronominal prefix on the accompanying verb is from Paradigm I (agent *ka-*) or Paradigm II (patient *io-*).

(13)   Noun prefix paradigm: independent of syntactic function
  a.   *Katákhe'*   *ne   otsinó:wen.*
       ka-takh-e'   *ne   o-tsinow-en'*
       NEUT.I-run-IMPERF   the NEUT.II-mouse-NOUN.SUFFIX
       "The mouse is running."

b. *Ió:ta's*   *ne otsinó:wen.*
   io-ta'-s   *ne o-tsinow-en'*
   NEUT.II-sleep-IMPERF the NEUT.II-mouse-NOUN.SUFFIX
   "The mouse is sleeping."

The shapes of the pronominal prefixes on verbs and gender prefixes on nouns are similar but not identical. A comparison of the prefixes in the left and right columns in (14) below shows that many of the verb prefixes contain an initial glide that is absent from noun prefixes. (The letter *i* represents the glide [y] before a vowel. Digraphs *en* and *on* represent nasalized vowels.)

(14)   Neuter prefixes on verbs and nouns

	Verbs	Nouns	
Paradigm I	*ka-*	*ka-*	(before consonants, *i*;
AGENT	*ka-tákhe'*	*ka-nákta'*	*a+i > en*)
	"it is running"	"bed"	
	w-	–	(before *a, e, en*)
	w-áhtons	*à:there'*	
	"it disappears"	"basket"	
	i-	–	(before *o, on*)
	i-onhe'	*ón:kwe*	
	"it is alive"	"person"	
Paradigm II	*io-*	*o-*	(before consonants,
PATIENT	*ió-:ta's*	*o-'nó:wa'*	*a, i, o, on* with loss)
	"it is sleeping"	"guitar"	
	iaw-	*aw-*	(before *e, en*)
	iaw-enhé:ion	*aw-enhnísera*	
	"it is dead"	"day"	

When verbs contain incorporated nouns, the choice of pronominal prefix paradigm is normally governed by the verb root, since it is the head of the word. The verb *-nor-* "be precious", for example, requires a Paradigm I pronominal prefix, as can be seen in (15a). When the noun "silk" is incorporated, as in (15b), the Paradigm I prefix *ka-* remains unchanged. When the noun "wood" is incorporated as in (15c), the Paradigm I prefix *ka-* still remains unchanged, even though the noun "wood" by itself appears with the Paradigm II prefix (*o-*).

(15)   Prefix paradigm governed by verb
   a.   *Kanó:ron.*
        ka-nor-on
        NEUT.I-be.precious-STATIVE
        "It is precious, dear, expensive."

b. _Ka'nhehsanó:ron._   _kà:nhehs_ "silk"
   ka-'nhehs-nor-on   Paradigm I
   NEUT.I-silk-be.precious-STATIVE
   "It is expensive silk."

c. _Kaientanó:ron._   _ó:iente'_ "wood"
   ka-ient-nor-on   Paradigm II
   NEUT.I-wood-be.precious-STATIVE
   "It is expensive wood."

In certain combinations, however, the prefix choice is now governed by the incorporated noun. These are combinations that have been lexicalized as nominals, like the term for "gold" in (16). Here the headedness relation has been reinterpreted: the incorporated noun is the head, and the incorporating verb a modifier.

(16)   Prefix paradigm determined by incorporated noun
   ohwistanó:ron   _ohwísta'_ "metal"
   o-hwist-nor-on   Paradigm II
   NEUT.II-metal-be.precious-STATIVE
   "it is precious metal" > "precious metal" = "gold"

Though the verb -_nor_- "be precious" normally requires the Paradigm I prefix _ka_-, the prefix on "gold" matches that of the incorporated noun "metal" (II). Furthermore, the prefix shows the shape used with nominals (_o_-), rather than that used with verbs (_io_-). There is also a shift in referentiality. When verbs function as predicates or clauses, it is the pronominal prefix which is referential: "it is precious metal". When they function as nominals, the whole construction is referential: "gold".

The government of prefix choice by the incorporated noun is not an across-the-board structural change in all verbs serving as nominals. It is limited to a subset of lexical items containing only certain stative roots. These roots have the kinds of meanings typical of adjectives found in languages with limited adjective categories: good/bad, large/small, long/short, old/new, etc. (Dixon 1977 [1982]). The Mohawk root -_as_- "be new/fresh" is also part of the set. It normally appears with Paradigm I prefixes.

(17)   Paradigm I verb: -_as_- "be new/fresh"
   _wá:se'_
   _w-as-e'_
   NEUT.I-be.new-STATIVE
   "it is new, fresh"

When the verb is reanalyzed as a modifier, the incorporated noun can govern prefix choice.

(18) Prefix determined by incorporated noun

    a.   _kaná:tase'_   _kaná:ta'_ "town"
        ka-nat-as-e'   Paradigm I
        NEUT.I-town-be.new-STATIVE
        "a new town"

    b.   _ka-nónhsase'_   _kanónhsa'_ "house"
        ka-nonhs-ase'   Paradigm I
        NEUT.I-house-be.new-STATIVE
        "a new house"

    c.   _ohserá:se'_   _óhsera_ "year"
        o-hser-as-e'   Paradigm II
        NEUT.II-year-be.new-STATIVE
        "New Year's day"

    d.   _onénhstase'_   _ó:nenhste'_ "corn"
        o-nenhst-as-e'   Paradigm II
        NEUT.II-corn-be.new-STATIVE
        "fresh corn" (as opposed to dried)

Apart from the fact that their prefix paradigm is governed by the incorporated noun rather than the verb root, these attributive adjective constructions still show the morphological structures and patterns of verbs with incorporated nouns. The incorporated element must either be a noun root or carry an overt nominalizing suffix.

(19) Overt nominalizer with _-iio_ "good"

    a.   _ka'serehtí:io_
        ka-'sere-ht-iio
        NEUT.I-drag-NOMINALIZER-be.nice.STATIVE
        "it's a nice car"

    b.   _watekhwahra'tsherí:io_
        w-ate-khw-hra-'tsher-iio
        NEUT.I-MIDDLE-food-set.on-NOMINALIZER-be.nice.STATIVE
        "it's a nice table"

(20) Overt nominalizer with _-ase'_ "new"

    a.   _ka'serehtasé'tsi_
        ka-'sere-ht-as-e'-tsi
        NEUT.I-drag-NOMINALIZER-be.new-STATIVE-INTENSIFIER
        "new car"

    b.   _atekhwahrà:tsheres_
        (zero)_-ate-khw-hra-'tsher-es_
        NEUT.I-MIDDLE-food-set.on-NOMINALIZER-be.long.STATIVE
        "long table"

Comparative constructions are formed with Mohawk adjectival verbs by means of the particle _sénha_ "more": _sénha kakowá:nen_ "it is bigger" (also _sénha kowá:nen_).

The particle does not appear with nominals containing attributive adjectival suffixes, however, perhaps for structural reasons. The particle "more" would modify the word as a whole, rather than just a portion of it (a dependent qualifier), and the result would make little sense.

The kinds of situations that might prompt the reversal in headedness are easy to find. Sentences like that (21), from a conversation, are potentially structurally ambiguous.

(21)   Structural ambiguity: Sha'tekenhatie' Phillips, speaker
        Né: ki' kheienté:ri,
        ne: ki' khe-ienter-i
        it.is just 1SG/INDEF-know-STATIVE
        "Those are the ones I used to know,

        iakotiohkowá:nen   *... Oaks.*
        iako-itiohkw-owan-en
        INDEF.II-group-large-STATIVE   (name)
        they were a large group, the Oaks family/a large group, the Oaks family".

The use of morphological verbs as syntactic nominals facilitated the reinterpretation of headedness in incorporating constructions. The lexicalization of such complex morphological structures as single units of expression dimmed speaker awareness of their internal structures.

Comparative evidence confirms the sequence of events. Cherokee, the sole member of the Southern branch of the Iroquoian family, does not show the same elaboration of noun incorporation as the Northern languages, nor the same reanalysis of certain stative verbs in certain contexts as attributive adjectives. An adjective category has begun to emerge in that language as well, but from a different diachronic source (Lindsey & Scancarelli 1985).

3.   Further grammaticalization

Lexicalization has moved the grammar of the Northern Iroquoian languages ahead still one more step, but only with a few morphemes that recur frequently in lexicalized constructions. The stative verb *-kowanen* "be.large", has also evolved a step further into a derivational clitic *=kó:wa*. This new marker functions as an augmentative nominalizer, which can be added to any lexicalized nominal, of either nominal or verbal origin, to create new lexical nominals.

(22)   Augmentative nominalizer

takò:s	"cat"	tako's=kó:wa	"wildcat, panther"
ò:niare'	"snake"	ohniare'=kó:wa	"serpent"
otsinó:wen	"mouse"	otsinowen'=kó:wa	"rat"
kahonwé:ia	"boat"	kahonweia'=kó:wa	"ship"
onon'ónsera	"squash"	onon'onsera'=kó:wa	"pumpkin"
kaniá:tara	"lake"	kaniatara'=kó:wa	"ocean"

Similar developments have occurred with several other markers that originated as incorporating stative verbs, including a diminutive and set of locatives.

4. Conclusion

The processes of lexicalization and grammaticalization have often been compared in recent work on the factors that shape language. Both involve a cognitive process of routinization, the automation of frequently recurring sequences, but they differ in their output: the first creates lexical items (such as *eggbeater* or *ohserá:se'* "New Year's Day"), while the second, as now more generally understood, creates grammar: grammatical markers and constructions (such as the oft-cited English "be going to" future or SVO word order). Neither process operates in isolation, apart from a linguistic and pragmatic context. Here we have seen an example of the potential role of the first (lexicalization) in providing an especially tight linguistic context for the second (grammaticalization). The routinization of recurring morpheme sequences as unitary lexical items resulted in a fading of their internal semantic and grammatical structure. This fading facilitated the reanalysis of the internal structure in terms of their external syntactic uses. The result was a new lexical category for certain stative verb roots as attributive adjectives. This process can still be seen to be constrained by lexicalization, occurring only with certain roots in certain lexical constructions. Finally, some lexicalized constructions containing these attributive adjectives provided the context for further grammaticalization. Some of the attributive roots are now evolving into derivational nominalizers.

Lexicalization is of course a gradient phenomenon. Morphological verbs used as syntactic nominals in Mohawk show varying degrees of lexicalization as nominals. Some, like *atekhwà:ra* "table", are so fully lexicalized as nominals that speakers no longer have conscious access to their verbal etymologies. Some, like *kà:sere* "car/it drags", are robustly lexicalized as nominals, so that speakers typically provide an English noun as the first translation ("car"), but their literal verbal origins are still accessible. Some verbs are used spontaneously to designate entities, and the nonce forms may or may not subsequently become routinized with this function. And of course lexicalization does not necessarily stop at word boundaries. As we know from English, recurring sequences of words may become lexicalized as idioms, though speakers typically retain access to their components longer than they may to morphemes within words, particularly in languages with extensive phonological fusion and little tradition of writing. But in all cases, lexicalization can dim the salience of internal grammatical and semantic structure, a development that can facilitate the reanalysis of the components of the construction and their functions.

Notes

* I am grateful to the Mohawk speakers from the communities of Kahnawake, Kanehsatake, Ahkwesahsne, Thaientaneken, Wahta, and Ohsweken, who have generously shared their expertise. I especially appreciate insightful comments provided by Kanerahtenhawi Nicholas and Skawennati Montour of Kanehsatake, Kaia'titahkhe Jacobs of Kahnawake, and Rokwaho Dan Thompson of Ahkwesahsne.

1. Material cited here is presented in the practical orthography adopted by all six Mohawk communities. Symbols *t* and *k* represent plain stops (voiced before voiced segments); *ts* is an alveolar affricate in Kahnawake, Kanehsatake, and Wahta, which corresponds to an alveopalatal affricate spelled *tsi* in Ahkwesahsne, Thaientaneken, and Ohsweken; *s* is a voiceless spirant; *n, r, w, i* are resonants, with *i* representing the glide [y] before vowels; *h* is always pronounced as a distinct segment (*th* = *t*+*h*); and the apostrophe ' represents glottal stop. The vowel symbols *i, e, a, o* have IPA values. Digraphs *en* and *on* represent nasal vowels: *en* is a low, central vowel (nasalized caret) and *on* is a high, back vowel (nasalized [u]). The colon : represents vowel length, the acute accent ´ stress with high or rising tone, and the grave accent ` stress with falling tone.

References

Dixon, R. M. W. 1977. "Where Have all the Adjectives Gone?" *Studies in Language* 1.1: 1–80. Reprinted with minor alternations and additional references in *Where Have all the Adjectives Gone? And other essays in semantics and syntax.* (= *Janua Linguarum, Series Maior*, 107.) Berlin & New York: Mouton de Gruyter, 1982.

Lindsey, Geoffrey & Janine Scancarelli. 1985. "Where Have all the Adjectives Come from? The Case of Cherokee". *Proceedings of the Eleventh Annual Meeting of the Berkeley Linguistics Society* ed. by Mary Niepokuj, Mary VanClay, Vassiliki Nikiforidou, & Deborah Feder, 207–215. Berkeley: Berkeley Linguistics Society.

Thomas, Elaine 1978. *A Grammatical Description of the Engenni Language.* Arlington, TX: University of Texas and Dallas, TX: Summer Institute of Linguistics.

Why "me" and "thee"?

Johanna Nichols
University of California, Berkeley

1. Introduction

Personal pronouns are usually inherited and rarely borrowed. When pronouns resemble each other in different languages, the usual assumption seems to be that we must decide whether the resemblances are due to inheritance, borrowing, universals, or chance. When macrocomparison is at issue, the debate generally seems to boil down to inheritance vs. universals, with conformity to universals taken to weaken the case for deep genetic relatedness. For instance, a number of language families of northern Eurasia have /m/ as the first or sole root consonant in first person pronouns and a dental or other anterior obstruent in the second person. To some linguists, this is evidence of genetic relatedness; others maintain that very basic consonants, in particular nasals, are likely to occur in personal pronouns and therefore their diagnostic value is weak. That is, a cross-linguistically favored consonantism reflects universal preferences. Just how the universal preferences might have become embedded in a vocabulary system considered resistant to borrowing is not clear, however.

Outside the domain of pronouns, the kin terms known as 'mama'–'papa' vocabulary, which display striking cross-linguistic resemblances around the globe, are generally regarded as universal-driven and phonosymbolic in their phonology (Jakobson 1960) and therefore largely irrelevant to genetic classification.

It happens, however, that the phonological shapes of personal pronouns and 'mama'–'papa' vocabulary are quite similar: both tend to involve nasals, labial and apical consonants, and assonance[1] in the form of rhyme, alliteration, shared syllable structure, and the like. Since pronouns are prone to be inherited while 'mama'–'papa' terms are prone to be reshaped, recreated, etc. and furthermore phonosymbolic, there is no a priori reason to expect these two classes of words to be phonologically similar.

This paper is a programmatic inquiry into these resemblances. It first seeks to determine whether in fact such resemblances exist, using a systematic cross-

Map 1. *m-* in 1SG independent form

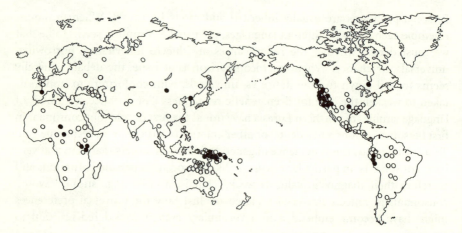

Map 2. *m-* in 2SG independent form

linguistic survey, a controlled vocabulary sample, and controlled phonological parameters. The resemblances do prove to exist, and thus personal pronouns and 'mama'–'papa' terms have an equal claim to be phonosymbolic.

Phonosymbolism of course does not mean that particular sounds carry particular meanings. The worldwide distribution of pronominal consonantism makes it clear that there is no straightforward association between particular nasals and particular meanings in personal pronouns. Maps 1 and 2 (from Nichols & Peterson 1996) illustrate this by plotting the distribution of /m/ as first root consonant in one or another person-number category: first person singular in Map 1, second person singular in Map 2. If there were any universal tendency, even a fairly weak one, to associate /m/ or nasals more generally with personal pronouns,

/m/ should be evenly, and rather thickly, distributed over the earth in both person categories. This is not the case, however. As the maps show, /m/ in the first person is common in northern Eurasia, and in the second person it is common in the western Americas. Apart from these two large clusters, /m/ is not particularly common in either pronoun. Continent-to-continent or area-to-area differences in the incidence of both of these patterns are statistically significant (Nichols & Peterson 1996). This means that the geographical distributions of both patterns are highly unlikely to have arisen by chance. If phonosymbolism were a simple matter of favoring one or another consonant or class of consonants, these significant geographical skewings would not be expected. These maps serve as a graphic indicator that phonosymbolism as it affects pronouns is not a simple matter of favoring one or another type of consonant.

2. Survey design

Some ten years ago I was struck by the fact that the Indo-European pronominal consonantism with first person singular oblique forms in *m- and second person singular forms in *t- was nearly the same as that of English mom and dad and their equivalents in several other languages. The survey reported here is a pilot study designed to indicate whether this is a fluke or a more systematic property of language.

Independent forms of first and second person singular pronouns were surveyed in 152 languages (using data from Nichols & Peterson 1996). Independent forms, rather than verb agreement affixes, possessive affixes, or some other series were used because, as self-standing lexemes, these are most comparable to the other items surveyed, and also because no other series is found in every language. (The independent forms are also strongly consistent with the consonantism found in other series, as Nichols & Peterson 1996 show.) The words for 'mother' and 'father' were surveyed in most of those languages (125 of them). They are proxies for mom and dad, mama and papa, and the like, which it was not possible to survey for a number of reasons. The sample languages were chosen first for their genetic classification and then for the quality of published grammatical description available on them, and not all of them have published dictionaries. It is almost always possible to find the words for 'mother' and 'father' in a grammar, but not always (in fact often not) 'mom' and 'dad'. Furthermore, even if found in glossaries or dictionaries, it is not always clear that they are cross-linguistically comparable in stylistics, function, etc. Hence the ordinary words 'mother' and 'father' were surveyed instead.

As a first stab at controls, two other potentially paired lexical sets were surveyed in 30 languages each: 'sun' and 'moon', and 'fire' and 'water'. The expectation was that 'sun' and 'moon' are a salient lexical pair and quite possibly a closed pair and might therefore sometimes show assonance, while the words for 'fire' and 'water', while occasionally found together, are much less likely to constitute a lexical pair and therefore much less likely to show assonance. In addition, neither of these two pairs of words is in any obvious way pragmatically or deictically laden, and there was no reason to believe that either pair would exhibit any cross-linguistic tendency to be phonosymbolic. Thus the hypotheses were that the pronouns and 'mother'–'father' would both show significant cross-linguistic tendencies for phonosymbolism and assonance, that the tendencies would be about equally strong for the two pairs, and that the formal symbolic means would be similar; that 'sun'–'moon' would show some weak tendency for assonance while 'fire'–'water' would not; and that neither 'sun'–'moon' nor 'fire'–'water' would exhibit phonosymbolism with any frequency. I further assumed that phonosymbolism would manifest itself in higher frequency of nasals, and also in what I call *counterposed* labial and dental consonants in the same phonotactic position: one member of the pair has a labial and the other a dental in the same position (as in English *mom* and *dad*, or *me* and *thee*, in which the first word of each has a labial and the second has a dental). The consequent hypothesis was that pronouns and 'mother'–'father' would have nasals and counterposed labials and dentals more frequently than the other sets. These hypotheses about consonant classes and their distribution were based on gut intuition, observation of consonants in pronoun systems, and reading of Jakobson 1960.

The lexical basis of the survey is summarized in (1), and the hypotheses are summarized in (2).

(1)   Lexical sets surveyed
      Pronouns: 1sG and 2sG independent forms (in nominative or citation case) in
      152 languages
      'mother', 'father' in 125 of those languages
      'sun', 'moon' in 30 of those languages
      'fire', 'water' in the same 30 languages

(2)   Hypotheses
      1.   Pronouns and 'mother'–'father' will contain nasals more frequently than the
           other pairs.
      2.   Pronouns and 'mother'–'father' will exhibit assonance more often than the
           others.
      3.   Pronouns and 'mother'–'father' will contain counterposed labial and dental
           consonants more often than the others.
      4.   'Sun'–'moon' will exhibit assonance to some observable extent, and more
           often than 'fire'–'water'.
      5.   Both 'sun'–'moon' and 'fire'–'water' will have similar and low frequencies
           of nasals.
      6.   Both 'sun'–'moon' and 'fire'–'water' will have similar and low frequencies
           of counterposed labials and dentals.

For the four lexical sets two things were surveyed: the first consonant of the root, specifically its membership in broad consonant categories: labial, dental/alveolar/ alveolopalatal, velar/uvular, and nasal vs. non-nasal (the same categories surveyed in Nichols & Peterson 1996); and assonance of various kinds. The types of assonance surveyed are shown in (3)–(7).

(3) Rhyme: Avar   1sg   dun   2sg   mun
              Finnish   1sg   minä   2sg   sinä

(4) Alliteration: Avar   1sg   di-   2sg du- (oblique stems)
              Avar   1pl Ex   niž   2pl nuž
              Diegueño   'mother' tal^y   'father' ta:t

Often a pronoun or kin term contains two tokens of the same consonant (as in English *mom* and *dad*) or even two identical syllables (as in *mama* and *papa*). If both forms of a pair had repetition and the syllable structure and/or vocalism were the same I counted the set as assonant; examples are in (5). If one form had a repeat and the other rhymed or alliterated with it, as in (6), I counted the set as assonant.

(5) Consonant or syllable repetition in both forms with minimal variation:
                           'mother'   'father'
     Fula   yaaye, daada   baaba
     Sulka   na:n   ti:t
     Sahu   meme   'ba'ba
     Cuzco Quechua   mama   tayta

(6) Consonant or syllable repetition in one form, some assonance with the other:
     Yoruba   'mother' ìyá   'father' bàbá

Less clearly assonant are pairs in which the two forms have the same syllable structure and the same class of consonant. (7) shows an example, in which both words have VCV structure where C is a nasal and both end in the same vowel but do not rhyme or alliterate. (Both words begin with vowels, but I did not code them as alliterating.)

(7) Variation on similar template (coded as 0.5 assonant):
     Tagalog   'mother' ina   'father' ama

(8) shows an example which is assonant in the sense that the syllable structure is identical and the consonantal templates near-identical. Furthermore, the vocalisms echo each other in that each word begins with the high vowel that constitutes the syllabic equivalent of the medial glide and each ends in a lower vowel.

(8) Trans-segmental or trans-syllabic phonological oppositions, similar template:
     Berik   'mother' iye   'father' uwa

(9) shows an illustrative fragment of the database. The two words of a pair are surveyed for phonological properties of the first consonant in each root: its broad

point of articulation and whether or not it is a nasal. The last three columns show whether the forms exhibit assonance, whether the pair contains at least one nasal, and whether the pair shows a counterposed labial and dental in similar phonotactic positions. The Avar pronouns have initial /d-/ and /m-/, and the Tagalog ones /-n-/ and -/m-/, and these are counterposed labial-dental sets. (The Warao forms have the same pattern in their second consonants, but only the first consonant in the root is surveyed here.)

(9)   Sample partial entries from actual database:

		First form:				Second form:						
		P	T	K	N	P	T	K	N	Asn	Nasal	P : T
Avar	dun, mun	0	1	0	0	1	0	0	1	1	1	1
Warao	dani, dima	0	1	0	0	0	1	0	0	1	0	0
Tagalog	ina, ama	0	1	0	1	1	0	0	1	0.5	1	1
Basque	eki, argizaki	0	0	1	0	0	1	0	0	0	0	0

Coding pertains to the first consonant in the word. P = labial, T = dental or alveolar, K = velar, N = nasal. Asn = assonant, Nasal = any nasal in either (or both) of the two forms, P : T = counterposed labial and dental. Categories are mixed here for illustrative purposes. Avar: first form = 1sg pronoun, second = 2sg; Warao and Tagalog first = 'mother', second = 'father'; Basque first = 'sun', second = 'moon'. 1 = yes, 0 = no.

3.   Results

(10) shows the frequency with which the four pairs tend to have at least one nasal. The pronouns and 'mother'–'father' sets contain one or more nasals about twice as often as the others, and the difference among the four sets is highly significant (based on a chi square test on the absolute frequencies worldwide). The differences between pronouns and 'mother'–'father', and those between 'sun'–'moon' and 'fire'–'water', are small and statistically not significant. Thus, Hypotheses 1 and 5 are strongly confirmed for the sample as a whole. However, the differences between the three parts of the world — the Old World, the Pacific, and the New World — for pronouns and for kin terms are significant, which weakens any claim for straightforward universality.

(10) Frequencies of nasals in the four pairs (a nasal in either or both forms):

	n	World	OW	Pac	NW	
Pronouns	152	70%	65%	84%	62%	$p < 0.05$
'mother'–'father'	125	63%	67%	70%	46%	$p < 0.05$
'sun'–'moon'	30	37%				
'fire'–'water'	30	33%				
		$p < 0.001$				

Entries are percents of languages in the sample having a nasal in the word pair. World =
entire sample; OW = Old World (Africa, Eurasia); Pac = Pacific (New Guinea, Australia,
islands); NW = New World (Americas). Significance levels given for worldwide differences
between the four lexical sets (at bottom of 'World' column) and inter-areal differences for
one set (at right).

(11) shows the frequency with which the four pairs exhibit assonance, worldwide and
hemisphere by hemisphere. The pronouns and the 'mother'–'father' pairs are often
assonant, and again the difference among the four sets is highly significant. Also, the
differences between the first two and between the second two were small and not
significant. For pronouns the differences between the three parts of the world are not
significant, and therefore the relatively high frequency of assonance in pronouns
may be a genuine universal. The differences are significant for 'mother'–'father',
though, so their relatively high frequency may not reflect universals.

(11) Frequencies of assonance in the four pairs surveyed:

	n	World	OW	Pac	NW	
Pronouns	152	49%	47%	53%	48%	n.s.
'mother'–'father'	125	50%	64%	35%	48%	$p < 0.05$
'sun'–'moon'	30	12%				
'fire'–'water'	30	17%				
		$p < 0.001$				

Conventions as in (10). n.s. = not significant

These counts support Hypotheses 1, 2, 5, and 6: personal pronouns and 'mother'–
'father' are prone to exhibit both nasals and assonance. Hypothesis 4 (that 'sun'–
'moon' will be assonant more often than 'fire'–'water') is not supported; the results
are in fact reverse, though the difference between the two sets is not significant.

Counterposed labials and dentals are of very nearly equal and fairly low frequency
in the four pairs, as shown in (12). The differences are not significant. Thus, hypothesis
3 is not supported. The differences between the three parts of the world are
significant (highly so for pronouns), though, pointing to areal tendencies. Even
assuming areal pressure, however, the highest figure on (12) — 41% for counterposed consonants in 'mother'–'father' in the Old World — is not a very strong showing.

(12)   Frequency of counterposed labial and dental in the four pairs:

	n	World	OW	Pac	NW	
Pronouns	152	25%	28%	4%	38%	$p < 0.001$
'mother'–'father'	125	26%	41%	15%	23%	$p < 0.05$
'sun'–'moon'	30	23%				
'fire'–'water'	30	30%				
		n.s.				

Conventions as in (10).

The four sets are not equally prone to contain labials, as shown in (13). Pronouns and 'mother'–'father' terms are fairly likely to contain labials, but the propensities are not evenly distributed worldwide: in the Old World and the Pacific, 'mother'–'father' terms are quite likely to contain labials, while pronouns are not; in the New World, pronouns are likely to contain labials while the kin terms are not. The 'fire'–'water' pair is also quite prone to contain a labial. The differences between the four lexical pairs are significant, but (unlike the figures for nasals and assonance) do not set pronouns and 'mother'–'father' apart from the others; rather, 'mother'–'father' and 'fire'–'water' are significantly more prone to contain labials than the others are. (The labial in 'mother'–'father' is disproportionately associated with 'father', as discussed below. Both 'fire' and 'water' have labials with exactly equal frequency: 33%.) The differences between the three parts of the world for both pronouns and 'mother'–'father' are highly significant.

(13)   Frequencies of labials in the four pairs (a labial in either or both forms):

	World	OW	Pac	NW	
Pronouns	41%	39%	16%	62%	$p < 0.001$
'mother'–'father'	56%	79%	64%	33%	$p < 0.001$
'sun'–'moon'	37%				
'fire'–'water'	57%				
	$p < 0.025$				

Conventions as in (10).

There appear to be some lexical universals, as shown in (14). In the 'mother'–'father' set, the word for 'father' is significantly prone to contain a labial; the tendency, however, is not even worldwide, but is found primarily in the Pacific. (The labial in 'father', incidentally, tends not to be a nasal.) Words for 'mother' tend very strongly to contain a nasal, overall and area by area. Neither trend is visible among pronouns. I interpret these differences between pronouns and 'mother'–'father' terms as due to the fact that pronouns are shifters and hence their reference is not constant, while 'mother' and 'father' are not shifters.

(14) Affinities of particular consonant classes for particular members of pairs:

	World	Old World	Pacific	Americas
Labial in 'father'	0.05	n.s.	0.025*	n.s.
Nasal in 'mother'	0.0001	0.0001	0.005*	0.005

Entries are levels of statistical significance (n.s. = nonsignificant conforming trend).
* = majority tendency.

Given that there are universal tendencies to place labials and nasals in certain words, are there any universals governing the place of articulation of nasals in particular sets? (15) shows that there are not. There are large-scale geographical preferences — 'mother' tends to contain a labial nasal in the Old World and a dental in the New World; 'you' tends to contain a labial in the New World — but no universals.

(15) High-frequency nasals, by place of articulation, lexical set, and area:

M:	1sg	2sg	'mother'	'father'	'sun'	'moon'	'fire'	'water'
Old World	26		38					
Pacific			18	18				
New World		39						
World		20	23				13	13

N:	1sg	2sg	'mother'	'father'	'sun'	'moon'	'fire'	'water'
Old World	28		21					
Pacific	33	42	18					
New World	31		25					
World	31	20	22		17			

Ng:	1sg	2sg	'mother'	'father'	'sun'	'moon'	'fire'	'water'
Old World								
Pacific			24					
New World								
World								

M = labial nasal, N = dental and alveolar, Ng = velar.

Several of the tendencies discussed above are heightened in pairs of words that are assonant. Recall the association of the word for 'mother' with a nasal consonant, shown in (14) above. (16) gives figures for this association in assonant and non-assonant sets. There is a clear and significant asymmetry.

(16) Nasal in 'mother', assonant vs. non-assonant sets:

	Assonant:		Total
	Yes	No	
Nasal in 'mother'	31	34	65
No nasal in 'mother'	18	42	60
Total	49	76	125	$p < 0.05$

(17) gives comparable data on all four pairs of words. It turns out that in each pair one member is prone — notably and often significantly prone — to contain a nasal in the assonant sets. The effect in the first person singular pronoun is weak and not disproportionately contributed by any one area, so it may be a general minor universal propensity. The effect in 'mother' is significant and contributed disproportionately by the languages of the Americas, though it is weakly evident in the other two areas as well; it is a stronger candidate for a universal.

(17) Higher frequency of nasals in particular words in assonant sets:

	World	OW	Pac	NW
1SG	0.08 *	n.s. *	n.s.	n.s.
'mother'	0.05 *	none *	none *	0.01
'moon'	yes			
'water'	yes			

Entries are levels of significance. * = majority tendency. none = no evident correlation either way. yes = clearly higher but sample too small for testing significance. Clear cases only were counted for pronouns and 'mother'–'father'; clear and uncertain cases for 'sun'–'moon' and 'fire'–'water'.

(18) gives the frequencies with which particular words tend to contain particular nasals (chiefly, a labial nasal or a dental nasal), in assonant sets. There are preferences for particular nasals in particular words, notably /m/ in 'mother', 'moon', and 'water', but no such preferences among pronouns — presumably because pronouns, and only they, are shifters, i.e., lack a constant reference.

(18)   Higher frequency of nasality in particular places of articulation with particular words, in assonant sets. Entries are the nasal categories that are higher in assonant sets:

	World	Old World	Pacific	New World
Pronouns:	varies	M 1sg	N 1sg	M, N 1sg
			Ng 2sg	
'mother'–'father':	M 'mother'	M 'mother'	M 'mother'	M, N 'mother'
'sun'–'moon':	M 'moon'			
'fire'–'water':	M 'water'			
	N 'fire'			

Conventions as in (15).

In addition to higher frequencies of nasals, assonant word pairs are more likely to have a counterposed labial and dental, while non-assonant sets do not. This tendency is clear for all words except 'mother'–'father', where counterposing is fairly frequent in non-assonant sets (and where, in addition, many languages have labials in both words).

(19)   Higher frequency of counterposed labial and dental in assonant sets. (One form of each pair contains a labial and the other a dental.)

		World	Old World	Pacific	Americas
Pronouns:	Assonant	33 ✓	47 ✓	5 ✓	50 ✓
	Non-assonant	18	20	0	41
	All	25	28	4	38
'mother'–'father':	Assonant	31 ✓	40	10	32 ✓
	Non-assonant	26	44	20	24
	All	26	41	15	23
'sun'–'moon':	Assonant	33 ✓			
	Non-assonant	21			
	All	23			
'fire'–'water':	Assonant	50 ✓			
	Non-assonant	25			
	All	30			

Entries are percents. ✓ = frequency is higher in assonant sets.

In a related trend, (20) shows that consistent with higher labial-dental counterposition among assonant sets, there is more polarization of places of articulation in words of assonant sets. This is measured by taking the standard deviation of the proportions in the sample of languages with labial, dental, and velar consonants for each set. All words except 2sg shower a higher standard deviation — more variation or less consistency — in the assonant sets. Velars have lowest frequency in all assonant sets.

(20)   Higher variation in frequencies in different places of articulation (P, T, K) in assonant sets (measured as standard deviation in the proportions of P, T, and K):

	St. dev.		High		Low	
	Asn	Non-asn	Asn	Non-asn	Asn	Non-asn
1SG	23	18	T	T	K	P
2SG	15	18	T	T	K	K
'mother'	20	11	P	T	K	P
'father'	27	14	P	P	K	K
'sun'	29	26	T	T	P=K	P
'moon'	33	13	T	T	K	P
'fire'	31	14	T	T	K	K
'water'	19	3	P	T	K	P=K

High, Low: the place of articulation with highest and lowest frequency. Based on entire sample (no areal breakdown). Asn = assonant.

4.   Discussion

The figures given in Section 3 show that there are significant trends which can safely be called phonosymbolic: preferences for a nasal in one or both forms of a pair, assonance between the two, and a counterposed labial and dental spanning the two. In their raw form these patterns primarily characterize the personal pronouns and 'mother'–'father', suggesting that those words are indeed more prone to be phonosymbolic than the other two. More pervasively, however, various asymmetries and preferences for one or another consonant can be observed at least as background tendencies in all four word pairs, provided the pair is assonant. These are preference for nasals and counterposition, and an association of a labial with one member of a pair, and they characterize both the personal pronouns and 'mother'–'father' sets (which are most prone to be assonant) and the others, provided they are assonant. Not all of these tendencies are equally strong worldwide, but for each of them there is evidence to be found in more than one of the three large parts of the world.

Assonance was defined above in phonetically neutral terms of rhyme, alliteration, and other forms of echo. As the evidence in this section shows, however, assonance is not phonetically neutral in its effects: it favors the presence within the assonant set of one or more nasals, counterposition, and association of a labial with a particular member of the set (except in the latter case for the personal pronouns, which as shifters have no fixed reference and perhaps for that reason have no preferred fixed position in the set for a labial).

Preference for a nasal, counterposition, and fixed position of a labial, all contingent on the presence of assonance, are properties I propose to identify as phonosymbolic. They all pertain to sets of words rather than to individual words, and I further propose that phonosymbolism of this type be considered an inherent tendency of close-knit sets of words. This study has focused on small closed sets of very basic words: the personal pronouns (which in addition to the first and second person singular surveyed here generally include plural forms, less often duals and/or inclusives, and sometimes third person forms as well), and the kin terms 'mother' and 'father' (proxies for 'mom' and 'dad', a set which in some languages may also include terms for grandparents, aunts and uncles, and 'baby'). The actual limits and bounds of these two sets in individual languages can be determined by surveying the morphological and syntactic properties of personal pronouns (in some languages, for instance, third person forms are essentially demonstratives, while in others they are true personal pronouns) and the morphological and semantic properties of words like 'mom' and 'dad' (for example, they may be inherent vocatives). 'Sun' and 'moon' seem to be a natural pair, and it may be that in languages where these words display assonance they are viewed as a pair. 'Fire' and 'water' seem less likely to be a natural pair (though they do seem to be paired at least in English). Natural pairing or association of words like these can be indicated by stability of collocation as in English, where the natural phrases are 'sun and moon', 'fire and water' (while 'moon and sun' and 'water and fire' are odd). Other indicators would presumably include their association in riddles, poetic texts, myth, etc.

I suggest the term *closed-set phonosymbolism* (or shorter forms *set symbolism* and adjectival *set-symbolic*) as labels for this kind of phonosymbolism. It is not the only kind of phonosymbolism: diminutive consonant shifting, associations of higher and/or front vowels with smaller referents, association of longer forms with more marked or complex morphological categories, onomatopoeia, and others would not seem to be logically connected to closed sets of forms.

Closed-set phonosymbolism is closely associated with assonance and is therefore a special type of what is traditionally called paronymy or paronomasia. Some of the assonant elements are what Bolinger (1965) has called *phonesthemes* or *phonetic intensives*, Hinton et al. (1994:5ff.) *non-arbitrary conventional sound symbolism*, and Bickel (1995) *paronymic eidemic resonance*. The phonology of closed-set phonosymbolism is more precise than is found in these other kinds of assonance, involving actual phonological classes (nasal, labial, dental/apical). Many studies of recurrent submorphemic partials in lexical or grammatical systems focus on their iconic nature; e.g., Rhodes (1994) associates particular onsets of English with particular acoustic and visual *image schemata* that they label. Bickel (1995) most explicitly de-emphasizes iconicity and focuses on the validity of the sound-meaning associations only within systems, and I am taking this approach even farther in defining closed-set symbolism as ultimately arbitrary sound-meaning correspondences in which a limited inventory of sounds with strict constraints on their distribution metalinguistically signals, or labels, not particular meanings but the fact of a closed system in the abstract and the status of the elements in it. Closed-set symbolism can be said to symbolize the bounds of the system, membership of elements in it, and relations among the elements of the system. It uses a limited set of phonological elements and patterns and is most likely to arise in particular lexical and grammatical domains (those that inherently take the form of small closed sets), but this does not mean that the sounds involved (such as nasals) signify or symbolize or otherwise 'mean' the susceptible lexical or grammatical sets or their members.

This inquiry was intended as programmatic and a pilot study, and the conclusions just summarized can now be rephrased as hypotheses for further study:

- Assonance and closed-set phonosymbolism are associated with small closed sets of words.
- Hallmarks of closed-set phonosymbolism are preference for a nasal in one or more forms, counterposed labial and dental or apical articulations, and a preferred place for a labial in non-shifter sets.
- These are universal tendencies, which may or may not be exploited by particular languages.
- One or another of the tendencies can be prominent in a large areal grouping of languages (on the order of a continent or larger, sampled genetically). These groupings are not demonstrably genetic and probably not genetic. (Certainly the larger-than-continental three-way division of the world used here does not produce sets of languages believed to be, or likely to be, macrogenetic.)

5.   The evolution of set-symbolic canon: Two case studies

How do set-symbolic canons form and how do they come to characterize large language areas? If they are universal, how does it happen that differences in their frequency from area to area are statistically significant, and how does it happen that, say, pronouns or 'mother'–'father' terms are highly set-symbolic in one language and not at all in another? This section presents two case studies showing how set-symbolic canons arise and spread.

The personal pronouns of the Nakh-Daghestanian (Northeast Caucasian) language family are a particularly clear example showing that assonance and closed-set phonosymbolism can be secondary in a language family. Table 1 shows personal pronouns of various languages of the family, and the reconstructable consonants of the protoforms (Nichols 1992). Nakh-Daghestanian is an old and ramified language family in which millennia of morphological change such as analogical extension, intraparadigmatic leveling, spread and loss of gender prefixation, reanalysis of unipartite verb stems as bipartite and vice versa, accretion of preverbs, reanalysis of stem extenders as root consonants, and the like have obscured the protoforms of many stems so that in most words the only element that displays regular sound correspondences and can be reconstructed is a single consonant, which in the daughter languages is usually the first postvocalic consonant but sometimes initial. The sound changes themselves are unremarkable, but the degree of morphological change impedes reconstruction of whole roots. (Work on Proto-Nakh-Daghestanian includes Nichols 1992; Schulze 1998 [and subsequent volumes to appear]; Nichols in press.) All of this pertains to personal pronouns as well; for most of them, all that can be reconstructed is a single consonant, which is variously initial and postvocalic depending on the language and the particular case form.

It can be seen from Table 1 that rhyme, alliteration, and nasals abound in the personal pronouns of the daughter languages. In Avar, for instance, the singular nominative forms rhyme and their obliques alliterate but do not rhyme, and both nominatives and obliques have the same vowels; the plural forms (nominative and oblique) alliterate but do not rhyme. In the Lezghian branch, singular forms rhyme and plural forms tend to rhyme. In Chirag Dargi the plurals rhyme. In Chechen the singular nominatives rhyme as in Avar, but the actual rhyming segments are different. In Lak the singulars neither rhyme nor alliterate nor share vocalism; the plurals either rhyme or alliterate depending on which variant of the second person plural is taken.

Thus the patterns of rhyme and alliteration vary from language to language and from branch to branch, and cannot be reconstructed. More precisely, there is no one pattern of rhyme or alliteration that can safely be reconstructed as ancestral; Proto-Nakh-Daghestanian may well have had some form of assonance among some or all of its pronouns, but nothing specific can be reconstructed.

Nasals occur in the singular nominatives of all the Daghestanian languages on the table except for Chirag Dargi, variously initial (Lak) or stem-final (elsewhere). The second person singular has a nasal initial in the Avar-Andic-Tsezic branch, as do all plurals of Avar and the second plural of Tsez. None of these nasals occur in the Nakh branch. The /n/ of the singular forms, at least where stem-final, may be a Proto-Daghestanian innovation, and initial /n/ in the first person plural likewise. The other nasals are subbranch or lower innovations. None of them is Proto-Nakh-Daghestanian.

The Avar-Andic-Tsezic branch, and some of the Lezgian languages, show counterposed dentals and labials, of which the Avar-Andic-Tsezic opposition of /d/ to /m/ is canonical but secondary; the /v/ or /w/ of the second person is a possible, though far from certain, reconstruction for Proto-Daghestanian but not for Proto-Nakh-Daghestanian. The initial /m/ of Avar-Andic-Tsezic cannot be reconstructed beyond that subbranch.

The history of these forms shows that assonance and closed-set symbolism, so

Table 1. Personal pronouns in selected Nakh-Daghestanian languages (after Nichols 1992)

Branches, languages	1SG		2SG		1PL Exclusive		1PL Inclusive		2PL	
	Nom	Obl	Nom	Obl	Nom	Obl	Nom	Obl	Nom	Obl
Nakh branch:										
Chechen	so	as	ħo	aħ	txo	uoxa	vaj[a]	—	šu	aš
Daghestanian branch:										
Avar-Andic-Tsezic:										
Avar	dun	di-	mun	du-	niž	—	nił	—	nuž / muž	—
Akhvakh	dene	di-	mene	du-	issi[□]	issi	iλλi	iλλi	uššdi	uššde-
Tsez	di	dä-	mi	deb-	eli	elu-	—	—	meži	mežu-
Lak	na	ttu-	ina	vi-	zhu	—	—	—	zu / žwi	—
Dargic										
Chirag	di-	di-	ʕa-	—	nussa	nussa	—	—	ʕussa	—
Lezghian										
Lezghi	zun	za	vun	(vu)na	čun	čna	—	—	kün	küne
N. Tabassaran	uzu		uwu		učtu		uxu		učtwu	
Agul (Richa)	zun		wun		in[a]		xin		čun	
Archi	zon		un		nen[a]		nen-t'u[a]		žwen	
Proto-Nakh-Daghestanian	*z/d	*-n?	*w? *ʕ?	*-n?	*(nV)λλ		—		*ž	

Daghestanian forms are from Kibrik & Kodzasov (1990) and reflect the dialects surveyed there. [a] full neologism. Proto-Nakh-Daghestanian had a single first person plural pronoun with no inclusive/exclusive distinction, but most daughter languages distinguish inclusive from exclusive. The PND first person plural pronoun is regularly reflected in the exclusive of Nakh but the inclusive of Daghestanian.

prominent among the modern pronouns, are secondary in Nakh-Daghestanian. None of the innovations are the result of borrowing; they reflect purely internal morphological changes. The implication is that assonance and the general set-symbolic principles of nasality, counterposition, and anchoring labial can arise purely internally, without external sources or models, as the result of quite ordinary morphological processes. The only open question is the source of the crucial nasals. The -*n* of the various Daghestanian singular forms may have been a stem formative, and the initial *m*- of second person forms in Avar-Andic-Tsezic may possibly have arisen through distant nasal assimilation of a labial element (cognate to the Lezgian *v*-/*w*-, or prefixal, as is plausible for the family) to the stem-final nasal. Both of these suggestions are speculative but plausible. In general it can be hypothesized that segments critical to closed-set symbolism are favored targets of sound change and sources of morphological analogy within closed sets, especially where the sets already have some degree of assonance.

The second case study involves the rise and consolidation, over a considerable span of time, of a canon of assonance and closed-set phonosymbolism among several language families that find their ultimate origins in the central to eastern part of northern Eurasia. The language families are Kartvelian, which originated in the Transcaucasus perhaps 4500 BP; Indo-European, which dispersed on the western to central steppe about 5500 BP and may have come there from farther east; Uralic, which dispersed from the vicinity of the western Siberian forest-steppe or forest belt at least 6000 BP; three smaller families generally believed related: Turkic (which spread from the north of Mongolia some 2000 years ago), Tungusic (which spread from northern Manchuria perhaps 3000–4000 years ago), and Mongolian (which spread from central Manchuria to Mongolia not quite 1000 years ago); the language isolate Yukagir of northeastern Siberia; and the Chukchi-Kamchatkan family of far northeastern Siberia, which spread from around the base of Kamchatka perhaps some 4000 years ago. (Fortescue 1998; Janhunen 1996; Nichols 1997, 1998 survey aspects of the histories of these families and refer to primary comparative literature. Another important source is Klimov 1998.)

The personal pronouns of these languages resemble each other, as has long been noted, and the resemblances take the form of assonance and closed-set symbolism. The assonant canon is briefly exemplified in Table 2. It involves a labial consonant in the first person pronoun and a dental or other apical in the second; a nasal in the first person and usually a form like *mVn* as oblique stem; and resemblant or even identical stems in singular and plural pronouns. The counterposed labial and dental, the nasal, and the similar stem shapes and frequent rhymes mark these shapes as set-symbolic.

This canon makes itself felt to different extents and in different ways in the eight families, and as a type of canon it exemplifies one of the roughly continent-sized spikes in adherence to set-symbolic patterns that made for area-to-area

Table 2. Conformity to the north Eurasian canon in personal pronouns

Language	Person	Singular		Plural	
		Nominative	Oblique	Nominative	Oblique
Chuvash	1	epĕ	man	epir, epĕr	pir
	2	esĕ	san	esir, esĕr	sir
Pre-Finnish	1	minä	min-	me	me-
	2	tinä	tin-	te	te-
Chukchi	1	γəm		muri	
	2	γət	γən-	turi	
Proto-Slavic	1	az-	m(e)n-	my, ny	nV-
	2	ty	te-	vy	vV-

Strong conformity shown by Chuvash and Pre-Finnish: 1SG has labial consonant, 2SG has dental; oblique has 1SG MEN, 2SG CEN; singular and plural have same stem. Weak conformity shown by Chukchi and Proto-Slavic: 1SG has M, 2SG has dental; partly resemblant oblique stems; plural stems more distant or entirely different.

differences described in Sections 2 and 3 above. These spikes show that, while following weak universals, set-symbolic paradigms can be good large-areal features. This means that the northern Eurasian canon can be assumed to have historical reality, including a time and place of origin, though the origin is so ancient that it cannot be dated or localized very precisely and there is no knowing whether it is genetic, areal, or a combination of the two. (Another canon with clear historical reality together with indeterminacy as to its origin and spread is the pattern of first person *n* and second person *m* found along the Pacific coast of the Americas: (Nichols & Peterson 1996).)

The rest of this section proposes an interpretation of how and when the shared canon may have arisen in this set of families, assuming the canon is historically related. An approximate chronology and geography can be established by assuming that if an aspect of the canon is shared by two families it arose before the older of the two families dispersed and in a location where the pre-protolanguages are likely to have been neighbors.[2]

Table 3 shows the protoforms or quasi-protoforms for the singular personal pronouns of these families.[3] In Table 3, families are listed in west-to-east order, i.e., beginning with those whose dispersals took place farther west and ending with those that originated farther east.[4] The oldest families of this group are Indo-European and Uralic, both about 6000 years old. The assonant pronominal canon must be older still, as it is firmly in place in both Proto-Indo-European and Proto-Uralic. This is true regardless of whether Indo-European and Uralic are deemed to be genetically related. (See Ringe 1998 for statistical evidence that they are related. The relatedness is slightly too ancient to be fully provable by current comparative-historical or statistical methods, but the evidence is qualitatively very good.) If they are related, the canon was inherited from the ancient protolanguage; if the canon is areal, it spread from one protolanguage to the other or to both from some third source. Whatever its origin it was firmly in place and well differentiated by the time of dispersal of the older of the two protolanguages, Proto-Uralic.

Table 3. Resemblant personal pronoun forms in north Eurasian families

	1SG	2SG
Kartvelian	*me(n)-	*sen-
Indo-European	*eg′o:, *me-	*tu:, *tew-, etc.
Uralic	*mun; #Vm (?)	*tun
Turkic	*bi-, *bän-; #eb- (?)	*si-, *sän-
Mongolian	*bi, *min-, *na-	*či, *čin-
Tungusic	#bi, #min-	*si, *sin-
Yukagir	met	tet
Chukchi-Kamchatkan	*kəm	*kəð

* = protoforms from published sources; # = quasi-protoforms. Forms shown are nominative and oblique (if any) stems of independent forms of the personal pronouns. Uralic protoforms from Janhunen (1981), Chukchi-Kamchatkan from Fortescue (1998: 98); others from more than one handbook. For the isolate, Yukagir, modern forms are given.

Table 4 rates the various families for conformity to a canon of stem shapes indicated by the oldest or reconstructable stages, and Table 5 rates them for conformity to a canon of assonance with counterposed dental and labial, a nasal, and resemblant stem shapes between the two persons and the two numbers. These two tables represent different ways of looking at the facts of assonant stems. In both tables, conformity is low in the families that originated to the far west (Kartvelian, Indo-European) and the far northeast (Chukchi-Kamchatkan) and highest in the central-eastern families. In addition, conformity is highest in the younger families; of the ancient families, only Uralic shows good conformity.

I suggest the following interpretation. There is a long-standing and roughly cigar-shaped language area in central Eurasia, running from the steppe due east to the middle and lower Amur and then trending northward, from which various language families dispersed. (For overviews of the history and prehistory of language families in these areas see, e.g., Janhunen 1996; Fortescue 1998; Nichols 1997, 1998; Sinor 1990.) In this area a canon of assonance for pronominals arose and consolidated, based on universals but with the specific areal choice to associate labials with first person. The canon continued to develop and strengthen over time, finally developing into one with rhyme between person categories, alliteration and rhyme between number categories, other forms of assonance, nasals, and counterposed labial and dental consonants, as well as other kinds of assonance. As the canon developed it made itself most strongly felt in those language families that

Table 4. 'Me'–'thee' pronouns: approximation to ancient pattern of stem shapes

Family	1SG: Nom. Suppl	Stop	*V-	B-	-N	mEn	2SG: Nom = T Obl		Sum	N	%
Kartvelian	1	0		0	0	0.5	0.5	1	3	7	43%
Indo-European	1	1	1	1	1	0.5	1	1	7.5	8	94%
Uralic	0.5	0	1	1	1	1	1	1	6.5	8	81%
Turkic	1	1	1	1	1	1	1	1	8	8	100%
Mongolian	1	1		1	1	1	1	1	7	7	100%
Tungusic	1	1		1	1	1	1	1	7	7	100%
Yukagir	0	0		1	1	0	1	1	4	7	57%
Chukchi-Kamchatkan	0	1		0	0	0	0	1	2	7	29%
Total	5.5	5	3	6	6	5	6.5	8			
Mean									5.6	7.4	75%

Nom. Suppl: Nominative and oblique stems are suppletive; Stop: First root consonant is a stop in at least one stem form; *V-: There is some evidence of a vowel-initial form among the daughter languages; B-: This form begins with a labial; -N: This form ends in a dental or alveolar nasal; mEn: A form such as *min*, *men*, or *man* is found in the oblique stem forms; Nom = Obl: Nominative and oblique have the same root; T: First root consonant is a voiceless dental or palato-alveolar obstruent.

originated in interior Siberia, in the central to eastern part of the area, and later in time. The canon arose over 6000 years ago, earlier than the dispersals of Indo-European and Uralic, as discussed above. It is viable to this day, in that levelings and analogical reshapings of first person singular nominative pronouns continue, or have continued until recently, in Turkic languages, changing 1SG.NOM *ben* to *men* individually in various branches. Over time, nasals increase and analogy regularizes stems, so that in the later stages, and in the eastern central part of the area, we find very strong conformity to the assonant canon. The pace of change is very slow. None of the conformities appear to be the result of simple borrowing of forms; nor are they traceable to inheritance from a single ancient ancestor (Proto-Nostratic or Proto-Eurasiatic), as the assonance increases over time within individual families. Rather, the canon seems to have arisen and diffused, favoring the same changes (be they phonological ones, such as distant nasality assimilation producing /mVn/ from *bVn, or morphological ones regularizing stems) independently in different families.

6. Conclusions

We have seen that phonosymbolism in personal pronouns and 'mama'–'papa' vocabulary is more indirect and abstract than has generally been believed. The essentials of this phonosymbolism are counterposed labials and dentals (or apicals),

Table 5. 'Me' – 'thee' pronouns: approximation to a standard pattern of stem regularization

| Family | 1SG: | | | 2SG: | | | | | | Total | N | % |
| | Nom | Obl | | Nom | | Obl | | 1 & 2 | | | | |
	M/B	m-	-D	T-	c/s-	T-	-D	rhyme	SG=PL			
Kartvelian	1	0	0	1	1	1	1	0	0	5	9	56%
Indo-European	0	1	0.5	1	0	1	0	0	0	3.5	9	39%
Uralic	1	1	1	1	0	?	?	1	1	5	6	83%
Turkic	1	1	1	1	1	1	1	1	1	9	9	100%
Mongolian	1	1	1	1	1	1	1	1	0.5	8.5	9	94%
Tungusic	1	1	1	1	1	1	1	1	1	9	9	100%
Yukagir	1	1	1	1	1	1	1	0	1	7	7	100%
Chukchi-Kamchatkan	1	0	0	0	0	0	1	1	1	3	9	33%
Total	6	6	5.5	6	4	6	6	5	5.5			
Mean										6.26	8.4	76%

M/B: labial of some kind in the stem; m-: This form begins in *m*; -D: This form ends in a dental; c/s-: This form contains an alveolar or palatal affricate or fricative; 1&2 rhyme: First and second person singular forms rhyme; SG=PL: Singular and plural forms of both pronouns have the same root. Other abbreviations as on Table 4.

at least one of them nasal, and various forms of assonance. The symbolic effect is not to mark extremely basic vocabulary as basic by using simple and basic consonants in them; nor is it to mark pronouns as pronouns, kin terms as kin terms, or whatever; much less is it to set off particular meanings or categories. There is no reason to link the nasal to infant vocalization or the counterposition to the stepwise mastery of phonemic oppositions (as Jakobson does), and in any case these things do not explain the other assonant properties. Rather, the symbolism pertains to the system itself: a small, closed system of basic lexemes, especially if they are deictic, is prone to be knitted together by assonant phonosymbolism. Closed-set symbolism is equally likely to affect the relatively stable parts of vocabulary such as personal pronouns and the much less stable 'mama'–'papa' terms, and it affects them in the same way. The only differences in the structure of set-symbolic systems between pronouns and 'mama'–'papa' terms have to do not with their relative stability but with the fact that pronouns are shifters while kin terms are not. Hence the labial has an affinity for 'father' and the nasal for 'mother' worldwide, while neither labial nor nasal has any worldwide affinity for any person or number category of pronouns.

The process that brings about conformity to a phonosymbolic canon over time must be a simple matter of selection: forms that correspond to the canon have a slight selectional edge, so that other things being equal they are likely to increase over time within languages or families. Phonosymbolic canons have some propensity for diffusion, so that the same selectional pressures shape different languages. The rate of such selection must be very slow, and the rate of diffusion likewise, at least in pronouns. Over enough time, when languages have been in long-standing contact, a phonosymbolic canon in personal pronouns can acquire a robust and durable macroareal distribution.

At the relatively shallow time depths at which the comparative method operates well and uncontroversially, assonance and phonosymbolism are easy to detect and unlikely to obscure the actual genetic picture. At great time depths, however, assonant systems are unreliable indicators of genetic affinity. Though personal pronouns are usually inherited and rarely borrowed, an inherited pronoun system can respond to the selectional pressure of assonance and, over time, come to approximate universal and areal symbolic canons. Thus, though resemblance of a whole system, as opposed to individual elements, is one of the most powerful indicators of genetic relatedness, a cautionary note needs to be raised: if the system is assonant or prone to closed-set phonosymbolism its value as a diagnostic of ancient common descent is dubious. The older the proposed relatedness, the less useful any vocabulary domain with set-symbolic properties.

The account of the Eurasian assonant pronominals given here is an attempt at cross-family comparison that is historical but not genetic, and it will probably take challenges to both method and interpretation. Its advantages are an improved account of sound symbolism and its function in small closed systems, an account of the geography of the central Eurasian pronominal canon and of its relative strength, and an explanation that recognizes the deep historical unity of the Eurasian pronominal systems without necessitating the drastic step of positing genetic unity for the language families involved. I hope the geographical and historical interpretation given here can provide useful hypotheses for further historical inquiry.

Notes

1. Some sources (e.g., Bolinger 1950) use *assonance* roughly in the set of *onset*. I use it to refer to phonological resemblances involving fairly specific recurrent elements.

2. The possibility always exists that the pronominal paradigm or parts of it were borrowed from one protolanguage to the other, e.g., from Proto-Uralic to Pre-Proto-Indo-European. I assume that if this had occurred it would long since have been evident to traditional comparative-historical method. (The pronouns of Proto-Uralic and Proto-Indo-European are resemblant in ways unlikely to be accidental, but are not identical, as they would be if Pre-Proto-Indo-European had borrowed them from Proto-Uralic, and do not demand reconstruction of a unique common ancestor to just these two families. Either of these two situations would long since have been recognized by traditional comparativists.)

3. A quasi-protoform is my own abstraction over the daughter forms, proposed on the basis of comparative method and understanding of morphological and phonological change but without determining regularity of correspondences. This practice is taken from Williamson (1989 — "Pseudo-reconstructions based on a quick inspection of a cognate set without working out sound correspondences are preceded by a #." — p. 253). Williamson uses this approach where reconstructions have not been worked out. I use them for some families for which at least some of the reconstructive work bases family protoforms on assumptions about deeper relatedness between families. The hatched forms here are meant not to bypass the existing literature but to point out what can be reconstructed on the evidence from just that family. They are meant to capture essential aspects of stem shape and broad classes of consonants, but are not offered as precise segmental reconstructions.

4. The only other language family known to have originated in this area — Yeniseian, whose sole survivor is Ket — bears no resemblances at all in its pronominals to the other families.

References

Bickel, Balthasar. 1995. "In the Vestibule of Meaning: Transitivity Inversion as a morphological phenomenon". *Studies in Language* 19: 1.72–128.
Bolinger, Dwight. 1950. "Rime, Assonance, and Morpheme Analysis". *Word* 6.117–136.
Bolinger, Dwight. 1965. "The Atomization of Meaning". *Language* 41.555–573.
Fortescue, Michael. 1998. *Language Relations Across Bering Strait: Reappraising the archaeological and linguistic evidence*. London & New York: Cassell.
Hinton, Leanne, Johanna Nichols, & John J. Ohala, eds. 1994. *Sound Symbolism*. Cambridge: Cambridge University Press.

Jakobson, Roman. (1960) 1971. "Why 'mama' and 'papa'". *Selected Writings of Roman Jakobson* I.538–545. The Hague: Mouton.

Janhunen, Juha. 1981. "Uralilaisen Kantakielen Sanastosta". *Journal de la Société Finno-ougrienne* 77: 9.219–274.

Janhunen, Juha. 1996. *Manchuria: An ethnic history.* (= *SUST*, 222.) Helsinki: Suomalais-ugrilaisen seura.

Kibrik, A. E. & S. V. Kodzasov. 1990. *Sopostavitel'noe izuchenie dagestanskix jazykov: Imja. Fonetika.* Moscow: Moscow State University.

Klimov, G. A. 1998. *Etymological Dictionary of the Kartvelian Languages.* Berlin & New York: Mouton de Gruyter.

Nichols, Johanna. 1992. "The Caucasus as a Linguistic Area, 1: Personal pronouns". *Caucasian Perspectives*, ed. by B. G. Hewitt. London: Lincom Europa.

Nichols, Johanna. 1997. "The Eurasian Spread Zone and the Indo-European Dispersal". *Archaeology and Language II: Correlating archaeological and linguistic hypotheses* ed. by R. M. Blench & Matthew Spriggs, 220–266. London & New York: Routledge.

Nichols, Johanna. 1998. "The Epicenter of the Indo-European Linguistic Spread". *Archaeology and Language I: Theoretical and methodological orientations* ed. by Roger Blench & Matthew Spriggs, 122–148. London & New York: Routledge.

Nichols, Johanna. In press. "The Nakh-Daghestanian Consonant Correspondences". To appear in a festschrift.

Nichols, Johanna & David A. Peterson. 1996. "The Amerind Personal Pronouns". *Language* 72: 2.336–371.

Rhodes, Richard. 1994. "Aural Images". Hinton et al. 1994.276–292.

Ringe, Don. 1998. "A Probabilistic Evaluation of Indo-Uralic". *Nostratic: Sifting the evidence*, ed. by Joseph C. Salmons & Brian D. Joseph, 153–198. Amsterdam & Philadelphia: John Benjamins.

Schulze, Wolfgang. 1998. *Person, Klasse, Kongruenz. Fragmente einer Kategorialtypologie des einfachen Satzes in den ostkaukasischen Sprachen. Vol. 1: Die Grundlagen, Part 1.* München: Lincom Europa.

Sinor, Denis, ed. 1990. *The Cambridge History of Early Inner Asia.* Cambridge: Cambridge University Press.

Williamson, Kay. 1989. "Benue-Congo Overview". *The Niger-Congo Languages* ed. by John Bendor-Samuel, 247–274. Lanham, New York, & London: University Press of America.

The English s-genitive

Animacy, topicality, and possessive relationship in a diachronic perspective[*]

Anette Rosenbach
Heinrich Heine University Düsseldorf

1. Introduction

The English language has two nominal constructions to encode possessive relationships, the s-genitive (*the girl's eyes*) and the of-genitive (*the eyes of the girl*).[1] Numerous factors have been reported to be responsible for the choice between these two constructions, such as, e.g., syntactic complexity, phonological, lexical, pragmatic or stylistic reasons. In this paper, I will focus on a possible cognitive-psychological motivation for the choice between the s-genitive and the of-genitive, analyzing the role of various conceptual factors in the long-term diachronic development of the genitive alternation, namely animacy, topicality, and the type of possessive relation. Among others, it has recently — and most prominently — been argued by Taylor (1989, 1996) that such conceptual-cognitive factors are highly relevant for the choice of the s-genitive.[2] In contrast to Taylor's (1989, 1996) account, which is exclusively synchronic and theoretical, i.e., from a Cognitive-Grammar point-of-view, and focuses on the s-genitive solely, the present paper sets out to explore empirically the relative importance of the factors animacy, topicality, and the type of possessive relation on the frequency of the s-genitive as opposed to its structural alternative, the of-genitive, from a long-term diachronic perspective, comparing data from late Middle English and Early Modern English (henceforth referred to as 'EModE data') with Modern English data (henceforth 'ModE data'). It will finally be argued that the observed effects point to iconically/psychologically-driven language change and incipient grammaticalization.

2.   Historical development of the *s*-genitive: A short overview

In Old English, which was still an inflectional language, the inflectional genitive was the almost exclusive nominal possessive construction, which, at that time, still had various inflectional endings — not only the *-s*. In the course of Middle English the *s*-suffix was generalized to all noun classes and became the only genitive suffix. While the periphrastic *of*-genitive was at best marginal at the end of the Old English period, in Middle English it increasingly replaced the *s*-genitive, a development that is well in accordance with the drift of English from a synthetic to a more analytic character.

In a recent study Rosenbach and Vezzosi (2000) have shown that the *s*-genitive increases again, at the expense of the *of*-genitive, from about 8% around 1400 to almost 20% in the early 17th century (see also Rosenbach, Stein, & Vezzosi 2000: §2.1). This is a development which seems to run *counter* to the typological development of English. If anything, one would have expected the *s*-genitive to be lost but not to be revived. Interestingly, this new productivity of the *s*-genitive correlates — at least chronologically — with the changing status of the *s*-genitive from an inflection to a clitic (see also Rosenbach & Vezzosi 1999). Evidence for a clitic-like behaviour of the *s*-genitive, e.g., the attachment of the *s*-suffix to whole phrases ([*the king of England*]*'s daughter*), is first attested in the late 14th century (see Allen 1997; Seppänen 1997). This change of the *s*-genitive from an inflection to a clitic has recently come into the limelight in discussions on the directionality of linguistic change (see, e.g., Lass 1997: §6.3.5; Tabor & Traugott 1998), because it would be one of the extremely rare cases where the grammaticalization process is reversed, going backwards from a more bound element (= inflection) to a less bound element (= clitic).

3.   Animacy, topicality, and possessive relationship: Empirical evidence

Before presenting the empirical evidence, a brief introduction of the terminology used is in order; for more detailed information on the definition and motivation of the categories used, particularly for the factors topicality and possessive relation, see Rosenbach, Stein, and Vezzosi (2000).

3.1 Terminology

The factor animacy refers to the distinction between [+animate] [+human] possessors and [−animate] possessors.

Topicality is used in the sense of the givenness and identifiability of the possessor, distinguishing between referentially given and new possessors. For the analysis of the EModE data, topicality/givenness is operationally defined in terms of referential definiteness. Within the 'given' category, a further distinction is made for the EModE data between more given/topical referents, i.e., referents highly accessible due to their ontological status (i.e., extracontextually known referents [*God's name; the mouth of our Saviour*], proper names [*Simon's father; the hand of Laertes*], and high-rank referents [*the king's ear; the Lord Chancellor's secretary; the authority of the true Pope*]) and less given referents, which are simply marked as formally definite (e.g., *his father's death; the cattle of this man; the violence of my said ancestors*). As [−topical] possessors, referential indefinite expressions are counted (e.g., *a poor man's leg; the image of a naked man*).[3]

Based on the framework of possession (cf., e.g., Seiler 1983; Taylor 1989; Heine 1997) the type of possessive relationship is split into [+prototypical] (i.e., kin terms [*his master's daughter*], body parts [*Falstaff's head*], and (permanent) ownership of concrete things [*Master Slender's purse*]) and [−prototypical] possessive relations, which cover the remaining possessive cases (in particular, social relations [*Saint Paul's teacher*], mental/physical states [*Hamlet's lunacy*] and abstract possession [*the man's name*]).[4]

Note at this point that animacy, topicality, and possessive relation are themselves closely interrelated factors: topics usually are animate, and only humans prototypically possess things. Taylor (1996) goes as far as to view animacy not as an independent factor but rather as a factor contributing to the inherent topicality of nouns. In the present study these three factors are treated as separate factors; to keep their effects logically and empirically apart they are analyzed in all possible combinations in which they can occur (for details, see further below).

3.2 EModE data: Corpus analysis (1400–1630)[5]

The analysis of the EModE data draws on the analyses presented in Rosenbach and Vezzosi (2000) and Rosenbach, Stein, and Vezzosi (2000). The relative frequency of the s-genitive vs. the of-genitive is analyzed. As shown by Rosenbach and Vezzosi (forthc.), in the period investigated (1400–1630) the s-genitive almost always occurs with [+animate] possessors. Therefore, topicality and the type of possessive relationship are quantified only for this context.[6] The results are summarized in Figure 1 below, where the relative frequency of the s-genitive (in %, calculated as opposed to the of-genitive) is given (a) for the six possible combinations of the factors topicality and possessive relation (for animate possessors only), and (b) for each of the four time intervals investigated. The absolute numbers for the s-genitive for each context are indicated at the top of each column.

In the following I will first anticipate how the data can be interpreted in terms of a hierarchical order of the factors investigated, thereby guiding the reader through the condensed and therefore complex presentation of the data in Figure 1.

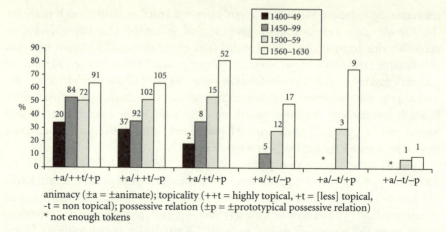

animacy (±a = ±animate); topicality (++t = highly topical, +t = [less] topical,
-t = non topical); possessive relation (±p = ±prototypical possessive relation)
* not enough tokens

Figure 1. Relative frequency of the *s*-genitive in Early Modern English: Interaction of
the factors animacy, topicality, and possessive relationship

In a nutshell, it can be observed that the data suggest the following hierarchy:

animacy > topicality > possessive relationship.

To illustrate how this hierarchy should be interpreted, I would like to suggest the
following preference structure, which needs to be read as a kind of decision tree.
Note that the order in which the possible combinations of the three factors is given
in Figure 1 corresponds to the order in this preference structure.[7]

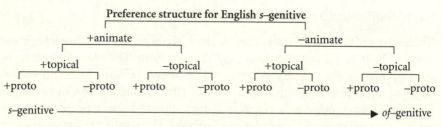

Figure 2. Preference structure for the English *s*-genitive

This preference structure gives the following information:

- First, it shows the possible contexts for the occurrence of the *s*-genitive,
  decreasing in preference from left to right.
- Second, it illustrates the relative frequency of the *s*-genitive, as compared to the
  of-genitive, decreasing from left to right.
- Third, it outlines the direction of the diachronic extension of the *s*-genitive,
  again from left to right.

Figure 1 shows that around 1400 the s-genitive is mainly restricted to the context [+animate] [+highly topical] possessor with a preference for [+prototypical] possessive relations. If it does occur with less topical possessors at all, then the type of possessive relation [+prototypical] is the decisive factor. However, even in the 'optimal' context, [+animate] [+highly topical] possessor, the s-genitive is less frequent than the *of*-genitive. In the second half of the 15th century and even more so throughout the 16th century the s-genitive extends notably to less and non-topical contexts, and at the turn of the 17th century the s-genitive is, except for [−prototypical] possessive relations in less and non-topical contexts, always the more frequent option than the *of*-genitive within the [+animate] domain. To sum up, for the period under investigation (1400 to 1630) two kinds of extension can be observed for the s-genitive: first, an extension of the possible contexts, in which the s-genitive can occur, and second, an increase in the relative frequency of the s-genitive. Note that all these extensions occur within the [+animate] domain only. The importance of animacy is confirmed by Altenberg's (1982) extensive corpus analysis for the 17th century:

> ... the great variation in GEN/OF selection gives an indication of the power and flexibility of the lexical factor. Its impact is most uncompromising at the inanimate end of the scale, where OF is practically obligatory with many noun classes und seldom replaced by GEN even in rhetorical or poetic contexts. (Altenberg 1982:148)

Moreover, Altenberg (1982:299ff.) notes that in his data the factor animacy seems to be more important than topicality:

> The most severe constraints on GEN/OF variation are exerted by an inanimate (especially concrete) Mod and an objective Mod-Head relation (both favouring OF), ... The least constraining factors are a subjective Mod-Head relation and a human individual Mod. Although they weakly promote GEN, their essential effect in the material is to provide freedom of variability, ie a fairly 'neutral' setting for the operation of communicative factors and certain minor grammatical factors, ... (Altenberg 1982:300)

Thus, Altenberg's 17th century data confirm the validity of the preference structure proposed for the period between 1400 and 1630 with respect to the relative importance of animacy and topicality: A [−animate] possessor is and remains the knock-out criterion for the occurrence of the s-genitive; only within the [+animate] domain do other factors, such as topicality and the kind of possessive relationship, further determine the occurrence and frequency of the s-genitive.[8]

3.3   Modern English data: Experimental study

The question now is whether this revival and extension of the *s*-genitive is a development restricted to the EModE period, or whether there has been further change, and if so, in which direction? For this purpose I will present new data from Modern English and compare them with the EModE data. In particular, I will try to answer the following questions:

1.   Is the preference structure found for the EModE data the same in Modern English, or has the relative importance of the factors animacy, topicality, and possessive relationship been reversed?
2.   In particular, are the contexts in which the *s*-genitive can occur the same, or not?
3.   And, what is the relative frequency of the *s*-genitive, as compared to the *of*-genitive in the given contexts?

3.3.1 *Previous studies*

There is indeed evidence which points to a further extension of the *s*-genitive in Modern English. For Modern English several empirical studies (e.g., Jahr Sorheim 1980; Jucker 1993; Raab-Fischer 1995; Anschutz 1997) report the use of the *s*-genitive with inanimate possessors; note that this was almost impossible during the EModE period. According to Jahr Sorheim (1980) and Jucker (1993) this use of the *s*-genitive with inanimate possessors is most frequent with certain noun classes, such as e.g., temporal nouns (*today's weather*) or geographical nouns (*London's citizens*). It seems to have spread from American English to British English and is most prevalent in the language of newspapers. Moreover, Anschutz (1997) shows in a corpus analysis of American English that today the factor animacy seems to be less important than topicality.

3.3.2 *Present study*

There are a multitude of factors involved in the choice between the *s*-genitive and the *of*-genitive, and it is therefore not easy to find 'neutral' contexts to investigate the factors animacy, topicality, and possessive relationship. Also, as said above, these factors often go hand in hand, and it is extremely difficult to study them in isolation. In contrast to previous empirical studies, which were all corpus analyses, I therefore used an experimental design, which allowed for a highly controlled investigation of the relative importance of these three conceptual factors.

3.3.2.1 *Experimental design.* My subjects were 56 British native speakers, aged between 18 to 81, all with higher education. As material I used a questionnaire containing short text passages providing contexts for the occurrence of nominal possessive constructions. The subjects had to choose as spontaneously as possible whether to use the *s*-genitive or the *of*-genitive in the given contexts. The following example from the questionnaire will illustrate what the task looked like:

He passed through the entrance where a sign identified the park as Island Gardens. At its far west end, a circular brick building stood, domed in glass and mounted by a white and green lantern cupola. A movement of white shimmered against the red bricks, and Lynley saw Jimmy Cooper trying [*the door of the building/the building's door*].[9]

According to the 3 nominal variables animacy, topicality, and possessive relationship there are 8 conditions, with at least 10 items per condition, altogether 93 items. The conditions are specified in Figure 3, which also gives an example for each condition.

+animate				−animate			
+topical		−topical		+topical		−topical	
+prototyp. possession	−prototyp. possession	+prototyp. possession	−prototyp. possession	+prototyp. possession	−prototyp. possession	+prototyp. possession	−prototyp. possession
the boy's eyes/the eyes of the boy	*the mother's future/the future of the mother*	*a girl's face/the face of a girl*	*a woman's shadow/the shadow of a woman*	*the chair's frame/the frame of the chair*	*the room's darkness/ the darkness of the room*	*a lorry's wheels/the wheels of a lorry*	*a car's fumes/the fumes of a car*

Figure 3. Experimental study: Conditions and items (examples)

In a short pilot study it was found that both the s-genitive and the of-genitive were always potential options, although—due to the different conditions—certainly with varying degrees of likelihood. Moreover, in order to test the productivity of the s-genitive and avoid any specific lexical effects, exclusively items with possessors of such noun classes were taken that have been reported to have the least propensity for taking the s-genitive. Thus, within the [+animate] conditions only items with personal nouns were chosen, but no proper names (see, e.g., Jucker's 1993 data, which shows that, apart from pronouns, proper names are most likely to take the s-genitive). Accordingly, within the [−animate] conditions only items with concrete nouns as possessors were selected, which have been shown by both Jucker (1993) and Jahr Sorheim (1980) to be among the least likely noun classes to take the s-genitive. Thus, if a difference is found between the [+animate] and [−animate] condition, this difference cannot be due to any lexical effects, but must be attributed to the factor animacy itself.

Topicality again refers to the identifiability of the possessor. In the [+topical] condition the possessor was always a second-mention definite expression; in the [−topical] condition the possessor was a first-mention, indefinite expression.

Although the concept of possession prototypically assumes a [+animate]

[+human] possessor (cf., e.g., Seiler 1983: 4; Taylor 1989: 679), it is also applicable to [−animate] possessors (see, e.g., Heine 1997: § 1.3). For the present analysis I will consider part/whole relations as prototypical instances of inanimate possession (e.g., *the chair's frame, the car's bonnet*), because they form an inherent, non-separable part with their possessum; non-part/whole possessive relations constitute non-proto-typical cases of inanimate possession (e.g., *the room's darkness, the pit's grime*).

Note that the structure and arrangement of the conditions in Figure 3 corresponds to the preference structure in Figure 2; i.e., they are — for the sake of illustration — already structured according to the proposed hierarchy: animacy > topicality > possessive relationship. If this hierarchy holds true for the ModE situation, the optimal context for the occurrence of the *s*-genitive should decrease from the most optimal context, namely, the +animate/+topical/+prototypical possessive relation condition, to the least optimal context, the −animate/−topical/ −prototypical possessive relation condition, which should also be reflected in the decreasing frequency of the *s*-genitive along this scale.

3.3.2.2 *Results.* Figure 4 shows the relative frequency of the *s*-genitive versus the *of*-genitive according to the eight conditions in the order given in Figure 3 above.

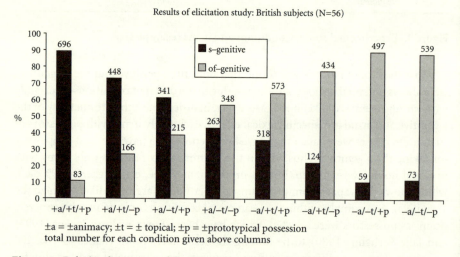

±a = ±animacy; ±t = ± topical; ±p = ±prototypical possession
total number for each condition given above columns

Figure 4. Relative frequency of the *s*-genitive vs. the *of*-genitive (in %)

As is apparent from Figure 4, the frequency of the *s*-genitive decreases steadily from left to right along the preference structure in Figure 2; the differences between the conditions are all highly significant (at least with χ^2, $p < 0.01$, using Yates' correction, df 1), except the difference between the last two conditions ([−a/−t/+p] vs. [−a/−t/−p], which is not significant. This confirms the hierarchy and preference structure proposed for the EModE data. Moreover, a clear extension of the s-genitive to the [−animate] domain can be observed, again with a decreasing frequency along the preference structure in Figure 2.

There is also evidence for ongoing change with the s-genitive in British English. To show this change in progress I would like to adopt the Labovian concept of change in apparent time (Labov 1972), dividing my subjects into older and younger subjects, drawing the line at the age of 40, the average age of the younger subjects being 23, that of the older subjects 54. The idea behind this is that the language of the older subjects should reflect an older language state, while the language of the younger subjects should represent more recent language usage. Figure 5 shows the relative frequency of the s-genitive according to the two age groups; the conditions are again arranged in the same order as in the previous figures.

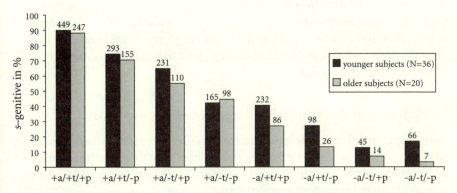

Figure 5. Frequency of the s-genitive (in%): Younger subjects vs. older subjects

Both age groups apparently use the s-genitive according to the same preference structure, i.e., the relative frequency of the s-genitive decreases steadily from left to right. There is, however, a clear difference in the frequency of usage between the two age groups, and this difference is most pronounced within the [−animate] conditions. The younger subjects use the s-genitive significantly more often with inanimate possessors than the older subjects. A χ^2-test shows that this difference between the two age groups is highly significant with χ^2, $p < 0.001$ (using Yates' correction, df 1) for the four [−animate] conditions; except for the [−a/-t/+p] condition, which was not significant but still showed a strong tendency (χ^2, $p < 0.10$, using Yates' correction, df 1). In light of the decreasing importance of the factor animacy with the younger subjects, it may also be no coincidence that in this age group the difference between the conditions at the borderline between the [+animate] and the [−animate] conditions ([+a/-t/-p] vs. [−a/+t/+p]) is no longer significant, as opposed to the older subjects.

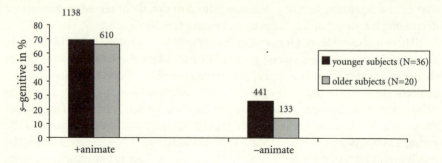

Figure 6. Animacy: Younger subjects vs. older subjects

In Figure 6 the relative frequency of the *s*-genitive for all animate conditions is summarized and compared to that of all inanimate conditions. While the difference in frequency of the *s*-genitive between the two age groups is not significant for the animate conditions, it is highly significant (χ^2, $p < 0.001$, using Yates' correction, df 1) for the inanimate conditions.

3.4 Summary of the empirical findings (EModE vs. ModE data)

Comparing the three conceptual factors animacy, topicality, and possessive relationship, there seems to be a rather stable ordering of their relative importance for the choice of the *s*-genitive, namely animacy > topicality > possessive relationship, as illustrated in the preference structure in Figure 2. The possible contexts for the occurrence of the *s*-genitive extend, diachronically, along this preference structure. Most importantly, while in Early Modern English the *s*-genitive was almost impossible with inanimate possessors, in Modern English the domain of the *s*-genitive has clearly extended to the [−animate] domain. Along this preference structure an increase in the frequency of the *s*-genitive has also been observed over time, both in the period from 1400 to 1630, and also as a change-in-progress phenomenon within the ModE data. While this increase in the frequency of the *s*-genitive took place in the [+animate] domain only in the EModE period, in Modern English it can mainly be observed for the [−animate] domain. A reason for this may be the fact that the *s*-genitive is already well established in the [+animate] domain, so that the increase in frequency — as an indicator for ongoing change — is confined to the more sensitive domain of inanimate possessors today. Note, finally, that although the importance of the factor animacy is certainly decreasing today in British English, the data presented in this study indicate that it still continues to be the most important factor.

Summing up the results of the EModE and ModE data, both elements of stability and change seem to be involved in the development of the English s-genitive: stability in the sense that the relative importance of the factors animacy, topicality, and possessive relationship seems to be approximately the same for Early Modern English and Modern English, i.e., animacy > topicality > possessive relationship. What has changed, however, are the contexts in which the s-genitive can occur and its relative frequency within these contexts. While the s-genitive was restricted to [+animate] possessors in the EModE period, it has now clearly extended to the [−animate] domain. And this process has not come to an end yet; it seems to be still ongoing, as the strikingly higher frequency of the s-genitive among the younger British subjects in the ModE data suggests.

4. Discussion: The role of animacy, topicality, and possessive relationship for the use of the English s-genitive: Iconic motivation?

The question remains *why* the investigated factors (animacy, topicality, and possessive relationship) play such a decisive role in the choice and diachronic extension of the English s-genitive? This is an ambitious question to ask, and it is certainly beyond the scope of this paper to present an ultimate answer to it. On a more speculative basis, however, I would like to draw attention to the concept of iconicity, which may — at least partly — account for the observed development of the s-genitive.

The basic assumption of iconicity is that the relationship between the signifier and the signified is not completely arbitrary, as was the basic tenet of Saussurean linguistics, but that there may be a correspondence between the linguistic sign and the underlying concept and that the structure and use of language can indeed be motivated. Several types of iconicity have to be distinguished;[10] for the present purpose I would like to focus on two specific notions of iconicity.

4.1 Linear sequencing

The first notion proceeds from the assumption that linear order may reflect the order of the concepts — or rather the order of their perception — in the world. This principle may account for the role of the animacy and topicality of the possessor and concerns the position of the possessor. The psycholinguist Kathryn Bock and associates (1982, and subsequent work) have put forward the argument that concepts are processed and then linearized in the order in which they become available to the mind. In particular, animate and otherwise highly salient and familiar concepts, such as topics, have been shown in a series of psycholinguistic experiments to be highly accessible and thus to occur early in utterances (see, e.g., Bock & Warren 1985; McDonald, Bock, & Kelly 1993). The two nominal possessive

constructions in English, the *s*-genitive and the *of*-genitive, provide two complementary positions for the possessor: in the *s*-genitive the possessor precedes the
possessum, while the order is reversed in the *of*-genitive. The *s*-genitive therefore
provides an opportunity to place highly accessible possessors, that is, [+animate]
[+topical] possessors, early in a possessive construction. While the existence of two
truly synonymous structures seems to be extremely uneconomic and to run counter
to the principle of isomorphism — i.e., one form for one meaning — in the present
argumentation, word order choices are motivated and are being utilized by
processing needs.[11]

4.2 Conceptual distance

Second, another iconic principle may account for the factor possessive relationship,
i.e., the principle of 'conceptual distance' (Haiman 1985).[12] According to this
principle, the distance between two concepts should be reflected in their linguistic
form: the closer the relation between two concepts, the closer they should be
linguistically expressed. Prototypical possessive relations represent close relations
between possessor and possessum and are therefore more likely to be encoded in
closer proximity than less prototypical possessive relations. Based on this principle
of conceptual distance and following Seiler (1983:80ff.) and Haiman (1985:130) I
would like to suggest the following scale for English possessive constructions:

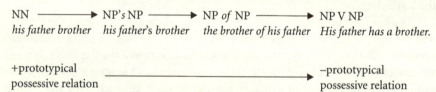

NN ————→ NP's NP ————→ NP *of* NP ————→ NP V NP
his father brother   *his father's brother*   *the brother of his father*   *His father has a brother.*

+prototypical   −prototypical
possessive relation ————————————————→ possessive relation

The closest linguistic expression between possessor and possessum is N-N juxtapo-
sition (*his father brother*).[13] These *s*-less forms were rather frequent in certain late
Middle English and EModE English dialects, where, according to Altenberg
(1982:13), they were used so extensively that the *s*-genitive was almost threatened
by extinction. *S*-less forms are also reported for Middle Scots (Rosenbach & Vezzosi
1999) and 20th century Northern English (see, e.g., Klemola 1997). At the other end
of the scale the possessive relationship is expressed with a full predicative structure
(*His father has a brother*). Accordingly, the *s*-genitive should be more likely to
encode more prototypical possessive relations than the *of*-genitive. This prediction
is indeed confirmed by the data presented in this paper: Both in Early Modern
English and Modern English, the *s*-genitive is used more often in prototypical
possessive relations than in less prototypical ones.

4.3 Possible outlook?

It has been argued that the impact of the factors animacy, topicality, and possessive relationship on the occurrence and the frequency of the English *s*-genitive may point to two different types of iconic motivation: linear sequencing and conceptual distance. Both types of iconicity, I would like to argue, facilitate language processing. Diachronically, such iconically-driven processing biases may lead to language change, as has been shown in the present paper by the comparison of the EModE and the ModE data. Figure 7 illustrates this kind of reasoning and gives a possible outlook on the future development of the *s*-genitive.

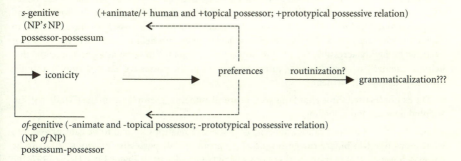

Figure 7. The English *s*-genitive: Iconically - driven language processing in a diachronic perspective

The English language provides two principally alternative constructions to encode possessive relationships, namely, the *s*-genitive and the *of*-genitive, which make it possible to process concepts in the order in which they become available to the mind and according to the principle of linguistic distance; the English *s*-genitive provides an opportunity to place highly accessible possessors, that is, [+animate] and [+topical] possessors, early and represents the more implicit linguistic structure to encode prototypical possessive relations.

Note, finally, that these are *preference* options and not *grammaticalized* options; it is always a question of more or less likely and never an either/or question. However, one may speculate whether the English *s*-genitive may be beginning to lose its originally iconic motivation and become grammaticalized. The extension and ongoing change of the *s*-genitive in the domain of [−animate] possessors may well point to the fact that it may be in the process of being automatized and routinized.

Notes

* This paper has greatly benefitted from discussions with Keith Brown, Martina Penke, Letizia Vezzosi, the participants of the research colloquium in the Department of General Linguistics at Heinrich Heine University Düsseldorf, and last, but certainly not least, from the comments of two anonymous reviewers. I am also indebted to all the British subjects who were willing to volunteer in the present study and to Keith Brown, Susan Dostert, Kerrie Elston-Güttler, Antje Hartmann, Verena Jung, and Simone Pesch for helping me find them. I am grateful to Dieter Stein for making this joint research on the English genitive constructions possible for me.

1. Throughout this paper I will refer to the head of a possessive construction (*the girl's eyes* versus *the eyes of the girl*) as the 'possessum' (*eyes*) and to the modifier as the 'possessor' (*the girl*).

2. According to Taylor (1989, 1996) two aspects seem to be important for the choice of the *s*-genitive: first, the prototypicality of the semantic relation that holds between the possessor and the possessum (Taylor 1989), and second, the accessibility of the possessor (Taylor 1996); in Taylor's (1996) account of the *s*-genitive as a device to ensure definite reference, the possessor needs to be highly accessible (i.e., highly topical and animate) to serve as a good 'anchor' that helps to mentally narrow down the intended referent of the possessive construction to a single, uniquely identifiable element.

3. The examples used throughout this section are all authentic examples from the EModE corpus, adapted here to Mod E spelling.

4. For the sake of quantification, the type of possessive relationship had to be categorized into what looks like two binary categories, i.e., [+/- prototypical] possessive relations. It has to be stressed, however, that in frameworks of possession (e.g., Seiler 1983; Taylor 1989; Heine 1997) the different types of possessive relationship are supposed to form a gradient scale, rather than a binary, categorical opposition.

5. The corpus consists of a variety of prose texts, mainly taken from the Helsinki Corpus, ranging from formal to informal genres and representing various authors, thereby avoiding a possible bias of the results towards the stylistic preferences of single authors or towards certain text types (cf., e.g., Jahr Sorheim 1980; Altenberg 1982; Jucker 1993, who show that the frequency of the *s*-genitive is to a large extent determined by genre and style). For the present analysis the corpus was narrowed down to 1,500 tokens; for more details on the corpus, the analyses and for the list of primary sources, I refer to Rosenbach and Vezzosi (2000) and Rosenbach, Stein, & Vezzosi (2000).

6. Note that only those contexts are quantified for which at least 10 obligatory contexts for the occurrence of the *s*-genitive or the *of*-genitive could be found.

7. For the sake of exposition and oversimplifying somewhat for topicality, a binary distinction is used here instead of the tripartite one presented in Figure 1. Since the number of overall obligatory contexts in the [−topical] contexts are much lower than for the other contexts, the results for this context must be taken cautiously; [−topical] as indicated in this preference structure should therefore read as less topical and non-topical (= new) possessors.

8. For this reason, animacy is considered the most important factor of the three conceptual factors investigated. The relative importance of topicality versus the type of possessive relation is such that topicality is clearly the more important factor throughout the 15th century, though it looks as if by the early 17th century the type of possessive relation may have become the stronger factor than topicality (cf., Rosenbach, Stein, & Vezzosi 2000: §2.4). Unfortunately, there is no comparable data for the later 17th century, which could validate this point.

9. The text passages used in the questionnaire are largely adaptations of novels by Elizabeth George (*Missing Joseph* [1993]; *Playing for the Ashes* [1994]) and Patricia Cornwell (*The Body Farm* [1994]).

10. For a good overview of the different types of iconicity I refer to Fischer and Nänny (1999) and Fischer (1999).

11. Note that also from a pragmatic point of view the s-genitive and the *of*-genitive are not truly synonymous but serve different communicative needs; see, e.g., Altenberg (1982:249–293) and Jucker (1993) or Rosenbach and Vezzosi (2000) for such an argument.

12. The notions of 'semantic bonding' (cf. Siewierska 1988:55–56) and 'proximity principle' (Givón 1996:437–438) express basically the same idea.

13. Note that in the examples given here the possessor (*father*) belongs to a noun class which already in Old English was s-less; that is, in this case it is a continuation of an older pattern. There is, however, also ample evidence that these s-less forms spread to nouns/noun classes historically not s-less (e.g., *the bucher wyff, Henry Winslow horse*); see Altenberg (1982:§2.4) and Wyld (1936:316–318) for further data and discussion.

References

Allen, Cynthia. 1997. "The Origins of the 'Group Genitive' in English". *Transactions of the Philological Society* 95: 1.111–131.

Altenberg, Bengt. 1982. *The Genitive v. the of-Construction: A study of syntactic variation in 17th century English*. Malmö: CWK Gleerup.

Anschutz, Arlea. 1997. "How to Choose a Possessive Noun Phrase Construction in Four Easy Steps". *Studies in Language* 21: 1.1–35.

Bock, J. Kathryn. 1982. "Toward a Cognitive Psychology of Syntax: Information processing contributions to sentence formulation". *Psychological Review* 89: 1.1–47.

Bock, J. Kathryn & R.K. Warren. 1985. "Conceptual Accessibility and Syntactic Structure in Sentence Formulation". *Cognition* 21.47–67.

Fischer, Olga. 1999. "On the Role Played by Iconicity in Grammaticalisation Processes". Nänny & Fischer 1999. 345–374.

Fischer, Olga & Max Nänny. 1999. "Introduction: Iconicity as a creative force in language use". Nänny & Fischer 1999. xv–xxxvi.

Givón, Talmy. 1996. *Functionalism and Grammar*. Amsterdam & Philadelphia: John Benjamins.

Haiman, John. 1985. *Natural Syntax*. Cambridge: Cambridge University Press.

Heine, Bernd. 1997. *Possession: Cognitive sources, forces, and grammaticalization*. Cambridge: Cambridge University Press.

Jahr Sorheim, Mette Catherine. 1980. *The s-Genitive in Present-Day English*. Department of English, Oslo University.

Jucker, Andreas. 1993. "The Genitive versus the of-Construction in Newspaper Language". *The Noun Phrase in English: Its structure and variability* ed. by Andreas Jucker, 121–136. Heidelberg: Winter.

Klemola, Juhani. 1997. "Dialect Evidence for the Loss of Genitive Inflection in English". *English Language and Linguistics* 1: 2.350–353.

Labov, William. 1972. *Sociolinguistic Patterns*. Philadelphia: University of Pennsylvania Press.

Lass, Roger. 1997. *Historical Linguistics and Language Change*. Cambridge: Cambridge University Press.

McDonald, Janet L., J. Kathryn Bock, & Michael H. Kelly. 1993. "Word and World Order: Semantic, phonological, and meterical determinants of serial position". *Cognitive Psychology* 25.188–230.

Nänny, Max & Olga Fischer, eds. 1999. *Form Miming Meaning: Iconocity in language and literature.* Amsterdam & Philadelphia: John Benjamins.

Raab-Fischer, Roswitha. 1995. "Löst der Genitiv die *of*-Phrase ab?" *Zeitschrift für Anglistik und Amerikanistik* 2.123–132.

Rosenbach, Anette & Letizia Vezzosi. 1999. "Was the *s*-Genitive a Traveller through England?" *LANA-Düsseldorf Working Papers on Linguistics 1.* (http://ang3-11.phil-fak.uni-duesseldorf.de/~ang3/LANA/LANA.html) ed. by Alexander Bergs, Monika S. Schmid, & Dieter Stein, 35–55.

Rosenbach, Anette & Letizia Vezzosi. 2000. "Genitive Constructions in Early Modern English: New evidence from a corpus analysis". *Stability, Variation and Change in Word-Order Patterns over Time* ed. by Rosanna Sornicola, Erich Poppe & Ariel Shisha-Halevy, 285–307. Amsterdam & Philadelphia: John Benjamins.

Rosenbach, Anette, Dieter Stein, & Letizia Vezzosi. 2000. "On the History of the *s*-Genitive". *Generative Theory and Corpus Study: A dialogue from 10ICEHL* ed. by Ricardo Bermúdez-Otero, David Denison, Richard M. Hogg, & C.B. McCully, 183–209. Berlin: Walter de Gruyter.

Seiler, HansJakob. 1983. *Possession as an Operational Dimension of Language.* Tübingen: Gunter Narr Verlag.

Seppänen, Aimo. 1997. "The Genitive and the Category of Case in the History of English". *Language History and Linguistic Modelling: A Festschrift for Jacek Fisiak on his 60th birthday* ed. by Raymond Hickey & Stanislaw Puppel, vol. I, 193–214. Berlin: Mouton de Gruyter.

Siewierska, Anna. 1988. *Word Order Rules.* London: Croom Helm.

Tabor, Whitney & Elizabeth C. Traugott. 1998. "Structural Scope Expansion and Grammaticalization". *The Limits of Grammaticalization* ed. by Anna Giacalone Ramat & Paul J. Hopper, 229–272. Amsterdam & Philadelphia: John Benjamins.

Taylor, John. 1996. *Possessives in English. An exploration in cognitive grammar.* Oxford: Clarendon.

Taylor, John. 1989. "Posessive Genitives in English". *Linguistics* 27.663–686.

Wyld, Henry Cecil. 1936. *A History of Modern Colloquial English.* 3rd ed. Oxford: Blackwell.

Default inheritance hierarchies and the evolution of inflectional classes

Gregory Stump
University of Kentucky

1. Gender, declension classes, and default inheritance hierarchies

In this article, I examine the historical evolution of three classes of nominals in Vedic: feminine *i*-stems, radical *ī*-stems, and derivative *ī*-stems. I argue that the analogical influences that affect these classes in later varieties of early Indic allow declensional systems to emerge whose alignment of gender distinctions with declensional distinctions makes them more highly valued than the original Vedic system in regard to the principles in (1).

(1) a. A declensional system is preferred if sameness of declension entails sameness of gender.
      b. A declensional system is preferred if sameness of gender entails sameness of declension.

This argument presupposes that a language's declension classes have a hierarchical organization in which classes may be nested (Corbett & Fraser 1993). This view is necessitated by the fact that within a language, two inflectional classes may be alike in some ways but different in others. In Vedic, for example, the *i*-stem, *a*-stem, and nonalternating C(onsonant)-stem declensions are alike in the suffixal morphology of the locative plural (e.g., *śúci-ṣu* "bright", *priyé-ṣu* "dear", *sumánaḥ-su* "well-disposed"); in the genitive plural, by contrast, the *i*-stem and *a*-stem declensions are alike in their suffixation (*śúcī-n-ām, priyá-ṇ-ām*), but differ from the nonalternating C-stem declension (*sumánas-ām*); and in the genitive singular, each of the three declensions exhibits a different suffix (*śúce-s, priyá-sya, sumánas-as*). The organization of these declension classes might therefore be represented by means of the network in Figure 1. In this network, each node houses the default declensional properties common to the lexemes that it dominates: the property of marking the locative plural with the suffix *-su* (or its sandhi form *-ṣu*) is situated at the 'Nominals' node; that of marking the genitive plural with *-n(-ām)* (sandhi form *-ṇ(-ām)*) is situated at the 'Vowel-stem nominals' node; and that of marking the genitive singular with -*sya* is situated at the '*a*-stem nominals' node. The network in Figure 1 is an inheritance hierarchy: dominated nodes inherit properties from dominating nodes. In natural language, inheritance relations of this kind are default relations: a dominated node N inherits properties from a dominating node unless those properties are overridden by stipulations at N. In Vedic, for instance, the ablative singular is generally syncretized with the genitive singular, but *a*-stem nominals instead form their ablative singular with a special suffix -*t*. Thus, although the property referring the form of the ablative singular to that of the genitive singular is situated at the 'Nominals' node in Figure 1, this property is not inherited by the '*a*-stem nominals' node, being overridden by the property of ablative singular -*t* suffixation that is situated at the latter node.

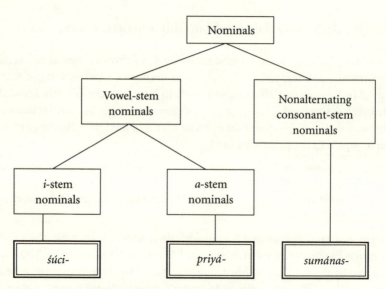

Figure 1. Partial hierarchy of declension classes in Vedic

Under this conception of a language's system of inflectional classes, the principles in (1) have two theorems: first, a declensional system is preferred if it allows a lexeme's gender and its declensional properties to be inherited from the same node in the declensional hierarchy; and second, a declensional system is preferred if it houses a given gender specification at a single preterminal node in the declensional hierarchy.

2. Vedic

The Vedic declensional system conforms to the principles in (1) to an extent, since some declension classes are associated with specific genders. This is most obviously so in the case of neuter nominals: whatever the declension of a neuter nominal, it is always distinct in various ways from that of any masculine or feminine nominal; the distinction is, moreover, a very salient one, being regularly made in the direct cases. There are also declension classes that are specifically associated with the feminine or the masculine gender. For example, all nominals belonging to the (non-neuter) *a*-stem declension are masculine (Macdonell 1910: § 369, § 371), and all nominals belonging to the derivative *ā*-stem declension are feminine (Macdonell 1910: § 373).

In some instances, the relation of a declension class to a specific gender is one of default rather than absolute association. For instance, the derivative *ī*-stem declension (that of *devī́*- "goddess" in Table 1) includes both feminine and masculine members, but the representation of these two genders is highly disproportionate — only seven masculine members are attested, of which five are proper names (Macdonell 1910: § 377); similarly, the derivative *ū*-stem declension includes only five attested masculines (Macdonell 1910: § 384), the remainder of its members being feminine. In such cases, the declension class is associated with a specific gender, but this association is subject to occasional, lexically stipulated override.

Despite such correlations between declension-class distinctions and gender-class distinctions, Vedic has declensions in which the masculine and feminine genders are both heavily represented. This is true of the (non-neuter) declension of nonalternating C-stems: the radical noun stems in this class are mostly feminine, but this class also includes a large number of adjectival compounds, whose feminine and masculine paradigms are identical. In Vedic, radical *ī*-stem nouns — which are generally feminine (Macdonell 1910: § 375) — follow the nonalternating C-stem declension; thus, the paradigm of the radical *ī*-stem noun *śrī́*- "glory" is parallel to that of *vā́c*- "speech" (Table 1). Moreover, certain *ī*-stem nouns which are not strictly radical (since they derive from other roots) nevertheless inflect in this same way rather than in the manner of *devī́*-. For instance, the noun *nadī́*- "stream" (Table 1) has fundamentally the same suffixal morphology as *śrī́*-, and the only necessary declensional differences between *śrī́*- and *nadī́*- are those that follow from the fact that *śrī́*- is monosyllabic and hence exhibits suffixal accent in the so-called 'weak' cases and stem-final *iy* before vowel-initial suffixes. Like true radical *ī*-stem nouns, 'pseudo-radical' *ī*-stem nouns such as *nadī́*- are nearly all feminine (Macdonell 1910: § 375).

In the nonalternating C-stem declension, masculine and feminine nominals are inflected identically. But even where feminines and masculines differ declensionally, the difference can be negligible. For instance, feminine *i*-stem nominals and masculine *i*-stem nominals generally inflect alike, the only invariable difference

Table 1. Vedic declension of *devī́-* "goddess" (a derivative *ī*-stem), *śrī́-* "glory" (a radical *ī*-stem), *vā́c-* "speech" (a nonalternating consonant-stem), *nadī́-* "stream" (a pseudo-radical *ī*-stem), and the *i*-stem adjective *śúci-* "bright" (feminine and masculine forms)

		devī́-	śrī́-	vā́c-	nadī́-	śúci- (feminine)	śúci- (masculine)
Singular	Nom.	devī́	śrī́-s	vā́k [< vā́c-s]	nadī́-s	śúci-s	} (same)
	Acc.	devī́-m	śriy-am	vā́c-am	nadi-am	śúci-m	
	Instr.	devy-ā́	śriy-ā́	vā́c-ā	nadi-ā́	śúcy-ā (~ śúcī ~ śúci)	śúcy-ā (~ śúci-n-ā́)
	Dat.	devy-ā́i	śriy-é	vāc-é	nadi-e	śúcay-e	
	Abl., Gen.	devy-ā́s	śriy-ás	vāc-ás	nadi-as	śúce-s	
	Loc.	devy-ā́m	śriy-í	vāc-í	[?]	śúcā ~ śúcau	
Dual	Nom., Acc.	devī́	śriy-ā́(u)	vāc-ā́(u)	nadi-ā́	śúcī	(same)
	Instr., Dat., Abl.	devī́-bhyām	śrī-bhyā́m	vāg-bhyā́m [< vāc-bhyā́m]	nadī́-bhyām	śúci-bhyām	
	Gen., Loc.	devy-ós	śriy-ós	vāc-ós	nadi-os	śúcy-os	
Plural	Nom.	devī́-s	śriy-as	vā́c-as	nadi-as	śúcay-as	
	Acc.	devī́-s	śriy-as	vā́c-as	nadi-as	śúci-s	śúci-n
	Instr.	devī́-bhis	śrī-bhis	vāg-bhís [< vāc-bhís]	nadī́-bhis	śúci-bhis	
	Dat., Abl.	devī́-bhyas	śrī-bhyás	vāg-bhyás [< vāc-bhyás]	nadī́-bhyas	śúci-bhyas	} (same)
	Gen.	devī́-nām	śriy-ā́m (~ śri-ṇ-ā́m)	vāc-ā́m	nadī́-n-ām	śúci-n-ām	
	Loc.	devī́-ṣu	śrī-ṣú [< śrī-sú]	vāk-ṣú [< vāc-sú]	nadī́-ṣu	śúci-ṣu	

being their accusative plural forms (e.g., *śúci-s* vs *śúcī-n*, Table 1). It is not clear that this single contrast is sufficient motivation to distinguish two *i*-stem declension classes, one feminine and one masculine; instead, one can easily assume a single declension class whose accusative plural inflection is gender-sensitive.[1]

These facts suggest the network in Figure 2 as a (partial) representation of the Vedic declensional system.[2] In this network, radical and pseudo-radical *ī*-stems do not inherit their declensional characteristics from the same node as derivative *ī*-stems, but instead pattern with nonalternating C-stems; and feminine *i*-stems inherit from the same node as their masculine counterparts (a node at which the affixal exponence of the accusative plural is gender-sensitive).

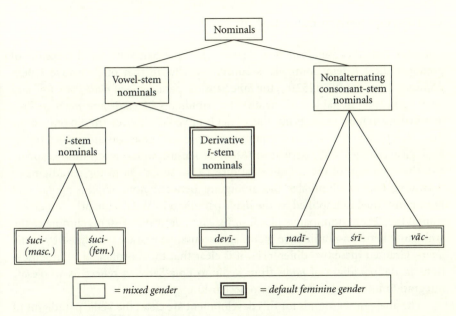

Figure 2. Partial hierarchy of declension classes in Vedic

Feminine gender is a default concomitant of membership in the class of derivative *ī*-stem nominals: thus, *devī́-* inherits its gender from the node which determines its declensional properties. But because the nonalternating C-stem nominals are heterogeneous with respect to gender, the gender of radical and pseudo-radical *ī*-stem nouns is not a concomitant of their declension-class membership: though nouns of these latter sorts are nearly all feminine, their gender is not inherited from the node determining their declensional properties, but must either be a matter of lexical stipulation or be deduced from other properties (e.g., the stem vowel *ī*, which, in nouns, correlates highly reliably with membership in the feminine gender). Similarly, the node determining the declensional properties of *i*-stem nominals fails to determine gender.

Because nominals which inherit their declensional properties from the 'non-alternating C-stem nominals' node or from the '*i*-stem nominals' node are heterogeneous with respect to gender, the network of declension classes in Figure 2 is dispreferred by principle (1a); that is, it would be consistent with (1a) for this network to be replaced, diachronically, by a more highly preferred network. This is, in fact, what happens: assuming that its linguistic antecedent is like Vedic in the relevant respects, Epic Sanskrit gives evidence of having undergone three analogical developments which result in a more highly preferred network of declension classes.

3.   Developments in Epic Sanskrit

Consider first the pseudo-radical *ī*-stems. In Epic Sanskrit, the declension of pseudo-radical *ī*-stem nominals is entirely parallel to that of derivative *ī*-stem nominals (Burrow 1973:252ff.); the Epic Sanskrit paradigms of *nadī-* "stream" and *devī-* "goddess" in Table 2 illustrate. The paradigms of *nadī-* and *devī-* in Epic Sanskrit are in most respects like that of *devī-* in Vedic, differing from it only in the dual direct-case form and in the nominative plural. These two differences reflect analogical changes in the derivative *ī*-stem declension whose motivation is apparent: the extension of the default dual direct-case suffix *-au* to the paradigms of derivative *ī*-stems eliminates the ambiguity between nominative singular and nominative dual exemplified by the *devī-* paradigm in Vedic; similarly, the extension of the default nominative plural suffix *-as* to derivative *ī*-stems eliminates the ambiguity between nominative plural and accusative plural exemplified by Vedic *devī-*. Granted these two differences, it is clear that the morphological modifications in the paradigm of *nadī-* from Vedic to Epic Sanskrit reflect its wholesale integration into the derivative *ī*-stem declension.

The analogical grounds for this development are clear: the Vedic paradigms of *devī-* and *nadī-* coincide in a number of cells, e.g., the oblique cases of the plural. But given this congruence, why did pseudo-radical *ī*-stem nominals come to follow the pattern of derivative *ī*-stems rather than the other way around: why weren't nominals like *devī-* instead integrated into the nonalternating C-stem declension? It's not that the pseudo-radical *ī*-stem nominals transferred because they constituted a marginal declensional type with few exemplars: there are over eighty stems of this type attested in Vedic (Macdonell 1910:§375), and the nonalternating C-stem declension which they follow in Vedic is firmly established throughout Old Indic. Instead, I claim that the direction of the analogical influence between *devī-* and *nadī-* is determined by the preference principle (1a). A transfer of *devī-*-type nominals to the *nadī-* declension would have resulted in a dispreferred system: in Vedic, the feminine gender of *devī-*-type nominals is a default concomitant of

Default inheritance hierarchies **299**

Table 2. The declension of *nadī-* "stream", *devī-* "goddess", and *śrī-* "glory" and the feminine and masculine paradigms of *śuci-* "bright" in Epic Sanskrit

		nadī-	*devī-*	*śrī-*	*śuci-* (feminine)	*śuci-* (masculine)
Singular	Nom.	nadī (a)	devī	śrī-s	śuci-s	śuci-s
	Acc.	nadī-m (a)	devī-m	śriy-am	śuci-m	śuci-m
	Instr.	nady-ā	devy-ā	śriy-ā	śucy-ā	śuci-n-ā
	Dat.	nady-ai (a)	devy-ai	śriy-e ~ śriy-ai (a)	śucay-e	śucay-e ~ śucy-ai (a)
	Abl., Gen.	nady-ās (a)	devy-ās	śriy-as ~ śriy-ās (a)	śuce-s	śuce-s ~ śucy-ās (a)
	Loc.	nady-ām (a)	devy-ām	śriy-i ~ śriy-ām (a)	śucau	śucau ~ śucy-ām (a)
Dual	Nom., Acc.	nady-au (a)	devy-au (a)	śriy-au	śucī	śucī
	Instr., Dat., Abl.	nadī-bhyām	devī-bhyām	śrī-bhyām	śuci-bhyām	śuci-bhyām
	Gen., Loc.	nady-os	devy-os	śriy-os	śucy-os	śucy-os
Plural	Nom.	nady-as	devy-as (a)	śriy-as	śucay-as	śucay-as
	Acc.	nadī-s (a)	devī-s	śriy-as	śuci-s	śuci-n
	Instr.	nadī-bhis	devī-bhis	śrī-bhis	śuci-bhis	śuci-bhis
	Dat., Abl.	nadī-bhyas	devī-bhyas	śrī-bhyas	śuci-bhyas	śuci-bhyas
	Gen.	nadī-nām	devī-nām	śriy-ām ~ śrī-ṇ-ām (a)	śucī-n-ām	śucī-n-ām
	Loc.	nadī-ṣu	devī-ṣu	śrī-ṣu	śuci-ṣu	śuci-ṣu

(a) = analogical innovation

membership in the derivative *ī*-stem declension class; but because the nonalternating C-stem class is a mixed-gender class, a transfer of *devī*-type nominals to the nonalternating C-stem class would have made it necessary to specify their gender independently of their declension-class membership.

In actuality, the pseudo-radical *ī*-stems left the mixed-gender declension of nonalternating C-stems to follow the derivative *ī*-stem declension; consequently, their feminine gender became a default concomitant of their new declension-class membership, in accordance with (1a).

Unlike pseudo-radical *ī*-stems, true radical *ī*-stems are not fully integrated into the derivative *ī*-stem declension in Epic Sanskrit. Although radical *ī*-stem nouns are (like derivative and pseudo-radical *ī*-stem nouns) mostly feminine, the class of radical *ī*-stem nominals also includes many adjectival compounds — specifically, bahuvrīhi compounds having a radical *ī*-stem noun as their final member (e.g., *veṣaśrī*- "beautifully adorned" < *véṣa*- "ornament" + *śrī*- "glory") and tatpuruṣa compounds having a verb root in *ī* as their final member (e.g., *yajñanī*- "leading the sacrifice" < *yajñá*- "sacrifice" + *nī*- "lead").[3] In the most conservative varieties of Old Indic, adjectival compounds such as *veṣaśrī*- and *yajñanī*- have identical feminine and masculine paradigms. Thus, while the integration of pseudo-radical *ī*-stem nominals into the derivative *ī*-stem declension helps satisfy (1a), that of radical *ī*-stem nominals — including adjectival compounds of the sorts at issue — would not, at least in conservative varieties; indeed, such a development would make the derivative *ī*-stem declension less homogeneous in gender.

This deterrent to the integration of the radical *ī*-stem nominals into the derivative *ī*-stem declension is, however, attenuated by an innovative tendency in Epic Sanskrit and even Vedic (Whitney 1889: § 354) to distinguish the feminine and masculine stems of adjectival compounds such as *veṣaśrī*- and *yajñanī*-; by virtue of this tendency, a compound's feminine stem (e.g., *veṣaśrī*-) follows the radical *ī*-stem declension, while its masculine stem, with shortened final stem-vowel (e.g., *veṣaśri*-), follows the *i*-stem declension. Thus, in varieties of Old Indic in which this innovation is elaborated, radical *ī*-stem nominals become more uniformly feminine.

This fact may be responsible for the emergence of a new, hybrid declension for radical *ī*-stem nominals in Epic Sanskrit: while radical *ī*-stem nominals simply follow the nonalternating C-stem declension in Vedic and in conservative varieties of Epic Sanskrit, their singular oblique paradigm comes to follow that of derivative *ī*-stem nominals in innovative varieties of Epic Sanskrit; the shaded portion of the paradigm of *śrī*- in Table 2 exemplifies this innovation. The analogical motivation for this development is the inherited parallelism of nonsingular oblique forms and that of instrumental singular forms. Here again, the direction of the analogical influence is the issue: why did the declension of radical *ī*-stems take on a partial resemblance to that of the derivative *ī*-stems rather than the other way around? The preference principle (1a) provides an answer. If the declension of derivative *ī*-stem nominals had taken on a partial similarity to that of radical ī-stem nominals (i.e., to the nonalternating C-stem declension), the resulting system wouldn't have satisfied (1a) any better than the historically antecedent system. The reverse development, however — the one that actually occurred — does yield a preferred system: prior to taking on the singular oblique declensional properties of derivative ī-stems, the radical ī-stems belong to a mixed-gender declension class; but once a new, hybrid declension class emerges having the radical ī-stem nominals as its membership, the feminine gender of these nominals becomes a default concomitant of their membership in this class.

In conservative varieties of Epic Sanskrit, feminine i-stem nominals remain essentially like their masculine counterparts in their declensional properties, as in Vedic. In innovative varieties, however, they exhibit a development similar to that of the radical ī-stem nominals: they come to follow a new, hybrid declension whose singular oblique forms are like those of derivative ī-stem nominals (Burrow 1973: 252 ff.). The shaded portion of the feminine paradigm of śuci- in Table 2 exemplifies this innovation. Exactly as in the case of the radical ī-stem nominals, the emergence of this new, hybrid declension class for feminine i-stem nominals finds its motivation in principle (1a): relinquishing their membership in a mixed-gender declension class, the feminine i-stems enter a new declension class where feminine gender is a concomitant of membership; the resulting system is thus more highly preferred.

The effect of these developments is a restructuring of that part of the Old Indic declensional hierarchy subsuming ī-stem nominals; the resulting Epic Sanskrit hierarchy is as in Figure 3.

As regards principle (1a), this Epic Sanskrit hierarchy is an improvement over the Vedic hierarchy in Figure 2: unlike those in the Vedic hierarchy, each of the feminine ī-stem nominals in the Epic Sanskrit hierarchy inherits its gender from the node determining its declensional properties. On the other hand, the Epic Sanskrit hierarchy is no better than the Vedic hierarchy at satisfying principle (1b): just as the paradigms of the feminine nouns devî-, nadî-, and śrî- and the feminine paradigm of śúci- embody three different declensions in Vedic, they continue to do so in Epic Sanskrit as well. Pāli, however, exhibits a further innovation in the inflection of ī-stem nominals that yields a declensional system better satisfying principle (1b).

4. Developments in Pāli

In Pāli, radical and pseudo-radical ī-stem nominals and feminine i-stem nominals are integrated into the derivative ī-stem declension (Bubenik 1996:79). Thus, consider the paradigms of sirī-, nadī-, and devī- and the feminine paradigm of suci- in Pāli (Table 3). If one takes account of (a) the regular sound correspondences

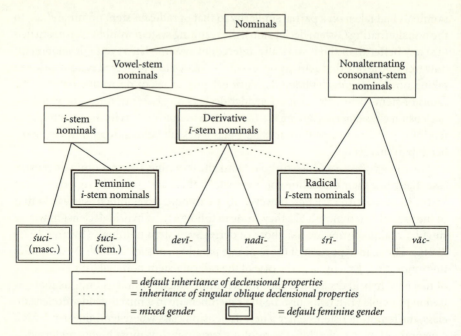

Figure 3. Partial hierarchy of declension classes in Epic Sanskrit

between Pāli and Old Indic (see Geiger 1994), (b) the absence of dual number in Pāli, and (c) the fact that the dative and the ablative are, by default, syncretized with the genitive and the instrumental in Pāli, the paradigm of *devī-* in Pāli can be seen to diverge from its Vedic counterpart in only two significant respects. First, in addition to assuming its "expected" form, the plural direct-case form of *devī-* may optionally carry *-o*, the Pāli reflex of *-as*, the default plural direct-case suffix in Old Indic. Second, the paradigm of *devī-* exhibits the pattern of phonologically conditioned stem alternation typical of radical *ī*-stems in Old Indic: stem-finally, preconsonantal *ī* alternates with prevocalic *iy* (Geiger 1994: §86).

With these modifications, the derivative *ī*-stem declension fully incorporates the radical and pseudo-radical *ī*-stem nominals and feminine *i*-stem nominals. In Table 3, *nadī-* inflects just like *devī-*, as earlier in Epic Sanskrit (Table 2). But here, *sirī-* likewise inflects like *devī-*, exhibiting not only an innovative set of singular oblique forms (as in Epic Sanskrit), but innovative direct-case forms as well, in both the singular and the plural. Similarly, the feminine paradigm of *suci-* exhibits innovative forms in the direct cases of the plural as well as in the singular oblique cases, and has the same stem-final vocalism as *devī-* in every form but that of the nominative singular. Thus, the Pāli declensional hierarchy has the configuration in Figure 4. In this hierarchy, the feminine *ĭ*-stem nominals inherit their gender from the node determining their declensional properties, satisfying principle (1a).

Table 3. The declension of *sirī-* "glory", *nadī-* "river", *devī-* "goddess", and *suci-* "bright" (feminine paradigm) in Pāli

		sirī-	*nadī-*	*devī-*	*suci-* (feminine)
Singular	Nom.	*sirī*	*nadī*	*devī*	*suci*
	Acc.	*siri-ṃ* (a)	*nadi-ṃ*	*devi-ṃ*	*suci-ṃ*
	Instr.	*siriy-ā*	*nadiy-ā*	*deviy-ā*	*suciy-ā* (a)
	Dat.	*siriy-ā* (a)	*nadiy-ā*	*deviy-ā*	*suciy-ā* (a)
	Abl., Gen.	*siriy-ā* (a)	*nadiy-ā*	*deviy-ā*	*suciy-ā* (a)
	Loc.	*siriy-ā* ~ *siriy-aṃ* (a)	*nadiy-ā* ~ *nadiy-aṃ*	*deviy-ā* ~ *deviy-aṃ*	*suciy-ā* ~ *suciy-aṃ* (a)
Plural	Nom., Acc.	*siriy-o* ~ (a) *sirī*	(a) *nadiy-o* ~ *nadī*	(a) *deviy-o* ~ *devī*	*suciy-o* ~ *sucī* (a)
	Instr.	*sirī-hi*	*nadī-hi*	*devī-hi*	*sucī-hi* (a)
	Dat.	*sirī-n-aṃ*	*nadī-n-aṃ*	*devī-n-aṃ*	*sucī-n-aṃ*
	Abl.	*sirī-hi*	*nadī-hi*	*devī-hi*	*sucī-hi* (a)
	Gen.	*sirī-n-aṃ*	*nadī-n-aṃ*	*devī-n-aṃ*	*sucī-n-aṃ*
	Loc.	*sirī-su*	*nadī-su*	*devī-su*	*sucī-su* (a)

(a) = analogical innovation

Moreover, this hierarchy does a better job of satisfying (1b) than either the Vedic hierarchy or the Epic Sanskrit hierarchy, since the identity in gender between *nadī-*, *devī-*, *sirī-*, and the feminine stem of *suci-* is matched by an identity in declension-class membership. Still, not even the Pāli hierarchy is in full conformity with the principles in (1); for instance, Pāli has feminine nouns whose stems are not *ī*-stems and which, contrary to (1b), follow other declensions. Only where sameness of gender coincides with sameness of stem-formation can one generally deduce sameness of declension in Pāli.

5. Discussion

In the foregoing sections, I have discussed four analogical developments in the declensional morphology of early Indic: the full integration of pseudo-radical *ī*-stem nominals into the derivative *ī*-stem declension in Epic Sanskrit; the emergence of two new, hybrid declensions — one for radical *ī*-stem nominals, the other for feminine *i*-stem nominals — in innovative varieties of Epic Sanskrit; and the full integration of radical *ī*-stem and feminine *i*-stem nominals into the derivative *ī*-stem declension in Pāli. My claim is that these developments all embody a single, general tendency in human language: a preference for declensional systems in which a nominal's membership in a particular declension class is both a necessary and a

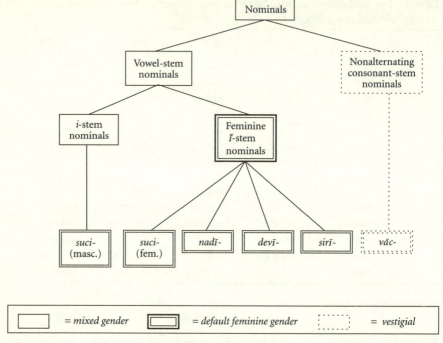

Figure 4. Partial hierarchy of declension classes in Pāli

sufficient correlate of its membership in a particular gender class. In particular, I have argued that the direction of the analogical influences in a language's declensional system is influenced if not fully determined by this preference: the Epic Sanskrit developments serve to heighten the deducibility of a nominal's gender from its declension-class membership; the Pāli development heightens the deducibility of a nominal's declension-class membership from its gender (together with its stem form).[4]

Other analogical developments in the early Indic declensional system provide additional evidence of the preference principles in (1a,b). Consider one additional example. In Vedic, the nonalternating C-stem declension includes a large number of adjectival compounds whose masculine and feminine forms are identical in their inflection. Despite its robustness in Vedic, this declension is virtually absent in Pāli (Geiger 1994:67): many of the Vedic lexemes belonging to this declension (e.g., *sumedhas-* "wise") have a Pāli reflex whose masculine subparadigm follows the (non-neuter) *a*-stem declension (stem *sumedha-* or *sumedhasa-*) and whose feminine subparadigm follows the *ā*-stem declension (stem *sumedhasā-*); unlike the nonalternating C-stem declension, the latter are both single-gender declensions.

This preference for one-to-one correlations between gender-class membership and declension-class membership can be plausibly motivated by considerations of learnability. In an 'ideal' system employing the same subclassification of nominals for both syntactic and purely morphological purposes, a nominal stem's gender and its declensional properties would always be mutually predictable; thus, an inflectional system in full conformity with these principles would be more learnable than a system in which gender-class membership and declension-class membership varied arbitrarily. Because conformity to the principles in (1) enhances a language's learnability, one would expect that in the evolution of a language having both gender classes and declension classes, membership in mixed-gender declension classes should tend to give way to membership in single-gender classes, and multideclensional gender classes should tend to give way to monodeclensional classes. An important goal for future research is that of determining the extent to which this expectation is satisfied among the world's languages.

The expectation does, in fact, seem clearly satisfied in the Romance languages. With the demise of the Latin neuter gender, the membership of the early Romance second declension becomes largely masculine: as a consequence, most second-declension feminines either become masculine (e.g., *fraxinus* "ash tree" > Port. *freixo*) or shift to the first declension (e.g., *amethystus* "amethyst" > Port. *ametista*); both sorts of developments promote greater conformity to principle (1a). Similarly, early Romance exhibits an overall decline in the extent to which nouns belonging to the same gender fall into distinct declensions. For instance, the fourth declension tends to be absorbed by the second declension, so that masculine nouns that were once declensionally distinct become declensionally alike (e.g., acc. pl. *passūs* "steps" but *amīcōs* "friends" > Port. *passos, amigos*); such developments promote greater conformity to principle (1b). At the same time, the longevity of the Latin third declension — whose membership is notoriously heterogeneous in gender — highlights the perennial problem of actuation: what is it that determines whether a declension class with only low conformity to the principles in (1) will undergo or fail to undergo analogical changes promoting greater conformity?

Declension-class membership is, of course, only one of the factors that may serve to determine a noun's gender in some language; thus, Corbett (1991) discusses diverse instances of semantic and phonological determination as well. Logically, any of these means of determining the gender of nouns enhances a language's learnability. Nevertheless, the principles in (1) cannot simply be equated with a more general principle such that a grammar is preferred if a noun's gender can be deduced from its other (morphological, semantic, or phonological) properties. The principles in (1) don't just favor deducibility; they favor a particular manner of deduction. Thus, recall that in Vedic, feminine gender is a default property of *ī*-stem nouns which follow the nonalternating C-stem declension (i.e., of radical and pseudo-radical *ī*-stem nouns); the gender of such nouns is, in Vedic, already predictable, at least by default. What changes in the development from Vedic to

Epic Sanskrit is not the predictability of such nouns' gender, but rather the possibility of predicting their gender from their declension-class membership.

Although the principles in (1) favor the eventual emergence of 'ideal' systems in which gender and declension class are always mutually predictable, this outcome is inevitably thwarted by independent tendencies of language change. For instance, a homogeneous, single-gender declension class may, as an effect of phonological changes, develop into two or more distinct declension classes, or it may merge with a declension class associated with a distinct gender. In these and other ways, one declensional system may be supplanted by another that is comparatively dispreferred by the principles in (1). These principles therefore cannot be seen as constraining every sort of change to which a language's declensional system is subject; rather, they serve more narrowly to determine the direction of analogical influences within that system.

Notes

1. I assume that gender-sensitivity within a single declension is in general minimized by language learners. In particular, I assume that a declension exhibiting a smaller degree of gender-sensitivity is more easily tolerated than one exhibiting a larger degree, and that intradeclensional gender-sensitivity is more easily tolerated in the exponence of a relatively marked morphosyntactic property set than in that of a relatively unmarked set. On this assumption, the masculine and feminine paradigms of śúci- can be seen as embodying the same declension more easily than, e.g., its masculine and neuter paradigms.

2. One might be tempted to claim that the 'i-stem nominals' and 'Nonalternating C-stem nominals' nodes in Figure 2 also specify default feminine gender, and that these defaults just happen to be overridden more often than the default feminine gender specified by the 'Derivative ī-stem nominals' node. But the number of masculine nominals in the i-stem and nonalternating C-stem declensions is of the same order of magnitude as the number of feminine nominals in these declensions, so if feminine gender were specified as the default for i-stem nominals and nonalternating C-stem nominals, overrides of these defaults would essentially be just as frequent as instances of conformity to the defaults; instances of conformity would therefore seemingly have to be learned no less consciously than instances of override. That is, for the language learner, the generalizations expressed by the purported defaults would be spurious, entailing no genuine economy.

3. Adjectival compounds of the analogous sorts do not appear in substantial numbers in the other classes of ī-stem nominals (Macdonell 1910: § 375; Whitney 1889: § 352, § 359, § 367).

4. In investigating these developments, I have devised morphological generation programs in the DATR language (Evans & Gazdar 1996) which make the patterns of inheritance represented in Figures 2–4 fully explicit; see http://www.cs.uky.edu/~gstump/indicfragments/.

References

Bubenik, Vit. 1996. *The Structure and Development of Middle Indo-Aryan Dialects.* Delhi: Motilal Banarsidass.

Burrow, T. 1973. *The Sanskrit Language.* 3rd, revised ed. London: Faber and Faber.

Corbett, Greville G. 1991. *Gender.* Cambridge: Cambridge University Press.

Corbett, Greville G. & Norman M. Fraser. 1993. "Network Morphology: A DATR account of Russian nominal inflection". *Journal of Linguistics* 29.113–142.

Evans, Roger & Gerald Gazdar. 1996. "DATR: A language for lexical knowledge representation". *Computational Linguistics* 22.167–216.

Geiger, Wilhelm. 1943. *Pāli Literature and Language* trans. by Batakrishna Ghosh. [1996 edition. New Delhi: Munshiram Manoharlal.]

Geiger, Wilhelm. 1994. *A Pāli Grammar* trans. by Batakrishna Ghosh, revised and edited by K. R. Norman. Oxford: Pali Text Society.

Macdonell, Arthur Anthony. 1910. *Vedic Grammar* (= *Grundriss der Indo-Arischen Philologie und Altertumskunde*, Band I, Heft 4.). Strassburg: Karl J. Trübner.

Whitney, William Dwight. 1889. *Sanskrit Grammar.* 2nd ed. Cambridge, MA: Harvard University Press.

On the eve of a new paradigm

The current challenges to comparative linguistics in a Kuhnian perspective

Marie-Lucie Tarpent
Mount Saint Vincent University

1. Introduction

1.1 Present position of historical linguistics

A recent and acclaimed textbook in historical linguistics describes the present situation of the field as follows (italics mine):

> More linguists list historical linguistics as one of their areas of specialisation (not necessarily their first or primary area of expertise) than any other subfield of linguistics (with the possible exception of sociolinguistics). That is, it is clear that there are many practising historical linguists, though this may seem to be in contrast to the perception one might get from a look at the lists of required courses in linguistics programmes, from the titles of papers at many professional linguistic conferences, and from the tables of contents of most linguistics journals; *nevertheless, historical linguistics is a major, thriving area of linguistics,* as well it should be, given the role it has played and continues to play in contributing towards the primary goals of linguistics in general.
> (Campbell 1998:2)

The statements contained in this paragraph can lead to a very different conclusion from that intended by its author. In "the lists of courses in linguistics programmes", those on historical linguistics appear more often as electives than as required courses; many linguistics majors will never go further in the subject than a single chapter in their introductory textbook, and even when there is a required historical component to a linguistics programme, it is rare for students to be taking more than one such course.

When there are few courses to be taught, there is little demand for teachers, so that even specialists in historical linguistics often teach mostly in other areas, and there is little incentive for students to choose this field as their area of specialization. Most "professional linguistics conferences" and "linguistics journals" focus on non-historical areas, so that linguists who are not already historicists are rarely aware of what is going on in our field, even when they do express an interest. Finally, when one has to appeal to the past greatness of a field to justify its continuing existence, it is clear that this field is not viewed as the wave of the future. Rather than *major* and *thriving*, historical linguistics today is largely *marginal*, and has been for several decades. As a result, with a few exceptions in the long-established specialties such as Indo-European and its best-known subfamilies, most contemporary linguists are only skimpily trained in historical work, they do not get much opportunity to sharpen their skills in this area through exposure to the work and opinion of their peers, nor to the questioning of their students, and very few of those students are receiving the thorough professional training needed if the work is to continue in the future. Our discipline still exists, and does have many distinguished full-time practitioners, but it survives mostly in the shadow of more prestigious, synchronically-oriented specialties.

1.2   Challenges to the field

If historical linguists are unused to being in the limelight within the discipline of linguistics as a whole, they are even less accustomed to the glare of publicity, in which they were thrust a few years ago after the publication of Greenberg's (1987) *Language in the Americas*. While devastating reviews of the book were published in the major linguistics journals (e.g., Rankin 1992), several wide-circulation magazines ran features on the current linguistic disputes and on the exciting challenges presented by Greenberg, Ruhlen, Shevoroshkin, and the Nostratic school[1] to the conventional wisdom of 'mainstream historical linguistics': Greenberg reduces the 200-odd accepted language families of the Americas to only three; the Nostraticists are relating Indo-European to a variety of language families of the Old World; and Shevoroshkin and his disciples even claim to be able to reconstitute some of the most ancient words of the human race (e.g., Shevoroshkin 1992). Much has been made in the press of remarks such as Campbell's call for Greenberg's classification of American Indian languages to be "shouted down" (Campbell 1986: 488), which has done nothing to enhance the public image of historical linguists; instead of the proud upholders of an unbroken tradition of exacting scholarship, historicists have been seen as diehard conservatives, wedded to outmoded and cumbersome techniques, seething with impotent fury while the young radicals were blazing a trail with a revolutionary new method, easily understood by the average person. Even worse, some of our own colleagues in linguistics and in related fields such as anthropology and archaeology have sometimes expressed sympathy and even admiration for the new approaches. This has been a rude awakening for many historicists, who may justifiably wonder what the future holds for the discipline, and whether potential students will also turn away from them and follow the new gurus.

1.3   A larger perspective

In order to gain some perspective on the situation, it is helpful to consider it in the wider context not only of the history of linguistics, but also of the history of science. By now most linguists have at least heard about Thomas Kuhn's *The Structure of Scientific Revolutions* (1970 [1962]), in which he proposes a new model to describe the process by which science evolves. Even though the model may not apply in every detail to every situation, its broad outlines provide a structured framework for analyzing specific cases such as that of historical linguistics. Seen in this larger perspective, the current challenges to the discipline can be seen as part of the growing pains to be expected at certain stages in the evolution of a scientific field.

2.   Kuhn's model of the life-cycle of scientific theories

Kuhn showed that what is commonly called scientific progress is not the linear, orderly, step-by-step process most of us have been taught to believe in; rather, science progresses through a series of cycles, each characterized by a specific 'paradigm', a body of knowledge including both theory and practice, which defines the domain of the discipline, shapes its major research questions, and prescribes the types of procedures it may follow. A very interesting part of Kuhn's model is that it considers not just the intellectual and technical aspects, but also the concomitant social aspects, as the characteristics of different stages in the evolution of a paradigm tend to attract researchers with similar characteristics, and the emergence of a new paradigm often faces bitter opposition from 'the establishment'.

While the cycles of the paradigm may be of greater or shorter duration, they follow a predictable pattern in three stages:

– *stage 1: trailblazing.* A paradigm arising from an original hypothesis wins over a significant group of members of a field by addressing questions hitherto neglected or poorly answered, both by the earlier paradigm and by competing hypotheses. This is a vigorous, optimistic period of growth and expansion, as creative scientists, mostly young and enthusiastic, are drawn to the explanatory power of the new hypothesis and explore its potential applications to yet more unsolved or unsuspected problems. Each problem solved provides new grounds to adopt the new approach, and the paradigm gains adherents. As time goes on, natural attrition removes the defenders of the earlier paradigm, and the new one emerges triumphant.

–   *stage 2: consolidation, establishment:* The scientific community, confident in its past achievement and future potential, is united by a singleness of purpose in its adherence to the paradigm, which is now the standard foundation, presented in textbooks, in which all new students are trained. Most scientific work at this stage consists of articulating the implications of the original concept, and discovering the full extension of its range by testing and experimenting within the paradigm. Any adjustments necessary in order to apply it to a greater variety of problems seem minor in the context of the achievements it has already led to. In this mature phase, diverse personalities are able to flourish and to contribute to the development of the field: the paradigm channels creativity within its guidelines, which are still flexible enough to leave a large part to hypothesis and imagination.

Eventually, though, the time comes when the paradigm is nearing the limits of its applicability; as most of the problems to which it was designed to apply have been solved, more difficult ones come to the fore as the next area of research. However, scientists increasingly face situations where the paradigm cannot be applied, or only through more and more awkward and complicated adjustments. In time, some scientists, especially the younger ones, have difficulty retaining a belief in the existing paradigm, and start searching elsewhere, while those whose own achievements have been tied to the success of the paradigm continue to adhere to it, believing that almost any problems in the field can be solved through faithfulness to the paradigm, and that other problems are either uninteresting or simply unsolvable.

–   *stage 3: rigidity and breakdown:* The last stage begins with a period of chaos and disarray as the existing paradigm is increasingly recognized as no longer satisfactory; some scientists now openly reject the paradigm and propose bold alternatives, while others cling desperately to the security of the old paradigm and reject any attempts at changing or even questioning the hallowed tradition handed down from the great pioneers of the past. As the old paradigm is increasingly challenged or rejected, there can be a multiplicity of competing theories, each vying to become the new paradigm. The turmoil will eventually die down as one of these theories triumphs, and the competitors are forgotten, as a new paradigm emerges in a 'scientific revolution'.

In every such revolution, the successful theory has two important characteristics: first, it begins by addressing and solving problems which had been ignored or neglected by the old paradigm; second, it is also able to incorporate the positive results achieved within the old paradigm, together with solving some new problems. Its success will attract more and more of the younger scientists, as well as those of the older generation who for one reason or another are not committed to the older paradigm. As the generations change, the old paradigm loses its last practitioners, and the cycle repeats until the new paradigm, now entrenched, becomes obsolete in its turn and is replaced by another.[2]

3.   Historical linguistics in a Kuhnian perspective

Many linguists have seen the relevance of Kuhn's model of scientific history to the recent history of linguistics: for instance, the phrase 'Chomskyan revolution' has been commonplace for a number of years, even if not all linguists agree that the influence of Chomsky's work truly merits the name of revolution (if we adopt one of Kuhn's criteria, namely, what model is presented as standard in student text-books, it is clear that pre-Chomskyan syntax rarely qualifies as suitable training for students today). In any case, it is difficult to deny that a major paradigm shift had earlier taken place in linguistics when the historical or diachronic orientation typical of the nineteenth century was largely replaced by the synchronic orientation typical of the twentieth century. As another century emerges, we are once again in a period of intellectual upheaval which may herald yet another revolution.

3.1   The nineteenth century

Let us go back then to the origins of the first scientific paradigm in Western linguistics. The beginning of linguistics as a science is usually traced to the famous statement by Sir William Jones, made in 1786, and repeated in practically all linguistics textbooks. The systematic exploration of the implications of the hypothesis of a common ancestor "which perhaps no longer exists" is what differentiated nineteenth century linguistic research from the more amateurish pursuits of an earlier period. No doubt the idea was not accepted by all scholars when it was first presented, but the possibility of reconstructing the common ancestor through the study of existing languages fired the imagination of a significant number of linguistic scholars, who became united in the pursuit of this goal.

The paradigm took some decades to develop, as did the techniques of the discipline. A major advance signalling the maturity of the discipline was the hypothesis of exceptionlessness of linguistic 'laws', which must be as precise as those being discovered in physics or chemistry. The English term 'Neo-Grammarian' fails to convey the excitement of the original name 'Junggrammatiker' adopted by those young scholars which saw themselves as creating a true science by rejecting the looser, less systematic principles of their older colleagues. At a time when the various sciences were accumulating discovery upon discovery, the historical approach to language was the only scientifically valid one, because it was the only one which rested upon a scientific paradigm, with its founding hypothesis, its corollary assumptions, and its own methods. The linguistics of those days was in the forefront of scientific thought, even influencing other sciences, and impressing other scholarly branches with the rigor of its methods.[3]

Yet it was in part this very success which caused the beginning of the decline of the discipline and resulted in the first scientific revolution in linguistics, with the shift from a diachronic to a synchronic approach in the twentieth century. Ferdinand de Saussure had been a brilliant young scholar, starting his career with a spectacular achievement at the height of the Neo-Grammarian period, yet he ultimately became dissatisfied with the diachronic paradigm, in which the focus of research was being more and more circumscribed, and meticulousness had replaced the earlier enthusiasm and questioning. While most other linguists were increasingly concerned with smaller and smaller details, and appeared "unaware of what they were doing" in theoretical terms, Saussure set out to investigate the properties of language from a different point of view, by considering the overall system revealed by a synchronic approach. It was this new and original approach, bolstered also by late nineteenth century studies of contemporary phenomena such as phonetics, and of languages with unwritten traditions such as those of the Americas, which eventually resulted in a new linguistic paradigm, with its own theoretical assumptions, types of data, and methods of research.

3.2   The twentieth century

3.2.1 *Two complementary but unequal paradigms*
With the paradigm shift in the twentieth century, historical linguistics has not disappeared, since synchronic linguistics has not been able to supplant it in its own domain, nor to incorporate it into a single, panchronic theory. In fact, there have been two paradigms, to some extent complementary, but by no means equal in terms of intellectual prestige and contribution to the development of the discipline of linguistics. For several decades all students of linguistics have been trained primarily if not exclusively in synchrony, and while the synchronic paradigm has gone through considerable evolution and renewal (and even revolution according to some estimates of Chomsky's role), the diachronic paradigm has remained basically that of the Neo-Grammarians. Cross-fertilization has been minimal. Of course, the diachronic paradigm has never outlived its usefulness for the type of problems it was designed to handle, and the power of its methods was demonstrated anew by their successful application to new sets of languages, starting most dramatically with the reconstruction of Proto-Algonquian (where the obstacles were not so much technical linguistic ones as preconceived ideas about the need of a written tradition). In so far as there are still many proto-languages to reconstruct in the world, and many unsolved problems within Indo-European and other well-known groupings, there is still plenty of room for the application of the diachronic paradigm as handed down from our predecessors.

3.2.2 *Marginalization of the diachronic paradigm and its consequences*
However, since diachronic studies have been overshadowed by synchronic studies, especially by formal theoretical preoccupations, historical linguistics has in fact lost

ground by standing still: the diminished diachronic community has tended to close ranks and to rest on its past glory, continuing in the footsteps of its revered predecessors, but rejecting most attempts to go beyond the paradigm established by them. Again, it is not that this paradigm has become outdated, or is inherently incapable of further development, but that it is less and less well mastered. Within the traditional historical subfields, principles and methods are so well-established that their theoretical underpinnings are rarely questioned, or even explicitly stated (cf. Lass 1997: 4–8) while outside of these fields, for instance in the Amerindian domain, many linguists (cf. Campbell quotation above) attempt to 'do' historical linguistics with inadequate understanding of those principles or training in those methods (cf. valid criticisms in, e.g., Greenberg 1987; Ruhlen 1994; but also Nichols 1992; Newman 1995). It is one thing to have spent a semester or two being taken through earlier scholars' reconstructions of, say, Proto-Indo-European or Proto-Finno-Ugric; it is quite another to attempt reconstruction oneself in a language family, let alone a larger grouping, with limited tools, where little or no prior historical scholarship is available or reliable. The diachronic paradigm is a difficult one which requires much time and application for its mastery, and in the present linguistic climate, few linguists have had the opportunity to devote themselves to acquiring this mastery, and to be guided in the process by a master.

Consider the question of relatedness between languages: two or more languages are related because they descend from a common ancestor, and it is reconstruction of the common ancestor which proves relatedness. But very few historical linguists bother to state what factors lead to the *hypothesis* that any two or more languages have a common ancestor, and that therefore it is appropriate to attempt reconstruction: most textbooks in historical linguistics do not mention this as a potential problem (e.g., Campbell 1998; Bynon 1977; Hock & Joseph 1996; Sihler 2000, to name a few). Of course, when some languages are so structurally as well as lexically similar that the question of distinguishing between language and dialect might well arise, genetic relationship can be taken for granted, but it is important to be explicitly aware of all the requisite criteria when dealing with the possibility of even slightly more distant relationships, or venturing into the uncharted waters of long-range proposals.

In fact, the very foundations of comparative linguistics were already stated very clearly in Sir William Jones' statement: consideration of structural resemblances (meaning mostly morphology), individual grammatical morphemes, and similar lexical items, in that order.[4] These were not so much meant to be applied *within* families such as Romance or Germanic, in which the genetic relationships had always been obvious to the most casual observer, as to relationships *between* such families, i.e., to what were then 'distant relationships'. But because lexical/phonological comparison makes up a large part of a historical linguist's work within the accepted paradigm, it is easy to forget about the importance of morphology, or to treat it as just an adjunct rather than a logical preliminary to lexical comparison.[5] This approach makes it practically impossible for the would-be historicist to go beyond the obvious cases and to entertain the possibility of more distant relationships, where the best evidence of relatedness often resides in relic morphs and irregular patterns. Indeed some linguists are even reluctant to consider morphological clues to potential relationships, because "they could be due to borrowing", although this possibility does not stop them from considering vocabulary, which is far more susceptible to borrowing.

Among the techniques of the comparative method, none is better-known than the search for regular correspondences. Linguists whose training has consisted largely of engaging in this search in closely related languages (where there are large numbers of cognates differing only in a few non-identical sounds), and of performing shallow-level lexical reconstruction, are out of their depth when faced with comparing languages with few shared resemblant forms; yet they cling to the only technique they know, in fear of "diluting the rigor of the comparative method" by going even slightly beyond what they have been taught. In the virtual absence of other grounds for relatedness, the search for phonological correspondences means an overemphasis on shared vocabulary to the detriment of morphological structure, even though it is well-known that languages sharing vocabulary through prior contact may have large numbers of apparent cognates showing regular sound correspondences, without being closely related (e.g., the large numbers of Old French loanwords in English could suggest 'Proto-Anglo-French' to the uninitiated; cf. Tarpent & Kendall 1998 for an analogous Amerindian example). This overemphasis on the comparison of lexical items also leads to endless agonizing over problems of "acceptability" or "leeway" in semantic or phonological correspondences, which would not occur nearly as often were the languages already demonstrably related on other grounds. And while sound correspondences may be the stated focus of comparison, consideration of lexical items one at a time in an alphabetical English list (e.g., *arm, arrow, bat, bee, boy,* etc.), rather than grouped according to phonological criteria, paradoxically often causes neglect of actual phonological correspondences, which may go unrecognized if they are not 'inspectionally obvious'.

In the Amerindian domain, where many specialists in the languages have been trained more often in anthropology than in historical methods, the question of genetic affiliation of most language families to each other is still open. If 'the comparative method' has not been able to do more in this area than confirm groupings which were already obvious even to relatively untrained persons more than a hundred years ago (Newman 1995), it is not because the method is largely inapplicable across the diversity of the language families, as the comparativists are saying,[6] nor because it is not needed for higher-level groupings, as Greenberg and Ruhlen's practice[7] implies, but because it has not often been applied to its fullest extent except within the individual families.[8] For more distant relationships, insisting that any proposal for considering two or more language families related should first be addressed through the use of 'the comparative method', mistakenly understood simply as as lexical and phonological comparison leading to reconstruction, is putting the cart before the horse, by requiring the reconstruction of individual lexical items before a hypothesis of relatedness has been supported adequately by other evidence. In the evaluation of proposals for even larger groupings such as Sapir's (1929) Amerindian 'phyla', the emphasis on lexical reconstruction at too early a stage, and the resulting predictable failure, discourages considering or developing other tools, especially non-lexical, for generating or testing hypotheses of less obvious relationship, and for clearing the ground for the eventual application of the comparative method where appropriate (cf. Tarpent 1997).

In all these cases, the problem is not the diachronic paradigm: it is much more the insecurity linked to incomplete understanding and control of the paradigm, both of its principles and of its methods. In any field, whether technical, athletic, artistic, intellectual, or any other, inadequate mastery of the relevant techniques leads to insecurity and to the fear of losing control: on the contrary, it is full control of a technique that makes creativity possible, and that gives the security and confidence needed to adjust to circumstances, to improve the technique if possible, and to take calculated risks. In an intellectual field, such risks include exploring fully the implications of different hypotheses, but incomplete mastery of the techniques, and lack of full understanding of the principles behind them, prevent creative scholarship except with the most obvious data.

3.3 Current challenges: Can we extend, or go beyond, the 19th century paradigm?

3.3.1 *Strength and perhaps limits of the old paradigm*
The nineteenth century diachronic paradigm allowed inference and reconstruction from first-order linguistic groupings (obvious families) to a second-order entity (e.g., PIE); much work still needs to be done *within* this paradigm, including using the comparative method appropriately, concentrating on its possibilities rather than its perceived limitations, including the identification of many non-obvious groupings throughout the world, and the reconstruction of their proto-languages.

The next goal then is eventually to reach a third order (e.g., identifying sisters to PIE and reconstructing the proto-proto-language), and even higher. But the very possibility of a third order is denied by many 'mainstreamers' for whom PIE and similar constructs appear as the very limits of the field, in spite of the fact that, for instance, the concept of 'Nostratic' was first proposed by Pedersen (1962 [1931]), one of the acknowledged masters of the Neo-Grammarian tradition. However, the appeal of going beyond the traditional paradigm or of finding exciting alternatives to it is always irresistible to some personalities.

3.3.2 Two vocal groups of challengers

The current challenges to the paradigm are coming from two opposite directions, but the goal of the two groups of challengers is the same: to find a way to go beyond the apparent limits of the historical paradigm, in order to investigate what are hypothesized as 'distant genetic relationships', which conservative opinion considers to be beyond the range of the comparative method. In other words, either to extend the paradigm, or to find a new paradigm. Both of these groups have recently come into open and public conflict with 'mainstream historical linguists'.

One group which we might call "reformers" seeks to extend the reach of the paradigm from within: this group includes the Nostraticists, many of whom have indeed been trained in the full version of the paradigm and in the subfield it was first applied to. But since such extension is discouraged or rejected by the "conservatives" in the profession, this research tends to be in the hands of the more adventurous among the 'reformers', detracting from their overall credibility even though they claim to use traditional methods. We might call the second group 'iconoclasts', who, in rejecting a simplified and rigid version which they appear to confuse with the actual paradigm, are trying for nth-order language groupings ('Amerind') and even ultimate reconstruction (the 'Mother Tongue' or 'Proto-World') even though many second-order groupings (on the order of Sapir's 'phyla') are still not established, or even considered possible (cf. fn. 6), let alone higher-order groupings. In the pursuit of this goal, they use simplistic methods which are a throwback to the period before the development of the historical paradigm.

The contradictions of such approaches, especially the second one, reflect and magnify some of the problems of the field today: it is revealing that both groups appear to be so influenced by the focus on lexical comparison and reconstruction, caused by a misunderstanding of the principles of the paradigm that they attempt immediate reconstruction of lexical items even when, like Greenberg and Ruhlen, they claim to reject traditional methods and to pursue different classificatory goals.[9]

3.4 The twenty-first century: Towards a new historical paradigm

Rising from the present confused situation, a new paradigm is likely to come from non-traditional directions rather than simply be a continuation of the present paradigm. The successful paradigm will not reject the achievements of its predecessors (including the true 'comparative method'), but incorporate them: this means that the current 'iconoclasts' are unlikely to provide the next paradigm. Although it would be risky to try to predict the new direction, there are some things that even mainstream linguists can pay attention to in order not to lose sight of the nature and genuine achievements of the current paradigm, and in order to make sure that their students are aware of them.

3.4.1 A scientific attitude

The discipline of historical linguistics developed at a time which saw considerable development in all current branches of science, and linguistic pioneers were very conscious of practicing a form of science. There is a need to emphasize the components of a genuinely scientific (not merely technical) attitude.

An indispensable feature of a scientific attitude is an open mind, a willingness to entertain hypotheses (cf. Newman 1995) and explore all their implications in a principled and systematic manner (cf. Tarpent 1997). The diffident attitude *If you allow X, you are opening the door to ...* effectively closes the door to potentially valuable research for fear of undesirable results which may not materialize, while the person who says *Let's see what happens if we allow X* remains open to discovery with full control and without prejudging the results. There is a well-known example of this in the history of mathematics, where for more than two thousand years there was a foundational axiom that nobody dared question: *parallels never meet.* At some point two mathematicians decided to explore the heretical hypothesis: *what if parallels were to meet? in one point? in two points?* The implications of these hypotheses, pursued with the same rigorous methods as had been used to establish the axiom, eventually led not to the collapse of geometry, but to a new, more inclusive geometry in which the axiom is a special case.

We must be willing to entertain and test hypotheses, but we also need to keep in mind the difference between hypothesis, support, and proof: for instance, standards of proof appropriate to the judicial system (where decisions are of the utmost practical consequences) are often required of the proponents of distant relationships, rather than scientific standards of support for likely hypotheses (Newman 1995). Insistence on proof rather than support, even at early stages of research, tends to discourage pursuit of the implications of hypotheses which might be promising but require long and patient research in order to accumulate pertinent evidence for them.

3.4.2 Technical considerations

In the mature, establishment stage of a paradigm, the foundations of a discipline are often taken for granted; for example, Indo-Europeanists need no longer bother to explain why they consider their languages related. In a period of upheaval, the foundations need to be reexamined. Since determination of relatedness is crucial to the comparative enterprise, and many groupings are still undetermined, we should insist on using explicit and independent (not circular) criteria for relatedness, so as to have a principled basis for hypothesizing relatedness even in non-obvious cases.

If reconstruction is logically the last step, not the first, in language comparison, then preliminary steps become important: some directions which are currently being explored will probably remain useful:

– general principles of language organization and change: better knowledge of typology, of substantive and implicational universals, of grammaticalization, to name a few, should reinforce historical work; so should better knowledge of the conditions and results of language contact and language transfer, as well as social variation;

– a scientific comparative approach need not be limited to the specific techniques of 'the comparative method', i.e., morphological and lexical comparison: we can additionally consider a variety of possible clues to common ancestry even if a relationship is not obvious from superficial observation. For instance, Nichols' global approach (1992, 1993), looking for characteristics which might survive when most other traces of relationship have been obscured by evolution, is likely to be of more lasting impact than the challengers' attempts at immediate reconstruction; clues to unsuspected relationships might yet be discovered, opening new avenues of more traditional research;

– much work can be done at the intermediate level between the 'inspectionally obvious' and the global; there is an especially pressing need to pay attention to morphology when investigating proposed relationships. Sapir's Amerindian 'phyla' (1929) are examples of proposals which were largely based on general morphological structure (rather than simply typology); such features might be areal, but they might also be survivals, hence suggest relationships worth researching even if the proposal is not acceptable in its entirety.[10]

Whichever direction new research may take, methods must be rigorous in the testing of hypotheses, but methods should be retained, modified, or developed according to the tasks to be done: there is no point in restricting ourselves in advance to a single method or interpretation of a method. There is also a difference between method (which has a scientific basis) and technique (which should be justified by the principles of the method), and a rigorous method does not necessarily mean a rigid, unchanging set of techniques.

3.4.3 *Other hopeful factors*

Among other hopeful factors, we should not discount the avid public interest in the past; in addition to the material past uncovered by archaeology and paleontology, which is reported in a growing number of popular publications, the general public is also very interested in the linguistic past, and the fact that the press reports and cites the work not only of Greenberg, Ruhlen, and Shevoroshkin but also of Nichols, shows that the public is eager for information, and not just for sensational information, on the topic of the origins of languages and of the people that speak them, in marked contrast to the decided lack of interest in the contortions of modern synchronic theory. This interest should bring in future students, and this should lead to more courses offered, more extensive programs, and ultimately a greater critical mass of properly trained scholars.

Even though some students' interests might be sparked by sensational but unsupported claims, the better students will eventually recognize the chaotic and unpredictable nature of what they are presented with, and will set themselves to introduce some order through the rediscovery or reinvention of a form of the comparative method. The time will come when *tik, pal,* and *maliq'a* will join *sal, ber, yon,* and *rosh* in the virtual museum of linguistic curiosities, just as the *phlogiston* and the *philosopher's stone* are now relegated to the museum of chemical curiosities.

4. Towards a panchronic linguistics

If historical linguistics is currently marginal within linguistics as a whole, a needed revitalization through renewed interest from outside and renewed attention to principles from inside should raise its profile, and lead ultimately to a reconciliation of the two branches. There are already some meeting grounds between synchrony and diachrony within linguistic theory. The generative approach to phonology and morphophonemics has contributed to some extent to blurring the distinction between synchrony and diachrony. While phonology is currently theoretically divided, a renewed emphasis on the notion of *system* and attention to patterns of change within systems should eventually reconcile short-term generative approaches with the needed long-range view. Sociolinguistics, a theoretically-unbiased field, has already contributed much to the understanding of the conditions of change. The current interest in morphology within linguistic theory is also a hopeful sign for more careful attention to morphology in the diachronic field. And while most scholars keep their synchronic and diachronic interests separate, a few insist on the necessity of keeping together these two aspects of the same linguistic reality (cf. Hagège & Haudricourt 1978; Burling 1992; Lass 1997).

Encouraged by the long-range view afforded by the Kuhnian model, I see the present crisis, not as the beginning of the end for historical linguistics, but as heralding a new beginning, and I am confident that the chaotic period we are going through will eventually result in the emergence of yet another paradigm, uniting the diachronic and synchronic branches.

Notes

1. Cf. this definition by Aharon Dolgopolsky, one of the most influential proponents of Nostratic: "Nostratic is a hypothetical macrofamily of languages which includes Indo-European, Hamito-

Semitic, Kartvelian, Uralic, Altaic [including Korean and Japanese], and Dravidian" (quoted in Fleming 1999:418; I omit specific language details within families). There are "other versions of that grand hypothesis" (Fleming 418), the best-known of which are those of Illič-Svityč and Bomhard.

2. Kuhn has been criticized, in my opinion unfairly, for implying that the appeal of competing paradigms is largely subjective, and therefore there is no such thing as scientific progress through the succession of paradigms. While subjectivity may play a part in the acceptance of a paradigm by individual scientists, the intellectual content and objective achievements of the paradigm are what matter for the discipline as a whole.

3. E.g., this quotation from Darwin: "The formation of different languages and of distinct species, and the proofs that both have been developed through a gradual process, are curiously parallel" (1871, quoted in Ruhlen 1994:262).

4. Cf. Nichols' description of the 'standard comparative-historical method' (1992:312). It is relevant to the thesis of this paper that Nichols felt the need to append to a book addressed to a linguist audience a section explaining what the method is and is not.

5. Cf. Nichols: "Lexical comparison has been the primary occupation of Indo-Europeanists for two centuries ... and this has led to the frequent use of the term 'comparative method' to refer only to the lexical comparison.... Perhaps this is why the same term is sometimes used to describe research that uses only lexical comparison, assuming any resemblant vocabulary is cognate but operating without a theory of grounds for assuming relatedness, and producing lexical 'reconstructions' without embedding them in grammatical accidence" (1992:312). See also Silverstein: "'There has been an unfortunate ... tendency in Amerindian linguistics, particularly debilitating in problems of remote relationship ... to see phonetic (i.e., phonemic) correspondences and the establishment of 'sound laws' using isolated lexical forms as something different from, or discontinuous with, or even opposed to consideration of morphosyntax" (1979:672).

6. E.g., Golla, claiming to present "the voice of mainstream historical linguistics" in a column defending the "conservative" classification of North American languages into 60-odd families: A "language family is either obvious — a skein of regular sound correspondences knitting together hundreds of etymologies and allowing unambiguous reconstructions in a rich morphological schema — or it is forever dubious" (1997:19). Such a picture fits an obvious, first-order family such as Germanic or Sahaptian, not a second-order one like Indo-European, some branches of which have not always been obvious even to specialists. The assumption that families, even second-order ones, should be immediately obvious, and reconstruction easy to do, is another fallacy resulting from misunderstanding of historical materials and methods. Cf. also Newman (1995).

7. Even though Greenberg and Ruhlen seem to imply that they are practicing the comparative method (e.g., Ruhlen 1997:passim; cf. also Rankin 1992), their reliance on unsystematized superficial similarities as providing proof of higher-level relatedness through "mass lexical comparison" bypasses all but the most elementary levels of linguistic comparison.

8. A prominent exception is Algic (Algonquian plus Yurok and Wiyot), but not every group has been studied by giants such as Bloomfield and Sapir.

9. E.g., Ruhlen's list of 2000-plus 'phonetic glosses' for Greenberg's Amerind "etymologies" (1994:135–155). Even though the term 'reconstructed form' is avoided, it seems that these forms, starred in other contexts, are intended as proto-language forms, e.g., "Nostratic *mene 'walk, step', Amerind *mina 'to go'" (228).

10. Cf. Tarpent (1997). The Penutian phylum, which had been looking less and less promising, is being taken more seriously even though its internal structure needs to be reorganized. What Silverstein says about Dixon & Kroeber's 1918 California Penutian also applies to some extent to

Sapir's enlarged Penutian 'phylum': even though ostensibly D & K's "grouping of languages was reached principally on the basis of counting lexical resemblances (and ... rather chaotic sound correspondences ...) ... [i]t seems clear ... that D & K's intuitions about the deep similarity of Penutian grammatical structures, based on years of typological investigation ... were probably decisive in their conclusions". (Silverstein 1979:651–652). Sapir's notes on lexical resemblances are full of gross errors, but his typological/morphological characterizations, based on a wide acquaintance with languages, are much more accurate.

References

Burling, Robbins. 1992. *Patterns of Language: Structure, variation, change*. San Diego: Academic Press.

Bynon, Theodora. 1977. *Historical Linguistics*. Cambridge: Cambridge University Press.

Campbell, Lyle. 1986. Comments on Greenberg, Turner & Zegura, *The Settlement of the Americas: A comparison of the linguistic, dental and genetic evidence*. *Current Anthropology* 27: 5.477–497.

Campbell, Lyle. 1998. *Historical Linguistics: An introduction*. Cambridge, MA & London: MIT Press.

Fleming, Harold. 1999. Review of *The Nostratic Macrofamily and Linguistic Palaeontology* by Aharon Dolgopolsky and of *Indo-European, Nostratic, and Beyond: Festschrift for Vitalij V. Shevoroshkin* ed. by I. Hegedűs, P. Michalove, & A. Manaster Ramer. *Anthropological Linguistics* 41: 3.417–426.

Golla, Victor. 1997. "Interplay of Language History and Typology in the Americas". *Anthropology Newsletter*. Arlington, VA: American Anthropological Association. 38: 2.18–19.

Greenberg, Joseph. 1987. *Language in the Americas*. Stanford: Stanford University Press.

Hagège, Claude & André Haudricourt. 1978. *La phonologie panchronique: Comment les sons changent dans les langues*. Paris: Presses Universitaires de France.

Hock, Hans Henrich & Brian D. Joseph. 1996. *Language History, Language Change and Language Relationship: An introduction to historical and comparative linguistics*. Berlin & New York: Mouton de Gruyter.

Kuhn, Thomas. 1970 [1962]. *The Structure of Scientific Revolutions*. 2nd ed. Chicago: University of Chicago Press.

Lass, Roger. 1997. *Historical Linguistics and Language Change*. (= *Cambridge Studies in Linguistics*, 81.) Cambridge: Cambridge University Press.

Newman, Paul. 1995. *On Being Right: Greenberg's African linguistic classification and the methodological principles which underlie it*. Bloomington: Indiana University Press.

Nichols, Johanna. 1992. *Language Diversity in Space and Time*. Chicago: University of Chicago Press.

Nichols, Johanna. 1993. "Diachronically Stable Structural Features". *Historical Linguistics 1993: Selected papers from the 12th International Conference on Historical Linguistics* (= *Current Issues in Linguistic Theory*, 124) ed. by Henning Andersen, 337–355. Amsterdam & Philadelphia: John Benjamins.

Pedersen, Holger. 1962 [1931]. *The Discovery of Language: Linguistic Science in the 19th Century* (= *Midland Books*, 40) translated by J. W. Spargo. Bloomington, IN: Indiana University Press.

Rankin, Robert. 1992. Review of Greenberg 1987. *International Journal of American Linguistics* 58: 3.324–351.

Ruhlen, Merritt. 1994. *On the Origins of Languages: Studies in linguistic taxonomy*. Stanford: Stanford University Press.

Sapir, Edward. 1929. "Central and North American Languages". *Encyclopedia Britannica*, 14th ed. Vol. 5, 138–141. [Rept. in *Selected Writings of Edward Sapir in Language, Culture and Personality* ed. by David G. Mandelbaum, 169–178. Berkeley & Los Angeles: University of California Press, 1949.]

Shevoroshkin, Vitaly. 1992. *The Mother Tongue*. Reading, MA: Addison-Wesley-Longman.

Sihler, Andrew. 2000. *Language History*. (= *Current Issues in Linguistic Theory*, 191.) Amsterdam & Philadelphia: John Benjamins.

Silverstein, Michael. 1979. "Penutian: An assessment". *The Languages of Native America: Historical and comparative assessment* ed. by Lyle Campbell & Marianne Mithun, 650–691. Austin: University of Texas Press.

Tarpent, Marie-Lucie. 1997. "Tsimshianic and Penutian: Problems, methods, results and implications". *International Journal of American Linguistics* 63: 1.65–112.

Tarpent, Marie-Lucie & Daythal Kendall. 1998. "On the Relationship between Takelma and Kalapuyan: Another look at 'Takelman'". Paper presented at the Winter meeting of the Society for the Study of the Indigenous Languages of the Americas (SSILA), at Linguistic Society of America meeting, New York, January 1998.

Modeling koineization

Donald N. Tuten
Emory University

1. Introduction

In recent decades, research focusing on the effects of language contact has led to ever more precise delimitation of the conditions and processes associated with different types of contact. Pidginization and creolization are perhaps the most thoroughly investigated of these, but others have been suggested as well (e.g., the work of Thomason & Kaufman 1988). The study of contact between unrelated language varieties has also led to increased interest in the effects of contact between related language varieties or dialects. While dialect contact has long been used by language historians to explain anomalous changes, only recently has it come to be seen as potentially significant for the explanation of more regular changes. Different types of dialect contact have been identified (Trudgill 1986), and among the most important of these is koineization, or the formation of a new dialect as a result of dialect mixing. Here I review and critique two frequently-cited versions of the model of koineization, Siegel (1985) and Trudgill (1986), and offer suggestions for refining the model.[1] These suggested changes lead in turn to a questioning of the widely-held view of koineization as mere reduction to a 'least common denominator'. Using the development of the marked feature of *leísmo* in Peninsular Spanish, I argue that koineization can also lead to the introduction of novel features not found in any of the established contributing dialects. I conclude by stipulating the components of a well-constructed explanation of change based on the model of koineization outlined here.

2. Siegel's model of koineization

Siegel (1985) begins with an enlightening review and critique of the many meanings that have been assigned to the term *koine*, including though not limited to: a mixed variety, a reduced and simplified variety, a lingua franca, and a standard. In seeking a technical definition of the term, he suggests that there is no way of identifying a koine without looking at its historical development; as a result, the term *koine* can only be used technically as a shorthand reference to any variety that has undergone the process of koineization. Siegel therefore moves to define a model of koineization, which he bases on the stage-based model of pidginization proposed by Mühlhäusler (1980). In Siegel's model, the stages of koineization neatly parallel those of pidginization, as illustrated in Table 1 (taken from Siegel 1985:374).

Table 1. Developmental continua of pidgins and koines

Process	Stage of development	
	Pidginization	Koineization
Initial Contact	prepidgin (jargon)	prekoine
Stabilization	stabilized pidgin	stabilized koine
Expansion	expanded pidgin	expanded koine
Nativization	creole	nativized koine

This proposal seems eminently reasonable, since pidgins, creoles, and koines all result from language contact and demographic mixing, and they are often found in similar colonial or post-colonial regions. However, there are good reasons to question the close association between pidginization and koineization. First, pidgins are generally understood to result from contact between typologically distant varieties, while koines result from contact between linguistic subsystems that are to some degree mutually comprehensible.[2] Since speakers in a koineizing context can usually understand each other, the need to communicate clearly — which clearly plays a key role in pidginization — cannot be the primary motive for alterations in speaker production.[3] Second, and more importantly, in pidginization/creolization speaker-learners are deprived of contact with native speakers of the language and/or of input for learning, even as they must try to use the target variety to communicate with its native speakers or, more importantly, use a new intermediate variety to communicate with others with whom a common language is not shared (Thomason & Kaufman 1988:174–175). In koineization, however, speakers have frequent contact with each other and thus to abundant though highly variable input.

As a result, it becomes difficult to accept Siegel's 1985 claim that both pidginization and koineization are characterized not only by mixing and simplification, but also by reduction (or impoverishment). Siegel borrows Mühlhäusler's (1980:21) definitions of simplification — "an increase in regularity or a decrease in markedness" — and reduction — "a decrease in the referential or non-referential potential of the language". But while simplification is indeed a linguistic process of koineization, reduction cannot be, for reduction as defined here refers to the extreme structural reduction of pidgins, which makes full comprehension difficult or impossible outside of contexts of direct oral communication, where gestures, intonation and the possibility of clarification substitute for structural complexity. Since learners in a koineizing situation are not deprived of input, there is no logical reason for extreme reduction to occur.[4]

If this is so, there is then no need for the stage of structural expansion. Siegel identifies this third stage with "informal standardization" (from Moag 1979) or the use of the koine as a literary or standard language.[5] The inclusion of standardization within the model is not entirely unwarranted, for it reflects a frequent reality: koines tend to be selected as standards, since standards also require the decrease in variation that characterizes koines. However, while standardization does include a process of elaboration of the lexicon and syntax, particularly of written language (Haugen 1966: 933), this is not the same as expansion in creolization, which refers primarily to an increase in morphological complexity. Moreover, standardization may enter into competition with koineization. For instance, Fontanella (1992: 42–54) argues that in the history of American varieties of Spanish, standardization has sometimes impeded koineization, as in the interior of Mexico, and sometimes reversed its effects, as in Buenos Aires.[6]

Another problem with the parallel models of pidginization and koineization is the timing and significance of nativization. In pidginization this marks the final stage in which the pidgin is converted into a creole. Siegel, aware that exact parallelism is not possible here, points out that nativization can occur at any stage of koineization. By doing so, however, he ignores the potential significance of child learning. In fact, nativization may be very important to selection of features and the stabilization or focusing of a koine (Mesthrie 1994: 1866). Petrini (1988: 42), for example, argues that the developing koine or pre-koine of the Italian region of Ticino has so far failed to stabilize because there are no native speakers of this variety (see below for further discussion of acquisition).[7]

Now, Siegel's understanding of koineization has certainly not remained static since the publication of his 1985 article. Indeed, in later publications, he has incorporated many aspects of Trudgill's work into his own approach (Siegel 1993), and he too has discussed the differences between koineization and creolization that I highlight here (e.g., Siegel 1995), but such reformulations have not led to a reevaluation of the original stage-based model (still frequently cited in the literature, but without full awareness of its implications[8]). The adherence to the pidginization paradigm which underpins Siegel's model may reflect his particular experience studying Fiji Hindi and other post-colonial language varieties, since some of these varieties appear to show the interaction of koineization with other processes. For example, Siegel himself (1988: 196) points out that one of the contributing varieties of Fiji Hindi was itself a pidgin, so we should not be surprised to find some effects of pidginization in the resultant koine (also suggested by Trudgill 1986: 106).

Of course, the challenge to defining koineization is the necessity of distilling a simplified theoretical model from very complex cases of real change. Nevertheless, Siegel's discussion, though partially in need of revision, represents a first systematic description of such a model, and from it we can retain useful insights, including the concept of pre-koine, or the highly variable initial stage of demographic and dialect mixing; the concept of stabilization, which refers to the process of focusing or establishment of new norms, and, most important, the definition of contributing varieties as mutually intelligible linguistic subsystems.

3. Trudgill's model of koineization

A year after the appearance of Siegel's article, Peter Trudgill published his book *Dialects in Contact* (1986), which includes an important discussion of koineization. Trudgill distinguishes contact between stable dialects from dialect mixing which leads to the creation of a new dialect, or koineization. Unlike Siegel, he focuses on the linguistic processes or results of koineization, which he defines as mixing, leveling, and simplification. Mixing refers to the survival in the resultant koine of features from different contributing varieties. Leveling is the reduction or attrition of marked variants (Trudgill 1986: 97), where "marked" means unusual or minority. Simplification is an increase in regularity or an increase in morphological and lexical transparency (Trudgill 1986: 103). Trudgill (1986: 109) also specifies another process, reallocation, which occurs when more than one competing variant in the pre-koine linguistic pool survives, but each with a different social or stylistic function. Trudgill analyzes numerous cases of each of these processes and his discussion of them is in little need of revision. However, the distinction between leveling and simplification may be unnecessary, since all the cases of leveling and simplification described by Trudgill involve a reduction in units, such as morpho-lexical items and phonemes, or a reduction in rules, such as those underlying morphophonemic alternations. It may therefore be more useful to conceive of simplification as a limited reduction in inventories of units and rules in those areas of the grammar which show variation in the different contributing dialects. Secondary effects of this limited reduction then may lead, as Trudgill and others have argued (e.g., Siegel 1985; Gambhir 1981), to loss of minority variants, regularization of paradigms, simpler morphophonemics, greater transparency, and/or analytization. Summing up and altering slightly Trudgill's categorization, we can define the linguistic processes or results of koineization as: (1) mixing with leveling to one variant, (2) mixing with reallocation, and (3) simplification understood as the limited reduction in inventories of units and rules.

Though Trudgill emphasizes linguistic processes and results, he does pay some attention to definition of the social context of koineization. For instance, he points out that the effects of koineization are most likely to be seen in relatively isolated new towns, frontiers, and colonies which have suffered large and rapid immigration of speakers of different dialects. For Trudgill (1986: 126), the "motor" of koineization is the linguistic activity of adults who are suddenly dependent on each other and who, in order to strengthen a new common identity, accommodate their speech to that of their new neighbors. The easiest strategy for such speakers is to eliminate or "accommodate out" the most marked variants in their own speech, and it is this speaker activity that eventually leads to limited reduction in the stabilized or focused koine. Adult speakers also may attempt to learn and use features that other speakers produce, a process which Trudgill terms long-term accommodation. The features that they learn will be the most salient, and Trudgill lists numerous linguistic and sociolinguistic factors — such as phonological difference, naturalness, and stereotyping — that may contribute to or detract from salience. However, he comes to no definitive conclusions about salience, and Kerswill (1994: 158–159) has pointed out the circularity of these definitions of salience and the problematic fact that the same factor can both favor and disfavor salience. The complex interplay and varied outcomes of so many factors suggest that their effects can only be explained in reference to particular contexts.

Also problematic is Trudgill's emphasis on long-term accommodation by adults. Adult accommodation probably leads to the quick elimination of some highly marked variants, the introduction of some novel interlanguage variants or 'interdialectalisms' (see below), and, as suggested in Mesthrie (1994: 1866), the neutralization of the social meaning attached to certain linguistic variants (i.e., as adults attempt to imitate the speech of interlocutors, variation ceases to correlate clearly with non-linguistic factors such as regional origin, social status, or style). However, from a purely logical perspective, adults could maintain their speech unchanged, and koineization would still occur, for what ultimately matters is the learning and behavior of succeeding generations.[9]

4. Towards an elaborated model: Social conditions and language acquisition

Trudgill's model adequately addresses the linguistic results of koineization, but in order to turn it into a useful explanatory model of historical sociolinguistics, it needs to be elaborated with further specification of the social conditions (Siegel 1993: 116), the role of acquisition by adults and children, as well as an overarching conceptualization of the relation among these various linguistic, social, and individual aspects. This last problem can be addressed by constructing a model of koineization within the 'invisible-hand' framework of explanation. Keller (1994) argues that any thorough explanation of linguistic change must have a micro-level that examines intentional speaker activity and the constraints upon that activity, as well as a macro-level where the collective consequences of speaker actions are manifested. Trudgill's work addresses primarily the collective or linguistic consequences of koineization. However, except for his discussion of accommodation, he largely ignores the micro-level, or the ecological conditions of speaker activity, and this lack undermines the usefulness of the model for developing explanations of change that adequately address issues of actuation and transmission. These problems can be partly remedied by defining more precisely the social context of koineization, primarily in terms of social network theory, and by considering more fully the impact of language acquisition on the introduction and selection of features.

The social context of koineization is often taken for granted: the mixing together of speakers of different though related language varieties. But, as James Milroy has indicated, if immigrants to a mixed community maintain closeknit social networks and strong ties, norm enforcement within groups will remain strong as well, and what will result is not koineization but rather stable mulit-lingualism or multidialectalism (Milroy 1992:200). For koineization to occur, conservative social networks must break down and weak ties predominate; speakers may then begin to interact, accommodate, and alter their speech. In addition, it is new social networks, particularly those of younger generations, that are responsible for the focusing or stabilization of a new koine. For example, in the new town of Milton Keynes, England, the weakness of adult networks and the strength of adolescent social networks have allowed the formation of a new simplified variety in only one generation (Kerswill 1996). Social networks are fundamental to accurate language learning, for a closeknit social network assures close adherence to estab-lished norms and thus more frequent and consistent input for child learners. Conversely, loose-knit social networks will be less successful at enforcing norms and ensuring learning of older norms.

In defining ecological conditions, it is also necessary to consider the constraints that language acquisition imposes upon speaker-learners, be they children, adoles-cents or adults. Trudgill does in fact discuss the importance of adult second dialect acquisition in his chapter dealing with contact between stable dialects, and suggests that adult "interdialect" forms — particularly "fudged" phonetic forms — can become established in stable transitional varieties. However, he is not able to identify any clear cases of interdialect in the cases of koineization he analyzes, and he discounts the likelihood of their survival during koineization (Trudgill 1986:65). Still, long-term accommodation as he defines it must be understood as adult second dialect acquisition (Chambers 1992), and we must therefore assume that speaker-learners engaging in long-term accommodation produce interlanguage forms. These include, significantly, forms resulting from interference with the native dialect/language, overgeneralizations (often leading to the elimination of irregular forms), and misanalyses or uncorrected abductions (which may lead to the creation of novel forms or uses). Since these learner interlanguages are in fact subsystems of the established contributing varieties, they must be included among the contributing varieties to the prekoine linguistic pool. Moreover, they may include the interlanguages of native speakers of typologically distant languages, as in the case of Basque speakers learning Romance in early Castile.

Language acquisition by children also contributes to the creation of new variants, but it also plays a key role in the selection and stabilization of features in the new koine. In the koineizing context, where variation peaks and norms decline, children do not always receive frequent and consistent input, and their most frequent overgeneralizations and misanalyses may well survive in the linguistic pool, particularly when they mirror those of at least some adults. Kerswill (1996) shows that young children up to age six learn to speak much like their parents, but that older children begin to speak more and more like their friends — if they can, since acquisition ability begins to decline at age 8–and that adolescents alter their speech even more towards that of their peers as they develop their own social networks. Indeed, for Kerswill, it is the young adolescents (and the older children who follow them) who actually define the new community norms.

5.   Koineization and novel features: The case of Spanish *leísmo*

While inclusion of social network theory can aid in the construction of more convincing explanations, inclusion of acquisition and interlanguage theory may also alter our understanding of the potential effects of koineization. Many scholars appear to think of koineization as mere reduction to a 'least common denominator'. For example, Rebecca Posner comments in her recent book on the Romance languages: "the Castilian dialect is deviant phonologically and innovating morphologically, and far from a koineized compromise between Iberian varieties" (Posner 1996: 208). However, I think this view is not quite correct. Its specific claim about Castilian and its more general assumptions about koineization are both problematic, for there may well be "deviant" and "innovating" features of Castilian that cannot be explained without reference to koineization. For example, *leísmo*, an unusual phenomenon of the Spanish of northern central Spain, is very likely the result of misanalyses of input by speaker-learners in a koineizing environment.[10]

In most varieties of Hispano-Romance, the system of oblique pronouns inherited from Latin has been preserved unaltered. This is known as the etymological system and is illustrated in Table 2.However, in dialects with *leísmo*, *le* is used to refer to masculine singular personal accusatives. This leads to noticeable differences between etymological and *leísta* dialects:

Table 2. Etymological system of oblique pronouns

	Singular		Plural	
	Masculine	Feminine	Masculine	Feminine
Accusative	*lo*	*la*	*los*	*las*
Dative	*le*	*le*	*les*	*les*

Etymological system: *no lo veo*
                       not him I-see
Leísmo: *no le veo*
                       not him I-see

Interestingly, we know that this phenomenon dates to the 12th century (Lapesa 1968; Sanchis Calvo 1991),[11] and that its present-day limits (Fernández-Ordóñez 1994) correspond closely to the early 12th century limits of the kingdom of Castile, which at the time was undergoing repopulation, with rapid and massive demographic movement and dialect mixing.[12] The demographic mix included a majority of Romance-speaking immigrants from across the Iberian north, newcomers from present-day France, as well as resident Mozarabs (Christians that had lived under Arab rule) and Mudejars (Arabs who remained under Christian rule). It is unlikely that any of the Romance speakers arrived using anything other than the etymological system, with *le* restricted to dative use, so *leísmo* must have arisen as a result of contact and mislearning in this unique social context.

Apparently, speaker-learners were faced with input that was difficult to analyze and therefore to learn. At the time, the early Castilian dialect was characterized by frequent apocope of final *-e* and less frequent lexically-restricted apocope of final *-o*. As a result both *lo* and *le* could both be reduced to a single consonant *l'*. Speaker-learners would have been presented with such difficult-to-analyze sequences as:

nol veo [no l̲o̲ veo]   *nol di nada* [no l̲e̲ di nada]
not-him I-see   not-to-him I-gave nothing

Since apocope of *-e* was far more frequent, speaker-learners may have overgeneralized and understood many instances of *l'* as *le* rather than *lo*.[13] Most of the time, however, the dative *le* is used for personal reference, so these speaker-learners may have made the simple abduction that *le* was used for *lo* when accusative reference was to a masculine person. Since norm enforcement was weakened, their own output based on this abduction would have remained uncorrected and could then have served as input for still more learners — particularly children and adolescents — eventually leading to the establishment of a new norm. As a result, *leísta* dialects ended up with a novel and marked feature that was present in none of the established contributing dialects.

6. Conclusion: When is a change a koineizing change?

While the above represents only the briefest outline of an explanation based on the model of koineization, it does reveal some of the model's potential for the construction of explanations of linguistic change. Still, any and all of the particular types of changes that characterize koineization can occur in language varieties where koineization clearly has not occurred. For example, the effects of borrowing and mixing could easily be confused. Let me conclude, then, by specifying the basic elements of a thorough, plausible and cogent explanation of koineizing linguistic change. On the micro-level, the following features must be demonstrated for the social context:

1. an increase in variation due to demographic and dialect mixing,
2. a breakdown in social networks and consequently in norm enforcement,
3. specification of the contributing varieties and the proportions of speakers of each,
4. a specification of the structures of the contributing varieties, including possible learner varieties.

Other situational and cultural factors may also be included, such as isolation from home communities or the unifying effect of an outside threat.[14] On the macro- or linguistic level, it must be shown that:

1. the changes reflect mixing or reduction,
2. several such changes co-occur, and
3. the features are selected and stabilize rapidly, probably over the course of just two or three generations.[15]

Finally, the explanation must include an analysis of speaker activity that links together the causal or ecological conditions with the linguistic consequences.

Notes

1. Basing his criticism on the occasional difficulty of distinguishing between dialects and languages, Mufwene (1997) has argued that "koine" and "koineization" are not conceptually useful since they cannot always be clearly distinguished from "creole" and "creolization". However, following Thomason (1997) and Siegel (1995), I hold that a model serves not to explain each and every particular case, but rather as a prototype of change against which real cases can be compared. There will be cases of close approximation to the model and others which correspond less neatly, where the boundaries between types of change will be "fuzzy". Siegel (1995) includes a detailed response to Mufwene.

2. Siegel (1985:375–376) originally specified that the contributing varieties must be language varieties that are either (a) mutually intelligible or (b) share the same genetically-related superposed language. In light of Mufwene's (1997) criticisms of the second criterion, Siegel (1995:9)

restricts the definition of contributing varieties to those that are mutually intelligible (and, presumably, genetically-related). Of course, speakers in a contact situation involving genetically-related varieties may at first believe that their varieties are mutually unintelligible, but later change their attitudes as they become more familiar with different speech forms and uses.

3. Siegel (1995: 10) argues similarly, and points out that in most cases of koineization there may be no clear target variety, even though there may exist a dominant base dialect.

4. Siegel (1987: 187) does not include radical "reduction" as a feature of koineization. I discuss it here because the 1985 stage-based model is partially based upon it.

5. Siegel (1987: 201) abandons use of the term "informal standardization". Nevertheless, expansion is exemplified there by use of a stabilized koine as a literary or standard language.

6. Specifically, Fontanella (1992) argued that the spread of consonant weakening that so typifies the Caribbean Spanish koine was largely impeded in Mexico because of the presence of the viceregal court, archbishopric, university, and other educational institutions from very early on. In Buenos Aires, however, the Caribbean-type features appear to have dominated up to the 18th century. At that time, the city became the capital of a new viceroyalty and developed into a wealthy commercial center. Subsequently the impact of education led to a decline in the frequency of consonant weakening and its elimination in some cases (e.g., syllable-final liquids).

7. This is a major point of difference between my own perspective and that of Siegel. Note that much of Siegel's work on Fiji Hindi focuses on morphosyntax and lexicon, whereas it is in the phonology that the impact of child learning is likely to be most evident.

8. For example, Kerswill and Williams (2000) begin by situating their study within this model.

9. In later work, Trudgill (1992, 1994, 1996) has continued to emphasize that only imperfect learning by adults can explain cases of simplification resulting from dialect contact. This seems unlikely, given the tendency of both child and adult learners to regularize and simplify (e.g., Bybee & Slobin 1982).

10. This discussion of the origins of leísmo is an extremely simplified presentation of arguments and research that I am now preparing for publication. For example, there probably existed more than one type of leísmo from its very origins; here, however, I describe only that type which developed in the area of Toledo.

11. Lapesa (1968) gives numerous examples from the Poema del Cid. These include: si ellos le vidiessen "if they saw him"; echastele de tierra "you expelled him from the land". Sanchis Calvo (1991) includes many more from the Fazienda de Ultramar, the manuscript of which can be more safely dated to around the year 1220.

12. Moxó (1979) provides significant historical evidence of the demographic movement and mixing that accompanied the expansion into Toledo. Penny (1987) posits this period as the second important stage of dialect mixing in the history of medieval Castilian; Penny (2000) offers a more detailed overview of the effects of dialect mixing on the entire history of Spanish.

13. The lack of clear distinction between apocopated lo and le has been identified by others as a possible factor in the rise of leísmo (e.g., Echenique Elizondo 1981). However, no one has shown why it should have led to leísmo when and where it did.

14. Kerswill and Williams (2000), which appeared after this talk was presented, provide quite a long list of such micro-level factors. They also present a model of koineization in terms of certain key principles of koineization, most of which serve to specify the micro-level ecological conditions of koineization.

15. Trudgill (1986: 96) reports that stabilization or focusing occurred within three generations in the new town of Høyanger in Norway. Kerswill and Williams (2000), however, have found that the

second generation (first generation of children) has already stabilized a koine in the new town of Milton Keynes, England.

References

Bybee, Joan L. & Dan Slobin. 1982. "Rules and Schemas in the Development and Use of the English Past Tense". *Language* 58.265–289.

Chambers, J. K. 1992. "Dialect Acquisition". *Language* 68.673–705.

Echenique Elizondo, María Teresa. 1981. "El sistema referencial en español antiguo". *Revista de filología española* 61.113–157.

Fernández-Ordóñez, Inés. 1994. "Isoglosas internas del castellano: El sistema referencial del pronombre átono de tercera persona". *Revista de filología española* 74.71–125.

Fontanella de Weinberg, María Beatriz. 1992. *El español de América.* Madrid: Mapfre.

Gambhir, S. K. 1981. *The East Indian Speech Community in Guyana: A sociolinguistic study with special reference to koine formation.* Ph. D. dissertation, University of Pennsylvania.

Haugen, Einar. 1966. "Dialect, Language, Nation". *American Anthropologist* 68.922–935.

Keller, Rudi. 1994. *On Language Change: The invisible hand in language.* London: Routledge.

Kerswill, Paul. 1994. *Dialects Converging: Rural speech in urban Norway.* Oxford: Oxford University Press.

Kerswill, Paul. 1996. "Children, Adolescents, and Language Change". *Language Variation and Change* 8.177–202.

Kerswill, Paul & Ann Williams. 2000. "Creating a New Town Koine: Children and language change in Milton Keynes". *Language in Society* 29.65–115.

Lapesa, Rafael. 1968. "Sobre los orígenes y evolución del leísmo, laísmo y loísmo". *Festschrift Walter von Wartburg* ed. by Kurt Baldinger, 523–551. Tübingen: Niemeyer.

Mesthrie, Rajend. 1994. "Koinés". *The Encyclopedia of Language and Linguistics* ed. by R. E. Asher, 1864–1867. Oxford: Pergamon Press.

Milroy, James. 1992. *Language Variation and Change: On the historical sociolinguistics of English.* Oxford: Blackwell.

Moag, Rodney. 1979. "The Linguistic Adaptations of the Fiji Indians". *Rama's Banishment: A century tribute to the Fiji Indians, 1879–1979* ed. by V. Mishra, 112–138. London: Heinemann.

Moxó, Salvador de. 1979. *Repoblación y sociedad en la España cristiana medieval.* Madrid: Rialp.

Mufwene, Salikoko. 1997. "Jargons, Pidgins, Creoles, and Koines: What are they?" Spears & Winford 1997.35–70.

Mühlhäusler, Peter. 1980. "Structural Expansion and the Process of Creolization". *Theoretical Orientations in Creole Studies* ed. by Albert Valdman & Arnold Highfield, 19–55. New York: Academic.

Penny, Ralph. 1987. *Patterns of Language-Change in Spain.* London: University of London, Westfield College.

Penny, Ralph. 2000. *Variation and Change in Spanish.* Cambridge: Cambridge University Press.

Petrini, Dario. 1988. *La koinè ticinese. Livellamento dialettale e dinamiche innovative.* Berne: Francke.

Posner, Rebecca. 1996. *The Romance Languages.* Cambridge: Cambridge University Press.

Sanchis Calvo, María del Carmen. 1991. *El lenguaje de la Fazienda de Ultramar.* Madrid: Anejos del Boleti'n de la Real Academia Española.

Siegel, Jeff. 1985. "Koines and Koineization". *Language in Society* 14.357–378.

Siegel, Jeff. 1987. *Language Contact in a Plantation Environment: A sociolinguistic history of Fiji.* Cambridge: Cambridge University Press.

Siegel, Jeff. 1993. "Dialect Contact and Koineization: A review of *Dialects in Contact,* by Peter Trudgill". *Koines and Koineization* ed. by Jeff Siegel. *International Journal of the Sociology of Language* 99.105–121.

Siegel, Jeff. 1995. "Koine Formation and Creole Genesis". Paper presented at the Amsterdam Creole Workshop 95.

Spears, Arthur K. & Donald Winford, eds. 1997. *The Structure and Status of Pidgins and Creoles.* Amsterdam & Philadelphia: John Benjamins.

Thomason, Sarah. 1997. "A Typology of Contact Languages". Spears & Winford 1997.71–88.

Thomason, Sarah & Terrence Kaufman. 1988. *Language Contact, Creolization and Genetic Linguistics.* Berkeley: University of California Press.

Trudgill, Peter. 1986. *Dialects in Contact.* Oxford: Blackwell.

Trudgill, Peter. 1992. "Dialect Typology and Social Structure". *Language Contact: Theoretical and empirical studies* ed. by Ernst Håkon Jahr, 195–211. Berlin: Mouton de Gruyter.

Trudgill, Peter. 1994. "Language Contact and Dialect Contact in Linguistic Change". *Dialektkontakt, språkkontakt och språkförändring i Norden: Föredrag från ett forskarsymposium* ed. by Ulla-Britt Kotsinas & John Helgander, 13–22. Stockholm: Stockholm University.

Trudgill, Peter. 1996. "Dialect Typology: Isolation, social network and phonological structure". *Towards a Social Science of Language* ed. by Gregory Guy et al., vol. 1, 3–21. Amsterdam & Philadelphia: John Benjamins.

Coreference in the Popolocan languages[*]

Annette Veerman-Leichsenring
University of Leiden

1. Introduction

The four Popolocan languages, Mazatec, Ixcatec, Chocho and Popoloc,[1] belong to the vast and highly differentiated stock of Otomanguean languages, which are mainly spoken in the central part of Mexico. Mazatec is genetically and geographically the most distant member of the family and has the largest group of speakers (about 80,000).[2] It is spoken in an area covering large parts of the States of Puebla, Oaxaca, and Veracruz. Popoloc and Chocho (about 8,000 speakers each) share the largest number of innovations (Fernández de Miranda 1951; Gudschinsky 1959a; Hamp 1958). Popoloc is spoken in the southern part of the State of Puebla, and Chocho in a more or less adjacent region in the northeastern part of the State of Oaxaca, traditionally known as the Mixteca Alta. Ixcatec is spoken only in the village of Santa María Ixcatlán, also situated in the Mixteca Alta. During my last visit to the village, in 1997, Ixcatec had no more than ten speakers left.

The Popolocan languages are tonal, with three or four tones having a lexical and a grammatical function. Especially relevant for this article is the historical VSO basic order of constituents which goes back to Proto-Popolocan (PPn) and the use of coreferential pronouns which are synchronically and/or diachronically related to a set of lexical classifiers. These classifiers are prefixed to nouns (but not all nouns) indicating the semantic class of the referent, such as "animate", "flower", "tree", "child", "male person", or "female person". Most of them double as autonomous nouns with a similar semantic value. The coreferential pronouns are used after the third person pronoun or nouns expressing a third person possessor, and after verbs inflected for the third person. In the last-mentioned position, the use of coreferential pronouns is related to word order. Namely, when a subject or object constituent is moved to initial position, it is repeated with a coreferential pronoun after the verb phrase, which is in agreement with the basic verb initial order.[3] Thus, the coreferential pronoun marks a sentence which has a non-basic word order. In some of the languages, the fronted constituent is frequently followed by a focus marker. In these cases, the non-basic word order is doubly marked.

Although coreferential pronouns occur in all of the four languages, differences in form, usage, and frequency are indicative of specific developments in each of the sister languages. My claim is that a verb medial word order is gaining ground as the basic order at the expense of a verb initial order and the use of coreferential pronouns in the verb phrase. Gradual stages of this development are apparently present in the Popolocan languages showing that a less frequent occurrence of coreferential pronouns is concomitant with a higher degree of acceptance of verb medial constructions as the basic order. Although coreferential pronouns are used in larger units than the sentence to corefer with constituents introduced earlier, I will focus in this article on coreference in the verb phrase in relation to word order, that is, within the limits of the sentence.

All four languages are severely affected by Spanish, not only lexically but also by the structure of the Spanish sentence. For example, pronominal object marking is often applied to Popoloc contradictory to the rules dictated by the inflectional class of the verb; Spanish prepositions are adopted in all four languages sometimes replacing autochthonous instrumental and comitative constructions.

For Popoloc the examples are taken from Veerman-Leichsenring (1991) and fieldnotes; for Chocho from De Angulo and Freeland (1935); for Ixcatec from Fernández de Miranda (1961) and my own fieldnotes; and for Mazatec from A.R. Jamieson (1977a), Jamieson and Tejeda (1978), C. Jamieson (unpublished) and Schram and Schram (1979).

2. Popoloc

The verb initial order is generally maintained as the unmarked, neutral sentence in Popoloc.

(1) kui^1-ci^1nga^3 ti^1 $čha^3n^2a^3$
     P-fall.3   the my.son
     "My son has fallen."

A focus subject or object constituent is moved to the sentence-initial position and repeated in a nominal or pronominal form (co) directly after the verb. A focus marker (M) generally but not obligatorily follows the fronted constituent.[4]

(2) ti^1 $čha^3n^2a^3$ na^3 $kui^1ci^1nga^3$ $čhā^3$
     the my.child M P-fall.3   co.child
     "My child has fallen." or "It is my child that has fallen."

(3) $tu^3t^2e^1na^1$ na^3 thu^1a^1 $tu^3t^2e^2$
     my.feet   M clean co.foot
     "My feet, they are clean."

(4) ti^1 ka^3-nia^3 na^3 $t^2a^2khia^2$ ka^3
      the cl-strawmat M I.sell   co.leaf
      "It is the strawmat that I sell."

In examples (2) and (3), it is the antecedent noun which is repeated after the verb in an unaccented and uninflected form. This type of coreference, by a full noun, is a characteristic of Popoloc which is not shared by the other languages. In the second example, coreference is expressed by a pronoun which is morphologically related to the classifier used in the antecedent noun. This is the more common form of coreference. Thus in Popoloc, there is always an overt formal relationship between the antecedent and the coreferential term. In this language, a relatively large set of classifiers is matched with an equally large set of related coreferential pronouns.

Table 1. Popoloc classifiers and coreferential pronouns

		Classifiers	CO pronouns
inanimates:	tree, wood	nda^3-	nda^3
	flower	su^3-	su^3
	leaf, herb	ka^3-	ka^3
	fruit, round shape	tu^3-	tu^3
	stone	$šu^3$-	$šu^3$
	earth	$nž\,e^3$-	$nž\,e^3$
	corn, tortilla	nu^3-	nu^3
animates:	animal	ku^2-	ba^2
	people, person	ni^2-	na^2
	young, unmarried male	$ši^1$-	$ša^1$
	young, unmarried female	nri^1-	nra^1
	married male	$č^2i^1$-	$č^2a^1$
	married female	tha^3-	tha^3
	respected person	se^1-	$sĕ^1$
	child	$ča^3$-	$čhā^3$

Table 1 shows that the classifiers and the related pronouns of the inanimate categories have identical forms. The classifiers for the animate categories in -*i*, however, are matched with coreferential pronouns ending in -*a*. It is plausible that the vowel -*a* of the coreferential pronouns represents a fusion of -*i* with a deictic element, such as the morpheme -*a* that is used in modern Popoloc to indicate locational or temporal remoteness in nouns. The added vowel -*a* contrasts in this function (5a–b) with the vowel -*i* expressing locational or temporal proximity (5c).

(5) a. $tí^1$ se^1-$čhĩ^3$-a^3
the CL-woman-there
"that lady"

b. ngu^2 ku^2-$tu^2ru^1ce^3$?-a^3
a   CL-rabbit-there
"a rabbit over there"

c. $tí^1$ nda^3-$n1ǯe^3$-i^3 nu^2i^2
the CL-sotolin-here high
"this high sotolin-tree"[5]

The vowel -a is present in all the pronouns for animate categories. However, it fuses without leaving a trace when the classifier already ends in -a, as in $tha^3 + a > tha^3$, or in -e where a regular progressive assimilation is involved, as in $se^1 + a > see^1 > se^1$. In the pronouns expressing inanimate categories, the vowel -a is not included.

The "animal" pronoun ba^2 seems to be the only one which is related in an irregular way to the "animal" classifier ku^2-.

(6) ku^2-$n?ie^1$ $ši^1$-Juan $k?uē$ ba^2
CL-dog.his CL-Juan died CO.animal
"John's dog died."

It may nevertheless be the case that this pronoun is also based on the same root as the classifier ku^2-. In this case, a form *kua^2 (<$ku^2 + a$) should underlie the coreferential pronoun ba^2, whose initial b can be interpreted as the result of a progressive articulation of closure with the subsequent drop of the velar. If this is right, and it seems plausible to me,[6] the form has undergone a considerable phonetic development which suggests a long history with the pronoun already in use in an early language stage. Furthermore, it may be assumed that in that time a deictic vowel was added to animate coreference pronouns distinguishing them morphologically from the inanimate pronouns.

The "person" pronoun na^2 is also used to mark the plural in verbs inflected for the non-reverential and not further defined third person. In these cases the presence of the ni^2- classifier is not required.

(7) $ča^1$ nda^1?a^3 na^3 asta letra gotika $kui^1č?e^1na^2$ na^2
more there   M even letter gothic made   3.plural
"In the past, they even wrote with gothic letters."

Two stages of grammaticalization can be observed with reference to the Popoloc coreferential term; it occurs as a grammatical word or as a pronominal enclitic.[7]

3.   Chocho

Coreference occurs in Chocho only by means of pronouns, and since the number of gender classes is smaller than in Popoloc, the number of coreferential pronouns is also smaller. The morphologically related pairs of classifiers and coreferential pronouns which I detected in the Ocotlán dialect are as follows:

Table 2. Chocho classifiers and coreferential pronouns[a]

		Classifiers	CO pronouns
inanimates:	tree, wood	nda^3-	nda^3
	flower	su^3-	su^3
	leaf, thing	ka^2-	ga^3
	fruit	t^yu^3-	ru^3
animates:	animal	u^2-	ba^3
	person, people	$\check{r}u^2$-	ri^3
	respected person	–	ni^2
	male person	$\check{r}i^1$-	ri^1
	female person	ci^1-	ci^1
	child	$\check{s}a^3$-	$\check{s}\bar{a}^3$

[a] Mock (1977:37) mentions in her list of pronominal forms specific third person pronouns which express an intimate relationship with a male person, $so^2a^1ga^1$, and a female person, $so^2a^1nu^2$. However, the involved pronominal morphemes ga^1 and nu^2 are absent in the material I collected during my last visit to the village in 1996/97. It seems that these forms are not used any longer in the Chocho dialect of Ocotlán.

Contrary to Popoloc, the pronouns which are used in coreference with the animate categories, viz., ni^2, ri^1 and ci^1, are not modified by a vowel -a. The exception is the 'animal' pronoun ba^3, which derives, as in Popoloc, from the proto form *ku, modified by the supposed deictic vowel -a.

The unclear relationship between the "fruit" classifier and the "fruit" coreferential pronoun is due to different phonetic developments. The classifier, as well as the coreferential pronoun, are reflexes of PPn **tyu "fruit" (Gudschinsky set 36). However, the unaccented pronoun suffered rhotacism,[8] whereas the consonant cluster is retained in the classifier forming part of an accented noun.

Another fundamental difference with Popoloc exists in the lack of a morphological relationship between the coreferential pronoun and the antecedent classifier, and in the fact that classifiers are optionally used in Chocho. For example, the coreferential pronoun ba^3 is used with animal names containing the classifier u^2-, but also with the classifier ri^1- (for non-domesticated animals) or when no classifier is used in the antecedent, as in the following example.

(8) ... $hngu^1$ n^ya^3 ka^3 xu^3na^1 be^2 ci^1nga^2 ba^3 nu^3nde^3
    one dog small never is lies   co.animal ground
    "... a little dog who never lies down on the ground"
    (De Angulo & Freeland 1935: 126; adapted transcription)

Other examples of pronouns which occur without morphological relatives are the pronouns ru^3 and ri^3. The "fruit" pronoun ru^3 is used in coreference with nouns denoting round-shaped things which lack the 'fruit' classifier or which contain an unrelated classifier. The pronoun ri^3 corefers with the classifier ru^2- for adult male persons but also with the reverential male and female classifiers ta^1- and na^1-, and various unclassified nouns, such as zu^3rxi^2 "person, people".

(9) su^3a^1 ru^2-*gringo* $cö^3$ ri^3
    this CL-gringo is.afraid CO.person
    "this American man is afraid."
    (De Angulo & Freeland 1935: 125, 126; adapted transcription)

Another case is the pronoun ni^2, which is nowadays used to express reverence towards a third person. The antecedent noun lacks a classifier or may contain a classifier which is not morphologically related, such as the already mentioned ta^1- and na^1- classifiers. Although I could not trace any classifier synchronically related to the pronoun ni^2, the "person" classifiers of Popoloc (ni^2-), Ixcatec (mi^2-), and Proto-Mazatec ($*hmi^4$-; Kirk set 138) lead to the hypothesis that in Chocho too, a classifier $*ni^2$- must have been in use during an earlier stage.

Therefore, in Chocho, a formal relationship between the coreferential pronoun and the antecedent is often lacking or rather loose as a consequence of a different and declining use of lexical classification. The fact that certain pronouns corefer with unrelated classifiers or with unclassified nouns signals that the lexical meaning of these pronouns have become weakened due to a process of grammaticalization, which is more advanced than in Popoloc. The reanalysis of the original "person" pronoun as a reverential pronoun is in agreement with this development and concomitant with a declining number of gender classes. Contrary to Popoloc, the Chocho animate coreferential pronouns lack the inclusion of a deictic vowel with the exception of the "animal" pronoun ba^3. Although a verb initial order of constituents still seems to be the basic one, the omission of a coreferential term when an argument is fronted to the verb indicates that a verb medial order is becoming an alternative basic order which does not require coreferential pronominal marking.

4. Ixcatec

The use and number of coreferential pronouns in Ixcatec is even more limited than in Chocho. Although several classifiers are used for animate as well as inanimate nouns, only three pronouns with an obvious coreferential function could be traced in the available materials. Moreover, the use of coreferential pronouns seems to be restricted to the animate categories.

Table 3. Ixcatec classifiers and coreferential pronouns[a]

		Classifiers	CO pronouns
inanimate:	herb, leaf	$\check{s}ka^2$-	–
	tree, wood	ya^3-	–
	etc.		
animate:	animal	$\hat{}u^2$-	ba
	man	di^2-	da
	woman	kua^2-	kua

[a] Tones are not marked in Ixcatec coreferential pronouns since they usually assimilate their tone to the last tone of the preceding word.

As in Popoloc, but different from Chocho, the coreferential pronouns are used only when the antecedent noun contains a generic noun or a classifier that is morphologically related to the pronoun. It is interesting, however, that the "animal" pronoun *ba* is also used frequently in Ixcatec and, as it seems, obligatorily when the "animal" classifier $\hat{}u^2$- is used.

(10) $tu^1nda^2\hat{}a^2$ $\hat{}u^2$-$\check{s}yee^1$ fi^2-ka^2hu^2 ba^3 ka^2hndu^3
he.has cl-his.ox goes-with co.animal mountain
"He (who) owns an ox, takes it to the mountain."
(Fernández de Miranda 1961: 178)

However, a pronoun coreferring with a preverbal classified noun is more often lacking.

(11) na^2-$\hat{}mi^1$ ci^1-$\check{s}ti^2h\tilde{a}^3$-$ke^2e^2$ $ku^2ra^1twe^3e^3$
cl-priest is.said-returned-again his.curacy
"The priest (they say) went back to his curacy."
(Fernández de Miranda 1961: 190)

Since the pronoun *ba* is cognate with the animal pronouns used in Popoloc and Chocho, a proto-from *ba* must have been in use in the proto-language ancestral of the three languages. The pronoun *ba* seems to be the only pronoun which has retained its original meaning in these three languages. The reason for this exceptional durability possibly has to do with the generic value of the animal category, which is, contrary to the human categories, not subject to social sub-categorization.

Whereas coreference in relation to word order is consistently applied with animal names, the occurrence of the two other coreferential pronouns traced is very limited. An example from my own fieldnotes is:

(12)   *kua²   ra² ce²xi² kua²*   *čhmi¹*
       woman this sells   co.woman fruit
       "This lady sells fruit."

In Fernández de Miranda's texts, a preverbal subject or object constituent is generally not repeated after the verb by a noun or a pronoun. This suggests that a verb medial order is now accepted as the basic order which does not require the use of coreferential pronouns to re-establish the grammatical word order.

The three attested pronouns are used in coreference with generic classes which are rather fundamental, the animal, the male and the female. This may indicate that they correspond to the remnants of an older language stage, which survived due to their frequent usage.

5.   Mazatec

Coreference is not analyzed as such in the descriptive studies of Mazatec, as far as I know. Therefore, the texts written in this language must give evidence of the use of coreferential pronouns. Such texts are available for the dialects of Chiquihuitlán, Jalapa de Díaz, and Huautla de Jiménez.

Some coreferential pronouns appear in the Chiquihuitlán texts. However, although the verb generally appears in sentence-initial position (C. Jamieson 1988: 17), the coreferential pronouns are seldom used when the verb-initial order is changed. In the five texts I had at my disposition (A. R. Jamieson 1977a,b; Jamieson & Tejeda 1978 and the unpublished text that Carole Jamieson generously allowed me to use), I detected the use of only two coreferential pronouns, *ča* for male persons and *ču* for animals. C. Jamieson (1988: 44) mentions a third pronoun, *na* for female persons, which I could not trace in the texts. The "male" pronoun *ča*, which is obviously related to the "male" classifier *ča-*, is an unambiguous reflex of the Proto-Mazatec classifier for singular male persons *ča¹* (Kirk set 55). The pronoun *ču*, which relates to the "animal" classifier *ču-*, is also applied when an unrelated classifier, or no classifier at all, is used in the animal name. These cases of the absence of a formal relationship between the antecedent and the coreferential pronoun is reminiscent of Chocho.

(13) sa^3kua^{234} hya^{34} $h\tilde{a}^2$ $n\tilde{e}^{24}$ $\check{s}i^3$ $skuae^{41}$ $\check{c}u^{14}$ la^3nka^{14} $n\tilde{e}^{24}$ ...
as   eagle he M   that will.see co.animal children M
"As the eagle will see the children ..."
(A.R. Jamieson 1977a: 175)

(14) $kui^4n\check{c}i^2ra^{24}$ $na^4\check{s}i^2$ $\check{s}i^3$ kua^4ni^{241} $\check{c}u^4$
he.will.look.for mule that will.transport co.animal
"He will look for mules for the transport."
(C. Jamieson, unpublished)

The initial consonant of the form $\check{c}u$ is the result of the development $^*k^y > \check{c}$ that had already taken place in Proto-Mazatec (Kirk set 107).

The following related pairs of lexical classifiers and coreferential pronouns occur in the one available Jalapa text (Schram & Schram 1979):

Table 4. Jalapa Mazatec classifiers and coreferential pronouns

	Classifiers	CO pronouns
male	nda^4-	ndo^3
people	ha^1-	ho^1o^3
tree	ya^1	yo^1o^3

Although the pronouns are used quite frequently for anaphoric reference in a postverbal position, their exact relationship to word order is not obvious. It is possible that more pairs exist in this dialect; however, it is not plausible that the number will be much larger than mentioned in Table 4.

An example of the occurrence of the pronoun ndo^3 coreferring with the noun nda^4, is given in the following example.

(15) nda^3 $\check{s}^2\tilde{a}^3$ $ha^2\tilde{a}^1$ ku^2ma^2 $ndyi^3na^1\check{s}u^1$ ndo^3
man poor then became rich   co.man
"The poor man became rich then."
(Schram & Schram 1979: 21; adapted transcription)

The paired terms are opposed by a vowel contrast $a : o$ which suggests that the roots of the classifiers are modified by a deictic vowel, as in Popoloc.

The use of coreferential terms is not attested in the Huautla texts at my disposal (E.V. Pike 1949; K. Pike 1948; F.H. Cowan 1963; G.M. Cowan 1965). Specific markers are used to indicate pragmatic functions in sentences which generally have a verb medial structure. The verb medial order of constituents has become the basic one in Huautla Mazatec, it seems. Since the position of the coreferential pronoun directly after the verb phrase is dictated by a basic verb initial order, the use of the pronoun in that position is no longer needed when a verb medial construction is accepted as the basic one. More insights, however, are needed into the syntax and pragmatic value of word order in Mazatec to make more conclusive statements.

6. Conclusions

Since pronouns that corefer with a preverbal argument are used in all four Popo-locan languages, this type of coreference was most probably already applied in Proto-Popolocan. The relationship of coreferential pronouns to lexical classifiers, which generally correspond to slightly modified forms of generic nouns, reveals the origin of the pronouns in lexical nouns and their inherently generic value.

The use of full nouns and the rather extensive set of coreferential pronouns that are used in Popoloc and in particular their transparent morphological relation to nouns or classifiers suggests that at least some of the pronouns correspond to classifiers that were introduced rather recently. That is to say, in Popoloc, the number of coreferential pronouns grows with the number of lexical classifiers. However, the number of pronouns shared by Popoloc and Chocho suggests that their common language already had a rich system of classifiers. Thus, it seems that Popoloc has a propensity to expand the classifier system triggering the development of coreferential pronouns, whereas Chocho shows a tendency to reduce the usage of classifiers. The decreasing number of lexical classifiers in that language parallels the decrease in the number of coreferential pronouns and a morphological dissociation of some pronouns from the noun in the antecedent.

The fusion of a deictic vowel in the coreferential pronouns occurs in three languages (Popoloc, Ixcatec, and Jalapa Mazatec), which gives the impression that the coreferential pronouns were already modified by a deictic vowel in PPn. However, a deictic vowel is not included in the Proto-Mazatec "animal" pronoun *$\check{c}u$, so the inclusion of the deictic vowel in the Jalapa pronouns probably corresponds to a local development. In that case, the inclusion of the deictic vowel in the coreferential pronouns is a characteristic of the common language after Mazatec split off. The vowel continues to be present in a lexicalized form in the animate pronouns in Popoloc and Ixcatec. The deictic lost this distribution in Chocho where it only survived in the "animal" pronoun ba^2.

The uses of coreference have an important concomitant in word order changes. In the languages where coreferential terms are not used when a subject or object constituent precedes the verb, i.e., where verb medial orders are no longer marked with a coreferential pronoun, the verb initial order seems no longer to be accepted as the only basic one. This is what happens in the Huautla variant of Mazatec. The very small number of coreferential pronouns that are used in Ixcatec and the Mazatec dialects of Jalapa and Chiquihuitlán are most probably the remains of an earlier language phase which was verb initial. Nowadays, the use of these pronouns seems to have a mere pragmatic function.

The basic mechanism of coreference was probably already present in the PPn language. In the modern Popolocan languages, various stages of further grammatic-alization are seen. Given the well-known cline of grammaticality: content item >

grammatical word > clitic > affix > lexicalization (Meillet 1958; Heine et al. 1991), it may be assumed that at the initial stage, the head noun or the content word of the preverbal argument was repeated after the verb, acquiring a grammatical function. This still happens in Popoloc, which is indicative of the vitality of the category in that language. The next step of the grammaticalization process, the cliticization of the grammatical word, happened in varying degrees in the four languages.

The loss of accent as a result of the enclitization of the coreferential term has resulted in significant phonemic differences between some pronouns and their related classifiers in Chocho, which can be considered a further step in the grammaticalization process. However, the stage of inflection or lexicalization seems not to be reached in any of the Popolocan languages.

Reanalysis is involved in Chocho, where the coreferential pronoun for person is now used to express reverence, and in Popoloc, where the original cognate term developed as a third person plural marker.

Instead of the earlier suggested loss of coreferential pronouns in Ixcatec and Mazatec, an alternative explanation of the very limited number of these pronouns could be that in these languages the stage of enclitization was not completed before word order changes started to develop. This might explain why only the more frequently used coreferential terms underwent a transition into clitics.

Although classifiers and the related pronouns may have appeared, disappeared, and changed their value in the course of time, my hypothesis that coreference was already expressed by generic terms in Proto-Popolocan supports the view that morphosyntactic categories are very persistent, and that changes within these categories are generally correlated with changes or innovative developments in other categories, in this case with changes in word order. This indicates that a holistic approach can be the only effective one in the reconstruction of morphosyntactic categories.

Since the influence of Spanish syntax is obviously present in Popolocan (refer to my introductory remarks), it seems plausible that the observed word order change is another effect of that influence.

Research in other Otomanguean languages may support the assumptions made in this article about the nature of coreference and its relationship to word order. It might reveal that coreferential terms were already used to mark verb medial word orders in a language phase older than PPn.

Notes

* I acknowledge the Netherlands Organization for Scientific Research (NWO) and the Research School for Asian, African and Amerindian Studies (CNWS) of Leiden University for providing the opportunity to do the necessary research. I wish to thank Søren Wichmann and two anonymous referees for their helpful comments and suggestions.

1. The name Popoloc refers to the language, in analogy with the language names Mazatec, Ixcatec, Mixtec, etc., whereas the name Popolocan refers to the language family.

2. The numbers of speakers mentioned for Mazatec, Chocho, and Popoloc are mostly based on information given by local authorities and personal observations during different field-work periods (see also Veerman-Leichsenring 1984). They differ significantly from the numbers given by the Mexican Government (www.sedesol.gob.mx/ini/len9095.htm), which are based on data collected in 1990 and 1995.

3. Subject and object constituents are fronted to the verb for focalization as well as topicalization. In a neutral (or basic) order of constituents, the verb may be preceded by the question marker and constituents indicating time, place, or instrument.

4. Abbreviations used in this article, many of which appear in the examples, are: PPn Proto-Popolocan, CL classifier, CO coreferential term, M focus marker. Proto-Popolocan reconstructions are indicated by a double asterisk, intermediate reconstructions by a single asterisk. Enclitics are separated from the preceding word by a space to distinguish them from affixes which form part of the word.

The following phonemic symbols are used: ^{1} indicates high tone, ^{2} mid tone, ^{3} low tone, and ^{4} lower than low tone; ^{t} is used to indicate any tone which is either not reconstructed or unknown. Long vowels and diphthongs are written as two vowels with one tone. Aspirated consonants are marked by *h*, prenasalized consonants by *n*; *š* and *č* are palatalized consonants; *c* and *ř* are retroflexed consonants, *ǯ* is a voiced palatal affricate. Gudschinsky's sets are taken from her 1959a publication, those of Kirk from his 1966 dissertation.

5. Were this a predicative construction, it would read:

ti^1 nda^{3}nǯe^3-i^3 na^3 nu^{2}i^2 nda^3
the sotolin.tree-here M high CO
"this sotolin tree is high."

6. A change from a labialized velar stop to a bilabial voiced stop has regularly taken place in the past tense forms of Chocho (see Veerman-Leichsenring 2000). A bilabial fricative is the regular reflex in Ixcatec (Veerman-Leichsenring forthc.).

"he swallowed":   *kui^{1}nga^2* (Popoloc)
                  bi^{2}ʔnga^3 (Chocho)
                  fʔi^{2}nga^2 (Ixcatec).

Similar developments are also observed in Nahuatl (Monzón & Roth Seneff 1984) and Zapotec (Suárez 1985).

7. Although the use of coreferential pronouns is evidenced by some examples given in the grammatical chapter included in Austin *et al.* 1995 (p. 308), the use of coreferential pronouns in verb medial constructions is not analyzed for Atzingo Popoloc nor for other Popoloc dialects than Metzontla.

8. Rhotacism is an innovation shared by Popoloc and Chocho which developed to a higher degree in the latter language (see Hamp 1960).

References

Austin Krumholz, Jeanne, Marjorie Kalstrom Dolson, & Miguel Hernández Ayuso. 1995. *Diccionario popoloca de San Juan Atzingo, Puebla*. Tucson: Instituto Lingüístico de Verano.

Cowan, Florence H. 1963. "La mujer del agua arrastradora: un texto mazateco". *Tlalocan* IV: 2.144–146.

Cowan, George M. 1965. *Some Aspects of the Lexical Structure of a Mazatec Historical Text*. Norman: Summer Institute of Linguistics & University of Oklahoma.

De Angulo, Jaime & L. S. Freeland. 1935. "The Zapotecan Linguistic Group: A comparative study of Chinanteco, Chocho, Mazateco, Cuicateco, Mixteco, Chatino, and especially Zapoteco proper and its dialects". *International Journal of American Linguistics*. 8.1–38, 111–130.

Fernández de Miranda, Maria Teresa. 1951. "Reconstrucción del protopopoloca". *Revista Mexicana de Estudios Antropológicos* 12.61–93.

Fernández de Miranda, Maria Teresa. 1961. *Diccionario ixcateco* (includes texts). Mexico: Instituto Nacional de Antropología e Historia.

Gudschinsky, Sarah C. 1958. "Mazatec Dialect History, A study in miniature". *Language* 34.469–481.

Gudschinsky, Sarah C. 1959a. "Proto-Popotecan: A comparative study of Popolocan and Mixtecan". (= *Indiana University Publications in Anthropology and Linguistics*, Memoir 15). *International Journal of American Linguistics* 25.2 (Supplement).

Gudschinsky, Sarah C. 1959b. "Mazatec Kernel Constructions and Transformations". *International Journal of American Linguistics* 25.81–89.

Hamp, Eric P. 1958. "Protopopoloca Internal Relationships". *International Journal of American Linguistics* 24.2.150–153.

Hamp, Eric P. 1960. "Chocho-Popoloca Innovations". *International Journal of American Linguistics* 26.62.

Heine, Bernd, Ulrike Claudi & Friederike Hünnemeyer. 1991. *Grammaticalization: A conceptual framework*. Chicago: University of Chicago Press.

Jamieson, Allan R. 1977a. "El origen del nombre del pueblo de Chiquihuitlán, Oaxaca". *Tlalocan* 7.173–179.

Jamieson, Allan R. 1977b. "Chiquihuitlán Mazatec Tone" (text). *Studies in Otomanguean Phonology* ed. by William R. Merrifield, 107–136. Dallas: Summer Institute of Linguistics & University of Texas.

Jamieson, Allan R. & Ernesto Tejeda. 1978. *Mazateco de Chiquihuitlán, Oaxaca*. (= *Archivo de lenguas indígenas de México* 5.) Mexico: Colegio de México, Centro de Investigación para la Integración Social & Summer Institute of Linguistics.

Jamieson, Carole. 1988. *Gramática mazateca del Municipio de Chiquihuitlán, Oaxaca*. Mexico: Instituto Lingüístico de Verano.

Jamieson, Carole. Not dated. *His father's mules* (a Chiquihuitlán text). Unpublished.

Kirk, Paul L. 1966. *Proto-Mazatec Phonology*. Ph. D. dissertation, University of Washington.

Meillet, Antoine. 1958. *Linguistique historique et linguistique générale*. Paris: Champion.

Mock, Carol. 1977. *Chocho de Santa Catarina Ocotlán*. (= *Archivo de lenguas indígenas de México*, 4.) Mexico: Colegio de México, Centro de Investigación para la Integración Social & Summer Institute of Linguistics.

Monzón, Cristina & Andrew Roth Seneff. 1984. "Notes on the Nahuatl Phonological Change k^w > *b*". *International Journal of American Linguistics* 50.456–461.

Pike, Kenneth L. 1948. *Tone Languages: A technique for determining the number and type of pitch contrasts in a language, with studies in tonemic substitution and fusion* (text on page 163). Ann Arbor: University of Michigan Press.

Pike, Eunice V. 1949. "Texts on Mazatec Food Witchcraft". *El México Antiguo* VII.287–294.

Pike, Eunice V. & Sarah C. Gudschinsky. 1957. *Vocabulario Mazateco* (Huautla). Revised ed. Mexico: Instituto Lingüístico de Verano.

Schram, Terry L. & Judith L. Schram. 1979. "Mazatec of Jalapa de Díaz: About the thunderman". *Discourse Studies in Mesoamerican Languages* ed. by Linda K. Jones, 2.15–27. Dallas: Summer Institute of Linguistics, University of Texas Press.

Suárez, Jorge A. 1983. *The Mesoamerican Indian Languages*. Cambridge: Cambridge University Press.

Suárez, Jorge A. 1985. "Loan Etymologies in Historical Method". *International Journal of American Linguistics* 51.574–575.

Veerman-Leichsenring, Annette. 1984. *El popoloca de Los Reyes Metzontla.* (= *Número especial,* 4.) Paris: Association d'Ethnolinguistique Amérindienne.

Veerman-Leichsenring, Annette. 1991. *Gramática del popoloca de Metzontla.* Amsterdam & Atlanta: Rodopi.

Veerman-Leichsenring, Annette. 2000. *Gramática del chocho de Santa Catarina Ocotlán, Oaxaca.* Leiden: Research School of Asian, African and Amerindian Studies of Leiden University & Instituto de Investigaciones Antropológicas de la Universidad Nacional Autónoma de México (UNAM).

Veerman-Leichsenring, Annette. Forthcoming. *Gramática del ixcateco.*

Atlantis Semitica

Structural contact features in Celtic and English

Theo Vennemann
University of Munich

Introduction

The European Atlantic Littoral was, at the dawn of history, explored and colonized by Mediterranean, probably Palaeo-Phoenician seafarers. To the Greeks, these western-most areas of Europe were located "am hesperischen Okeanos, an der Atlantis, wo auch der Himmelsträger Atlas haust" [on the Hesperian Okeanos, at the Atlantis, where also the sky-bearer Atlas dwells] (cf. Pauly/Wissowa 1893 ff.: s.v. *Hesperiden*).[1]

The Old Testament refers to trading relations with this region, namely with Tartessos on the Atlantic coast of the Iberian Peninsula. The prophet Ezekiel (Chapter 27) says, praising the Phoenician city of Tyre, "merchant of the people for many isles" (v. 2): "Tarshish [i.e., Tartessos] was thy [i.e., Tyre's] merchant by reason of the multitude of all kind of riches; with silver, iron, tin, and lead, they traded in thy fares" (v. 12), "the ships of Tarshish did sing of thee in thy market: and thou wast replenished" (v. 25). The prophet could have added copper. The copper trade from Ireland, where industrial copper mining for export has been demonstrated by archaeologists for the second millennium BC, was in the hands of the Phoenicians.[2]

There is some evidence that parts of the Atlantic littoral were linguistically Hamito-Semitic. For Insular Celtic an Hamito-Semitic[3] substratum has been demonstrated, e.g., by Morris Jones (1900), Pokorny (1927–30), Gensler (forthc.), cf. also Wagner (1959), Vennemann (1994: Appendix), Shisha-Halevy (1995). For Proto-Germanic I have collected evidence that it developed under a Semitic superstratum (Vennemann 1995, 1998a, b). The general theory of stratal language contact (Thomason & Kaufman 1988: ch. 5 et passim) predicts on the evidence of case studies that more structural Semitic influence should be found in Celtic than in Germanic but more lexical Semitic influence in Germanic than in Celtic (Vennemann 1998b: 245–248).

The latter prediction has been shown in some measure to be correct: Germanic has words with Semitic etymologies that are not shared by other Indo-European languages including Celtic. One example is the military term for a division of an army, Old Germanic *fulka- (cf. Hebr. *plC*, a family of related roots including *plg*, all meaning 'to divide') which survives in G *Volk* 'people', E *folk*; *fulka- 'division of an army' is a typical superstratal term, as the French borrowings *Division* (of an Armee), *division* (of an army or fleet) in modern German and English clearly show (Vennemann 1998b). Another example is OE *ymbe*, OHG *imbi* 'swarm of bees', or rather 'people of bees' (cf. G *Bienenvolk*), a cultural borrowing (like the *bee*-word itself) from the advanced superstratal civilization; cf. Semit. ʿ*Vm*- 'Volk, people' with various vocalizations and Egypt. *bi.t* 'bee' (Vennemann 1998d).

The following are some further superstratal loan-words occurring in Germanic but not in Celtic for which a Semitic origin has been proposed (cf. Vennemann 1995, 1997 for analyses and references): *harp* (only Germanic), together with *harfest* and related but non-native words in other Indo-European languages, cf. Semit. *hrp* 'to pluck, collect fruit'; OE *sūl*, G *Säule* and the irregular Goth. *sauls* 'pillar' (only Germanic), cf. Hebr. *selaʿ* 'rock' and, if Coates (1988a) is right, maritime place-names throughout the Mediterranean (and one in Great Britain) of the form *Solentia* and referring to cliffs (cf. the Pillars of Hercules), names which may contain the ablaut variant *sol*; *earth* (in this form only Germanic), cf. Proto-Semit. *ʾrḍ* in Akkad. *erṣetu*, Hebr. *éreṣ*, Aram. *arʿā*, South Arab. *ʾrḍ*, North Arab. *arḍun*, all meaning 'land, earth'; E *fright*, G *Furcht* 'fear', cf. Semit. roots like *plḥ*, *prḥ* 'to fear', in particular the Akkadian derived noun *puluḥtu(m)* 'fear'; E *to wake*, G *wachen* 'to wake', *Wächter* 'guard' etc., a word family which is highly irregular in Germanic and has a reasonably certain relative only in Lat. *vegēre* 'to be lively', *vigil* 'awake, on the watch, alert; watchman, sentinel', cf. Semit. *wqī* 'to keep, preserve', e.g., Old Assyr. *waqāʾum* 'to wait, wait for, keep/preserve, attend to, pay attention'.[4] But the picture is far from complete. In particular, similar investigations into the unexplained parts of the Insular Celtic lexicon seem to be lacking.

The present paper is addressed to the former of the two predictions, that of structural Semitic influence in Celtic. Whereas the Insular Celtic lexicon and morphology have remained Indo-European, the syntactic transformation of Insular Celtic in the British Isles has been radical, to the point that Insular Celtic syntax, except for traces in the oldest poetic and "rhetorical" Irish, no longer shows the Indo-European head-final word order and in this and many other regards gives the impression of a non-Indo-European language. It is structurally similar to the Hamito-Semitic type represented by Berber, Egyptian, and Semitic (the latter in the narrower sense[5]).

Indeed, the Insular Celtic languages are syntactically much more similar to Arabic and Biblical Hebrew than to Latin and German.[6] That this is not a matter of accident, of internally motivated development, or of typological convergence but a result of prehistoric language contact is shown in the comparative work of John Morris Jones (1900) and Julius Pokorny (1927–30) as well as, most recently and most forcefully, in a global comparative linguistic study carried out by Orin David Gensler (forthc.).

I cannot present all aspects of these reconstructions in the few pages allotted for my presentation. Therefore, I will concentrate on a few aspects that I am presently working on and that may be interesting to an audience fluent in English, namely, certain syntactic features that have carried through, by twofold substratal influence, from the Semitic substratum into Insular Celtic and from there into English, dragging first Celtic and then English away from the European, mostly Indo-European sprachbund and into an Atlantic sprachbund. In so doing I can take up, and develop, ideas already found in Pokorny's work, succinctly summarized in Pokorny (1959). There, after characterizing about twenty syntactic properties of Insular Celtic which are not Indo-European but have counterparts in the Hamito-Semitic languages, Pokorny says in passing:

> Interessant ist übrigens festzustellen, daß sehr viele der oben angeführten nichtidg. Elemente des Inselkeltischen auch auf dem Umwege des Keltischen ins Englische gedrungen sind, das dadurch ein ungermanisches, ja sogar direkt nichtindogermanisches Gepräge erhalten hat (Pokorny 1959: 161).

> [It is interesting to note that very many of the above-mentioned non-Indo-European elements of Insular Celtic have also, via Celtic, passed into English which has thereby received an un-Germanic, even a downright non-Indo-European character.]

I will address two of Pokorny's features that have passed all the way from the Semitic substratum through Insular Celtic into English,[7] one which is well-known in this context and needs no lengthy exposition, the rise of the verbal noun, another which is less commonly referred to but is treated in some detail in Vennemann (forthc.), the decline of the external affected possessor construction and the rise of the internal genitive possessor construction. Between these two points I will briefly summarize a less well-known phenomenon, the Northern subject rule as discussed by Klemola (2000).

1. The rise of the verbal noun

Pokorny's 7th point concerning non-Indo-European syntactic properties shared by Insular Celtic and Hamito-Semitic reads as follows:

Das Inselkeltische besitzt kein Partizipium Präsentis (wenngleich dessen Form in anderer Funktion erhalten blieb ...). ... Seine Funktion wird, wie im Ägyptischen und Berberischen, durch das Verbalnomen ausgedrückt. Vgl. nir. *tā sē ag teacht* 'er ist kommend' = 'beim Kommen' (Pokorny 1959: 155).

[Insular Celtic does not possess a present participle (even though its form has been preserved with a different function ...). ... As in Egyptian and Berber, its function is expressed by the verbal noun. Cf. ModIr. *tā sē ag teacht* 'he is coming' = 'on coming' (literally 'at coming').]

Concerning the verbal noun, Pokorny's 6th point says the following:

Das inselkeltische System der Zeiten und Aspekte, besonders der Gebrauch der sogenannten progressiven Formen zur Bezeichnung des Aspektes durch das Verbum 'sein' + Präposition + Verbalnomen ist gewiß nicht idg., findet sich aber im Baskischen und Ägyptischen (Pokorny 1959: 155).

[The Insular Celtic system of tenses and aspects, especially the use of the so-called progressive forms as an expression of the aspect by means of the verb 'to be' + preposition + verbal noun, certainly is not Indo-European but is found in Basque and Egyptian.]

The same example as in the 7th point (see above) follows, as well as several others.

Wagner (1959), after comparing the Insular Celtic innovations to Hamito-Semitic, carries the areal interpretation one step further into English:

Diesem semantischen, die Verbalkategorien (Tempus, Aspekt) in den Hinter-grund drängenden, stark nominalen Verbum [des Angelsächsischen] steht das aspektive neuengl. Verbum mit starrer oder syntaktisch bedingter Wort-bedeutung gegenüber, das auf Grund seiner flexions- und bedeutungs-isolierenden Züge (vgl. Progressivform) auch formell deutlich vom angel-sächsisch-urgermanischen Verbum absticht. Die typologische Umschichtung des Angelsächsischen erfolgt auf den brit. Inseln, geht parallel mit der Entwick-lung der inselkelt. Sprachen, und führt ... zu der Ausbildung eines typisch britischen, die keltischen Sprachen und das Englische umfassenden Verbal-typus, innerhalb dessen es geographisch gebundene Variationen gibt. Das Englische zeigt, wie eine einheitliche Sprachmaterie auf Grund ihrer geograph-ischen Verpflanzung Stadien zweier, einander absolut entgegengesetzter Sprachtypen durchlaufen kann (Wagner 1959: 150 f.).

[This semantic, strongly nominal verb of Anglo-Saxon which pushes the verbal categories (tense, aspect) into the background, is opposed by the aspective Modern English verb with rigid or syntactically conditioned word meaning, which on grounds of its flexion- and meaning-isolating traits (cf. the progres-sive form) shows a clear difference, also formally, to the Anglo-Saxon, Proto-

Germanic verb. The typological restructuring of Anglo-Saxon takes place in the British Isles, paralleling the development of the Insular Celtic languages, and leads to the formation of a typically British verbal type (including geographic variation), where British comprises the Celtic languages and English. English shows how a uniform language material, by its geographic transplantation, can pass through two absolutely opposite language types.]

Much has been written about the rise of the progressive aspect in English; cf., e.g., Mustanoja (1960:584–590), Faiß (1989:242ff. [§4.4.13f.]), recently Grzega (1999), and Celtic influence in particular has also been claimed to have played a role (cf. the references in Mustanoja 1960:590). Recently Mittendorf and Poppe have studied the question by comparing medieval texts and have cautiously formulated the following result:

> In addition to the striking formal similarities between the Insular Celtic and English periphrastic constructions, striking similarities also exist between their functional ranges in the medieval languages. This is perhaps not enough to argue decisively one way or the other with regard to the likelihood of Celtic contacts of the English progressive, but it adds another, new perspective to the problem (Mittendorf & Poppe 2000:139).

This is certainly correct. However, in my view the matter was settled with Preusler's detailed account of the English verbal noun and the English progressive. Preusler (1956:327–331, 331–334), who also considers Mossé's (1938:§§165ff.) contrary position, in my view leaves no room for doubt that in view of the exactness of their formal and functional correspondence and their temporal development, the English verbal noun and the English progressive have to be explained as influence of the parallel Welsh constructions. Concerning "das heutige übermaß der umschreibenden form im irischen, schottischen und walisischen englisch" [the current excessive measure of the periphrastic form in Irish, Scottish, and Welsh English], even Mossé (1938:§105) realized the necessity of admitting "die wahrscheinlichkeit keltischen einflusses" [the likelihood of Celtic influence] (Preusler 1956:333). In my view the essential English innovation consists in the victory of the Celtic-motivated verbal noun construction (suffix -ung/-ing) over the Anglo-Saxon present participle construction (suffix -inde/-ande), where even the frequent use of the latter may have been provoked by attempts to integrate the Celtic aspect into English.

One may object that the progressive, as a universally available verbal category belonging to the wider range of "continuous" or "imperfective" aspect (cf. Bybee 1985:141–146), may have originated in English independently of its existence in Insular Celtic. However, the explanandum remains that among all the Germanic languages, only English has undergone this development, plus certain continental dialects close to the coast, i.e., exactly those regions which, according to the theory, had been colonized by the prehistoric Semitic-speaking seafarers. It must also be noted that whereas the Rhenish progressive is formed with the nominalized infinitive (*er ist am lesen* "he is (at the) to-read", 'he is reading'), the English progressive has developed from a construction with the verbal noun (of the type *he is on reading* > *he is a-reading* > *he is reading*). The reason is evident: Insular Celtic does not possess an infinitive.[8]

Looking for more recent support of Pokorny's comparison of the Celtic and English verbal noun constructions with Egyptian, I found the following passages in Loprieno (1995):

> Later Egyptian develops periphrastic verbal forms based on the verb *jrj* 'to do' (*sdm.n=f* 'he heard' > *jr=f sdm*, lit. 'he did the hearing' ...). ... The earlier Egyptian opposition between the initial *jrr=f* and its non-topicalized counterpart *jrj=f*, rather than by different morphological *sdm.n=f*-patterns, is conveyed in later Egyptian by the use of the two distinct forms *j.jr=f-sdm*, lit. '(the fact) that he does a hearing' ... vs. *jw=f-ḥr-sdm*, lit.: 'while he is on hearing' (Loprieno 1995: 91).

My impression is that there does exist some similarity between the use of a verbal noun in Egyptian and Insular Celtic verbal periphrasis, just as there is a very transparent similarity between Insular Celtic and English in this regard.

2.   The Northern subject rule

Klemola (2000) studies the question of the origin of the Northern subject rule, which he formulates as follows:

> **The Northern subject rule:**
> In the present tense, the verb takes the *-s* ending in all persons, singular and plural, unless it is adjacent to a personal pronoun subject (Klemola 2000: 330).

He illustrates the rule with the following examples: *They peel them and boils them* and *Birds sings.* The rule is followed most consistently in "the North proper (Northumberland, Cumberland, Durham, Westmoreland)" and "was already fully established at the time during the 14th century when Northern Middle English texts become more common", if not much earlier. These originally Welsh areas were Anglicized in the second half of the 7th century and were probably bilingual until the end of the 8th century, in part longer.

It so happens that the strange Northern subject rule has a rather close counterpart in the Brythonic languages, Welsh, Cornish, and Breton. Citing King (1993: 137), Klemola states the rule for both spoken and written Welsh as follows, making his own addition:

The Welsh rule:
3rd pers. pl. forms are only used when the corresponding pronoun *nhw* 'they' is explicitly stated. In all other cases where the subject is 3rd pers. pl., the 3rd pers. sing. form must be used. [Addition:] When there is no overt subject, 3rd person plural agreement is used (Klemola 2000: 337).

Klemola cites the following examples from King (1993):

Maen   nhw'n dysgu   Cymraeg.
are-PL-VERB they a-learning Welsh
"They are learning Welsh."

Mae   Kev a   Gina yn dysgu   Cymraeg.
is-SG-VERB Kev and Gina a-learning Welsh
"Kev and Gina are learning Welsh."

Gân   nhw ailwneud y   gwaith 'ma yfory.
can-PL-VERB they redo   this work   tomorrow
"They can redo this work tomorrow."

Geith   y   myfyrwyr ailwneud y   gwaith 'ma yfory.
can-SG-VERB the students   redo   this work   tomorrow
"The students can redo this work tomorrow."

He tabulates the paradigm for Modern Welsh as follows:

1. maent   '[they] are'
2. maent hwy   'they are'
3. mae 'r bechgyn   'the boys are'

"where 1. (no overt subject) and 2. (adjacent personal pronoun subject) are grouped together as against 3. (full noun phrase subject)"

Klemola (2000: 337) says about the distribution of such rule systems: "From a typological point of view, agreement systems of the type exemplified by the northern subject rule appear to be extremely rare." Indeed, after mentioning the Celtic parallel he adds in a footnote (n. 7): "The only other languages where a somewhat similar agreement paradigm is found are, to the best of my knowledge, Hebrew (cf. Evans 1971: 42) and Arabic (Bernard Comrie, p.c.)."

The following statement made with reference to the Semitic languages and focussing on Arabic may serve as support of the similarity claim:

The Arabic rule:
Concord of Subject and Predicate. … The predicate agrees generally with the subject in gender and number. However, if the plural subject is definitely expressed and follows the verb [which is the basic word order], it is optional in Arabic whether the verb is in the plural or singular; e.g., *qad ǧā'akum rusulun*, 'messengers arrived for you', with the verb in the singular. Such a lack of grammatical concord sporadically occurs also in other Semitic languages, but

its frequency in old Arabic texts must result from a particular usage which did not take root in Neo-Arabic; e.g., *it'allamū l-wilād,* 'the children did learn' (Lipiński 1997:491f.).

The following quotation from a Hebrew textbook likewise supports the Semitic case:

The Hebrew rule:
Normalerweise kongruiert das Verbum in Geschlecht und Zahl mit seinem Subjekt. Doch kann das voranstehende Verbum auch im Singular angetroffen werden, wenn es sich in gleicher Weise auf verschiedene Subjekte bezieht (Jenni 1981:§6.3.1.2).

[Normally the verb agrees with its subject in gender and number. But a verb preceding several subjects which it governs in a parallel manner may occur in the singular.]

The example given by Jenni shows the following structure: $(saw)_{\text{V-Sing}}$ *(Aaron and all the Isrealites)*$_{\text{Subj-Plur}}$ *(Moses)*$_{\text{Obj}}$.

Klemola argues convincingly that despite the differences of detail, Northern English has borrowed the Northern subject rule from Celtic; he cites Hamp (1975–76:73) as an author likewise "suggest[ing] that the northern subject rule in Northern varieties of English could be a substratum feature from Cumbrian" (Klemola 2000:338). I would like to suggest, with the same kind of argument, that the Celtic subject rule is likewise a substratum feature, developed in Insular Celtic on the prehistoric Semitic substratum of the British Isles. Both the Northern English and the Insular Celtic subject rules are non-Indo-European and indeed unique in the Indo-European world, so that their origin in language contact is a priori likely. Since Semitic languages, members of the language family assumed to have been in contact with Celtic in the Isles on independent grounds, do have analogs of these strange and rare agreement rules, one does not have to look any further.

3.   The replacement of the sympathetic dative by the internal possessor construction[9]

In this section I would like briefly to consider an especially transparent case of transitive substratal influence of Semitic through Celtic on English, the rise of the possessive genitive for affected possessors,[10] i.e., the possessive genitive, inasmuch as it has replaced an earlier, non-genitival construction of the affected possessor, an "external possessor" construction, viz., in the case on hand, the "sympathetic dative".[11]

3.1 Illustrating external possessor construction: Modern German

Compare English sentences such as those in (1) and (2) to their German equivalents:

(1) The queen cut off the king's head.
     Die Königin schlug dem König   den Kopf   ab.
     the queen cut   the king-DAT the head-ACC off

(2) Mary broke her neck.
     a. *Maria brach sich   das Genick.*
         Mary$_i$ broke herself-DAT$_j$ the neck-ACC (i=j)
     b. *Maria brach ihr   das Genick.*
         Mary$_i$ broke her-DAT$_j$ the neck-ACC (i≠j)

The use of the possessive genitive here appears absolutely normal in a Modern English perspective. But it does not in a German perspective; as a matter of fact, in the intended sense the genitive is impossible in German. In English, the external possessor construction only survives residually in expressions such as *He looked her in the eyes, She stared him in the face* (König & Haspelmath 1997: 554).

Comparison with the older Germanic and Indo-European languages shows that German continues the inherited Germanic and, indeed, Indo-European construction.[12] The Modern English construction is not Germanic, and it is not Indo-European.

3.2 The external possessor construction in Old and Middle English

As a matter of fact, the Modern English construction is not Anglo-Saxon either. Typical of Old English are sentences with the sympathetic dative such as that in (3).

(3) *seo cwen het   þa þæm cyninge   þæt heafod   of aceorfan*[13]
     the queen ordered then the king-DAT the head-ACC off off-to-cut
     "The queen then ordered the king's head to be cut off."

This construction is also found throughout Middle English, as is evident in (4) and (5).

(4) *Sir Willam Mautrauers Carf him   of fet &   honde*[14]
     Sir W. M.   cut him-DAT off feet and hands-ACC
     "Sir W. M. cut off his feet and hands."

(5) *it com hire to minde*[15]

3.3 The internal possessor construction in Old and Middle English

However, as early as late Old English we also find the "internal possessor" construction that we know from Modern English. The oldest attestation of the replacing genitive could be that in (6); at least it seems to be the oldest for the verb *ofceorfan*.

(6)   *He cearf of* **heora** *handa 7*   **heora** *nosa*[16]
he cut   off their   hands and their   noses
"He cut off their hands and their noses."

That this is also a possible construction in Middle English and early Modern English is shown by the examples in (7) and (8).

(7)   *Hys legges hy   corven of anon*[17]
his legs   they cut   off immediately
"His legs they cut off immediately."

(8)   Though thou cut of **my** heed[18]

Mustanoja (1960:98) says about the inherited dative construction: "This construction, common in OE ..., is comparatively infrequent in ME and loses ground steadily". It is almost unknown in standard varieties of Modern English.[19]

3.4 A possible reason for the rise of the internal possessor construction

In Vennemann (forthc.) it is shown that the loss of the external possessor construction in English cannot be explained as a consequence of the loss of case distinctions. The main arguments are first, that the sympathetic dative could have survived just like the directional dative, e.g., with verbs of giving, as in (9) and (10), but did not;

(9)   Mary gave her husband the book. Mary gave him the book.

(9')   *Mary broke her husband the arm. *Mary broke him the arm.

(10)   Mary gave the book to her husband. Mary gave the book to him.

(10')   *Mary broke the arm to her husband. *Mary broke the arm to him.

and second, that in the Scandinavian Germanic languages where the cases were neutralized as in English, the external possessor construction is not at all lost but transformed into locative ("superessive") prepositional phrases, as in the examples (11) and (12) taken from König and Haspelmath (1997:559):

(11)   **Swedish**
Någon   brött   armen   på honom.
someone broke arm-the on him
"Someone broke his arm."

(12)   **Norwegian**
Legen   røntgenfotograferte magen   på dem.
physician-the X-rayed   stomach-the on them
"The physician X-rayed their stomachs."

This developmental option is available even in languages which still preserve case distinctions, such as in (13).

(13)   **Icelandic**
       Han nuddaði á henni   fætur-na
       he   massaged on her-DAT feet-the-ACC
       "He massaged her feet."

One may also point to the fact that even in English the sympathetic dative survives residually, cf. Section 3.1 above, despite the loss of case distinctions. In short, there was no need to give up the external possessor construction merely because morphological case distinctions eroded. So this is not an acceptable explanation.

3.5   The English internal possessor construction as a contact feature

König and Haspelmath (1997) and Haspelmath (1998:277f.) stress the fact that the elimination of the external possessor construction is, among all the European languages, strictly limited to the languages of the British Isles: except for Lezghian and Turkish, the only languages in Europe lacking external possessors are English and Celtic. Clearly the different ways affected possessors are expressed in the languages of Europe mark sprachbunds rather than language families: affected possessor construction is areal. Excepting the case where closely related languages have preserved an inherited model, sharing the same affected possessor construction type is a contact phenomenon.

The message of this fact for the present discussion seems clear: English and Insular Celtic stand alone against the rest of Europe. The examples in (14) to (19) may serve to illustrate the "Celtic" way of constructing affected possessors.[20]

(14)   **Middle Welsh** (Havers 1911:250f.)
       llad   y benn
       he-cut-off his head
       "he cut off his head."

(15)   *ae   vedru yn y lygat*
       and-he thrust into his eye
       "and he thrust into his eye."

(16)   **Modern Welsh** (textbook example)
       Mae e wedi torri ei fraich.
       is   he ADJ   break his arm
       "He has broken his arm."

(17)   **Old and Early Middle Irish** (Havers 1911:242)
       benaid   -sium a chend
       he-cut-off PART his head
       "He cut off his head."

(18)   *ben   mo chend dím*
       cut-off my head from-me
       "Cut off my head!"

(19)   *ro-s-bensat*   *a   leth-shuil*   *ńdeiss as*   *a   chend*
they-her-knocked-out his half-eye (fem.) right   out-of his head
"They knocked out his right eye (from his head)."
But cf. German:
Sie   schlugen   ihm   das rechte Auge aus.
they knocked him the right   eye   out

In Modern Irish the construction type with a locative prepositional phrase has been further developed into an external possessor construction similar to the type illustrated above in (11)–(13) for Modern Scandinavian Germanic. In view of the observation that innovations in the affected possessor construction tend to be contact phenomena, it appears likely that the Irish development occurred under Scandinavian influence in the Viking period.

The interpretation of the generalization of the English internal possessor construction as a "Celtic" borrowing is supported by the external histories of these languages and the general theory of language contact.

As a kind of "negative control" (as natural scientists say) of the thesis that the loss of external possessors in English is a contact phenomenon, one may check if the absence of external possessors from a language is in any way the normal state of affairs, the loss of external possessors therefore something natural or expected. The essays in Payne and Barshi, eds. (1999), and in particular the introduction by the editors (Payne & Barshi 1999), show that this is not the case; on the contrary:

> *External possession* is found in all parts of the globe: Asia ..., the Pacific region ..., Australia ..., all across the Americas from North America ..., through Meso-America ..., and in South America ..., Europe ..., and Africa ... [the three dots stand for omitted specifications and references]. It seems safe to say that there is no geographical area of the world where the phenomenon does not occur, and it is hardly exotic. Its sheer ubiquity suggests it must be a linguistically natural phenomenon, serving some central human communicative need (Payne & Barshi 1999:6).

It would therefore not be explanatory to assume that English lost its external possessors as a matter of course; those who want to claim this would first have to show that such a change, by internal motivation and within a few centuries, is at all possible.

3.6 The Semitic origin of the generalized Celtic internal possessor construction

Asking finally how the non-European, non-Indo-European generalized internal possessor construction arose in Celtic in the first place, we find the same answer as in the first two sections above. Except for Europeanized Maltese and Modern

Hebrew, Semitic totally lacks external possessors. The examples in (20) to (24) are representative.

Hebrew

(20)   *wajjikrā̆ṯ*   *-bah*   *'æṯ -rōšō*[21]
       and-cut-off-he with-her[22] ACC head-his
       "and he cut off his head with it"

(21)   *wajjikrᵉṯū*   *'æṯ -rōš Šæḇar*   *bæn-Bikrī*[23]
       and-cut-off-they ACC head of-Sheba son-of-Bichri
       "and they cut off the head of Sheba, the son of Bichri."

Arabic

(22)   qaṭaʿati l-malikatu ra'sa   l-maliki
       cut-off the-queen (the-)head (of-)the-king
       "The queen cut off the king's head."

(23)   qaṭaʿtu   ra'sahū
       cut-off-I head-his
       "I cut off his head."

(24)   kasarat Mary raqabatahā
       broke   Mary$_i$ neck-her$_j$ (i=j, i≠j)
       "Mary broke her neck."

We have to assume that Celtic in the Isles lost its external possessor construction on the Semitic substratum. It so happens that Old Irish still showed traces of the inherited external possessor type, the sympathetic dative, but soon lost it altogether, as did Insular Celtic generally:

> Dans les plus anciens textes celtique (vieil-irlandais), on trouve encore des exemples de datif sympathique, mais dès l'origine, il n'a qu'un rôle tout à fait marginal. Dans les langues celtiques actuelles, il n'existe plus du tout (König & Haspelmath 1997: 583).

> [In the most ancient Celtic (Old Irish) texts, one still finds examples of the sympathetic dative, but from the very beginning it only plays a completely marginal role. In the present Celtic languages it no longer exists at all.]

This has its parallel in the English development: Exactly as the Hamito-Semitic internal possessor construction gradually ousted the sympathetic dative from Celtic, leaving vestiges in early Old Irish, so the newly acquired and generalized "Celtic" internal possessor construction gradually ousted the sympathetic dative from English, leaving vestiges in Modern English. Old Irish and Modern English resemble each other in that they completed certain developments which in either case had begun, more than a thousand years earlier, by the first contacts with their respective substrates.

4.   Why did the Atlantic type rise in Middle English?

It may be asked why all three instances of Semiticizing-Celticizing syntactic influence illustrated here, after centuries of no or only sporadic attestation, rose almost suddenly in Middle English. The answer is provided by the theory of language contact: substratal influence originates in the lower strata of a society and usually takes centuries to reach the written language, and regularly only after a period of social upheaval. That this applies to Irish was argued by Pokorny (1927–30), and that it applies to English is a fact well known to every Anglicist: Middle English is the period during which the language of the old ruling class dies out because the new ruling class speaks French; and when this French-speaking ruling class switches to English, that English is the Celticized English of the lower strata. This was most succinctly summarized by Wagner:

> Daß sich das Germanische im angelsächsischen England einige Jahrhunderte ziemlich gut erhalten konnte, hängt mit dem Vorhandensein einer ags. Aristokratie und einer ags. Schrift- und Dichtersprache zusammen. Mit der normannischen Eroberung wird dieser germanischen Herrenschicht die Spitze gebrochen und der Entwicklung einer britischen Sprache freier Lauf gewährt (Wagner 1959: 151).

> [That Germanic was preserved in Anglo-Saxon England for several centuries is connected to the existence of an Anglo-Saxon aristocracy and an Anglo-Saxon written and poetic language. The Norman conquest broke the supremacy of this ruling class and paved the way for the development of a British language.]

5.   Conclusion

In this short paper I have presented three grammatical features which unite English and Insular Celtic with Semitic in a single sprachbund-like group of languages. More such features can be gained by comparing the research results of Morris Jones, Pokorny, and Gensler combining Hamito-Semitic and Insular Celtic, with those of Preusler combining Insular Celtic and English. I am convinced that an extension of this line of research to the entire grammar of English and to Insular Celtic and Semitic will reveal that English shares many distinctive properties with Semitic, and that it does so precisely because English was substratally Semiticized, namely by transitive loaning of Semitic structure, with Insular Celtic as mediator. Skipping the Celtic layer, and integrating the superstratal influence of Norman French after the Conquest of 1066,[24] we can succinctly characterize English as a structurally Semiticized, lexically Romanized German dialect.

Norman-French
$\Downarrow$

Saxon[25] > Anglo-Saxon → English
$\Uparrow$

Celtic → Insular Celtic
$\Uparrow$

Semitic

Explanation of symbols:
  $\Downarrow$: superstratal influence on
  $\Uparrow$: substratal influence on
  >: regional development into
  →: transformation into

I consider this a pedigree worthy of a truly cosmopolitan language.

Notes

1. Translations of foreign quotations are marked by square brackets throughout the article. They are my own.

2. I have presented arguments (cf. Vennemann 1998c) that even the name of Ireland is Semitic, together with several further place-names of a maritime significance in the British Isles (cf. Coates 1988a,b; Vennemann 1999).

3. I will often simply say Semitic; cf. note 5 below.

4. The fact that the verb is strong in English (OE *wōc, wōcum*, also ON *vakenn* 'awake') is not detrimental to the assumption of a loan-word. As a matter of fact, most strong verbs have no — or no good — etymologies and are therefore likely to be loan-words, among them the numerous verbs containing a ^+p (cf. Vennemann 1998a: 42–43 and, for ^+plegan 'to cultivate', Vennemann 1998b: 252–254).

5. There are two conceptions of Semitic, the majority view according to which Egyptian and Libyco-Berber are Hamitic — and thus non-Semitic — languages, though the ones most closely related to Semitic (in the narrower sense), and the minority view according to which Egyptian and Libyco-Berber *are* Semitic languages (e.g., Rössler 1950, 1952). Cp. the short overview in Moscati et al. (1964 [1980]: 16f.) and the most recent comprehensive presentation in Lipiński (1997: 23–47).

6. Even in papers not addressed to the question of why Insular Celtic has developed in its peculiar way, or specifically to the question of outside influence, one can read such descriptions as "the exotic characteristics of the Celtic languages from an Indo-European perspective" (Eska 1999: 155).

7. The question of the Celtic population substratum in early Anglo-Saxon England is addressed in German (2000) and Viereck (2000).

8. Cf. Russell (1995: Ch. 8) for the Insular Celtic verbal noun, and p. 258 for the lack of an infinitive. Since infinitives in the Indo-European languages are by origin nominal derivates of verbs, the difference between a "verbal noun" (a noun which happens to be derived from a verb,

e.g., G [*die*] *Tötung* '[the] killing') and an "infinitive" (a deverbal nominal integrated into the verbal paradigm, e.g., G [*das*] *Töten* '[the] killing' alongside [*er*] *wird töten* '[he] will kill'), though easy to grasp intuitively, is difficult to define in general terms. But this is not the place to address the general problem. (Cf. Mayerthaler, Fliedl, & Winkler 1993–97, 1998: s.v. *Infinitiv*.) Note further that Insular Celtic does not possess a present participle (ibid.), which explains the merger of the English present participle with the gerund, the central formal process in the development of the English progressive, as yet another manifestation of Celtic influence.

9. This development is illustrated and discussed more fully in Vennemann (forthc.)

10. I adopt the term *affected possessor* in this connection from Vandeweghe (1987:139) who presents it as established in the literature.

11. The term "sympathetic dative" (*Dativus sympatheticus*) was coined by Havers (1911:2); cf. König and Haspelmath (1997:551). The conditions for the use of the external possessor construction, such as the sympathetic dative, differ from language to language; see König and Haspelmath (1997).

12. The first and best exploration of the sympathetic dative in Indo-European, as is also stressed by Vandeweghe (1986:128, note 3) and by König and Haspelmath (1997:551), is Havers (1911).

13. Cf. Mustanoja (1960:98).

14. Robert of Gloucester (1810) 560 [a. 1297]; cf. OED: s.v. *carve* v. I.1.b.

15. Geoffrey Chaucer, *Troilus and Criseyde* ii. 602; cf. Mustanoja (1960:99). The predicate *com hire to minde* is glossed 'came to her mind' in *The Riverside Chaucer*.

16. OE Chron., a. 1014 [ca. 1025]; cf. OED: s.v. *carve*.

17. *Chronicle of England* 757 [ca. 1325], in Ritson *Metr. Rom.* II. 301; cf. OED: s.v. *carve*.

18. *The pilgrimage of perfection* (W. de W. 1531) 177 b [a. 1526]; cf. OED: s.v. *cut* v., no. 56. *cut off.*

19. The most comprehensive documentation of the external possessor construction is Ahlgren (1946).

20. I have to thank Stephen Laker (Munich) for the Celtic examples of this section as well as for the Semitic examples in Section 3.6 below.

21. Sam. I 17,51.

22. The reference is to 'sword' which is feminine in Hebrew.

23. Sam. II 20,22.

24. And simplifying matters by omitting other influences, such as those arising from Scandinavian contacts.

25. More precisely, Saxon and closely related Continental West Germanic dialects.

References

Ahlgren, Arthur. 1946. *On the Use of the Definite Article with "Nouns of Possession" in English.* (= *Stockholm Studies in English*, 2.) [Ph.D. dissertation, University of Uppsala.] Uppsala: Boktryckeriaktiebolag.

[Chaucer, Geoffrey.] 1987. *The Riverside Chaucer*, 3rd ed. ed. by Larry D. Benson, based on *The works of Geoffrey Chaucer* ed. by F. N. Robinson. Boston, MA: Houghton Mifflin.

Bybee, Joan L. 1985. *Morphology: A study of the relation between meaning and form.* (= *Typological Studies in Language*, 9.) Amsterdam: John Benjamins.

Coates, Richard. 1988a. "Periplus: A voyage round the Solent". Coates 1988c.1–20.

Coates, Richard. 1988b. "Uist = Ibiza". Coates 1988c. 21–23.

Coates, Richard. 1988c. *Toponymic Topics: Essays on the early toponymy of the British Isles*. Brighton: Younsmere Press.

Eska, Joseph F. 1999. Review of *Progress in Medieval Irish studies* ed. by Kim McCone & Katharine Simms. *Kratylos* 44.154–157.

Evans, D. S. 1971. "Concord in Middle Welsh". *Studia Celtica* 6.42–56.

Faiß, Klaus. 1989. *Englische Sprachgeschichte*. Tübingen: A. Francke.

Gensler, Orin David. Forthcoming. *The Celtic-North African Linguistic Link: Substrata and typological argumentation*. Oxford: Oxford University Press. [Rev. version of unpubl. Ph. D. dissertation, University of California, Berkeley, 1993.]

German, Gary D. 2000. "Britons, Anglo-Saxons and Scholars: 19th century attitudes towards the survival of Britons in Anglo-Saxon England". Tristram 2000.347–374.

Grzega, Joachim. 1999. "A New View on Why, How and in How Far -*ing* Prevailed over -*ind*". *Views: Vienna English Working Papers* 8: 1.34–42.

Hamp, Eric P. 1975–76. "Miscellanea Celtica I, II, III, IV". *Studia Celtica* 10/11.54–73.

Haspelmath, Martin. 1998. "How Young is Standard Average European?" *Language Sciences* 20.271–287.

Havers, Wilhelm. 1911. *Untersuchungen zur Kasussyntax der indogermanischen Sprachen*. (= *Untersuchungen zur indogermanischen Sprach- und Kulturwissenschaft*, 3.) Straßburg: Karl J. Trübner.

Jenni, Ernst. 1981. *Lehrbuch der hebräischen Sprache des Alten Testaments*. Basel: Helbing & Lichtenhahn.

King, G. 1993. *Modern Welsh: A comprehensive grammar*. London: Routledge.

Klemola, Juhani. 2000. "The Origins of the Northern Subject Rule — A case of early contact?" Tristram 2000.329–346.

König, Ekkehard & Martin Haspelmath. 1997. "Les constructions à possesseur externe dans les langues d'Europe". *Actance et valence dans les langues d'Europe* ed. by J. Feuillet, 525–606. Berlin: Mouton de Gruyter.

Lipiński, Edward. 1997. *Semitic Languages: Outline of a comparative grammar*. Leuven: Peeters.

Loprieno, Antonio. 1995. *Ancient Egyptian: A linguistic introduction*. Cambridge: Cambridge University Press.

Mayerthaler, Willi, Günther Fliedl, & Christian Winkler. 1993–97. *Infinitivprominenz in den europäischen Sprachen*. 3 parts. Tübingen: Gunter Narr.

Mayerthaler, Willi, Günther Fliedl, & Christian Winkler. 1998. *Lexikon der Natürlichkeitstheoretischen Morphosyntax*. Tübingen: Stauffenburg.

Mittendorf, Ingo & Erich Poppe. 2000. "Celtic Contacts of the English Progressive?" Tristram 2000: 117–145.

Morris Jones, John. 1900. "Pre-Aryan Syntax in Insular Celtic". *The Welsh People: Chapters on their origin, history, laws, language, literature and characteristics* ed. by John Rhys & David Brynmor-Jones, Appendix B, 617–641. London: T. Fisher Unwin.

Moscati, Sabatino, Anton Spitaler, Edward Ullendorf, & Wolfram von Soden. 1964. *An Introduction to the Comparative Grammar of the Semitic Languages: Phonology and morphology*. (= *Porta Linguarum Orientalium, Neue Serie*, 6.) 1980 reprint. Wiesbaden: Otto Harrassowitz.

Mossé, Fernand. 1938. *Histoire de la forme périphrastique être et participe présent en Germanique*. Paris: Klincksieck.

Mustanoja, Tauno F. 1960. *A Middle English Syntax*. Part I: *Parts of speech*. Helsinki: Société Néophilologique.

[Pauly/Wissowa] 1893 ff. *Paulys Realencyclopädie der classischen Altertumswissenschaft,* neue Bearbeitung begonnen von Georg Wissowa. Stuttgart: Alfred Druckenmüller.

Payne, Doris L. & Immanuel Barshi. 1999. "External Possession: What, where, how, and why". Payne & Barshi 1999.3–29.

Payne, Doris L. & Immanuel Barshi, eds. 1999. *External Possession.* (= *Typological Studies in Language,* 39.) Amsterdam: John Benjamins.

Pokorny, Julius. 1927–30. "Das nicht-indogermanische Substrat im Irischen". *Zeitschrift für celtische Philologie* 16.95–144, 231–266, 363–394; 17.373–388; 18.233–248.

Pokorny, Julius. 1959. "Keltische Urgeschichte und Sprachwissenschaft". *Die Sprache* 5.152–164.

Preusler, Walther. 1956. "Keltischer Einfluß im Englischen". *Revue des Langues Vivantes* 22.322–350.

Rössler, Otto. 1950. "Verbalbau und Verbalflexion in den semitohamitischen Sprachen". *Zeitschrift der Deutschen Morgenländischen Gesellschaft* 100.461–514.

Rössler, Otto. 1952. "Der semitische Charakter der libyschen Sprache". *Zeitschrift für Assyriologie und verwandte Gebiete* 50.121–150.

Russell, Paul. 1995. *An Introduction to the Celtic Languages.* London: Longman.

Shisha-Halevy, Ariel. 1995. "Structural Sketches of Middle Welsh Syntax (I)". *Studia Celtica* 29.127–223.

Thomason, Sarah Grey & Terence Kaufman. 1988. *Language Contact, Creolization, and Genetic Linguistics.* Berkeley: University of California Press.

Tristram, Hildegard L.C., ed. 1997. *The Celtic Englishes.* (= *Anglistische Forschungen,* 247.) Heidelberg: Carl Winter.

Tristram, Hildegard L.C., ed. 2000. *The Celtic Englishes II* (= *Anglistische Forschungen,* 286.) Heidelberg: Carl Winter.

Vandeweghe, Willy. 1986. "De zogenaamde possessieve datief en configuraatieherschikking". *Syntaxis en lexicon: Veertien artikelen bij gelegenheid van het emeritaat van Albert Sassen* ed. by Cor Hoppenbrouwers et al., 117–131. Dordrecht: Foris.

Vandeweghe, Willy. 1987. "The Possessive Dative in Dutch: Syntactic reanalysis and predicate formation". *Ins and Outs of Predication* ed. by Johan van der Auwera & Louis Goossens, 137–151. Dordrecht: Foris.

Vennemann, Theo. 1994. "Die mitteleuropäischen Orts- und Matronennamen mit *f, þ, h* und die Spätphase der Indogermania". *Früh-, Mittel-, Spätindogermanisch: Akten der IX. Fachtagung der Indogermanischen Gesellschaft vom 5. bis 9. Oktober 1992 in Zürich* ed. by George E. Dunkel, Gisela Meyer, Salvatore Scarlata, & Christian Seidl, 403–426. Wiesbaden: Ludwig Reichert.

Vennemann, Theo. 1995. "Etymologische Beziehungen im Alten Europa". *Der GinkgoBaum: Germanistisches Jahrbuch für Nordeuropa* 13.39–115.

Vennemann, Theo. 1997. "Some West Indo-European Words of Uncertain Origin". *Language History and Language Modelling: A festschrift for Jacek Fisiak on his 60th birthday* (= *Trends in Linguistics: Studies and Monographs,* 101) ed. by Raymond Hickey & Stanisław Puppel, vol. I.879–908. Berlin: Mouton de Gruyter.

Vennemann, Theo. 1998a. "Andromeda and the Apples of the Hesperides". *Proceedings of the Ninth Annual UCLA Indo-European Conference, 1997* (= *Journal of Indo-European Studies Monograph Series,* 27) ed. by Karlene Jones-Bley, Angela Della Volpe, Miriam Robbins Dexter, & Martin E. Huld, 1–68. Washington, D.C.: Institute for the Study of Man.

Vennemann, Theo. 1998b. "Germania Semitica: ⁺*plög-*/⁺*pleg-*, ⁺*furh-*/⁺*farh-*, ⁺*folk-*/⁺*flokk-*, ⁺*felh-*/⁺*folg-*". *Deutsche Grammatik — Thema in Variationen: Festschrift für Hans-Werner Eroms zum 60. Geburtstag* ed. by Karin Donhauser & Ludwig M. Eichinger, 245–261. Heidelberg: Carl Winter.

Vennemann, Theo. 1998c. "Zur Etymologie von *Éire*, dem Namen Irlands". *Sprachwissenschaft* 23.461–469.

Vennemann, Theo. 1998d. "Germania Semitica: *Biene* und *Imme*. Mit einem Anhang zu lat. *apis*". *Sprachwissenschaft* 23.471–487.

Vennemann, Theo. 1999. "Remarks on some British Place Names". *Interdigitations: Essays for Irmengard Rauch* ed. by Gerald F. Carr, Wayne Harbert, & Lihua Zhang, 25–62. Berne: Peter Lang.

Vennemann, Theo. Forthcoming. "On the Rise of 'Celtic' Syntax in Middle English". *Middle English from Tongue to Text: Selected papers from the Third International Conference on Middle English: Language and text, held at Dublin, Ireland, 1–4 July 1999*, ed. by Peter J. Lucas. Bern: Peter Lang.

Viereck, Wolfgang. 2000. "Celtic and English — An intricate interrelationship". Tristram 2000.375–398.

Wagner, Heinrich. 1959. *Das Verbum in den Sprachen der Britischen Inseln*. (= *Buchreihe der Zeitschrift für celtische Philologie*, 1.) Tübingen: Max Niemeyer.

Index of languages and language families

Index of names

Index of subjects

CURRENT ISSUES IN LINGUISTIC THEORY

E. F. K. Koerner, Editor
Department of Linguistics, University of Ottawa
OTTAWA, Canada K1N 6N5
koerner@uottawa.ca

The *Current Issues in Linguistic Theory* (CILT) series is a theory-oriented series which welcomes contributions from scholars who have significant proposals to make towards the advancement of our understanding of language, its structure, functioning and development. CILT has been established in order to provide a forum for the presentation and discussion of linguistic opinions of scholars who do not necessarily accept the prevailing mode of thought in linguistic science. It offers an alternative outlet for meaningful contributions to the current linguistic debate, and furnishes the diversity of opinion which a healthy discipline must have. In this series the following volumes have been published thus far or are scheduled for publication:

1. KOERNER, Konrad (ed.): *The Transformational-Generative Paradigm and Modern Linguistic Theory*. 1975.
2. WEIDERT, Alfons: *Componential Analysis of Lushai Phonology*. 1975.
3. MAHER, J. Peter: *Papers on Language Theory and History I: Creation and Tradition in Language*. Foreword by Raimo Anttila. 1979.
4. HOPPER, Paul J. (ed.): *Studies in Descriptive and Historical Linguistics. Festschrift for Winfred P. Lehmann*. 1977.
5. ITKONEN, Esa: *Grammatical Theory and Metascience: A critical investigation into the methodological and philosophical foundations of 'autonomous' linguistics*. 1978.
6. ANTTILA, Raimo: *Historical and Comparative Linguistics*. 1989.
7. MEISEL, Jürgen M. & Martin D. PAM (eds): *Linear Order and Generative Theory*. 1979.
8. WILBUR, Terence H.: *Prolegomena to a Grammar of Basque*. 1979.
9. HOLLIEN, Harry & Patricia (eds): *Current Issues in the Phonetic Sciences. Proceedings of the IPS-77 Congress, Miami Beach, Florida, 17-19 December 1977*. 1979.
10. PRIDEAUX, Gary D. (ed.): *Perspectives in Experimental Linguistics. Papers from the University of Alberta Conference on Experimental Linguistics, Edmonton, 13-14 Oct. 1978*. 1979.
11. BROGYANYI, Bela (ed.): *Studies in Diachronic, Synchronic, and Typological Linguistics: Festschrift for Oswald Szemerényi on the Occasion of his 65th Birthday*. 1979.
12. FISIAK, Jacek (ed.): *Theoretical Issues in Contrastive Linguistics*. 1981. Out of print
13. MAHER, J. Peter, Allan R. BOMHARD & Konrad KOERNER (eds): *Papers from the Third International Conference on Historical Linguistics, Hamburg, August 22-26 1977*. 1982.
14. TRAUGOTT, Elizabeth C., Rebecca LaBRUM & Susan SHEPHERD (eds): *Papers from the Fourth International Conference on Historical Linguistics, Stanford, March 26-30 1979*. 1980.
15. ANDERSON, John (ed.): *Language Form and Linguistic Variation. Papers dedicated to Angus McIntosh*. 1982.
16. ARBEITMAN, Yoël L. & Allan R. BOMHARD (eds): *Bono Homini Donum: Essays in Historical Linguistics, in Memory of J.Alexander Kerns*. 1981.
17. LIEB, Hans-Heinrich: *Integrational Linguistics. 6 volumes. Vol. II-VI n.y.p.* 1984/93.
18. IZZO, Herbert J. (ed.): *Italic and Romance. Linguistic Studies in Honor of Ernst Pulgram*. 1980.
19. RAMAT, Paolo et al. (eds): *Linguistic Reconstruction and Indo-European Syntax. Proceedings of the Colloquium of the 'Indogermanischhe Gesellschaft'. University of Pavia, 6-7 September 1979*. 1980.
20. NORRICK, Neal R.: *Semiotic Principles in Semantic Theory*. 1981.
21. AHLQVIST, Anders (ed.): *Papers from the Fifth International Conference on Historical Linguistics, Galway, April 6-10 1981*. 1982.

22. UNTERMANN, Jürgen & Bela BROGYANYI (eds): *Das Germanische und die Rekonstruktion der Indogermanischen Grundsprache. Akten des Freiburger Kolloquiums der Indogermanischen Gesellschaft, Freiburg, 26-27 Februar 1981.* 1984.

23. DANIELSEN, Niels: *Papers in Theoretical Linguistics. Edited by Per Baerentzen.* 1992.

24. LEHMANN, Winfred P. & Yakov MALKIEL (eds): *Perspectives on Historical Linguistics. Papers from a conference held at the meeting of the Language Theory Division, Modern Language Assn., San Francisco, 27-30 December 1979.* 1982.

25. ANDERSEN, Paul Kent: *Word Order Typology and Comparative Constructions.* 1983.

26. BALDI, Philip (ed.): *Papers from the XIIth Linguistic Symposium on Romance Languages, Univ. Park, April 1-3, 1982.* 1984.

27. BOMHARD, Alan R.: *Toward Proto-Nostratic. A New Approach to the Comparison of Proto-Indo-European and Proto-Afroasiatic. Foreword by Paul J. Hopper.* 1984.

28. BYNON, James (ed.): *Current Progress in Afro-Asiatic Linguistics: Papers of the Third International Hamito-Semitic Congress, London, 1978.* 1984.

29. PAPROTTÉ, Wolf & René DIRVEN (eds): *The Ubiquity of Metaphor: Metaphor in language and thought.* 1985 (publ. 1986).

30. HALL, Robert A. Jr.: *Proto-Romance Morphology. = Comparative Romance Grammar, vol. III.* 1984.

31. GUILLAUME, Gustave: *Foundations for a Science of Language.*

32. COPELAND, James E. (ed.): *New Directions in Linguistics and Semiotics.* Co-edition with Rice University Press who hold exclusive rights for US and Canada. 1984.

33. VERSTEEGH, Kees: *Pidginization and Creolization. The Case of Arabic.* 1984.

34. FISIAK, Jacek (ed.): *Papers from the VIth International Conference on Historical Linguistics, Poznan, 22-26 August. 1983.* 1985.

35. COLLINGE, N.E.: *The Laws of Indo-European.* 1985.

36. KING, Larry D. & Catherine A. MALEY (eds): *Selected papers from the XIIIth Linguistic Symposium on Romance Languages, Chapel Hill, N.C., 24-26 March 1983.* 1985.

37. GRIFFEN, T.D.: *Aspects of Dynamic Phonology.* 1985.

38. BROGYANYI, Bela & Thomas KRÖMMELBEIN (eds): *Germanic Dialects:Linguistic and Philological Investigations.* 1986.

39. BENSON, James D., Michael J. CUMMINGS, & William S. GREAVES (eds): *Linguistics in a Systemic Perspective.* 1988.

40. FRIES, Peter Howard (ed.) in collaboration with Nancy M. Fries: *Toward an Understanding of Language: Charles C. Fries in Perspective.* 1985.

41. EATON, Roger, et al. (eds): *Papers from the 4th International Conference on English Historical Linguistics, April 10-13, 1985.* 1985.

42. MAKKAI, Adam & Alan K. MELBY (eds): *Linguistics and Philosophy. Festschrift for Rulon S. Wells.* 1985 (publ. 1986).

43. AKAMATSU, Tsutomu: *The Theory of Neutralization and the Archiphoneme in Functional Phonology.* 1988.

44. JUNGRAITHMAYR, Herrmann & Walter W. MUELLER (eds): *Proceedings of the Fourth International Hamito-Semitic Congress.* 1987.

45. KOOPMAN, W.F., F.C. Van der LEEK , O. FISCHER & R. EATON (eds): *Explanation and Linguistic Change.* 1986

46. PRIDEAUX, Gary D. & William J. BAKER: *Strategies and Structures: The processing of relative clauses.* 1987.

47. LEHMANN, Winfred P. (ed.): *Language Typology 1985. Papers from the Linguistic Typology Symposium, Moscow, 9-13 Dec. 1985.* 1986.

48. RAMAT, Anna G., Onofrio CARRUBA and Giuliano BERNINI (eds): *Papers from the 7th International Conference on Historical Linguistics.* 1987.

49. WAUGH, Linda R. and Stephen RUDY (eds): *New Vistas in Grammar: Invariance and*

Variation. Proceedings of the Second International Roman Jakobson Conference, New York University, Nov.5-8, 1985. 1991.

50. RUDZKA-OSTYN, Brygida (ed.): *Topics in Cognitive Linguistics.* 1988.
51. CHATTERJEE, Ranjit: *Aspect and Meaning in Slavic and Indic. With a foreword by Paul Friedrich.* 1989.
52. FASOLD, Ralph W. & Deborah SCHIFFRIN (eds): *Language Change and Variation.* 1989.
53. SANKOFF, David: *Diversity and Diachrony.* 1986.
54. WEIDERT, Alfons: *Tibeto-Burman Tonology. A comparative analysis.* 1987
55. HALL, Robert A. Jr.: *Linguistics and Pseudo-Linguistics.* 1987.
56. HOCKETT, Charles F.: *Refurbishing our Foundations. Elementary linguistics from an advanced point of view.* 1987.
57. BUBENIK, Vít: *Hellenistic and Roman Greece as a Sociolinguistic Area.* 1989.
58. ARBEITMAN, Yoël. L. (ed.): *Fucus: A Semitic/Afrasian Gathering in Remembrance of Albert Ehrman.* 1988.
59. VAN VOORST, Jan: *Event Structure.* 1988.
60. KIRSCHNER, Carl & Janet DECESARIS (eds): *Studies in Romance Linguistics. Selected Proceedings from the XVII Linguistic Symposium on Romance Languages.* 1989.
61. CORRIGAN, Roberta L., Fred ECKMAN & Michael NOONAN (eds): *Linguistic Categorization. Proceedings of an International Symposium in Milwaukee, Wisconsin, April 10-11, 1987.* 1989.
62. FRAJZYNGIER, Zygmunt (ed.): *Current Progress in Chadic Linguistics. Proceedings of the International Symposium on Chadic Linguistics, Boulder, Colorado, 1-2 May 1987.* 1989.
63. EID, Mushira (ed.): *Perspectives on Arabic Linguistics I. Papers from the First Annual Symposium on Arabic Linguistics.* 1990.
64. BROGYANYI, Bela (ed.): *Prehistory, History and Historiography of Language, Speech, and Linguistic Theory. Papers in honor of Oswald Szemérenyi I.* 1992.
65. ADAMSON, Sylvia, Vivien A. LAW, Nigel VINCENT and Susan WRIGHT (eds): *Papers from the 5th International Conference on English Historical Linguistics.* 1990.
66. ANDERSEN, Henning and Konrad KOERNER (eds): *Historical Linguistics 1987.Papers from the 8th International Conference on Historical Linguistics,Lille, August 30-Sept., 1987.* 1990.
67. LEHMANN, Winfred P. (ed.): *Language Typology 1987. Systematic Balance in Language. Papers from the Linguistic Typology Symposium, Berkeley, 1-3 Dec 1987.* 1990.
68. BALL, Martin, James FIFE, Erich POPPE &Jenny ROWLAND (eds): *Celtic Linguistics/ Ieithyddiaeth Geltaidd. Readings in the Brythonic Languages. Festschrift for T. Arwyn Watkins.* 1990.
69. WANNER, Dieter and Douglas A. KIBBEE (eds): *New Analyses in Romance Linguistics. Selected papers from the Linguistic Symposium on Romance Languages XVIIII, Urbana-Champaign, April 7-9, 1988.* 1991.
70. JENSEN, John T.: *Morphology. Word structure in generative grammar.* 1990.
71. O'GRADY, William: *Categories and Case. The sentence structure of Korean.* 1991.
72. EID, Mushira and John MCCARTHY (eds): *Perspectives on Arabic Linguistics II. Papers from the Second Annual Symposium on Arabic Linguistics.* 1990.
73. STAMENOV, Maxim (ed.): *Current Advances in Semantic Theory.* 1991.
74. LAEUFER, Christiane and Terrell A. MORGAN (eds): *Theoretical Analyses in Romance Linguistics.* 1991.
75. DROSTE, Flip G. and John E. JOSEPH (eds): *Linguistic Theory and Grammatical Description. Nine Current Approaches.* 1991.
76. WICKENS, Mark A.: *Grammatical Number in English Nouns. An empirical and theoretical account.* 1992.
77. BOLTZ, William G. and Michael C. SHAPIRO (eds): *Studies in the Historical Phonology of Asian Languages.* 1991.

78. KAC, Michael: *Grammars and Grammaticality.* 1992.
79. ANTONSEN, Elmer H. and Hans Henrich HOCK (eds): *STAEF-CRAEFT: Studies in Germanic Linguistics. Select papers from the First and Second Symposium on Germanic Linguistics, University of Chicago, 24 April 1985, and Univ. of Illinois at Urbana-Champaign, 3-4 Oct. 1986.* 1991.
80. COMRIE, Bernard and Mushira EID (eds): *Perspectives on Arabic Linguistics III. Papers from the Third Annual Symposium on Arabic Linguistics.* 1991.
81. LEHMANN, Winfred P. and H.J. HEWITT (eds): *Language Typology 1988. Typological Models in the Service of Reconstruction.* 1991.
82. VAN VALIN, Robert D. (ed.): *Advances in Role and Reference Grammar.* 1992.
83. FIFE, James and Erich POPPE (eds): *Studies in Brythonic Word Order.* 1991.
84. DAVIS, Garry W. and Gregory K. IVERSON (eds): *Explanation in Historical Linguistics.* 1992.
85. BROSELOW, Ellen, Mushira EID and John McCARTHY (eds): *Perspectives on Arabic Linguistics IV. Papers from the Annual Symposium on Arabic Linguistics.* 1992.
86. KESS, Joseph F.: *Psycholinguistics. Psychology, linguistics, and the study of natural language.* 1992.
87. BROGYANYI, Bela and Reiner LIPP (eds): *Historical Philology: Greek, Latin, and Romance. Papers in honor of Oswald Szemerényi II.* 1992.
88. SHIELDS, Kenneth: *A History of Indo-European Verb Morphology.* 1992.
89. BURRIDGE, Kate: *Syntactic Change in Germanic. A study of some aspects of language change in Germanic with particular reference to Middle Dutch.* 1992.
90. KING, Larry D.: *The Semantic Structure of Spanish. Meaning and grammatical form.* 1992.
91. HIRSCHBÜHLER, Paul and Konrad KOERNER (eds): *Romance Languages and Modern Linguistic Theory. Selected papers from the XX Linguistic Symposium on Romance Languages, University of Ottawa, April 10-14, 1990.* 1992.
92. POYATOS, Fernando: *Paralanguage: A linguistic and interdisciplinary approach to interactive speech and sounds.* 1992.
93. LIPPI-GREEN, Rosina (ed.): *Recent Developments in Germanic Linguistics.* 1992.
94. HAGÈGE, Claude: *The Language Builder. An essay on the human signature in linguistic morphogenesis.* 1992.
95. MILLER, D. Gary: *Complex Verb Formation.* 1992.
96. LIEB, Hans-Heinrich (ed.): *Prospects for a New Structuralism.* 1992.
97. BROGYANYI, Bela & Reiner LIPP (eds): *Comparative-Historical Linguistics: Indo-European and Finno-Ugric. Papers in honor of Oswald Szemerényi III.* 1992.
98. EID, Mushira & Gregory K. IVERSON: *Principles and Prediction: The analysis of natural language.* 1993.
99. JENSEN, John T.: *English Phonology.* 1993.
100. MUFWENE, Salikoko S. and Lioba MOSHI (eds): *Topics in African Linguistics. Papers from the XXI Annual Conference on African Linguistics, University of Georgia, April 1990.* 1993.
101. EID, Mushira & Clive HOLES (eds): *Perspectives on Arabic Linguistics V. Papers from the Fifth Annual Symposium on Arabic Linguistics.* 1993.
102. DAVIS, Philip W. (ed.): *Alternative Linguistics. Descriptive and theoretical Modes.* 1995.
103. ASHBY, William J., Marianne MITHUN, Giorgio PERISSINOTTO and Eduardo RAPOSO: *Linguistic Perspectives on Romance Languages. Selected papers from the XXI Linguistic Symposium on Romance Languages, Santa Barbara, February 21-24, 1991.* 1993.
104. KURZOVÁ, Helena: *From Indo-European to Latin. The evolution of a morphosyntactic type.* 1993.
105. HUALDE, José Ignacio and Jon ORTIZ DE URBANA (eds): *Generative Studies in Basque Linguistics.* 1993.
106. AERTSEN, Henk and Robert J. JEFFERS (eds): *Historical Linguistics 1989. Papers from the 9th International Conference on Historical Linguistics, New Brunswick, 14-18 August 1989.* 1993.

107. MARLE, Jaap van (ed.): *Historical Linguistics 1991. Papers from the 10th International Conference on Historical Linguistics, Amsterdam, August 12-16, 1991.* 1993.
108. LIEB, Hans-Heinrich: *Linguistic Variables. Towards a unified theory of linguistic variation.* 1993.
109. PAGLIUCA, William (ed.): *Perspectives on Grammaticalization.* 1994.
110. SIMONE, Raffaele (ed.): *Iconicity in Language.* 1995.
111. TOBIN, Yishai: *Invariance, Markedness and Distinctive Feature Analysis. A contrastive study of sign systems in English and Hebrew.* 1994.
112. CULIOLI, Antoine: *Cognition and Representation in Linguistic Theory. Translated, edited and introduced by Michel Liddle.* 1995.
113. FERNÁNDEZ, Francisco, Miguel FUSTER and Juan Jose CALVO (eds): *English Historical Linguistics 1992. Papers from the 7th International Conference on English Historical Linguistics, Valencia, 22-26 September 1992.* 1994.
114. EGLI, U., P. PAUSE, Chr. SCHWARZE, A. von STECHOW, G. WIENOLD (eds): *Lexical Knowledge in the Organisation of Language.* 1995.
115. EID, Mushira, Vincente CANTARINO and Keith WALTERS (eds): *Perspectives on Arabic Linguistics. Vol. VI. Papers from the Sixth Annual Symposium on Arabic Linguistics.* 1994.

116. MILLER, D. Gary: *Ancient Scripts and Phonological Knowledge.* 1994.
117. PHILIPPAKI-WARBURTON, I., K. NICOLAIDIS and M. SIFIANOU (eds): *Themes in Greek Linguistics. Papers from the first International Conference on Greek Linguistics, Reading, September 1993.* 1994.
118. HASAN, Ruqaiya and Peter H. FRIES (eds): *On Subject and Theme. A discourse functional perspective.* 1995.
119. LIPPI-GREEN, Rosina: *Language Ideology and Language Change in Early Modern German. A sociolinguistic study of the consonantal system of Nuremberg.* 1994.
120. STONHAM, John T. : *Combinatorial Morphology.* 1994.
121. HASAN, Ruqaiya, Carmel CLORAN and David BUTT (eds): *Functional Descriptions. Theorie in practice.* 1996.
122. SMITH, John Charles and Martin MAIDEN (eds): *Linguistic Theory and the Romance Languages.* 1995.
123. AMASTAE, Jon, Grant GOODALL, Mario MONTALBETTI and Marianne PHINNEY: *Contemporary Research in Romance Linguistics. Papers from the XXII Linguistic Symposium on Romance Languages, El Paso//Juárez, February 22-24, 1994.* 1995.
124. ANDERSEN, Henning: *Historical Linguistics 1993. Selected papers from the 11th International Conference on Historical Linguistics, Los Angeles, 16-20 August 1993.* 1995.
125. SINGH, Rajendra (ed.): *Towards a Critical Sociolinguistics.* 1996.
126. MATRAS, Yaron (ed.): *Romani in Contact. The history, structure and sociology of a language.* 1995.
127. GUY, Gregory R., Crawford FEAGIN, Deborah SCHIFFRIN and John BAUGH (eds): *Towards a Social Science of Language. Papers in honor of William Labov. Volume 1: Variation and change in language and society.* 1996.
128. GUY, Gregory R., Crawford FEAGIN, Deborah SCHIFFRIN and John BAUGH (eds): *Towards a Social Science of Language. Papers in honor of William Labov. Volume 2: Social interaction and discourse structures.* 1997.
129. LEVIN, Saul: *Semitic and Indo-European: The Principal Etymologies. With observations on Afro-Asiatic.* 1995.
130. EID, Mushira (ed.) *Perspectives on Arabic Linguistics. Vol. VII. Papers from the Seventh Annual Symposium on Arabic Linguistics.* 1995.
131. HUALDE, Jose Ignacio, Joseba A. LAKARRA and R.L. Trask (eds): *Towards a History of the Basque Language.* 1995.

132. HERSCHENSOHN, Julia: *Case Suspension and Binary Complement Structure in French*. 1996.
133. ZAGONA, Karen (ed.): *Grammatical Theory and Romance Languages. Selected papers from the 25th Linguistic Symposium on Romance Languages (LSRL XXV) Seattle, 2-4 March 1995.* 1996.
134. EID, Mushira (ed.): *Perspectives on Arabic Linguistics Vol. VIII. Papers from the Eighth Annual Symposium on Arabic Linguistics.* 1996.
135. BRITTON Derek (ed.): *Papers from the 8th International Conference on English Historical Linguistics.* 1996.
136. MITKOV, Ruslan and Nicolas NICOLOV (eds): *Recent Advances in Natural Language Processing.* 1997.
137. LIPPI-GREEN, Rosina and Joseph C. SALMONS (eds): *Germanic Linguistics. Syntactic and diachronic.* 1996.
138. SACKMANN, Robin (ed.): *Theoretical Linguistics and Grammatical Description.* 1996.
139. BLACK, James R. and Virginia MOTAPANYANE (eds): *Microparametric Syntax and Dialect Variation.* 1996.
140. BLACK, James R. and Virginia MOTAPANYANE (eds): *Clitics, Pronouns and Movement.* 1997.
141. EID, Mushira and Dilworth PARKINSON (eds): *Perspectives on Arabic Linguistics Vol. IX. Papers from the Ninth Annual Symposium on Arabic Linguistics, Georgetown University, Washington D.C., 1995.* 1996.
142. JOSEPH, Brian D. and Joseph C. SALMONS (eds): *Nostratic. Sifting the evidence.* 1998.
143. ATHANASIADOU, Angeliki and René DIRVEN (eds): *On Conditionals Again.* 1997.
144. SINGH, Rajendra (ed): *Trubetzkoy's Orphan. Proceedings of the Montréal Roundtable "Morphophonology: contemporary responses (Montréal, October 1994).* 1996.
145. HEWSON, John and Vit BUBENIK: *Tense and Aspect in Indo-European Languages. Theory, typology, diachrony.* 1997.
146. HINSKENS, Frans, Roeland VAN HOUT and W. Leo WETZELS (eds): *Variation, Change, and Phonological Theory.* 1997.
147. HEWSON, John: *The Cognitive System of the French Verb.* 1997.
148. WOLF, George and Nigel LOVE (eds): *Linguistics Inside Out. Roy Harris and his critics.* 1997.
149. HALL, T. Alan: *The Phonology of Coronals.* 1997.
150. VERSPOOR, Marjolijn, Kee Dong LEE and Eve SWEETSER (eds): *Lexical and Syntactical Constructions and the Construction of Meaning. Proceedings of the Bi-annual ICLA meeting in Albuquerque, July 1995.* 1997.
151. LIEBERT, Wolf-Andreas, Gisela REDEKER and Linda WAUGH (eds): *Discourse and Perspectives in Cognitive Linguistics.* 1997.
152. HIRAGA, Masako, Chris SINHA and Sherman WILCOX (eds): *Cultural, Psychological and Typological Issues in Cognitive Linguistics.* 1999.
153. EID, Mushira and Robert R. RATCLIFFE (eds): *Perspectives on Arabic Linguistics Vol. X. Papers from the Tenth Annual Symposium on Arabic Linguistics, Salt Lake City, 1996.* 1997.
154. SIMON-VANDENBERGEN, Anne-Marie, Kristin DAVIDSE and Dirk NOËL (eds): *Reconnecting Language. Morphology and Syntax in Functional Perspectives.* 1997.
155. FORGET, Danielle, Paul HIRSCHBÜHLER, France MARTINEAU and María-Luisa RIVERO (eds): *Negation and Polarity. Syntax and semantics. Selected papers from the Colloquium Negation: Syntax and Semantics. Ottawa, 11-13 May 1995.* 1997.
156. MATRAS, Yaron, Peter BAKKER and Hristo KYUCHUKOV (eds): *The Typology and Dialectology of Romani.* 1997.
157. LEMA, José and Esthela TREVIÑO (eds): *Theoretical Analyses on Romance Languages. Selected papers from the 26th Linguistic Symposium on Romance Languages (LSRL XXVI), Mexico City, 28-30 March, 1996.* 1998.
158. SÁNCHEZ MACARRO, Antonia and Ronald CARTER (eds): *Linguistic Choice across Genres. Variation in spoken and written English.* 1998.

159. JOSEPH, Brian D., Geoffrey C. HORROCKS and Irene PHILIPPAKI-WARBURTON (eds): *Themes in Greek Linguistics II*. 1998.

160. SCHWEGLER, Armin, Bernard TRANEL and Myriam URIBE-ETXEBARRIA (eds): *Romance Linguistics: Theoretical Perspectives. Selected papers from the 27th Linguistic Symposium on Romance Languages (LSRL XXVII), Irvine, 20-22 February, 1997*. 1998.

161. SMITH, John Charles and Delia BENTLEY (eds): *Historical Linguistics 1995. Volume 1: Romance and general linguistics*. 2000.

162. HOGG, Richard M. and Linda van BERGEN (eds): *Historical Linguistics 1995. Volume 2: Germanic linguistics.Selected papers from the 12th International Conference on Historical Linguistics, Manchester, August 1995*. 1998.

163. LOCKWOOD, David G., Peter H. FRIES and James E. COPELAND (eds): *Functional Approaches to Language, Culture and Cognition*. 2000.

164. SCHMID, Monika, Jennifer R. AUSTIN and Dieter STEIN (eds): *Historical Linguistics 1997. Selected papers from the 13th International Conference on Historical Linguistics, Düsseldorf, 10-17 August 1997*. 1998.

165. BUBENÍK, Vit: *A Historical Syntax of Late Middle Indo-Aryan (Apabhramśa)*. 1998.

166. LEMMENS, Maarten: *Lexical Perspectives on Transitivity and Ergativity. Causative constructions in English*. 1998.

167. BENMAMOUN, Elabbas, Mushira EID and Niloofar HAERI (eds): *Perspectives on Arabic Linguistics Vol. XI. Papers from the Eleventh Annual Symposium on Arabic Linguistics, Atlanta, 1997*. 1998.

168. RATCLIFFE, Robert R.: *The "Broken" Plural Problem in Arabic and Comparative Semitic. Allomorphy and analogy in non-concatenative morphology*. 1998.

169. GHADESSY, Mohsen (ed.): *Text and Context in Functional Linguistics*. 1999.

170. LAMB, Sydney M.: *Pathways of the Brain. The neurocognitive basis of language*. 1999.

171. WEIGAND, Edda (ed.): *Contrastive Lexical Semantics*. 1998.

172. DIMITROVA-VULCHANOVA, Mila and Lars HELLAN (eds): *Topics in South Slavic Syntax and Semantics*. 1999.

173. TREVIÑO, Esthela and José LEMA (eds): Semantic Issues in Romance Syntax. 1999.

174. HALL, T. Alan and Ursula KLEINHENZ (eds): *Studies on the Phonological Word*. 1999.

175. GIBBS, Ray W. and Gerard J. STEEN (eds): *Metaphor in Cognitive Linguistics. Selected papers from the 5th International Cognitive Linguistics Conference, Amsterdam, 1997*. 2001.

176. VAN HOEK, Karen, Andrej KIBRIK and Leo NOORDMAN (eds): *Discourse in Cognitive Linguistics. Selected papers from the International Cognitive Linguistics Conference, Amsterdam, July 1997*. 1999.

177. CUYCKENS, Hubert and Britta ZAWADA (eds): *Polysemy in Cognitive Linguistics. Selected papers from the International Cognitive Linguistics Conference, Amsterdam, 1997*. 2001.

178. FOOLEN, Ad and Frederike van der LEEK (eds): *Constructions in Cognitive Linguistics. Selected papers from the Fifth International Cognitive Linguistic Conference, Amsterdam, 1997*. 2000.

179. RINI, Joel: *Exploring the Role of Morphology in the Evolution of Spanish*. 1999.

180. MEREU, Lunella (ed.): *Boundaries of Morphology and Syntax*. 1999.

181. MOHAMMAD, Mohammad A.: *Word Order, Agreement and Pronominalization in Standard and Palestinian Arabic*. 2000.

182. KENESEI, István (ed.): *Theoretical Issues in Eastern European Languages. Selected papers from the Conference on Linguistic Theory in Eastern European Languages (CLITE), Szeged, April 1998*. 1999.

183. CONTINI-MORAVA, Ellen and Yishai TOBIN (eds): *Between Grammar and Lexicon*. 2000.

184. SAGART, Laurent: *The Roots of Old Chinese*. 1999.

185. AUTHIER, J.-Marc, Barbara E. BULLOCK, Lisa A. REED (eds): *Formal Perspectives on Romance Linguistics. Selected papers from the 28th Linguistic Symposium on Romance Languages (LSRL XXVIII), University Park, 16-19 April 1998*. 1999.

186. MIŠESKA TOMIĆ, Olga and Milorad RADOVANOVIĆ (eds): *History and Perspectives of Language Study*. 2000.
187. FRANCO, Jon, Alazne LANDA and Juan MARTÍN (eds): *Grammatical Analyses in Basque and Romance Linguistics*. 1999.
188. VanNESS SIMMONS, Richard: *Chinese Dialect Classification. A comparative approach to Harngjou, Old Jintarn, and Common Northern Wu*. 1999.
189. NICHOLOV, Nicolas and Ruslan MITKOV (eds): *Recent Advances in Natural Language Processing II. Selected papers from RANLP '97*. 2000.
190. BENMAMOUN, Elabbas (ed.): *Perspectives on Arabic Linguistics Vol. XII. Papers from the Twelfth Annual Symposium on Arabic Linguistics*. 1999.
191. SIHLER, Andrew L.: *Language Change. An introduction*. 2000.
192. ALEXANDROVA, Galina M. and Olga ARNAUDOVA (eds.): *The Minimalist Parameter. Selected papers from the Open Linguistics Forum, Ottawa, 21-23 March 1997*. 2001.
193. KLAUSENBURGER, Jurgen: *Grammaticalization. Studies in Latin and Romance morphosyntax*. 2000.
194. COLEMAN, Julie and Christian J. KAY (eds): *Lexicology, Semantics and Lexicography. Selected papers from the Fourth G. L. Brook Symposium, Manchester, August 1998*. 2000.
195. HERRING, Susan C., Pieter van REENEN and Lene SCHØSLER (eds): *Textual Parameters in Older Languages*. 2000.
196. HANNAHS, S. J. and Mike DAVENPORT (eds): *Issues in Phonological Structure. Papers from an International Workshop*. 1999.
197. COOPMANS, Peter, Martin EVERAERT and Jane GRIMSHAW (eds): *Lexical Specification and Insertion*. 2000.
198. NIEMEIER, Susanne and René DIRVEN (eds): *Evidence for Linguistic Relativity*. 2000.
199. VERSPOOR, Marjolijn H. and Martin PÜTZ (eds): *Explorations in Linguistic Relativity*. 2000.
200. ANTTILA, Raimo: *Greek and Indo-European Etymology in Action. Proto-Indo-European *aǵ-*. 2000.
201. DRESSLER, Wolfgang U., Oskar E. PFEIFFER, Markus PÖCHTRAGER and John R. RENNISON (eds.): *Morphological Analysis in Comparison*. 2000.
202. LECARME, Jacqueline, Jean LOWENSTAMM and Ur SHLONSKY (eds.): *Research in Afroasiatic Grammar. Papers from the Third conference on Afroasiatic Languages, Sophia Antipolis, 1996*. 2000.
203. NORRICK, Neal R.: *Conversational Narrative. Storytelling in everyday talk*. 2000.
204. DIRVEN, René, Bruce HAWKINS and Esra SANDIKCIOGLU (eds.): *Language and Ideology. Volume 1: cognitive theoretical approaches*. 2001.
205. DIRVEN, René, Roslyn FRANK and Cornelia ILIE (eds.): *Language and Ideology. Volume 2: cognitive descriptive approaches*. 2001.
206. FAWCETT, Robin: *A Theory of Syntax for Systemic-Functional Linguistics*. 2000.
207. SANZ, Montserrat: *Events and Predication. A new approach to syntactic processing in English and Spanish*. 2000.
208. ROBINSON, Orrin W.: *Whose German? The ach/ich alternation and related phenomena in 'standard' and 'colloquial'*. 2001.
209. KING, Ruth: *The Lexical Basis of Grammatical Borrowing. A Prince Edward Island French case study*. 2000.
210. DWORKIN, Steven N. and Dieter WANNER (eds.): *New Approaches to Old Problems. Issues in Romance historical linguistics*. 2000.
211. ELŠÍK, Viktor and Yaron MATRAS (eds.): *Grammatical Relations in Romani. The Noun Phrase*. 2000.
212. REPETTI, Lori (ed.): *Phonological Theory and the Dialects of Italy*. 2000.
213. SORNICOLA, Rosanna, Erich POPPE and Ariel SHISHA-HALEVY (eds.): *Stability, Variation and Change of Word-Order Patterns over Time*. 2000.
214. WEIGAND, Edda and Marcelo DASCAL (eds.): *Negotiation and Power in Dialogic Interaction*. 2001.

215. BRINTON, Laurel J.: *Historical Linguistics 1999. Selected papers from the 14th International Conference on Historical Linguistics, Vancouver, 9-13 August 1999.* 2001.

216. CAMPS, Joaquim and Caroline R. WILTSHIRE (eds.): *Romance Syntax, Semantics and L2 Acquisition. Selected papers from the 30th Linguistic Symposium on Romance Languages, Gainesville, Florida, February 2000.* n.y.p.

217. WILTSHIRE, Caroline R. and Joaquim CAMPS (eds.): *Romance Phonology and Variation. Selected papers from the 30th Linguistic Symposium on Romance Languages, Gainesville, Florida, February 2000.* n.y.p.

218. BENDJABALLAH, S., W.U. DRESSLER, O. PFEIFFER and M. VOEIKOVA (eds.): *Morphology 2000. Selected papers from the 9th Morphology Meeting, Vienna, 25-27 February 2000.* n.y.p.

219. ANDERSEN, Henning (ed.): *Actualization. Linguistic Change in Progress. Selected papers from the Workshop on Patterns of Actualization in Linguistic Change, Vancouver, B.C., 14 August 1999.* n.y.p.

220. CRESTI, Diana, Christina TORTORA and Teresa SATTERFIELD (eds.): *Current Issues in Romance Languages. Selected papers from the 29th Linguistic Symposium on Romance Languages (LSRL), Ann Arbor, 8-11 April 1999.* n.y.p.